To Neil Alexander
Colleague & friend of Albert Outler

Albert C. Outler
The Gifted Dilettante

by

Bob Parrott, D.Min.

Albert C. Outler: The Gifted Dilettante

By Bob W. Parrott

© July 1999 by Bob W. Parrott
Published by Bristol Books, an imprint of Bristol House, Ltd.

First Edition, July 1999

ISBN: 1-885224-28-1

Printed in the United States of America

Bristol House, Ltd.
P.O. Box 4020
Anderson, Indiana 46013-4020

To order call: 1-800-451-READ (7323)

Table of Contents

Foreword

Albert Outler would have abhorred the concept and the word *postmodernity*. Not that this sophisticated theologian and historian, the subject of this biography, did not believe that our times were "post" some other times, even, quite possibly modern times. Highly aware of the way historians and nonhistorians alike construct the story of the past periods of time in contrast to our own, he would not have been inordinately upset by the notion that ours left behind many distinctive features of our pasts, including that of Christen*dom* or Protestant*dom* or Wesleyan*dom*. Much of his writing was in an elegiac mode, evocative of autumn and evening and filled with the sense of transience.

The feature of postmodernity that he would have found uncongenial appears at first glance, but only at first glance, to characterize this book. In the modern style of architecture, the elements come together in rational constructs. They are international, able to be uprooted or reproduced whether in New Delhi or Venice; Madison, Wisconsin; or Tokyo. The region, environment, and context mean little while rationality governs. The modern in art might be grasped normatively in Mondrian's or Albers's or Stella's or Noland's geometrically balanced and perfected linearity.

Postmodernity shakes that all up. In architecture, there may be elements of the Gothic, Byzantine, Romanesque, Norman, Classical, Neo-Penal, and Modern juxtaposed on the same facade or in a single interior. This is an example of postmodernity. Yet the result, when a master is at work, is not jarring. In visual arts, postmodernity has the artist putting together bits of what will make an aesthetic or expressive whole, even if the parts are no longer rationally and logically related. Somehow the postmodern terms in art tend to end in -*age*, as in montage, assemblage, collage, bricollage, and—adds a wag—garbage. Bob Parrott's book certainly includes enough in the sequence of chronology to give it a plot and help readers work through the trajectory of a life well lived. But he does not find it important to stick to that plot. One glimpse leads to another; one reminiscence to another; one topic to another, and we move, not ill at ease, with the author. One visits and revisits themes in different contexts, and is reminded of something important in the new place, even if it had appeared before.

A composition teacher would have trouble with such a plot outline. But the teacher is not dealing with the life and thought of Albert Outler, as Parrott chose to and now must. The myriad interests and styles of expertise displayed by this gracious Georgian-turned-Texan, this provincial Wesleyan and passionately ecumenical and cosmopolitan citizen, cannot be treated in simple logical sequence. There was anything but chaos in Outler's life, and that life visited on these pages is not the victim of chaos in Parrott's eye and soul.

Maybe a different word from the -*age* words would do, and help us cast this work not in post- or modern times but almost in a medieval matrix. Think of the mosaic. Parrott has done more than yeoman work with the archives, letters, interview processes, and papers. He finds a bit that by itself does not seem to fit the pattern, but then surrounds it with pieces that can relate and help form a design. Out of this piecing together comes the picture of that life well lived.

A second feature of this book that has to be anticipated—isn't anticipating what forewords are for?—has to do with the hundreds of quotations. I cannot recall reading a biography in recent times that has more paragraphs of direct quotation, both from Outler and from his correspondents, admirers, and antagonists. One side of me wishes that Parrott had internalized more of his reading and chosen to show a bit more *chutzpah*, sureness with himself—

Outler style?—to do more shaping. Then I come across another long passage of Outleriana and it occurs to me, as it must to many a reader, that this citing represents a creative way to go about the task. Could any of us have said better the things we read Outler saying? And many of his correspondents, family members, and other interviewees seem to shape up in the context of what Albert would expect of them. The quoted passages from their work become part of this mosaic, this single pattern.

I have stressed genre so much because I resolved in advance to be the first person ever to resist the temptation to match Outler stories, as Parrott presents them, with other Outler stories. Not that a lot of them do not come to mind; they do. But they need to be suppressed, both because the book is already long and because addition of this or that piece to the mosaic would do little to improve the central theme. Outler was the sort of person who told stories, lived them, and inspired them. Many who do that are not literarily productive. I think of my hero Joseph Sittler, who is grasped through tape recordings of lectures and anecdota more than in his slim corpus of writings. Outler brings to mind Sir Isaiah Berlin, reputed to be as exciting a conversationalist as this late century has known but also author of numerous essays now collectible into books. Outler did sit still to edit the huge Wesley edition, and he did write a number of systematic and coherently sustained works. But much of what he stood for is fugitive, dispensed almost casually in lectures that seemed to be delivered effortlessly, but manifest effort and learning. So get used to quotation marks.

My third theme: Does the real Albert Outler emerge on these pages? I am not sure that any twenty Outler students could agree on who the real professor was. Not that he was confused about himself, lacked identity, was incapable of loyalty, or did not have commitments. It is that he was able to sustain contradictions within himself because he Christianly saw the world as being complex and ambiguous in most of its signs.

Here's a challenge to anyone who has read these pages: Was Outler optimistic or pessimistic, liberal or conservative, humble or proud, sure of himself or insecure, envious of others or aware that he attracted envy, content with his achievement or restless, concerned about his place in modern Christian history or so concerned with his subject that he could work heedlessly of reputation? The answer to all seven is yes. It depends upon the eye of the beholder, the context of the moment, the side of himself that Outler chose to reveal at any encounter.

Having raised questions about his complexity, let me also suggest that readers trace continuities through it all. For one sample: His devotion to Wesley marks all his mature years. One can make the case that Wesley is the one Protestant genius between the first generation of the Reformation and now. He symbolized and shaped the modern style of being a Protestant Christian. While many in his generation worked on Luther and Calvin or spent part of their careers on Jonathan Edwards or Puritan divines, Outler found reason again and again to engage in *resourcement* at the Wesleyan fount. Yet he could feel at home with Georges Florovsky in Orthodoxy and with the Vatican lights at the Second Vatican Council.

Whatever else he stood for, Outler proved to the rest of us that the deeper one goes into a Christian tradition, the more likely one will meet others who probe deeply into another element of that tradition—and still have generosity of spirit to reach beyond such boundaries to Jews and to people of nonfaith, while keeping to the integrity of his own.

Parrott shows Outler reflecting on how the age of giants who stalked the Christian theological scene at midcentury was past. [Outler] did not say "we shall not see their kind again," though in faith he seemed to indicate that we might have to wait for another epoch, *kairos,* or unfolding. Maybe so. In the mean time, there is as much to learn from Outler as from anyone else in the in-between times, and I commend Parrott's version of him to you.

Martin E. Marty
The University of Chicago, emeritus

Preface

hile this book begins with the birth of Albert Outler, the book idea began with a rebirth experience—mine! It was in the fall of 1956, my first year in Perkins School of Theology, that a life-threatening ecstatic experience came upon me that I could not handle. I sought help from Perkins Counselor Professor Robert Elliot who took me to see Herndon Wagers, professor of Western Philosophy and Theology, who in turn (and on the same day) escorted me into the office of Albert C. Outler, whom I had never heard of at that time.

Outler heard my "unheard of" story (of *being* in the presence of Being-itself, followed by *its* absence in the indescribably horrible state of a consciousness of nothingness) and calmly said: "Mr. Parrott, you are not the first to have had such a dark-night-of-the-soul experience. I suggest you read St. John of the Cross, who wrote the book *The Dark Night of the Soul*, St. Augustine, St. Bonaventura, Thomas à Kempis, and others." He wrote out the list. Then he said: "I also suggest you go buy and read *all* the books written by Paul Tillich." Which I did.

This reading (and Outler's unflinching confidence and faith) made me realize that there were others before my time who, by divine intervention, found themselves on the brink of insanity; the ontological impact is too much for a *human* being to handle alone. God used the man's faith and knowledge to give me hope to live again. From that moment on, our lives were destined to cross many times in ways beyond the manipulations of either of us. The spirit in which this book is written rises out of that initial meeting. My gratitude to God for the man motivates me to write this book of his life.

This grateful posture before God allows me to be candid without being embarrassing, truthful without being destroying, respectful without being obsequious, conversant with the subject without being condescending, loving without being sentimental, and contributing without being self-serving. (This biography comes at a time in my life when high marks with anybody on this earth are meaningless; proceeds from book sales go into an archives fund at Bridwell Library, Perkins School of Theology.) Further still, it guards against that illusion called "objectivity," which some biographers struggle to project. If any two people cannot give the same objective account of a baby's birth, how can anyone ever think of writing a biography of one as complex as Albert Cook Outler *objectively?* Avoided is a squint-eyed, pursed lips look *at* the man.

Further still, everybody, knowingly or unknowingly, puts one's own spin on every event. My spin will be to write *about* Albert Outler in the same manner I approached him when he was alive. And that is a serious search for truth in dialogue with him in all aspects of his life. No attempt will be made to unravel the complexities of his makeup. This is an effort to be truthful, which is more than being *factful.* The *facts* expressed in this biography are imperfect observations by persons who knew him well. But never well enough to play God. The seeking of truth in the spirit of love and appreciation for the man allows for the candid approach that this writing takes.

In spite of the posture (before God) expressed earlier, some will say that this is but another hagiography by a subservient student paying reverent homage to his master teacher. While this man was my teacher (and the best I ever had), my relationship with him was not a matter of hero-worship. I am conscious of no inhibition, no obligations of fealty. In no way are these previous comments to be taken as apologies for my affection for the man. If affection for one's subject disqualified a biographer, the field indeed would be much impoverished.

His own comment offers a sobering thought for this biographer who searches with him for the truth of his life: "Kind words from good friends are like perfume; enjoy them but don't inhale deeply." The disclosures of this post-humously written biography are not for Outler to inhale. They are written for the reader to know and digest, and under the illumination of truth come to appreciate the mystery of the man and the grace-full contributions he made in this life.

The following letter written by me on June 16, 1972, and his answer to my letter indicate a relationship of mutual respect and affection:

"Dear Dr. Outler: Some of us will love you in spite of your lack of understanding on COCU! (Dig! Dig!) No, seriously, COCU [the mainline churches' Consultation On Church Union] has about as much excitement for me and the majority of the 'pew people' I know as a corporation merger of nine manufacturers of panty hose.

"Isn't it awful to have an 'old' student whack you like this? If this previous comment spins you, wait until you hear this next comment: *if* my publisher would go along with the idea, and *if* you concur, I would like to write Dr. Albert Outler's biography. So help me, I would even include your commitment to COCU!

"If this idea should interest you, let me know. If it does not interest you, I hope you will let somebody do this, or autobiograph yourself. You owe this to your public. Of that I am convinced."

When he was reminded of that dig at the Jurisdictional Conference in Houston during July 1972, he replied with this answer: "Friend, for *you* to pick the analogy of the panty hose, I would say that something exciting must be happening in the panty hose industry!"

One can readily see by this note that I respected him but was independent of him. And he of me. Dr. Outler more than once commented: "I've had more than my share of praise, but I've had far less than I needed of friendly, unselfish, negotiable criticism." Obviously, to him I answered a need.

Dr. Outler invited me to his office to hear me out concerning the biography. At that time he decided that, if it were to be done, I would be an acceptable biographer but that it should not be written in his lifetime. And that it should be in God's good time. That "good time" is *now*. A decade following his death has allowed the dust to settle following his illustrious yet sometimes stormy career as a churchman/theologian. And writing now permits some key players in his life to participate in the biography.

After he made me the executor/custodian of his papers, letters, and personalia, I met with him in Bradenton, Florida, during the spring of 1989 (just months before his death), and informed him of plans to publish eight books that would make up *The Albert Outler Library* (three books of his edited sermons/lectures and five books by scholars in specialized areas of Outler's scholarship). And then after he "falls off the perch" would come the biography. That now has come after six years of research and writing.

My calling was to do for the church what Dr. Outler would not do himself. Dean Joseph Quillian complained more than once: "Albert has about five books in his hide which I want him to write, if I could just keep him locked in his office away from every women's group that wants to hear about the Second Vatican Council!" If something of his was to be published, the publisher had to approach him. And you can tell by the bibliography at the end of this book that, indeed, many did. But there was so much not published. And still is. My mission is to get this material out of archival darkness into the light of day. I have and will continue to do that. This biography will bring to the readers of his scholarly works *the man*.

My efforts will, I hope, be in keeping with Albert's older sister, Fan, who wrote me on February 24, 1973:

"Dear Brother Parrott—I wish to thank you for your beautiful letter and your gracious gifts of your two impressive books [*A Man Talks With God* and *Earth, Moon, and Beyond*, Word Books] and to tell you that I am naturally interested in the suggestion that you wish to make my brother, Albert, the subject of a biography.

"I gather from your incisive style (more evident in your second book because of your growing self-confidence in the wondrous unfolding of the mysteries of 'our' universe through the NASA experience) that such a biography would be unstuffy, unambiguous, and unbeclouded by theological verbosity, and that you would be seeking to account for Albert to the (quote) 'average layman' (unquote) in a way he could never explain himself."

Sister Fan, with a Master of Arts degree from Emory University and a Ph.D. in Education from the Division of Humanities of the University of Chicago, described how the biography should read. I shall strive to make the book "unstuffy, unambiguous, and unbeclouded by theological verbosity." If the book is not readable for the average lay-person, I will have failed. I do not know that Albert Outler could not explain himself (as she mentioned), but I do know that he would never attempt it. I have heard people ask him: "Tell us how you got to where you are." He was always at a loss for words. He would not even attempt to make a start. This writing is an attempt to do something for him that he would never attempt for himself.

It is being done in the same vein as what was done with some of his works before he died. In a letter dated August 3, 1988, he wrote:

"Dear Bob and Doris, It suddenly occurred to me the other morning that, in all the hubbub of these last three months, I let something very fundamental slide (in all these bewilderments and unsettlings): a word of sincerest thanks to you two for your role and achievement in getting that volume of sermon notes into print and into the light of day. Our original compact was that you were welcome to work on the sermons project, so long as I was left free to con-tinue with the unmanageable pile of 'unfinished business' always on the desk. You and Doris and Carla have hon-ored this compact in letter and spirit. Thus it is that I have still no clear idea as to how you got it [*Albert Outler the Preacher*] finally into print. The practical upshot of this is that you now have the most nearly complete collection of my 'literary remains' that exists. I have no reliable way of judging how significant this material is—whether it may become more of an attic-stuffer than an archive."

His papers have been and are being published; the writing of this biography, which gives exposure to his let-ters and personalia, is my calling to fulfill. Quotes from his letters and papers in this biography offer a better view of the man than my words *about* him could ever accomplish. Those letters, which reveal warts 'n all, serve the purpose that he intended them to serve as he saved them. *His* letters offer an honest look at who he was. While I use them, I would never abuse them with a "gotcha" mentality. He had enough of that to deal with in theologians of all stripes while he was alive. He certainly would not appreciate that characteristic in his biographer, especially since he is unable to speak up and set his critic straight. Neither will the biography be filled with "fluff and puffery" (these are Outler's words describing those biographies that describe the subject as if *he is* as he *ought to be*).

My calling will be fulfilled if the writing fulfills what Albert Outler said in that same letter of August 3, 1988:

"Over the years and over the world, I have an abundance of academic colleagues who have kept me stretched in study, dialogue, and writing. Likewise, there have also been ecumenists in plenty to keep me busy and growing and loaded with unbelievable opportunities for cross-cultured contacts and world travel. But only a few UMC [United Methodist Church] churchmen have done more than 'admire' at a safe distance, or 'used' me when it suited them; they seemed not to have realized that it was the *church* that has always been my real 'home' and 'workplace'; you have been one of the few who have understood what I have meant by 'church.' I have known all this and have supposed all along that you knew this, but I have never said it out loud before, and it is way past due the time that I should have."

That is indeed how I continue to "see" Albert Outler. In this letter he did not define what either he nor I fully meant by the *church.* That is what this biography is about. You will read, from the beginning to the end, about how he lived in his real "home" and "workplace," the church.

I offer my grateful appreciation to the librarians of Candler School of Theology; Princeton Theological Seminary; Union Theological Seminary at Columbia University; Boston University School of Theology; Yale Divinity School; The Divinity School of Duke University; The Theological School of Drew University; Wofford College; St. Paul's

School in Washington, D.C. (Roman Catholic); St. John's Abbey (Collegeville, Minnesota); Perkins School of Theology; Cambridge University and Oxford University, England; World Council of Churches in Geneva, Switzerland; the Waldensian Seminary in Rome; and the Vatican. All of these, upon my visits, offered more than mere helping hands. They gave of themselves. But I am indebted to none more than to Page Thomas at Bridwell Library of Perkins School of Theology, who was at one time Albert Outler's research assistant. My thanks also to Glenn Morrison for his counsel concerning Outler's genealogy; to Wanda Smith and Les Longden for their bibliographical contributions; to Helen Lankford, Albert Outler's niece who got on board this writing joyfully and exhibited an intelligence, enthusiasm, and charm that has made its way into the stories she told about "Uncle Albert." To those I interviewed, whose names would more than fill a page (many of whose words, to my chagrin, had to be excluded because of manuscript length limitations), I am in debt. Many thanks to Professor Martin Marty who wrote the Foreword as a labor of love and appreciation for Albert Outler. And finally to my wife, Doris, whom Albert Outler always included as he addressed his letters to me, a loving thank you. He said that he trusted her judgment more than mine about what was readable and acceptable to the laity. The printed text has now passed the perfecting scrutiny of her eyes, plus those of the publisher's editors, and has been handed to you, the reader, to find, not errors in print (though some of those little "demons" will inevitably pop up), but to find the truth—the truth *about* Albert Outler and the truth *of* Albert Outler—the Truth, who *is* God the Father, the Son, and the Holy Spirit, the agent of *grace,* the theme that dominated the life of the man.

Bob Parrott
General Editor
The Albert Outler Library

PART 1

A Story of His Life

1

Albert Finds the Church at Home

The church was Albert's "home" and "workplace." While those two terms may seem to conflict, in Albert's experience they did not. He chose his words carefully. He understood what church as "home" meant because he experienced from the beginning of his life that there is no place like home. (Later the church as "workplace" will be discussed.)

Mother Outler

Albert Cook Outler was born on November 17, 1908, at 2:00 A.M. "in a big white two-story house next door to the big two-story brick white-steepled Methodist Church in Thomasville, Georgia"[1] where his father, the Reverend John Outler, was pastor. "Georgia-born and parsonage-bred" was Albert's own proud statement. His parents, John Morgan Outler and Gertrude Flint (Dewberry) Outler, were married on December 4, 1889. His mother's original name was *Gir*trude, but she did not like it. She changed the spelling to Gertrude, and did not like that either. It looked better on paper but still sounded the same. She simply would not allow others to call her by that name. People called her "Mrs. Outler."[2] Family members often referred to her as "The Little General."[3]

Here is how Mother Outler described parsonage life:

"I did not go into a parsonage as a bride, for my husband did not have 'the call' or urge to preach until after we had been married for two years. We had our own house, and had two very happy years in it, planning and building (as we thought) a home for ourselves and our children; but it wasn't in me to feel cheated or to rebel when I knew that I would have to give up our home and live in a parsonage. When I come to think of it, we gave up nothing at all, really, for the Dear Lord has more than compensated us for what was then a trying sacrifice.

"My husband was a 'circuit rider' for eight years before his salary equalled what he had been making before entering the ministry; and in those years there were four children to feed, clothe, and send to school; and there was an endless procession of perennial 'visitors' for us to house, feed and 'entertain.' The custom of constantly expecting and staying ready for visitors took away the precious privilege of privacy and contributed to the inability to relax. That left its mark on all of us. What may have begun as frontier hospitality may have survived from the days when the only news people had of other people or other countries was brought by itinerant peddlers. Where we lived there was no daily paper. Our children quickly learned that visitors were to be an inescapable part of our daily life; and it became a matter of interest to them to discover the unique pattern each newcomer would reveal of oddities and whims.

"About the time that the Indian Territory was being changed into the state of Oklahoma, there were numerous missionaries who had been released, and as they had to go somewhere, most of them were working their way back to the [Methodist] conference that had originally sent them out. Though all too often they were dirty and ill-kempt, they were travelers in need of shelter; and shelter was our job. In our parsonage lifetime we have entertained every sort of missionary, since quartering one at a hotel was never thought of. Of course, at the yearly conference, we would always have one or two 'just back from the missions field for a year's rest or vacation.' The term 'vacation' was a misnomer, for they spoke oftener back home than they did in the mission field. Without their interpreters, they were good speakers, and the tales they told were always thrilling, especially if the listener had never been outside his own county. At the yearly conference, the entertainment was always free and cordial; consequently, the delegation was always large.

"Our house was very small at that time, and in addition to caring for our quota of delegates, we were also expected to house the 'connectional officers' who, as mere overnight visitors, could be crammed into a makeshift bedroom originally our living-room. The rest of the house was packed to the rafters.

"I was made chairman of the committee on homes, by reason of the fact that I had been around over the conference and would be expected to know, better than a local person might, the types of delegates and the suitability of assignments of homes. I did indeed know by name and fame all the conference officers; but I was appalled by the number of women delegates who had so recently had an operation or were in such need of one that they were practically invalids and would require a separate room.

"We had many a letter that requested special accommodations, 'very close to the church and with someone who owns a conveyance' so that my four-year old son, not being able to manage to pronounce the letter 'g' very well, began to refer to the guests as 'delicates' until it really became a fact."[4]

Dad Outler

In the 1880 census nine-year-old John was listed as John Outlaw.[5] When John entered the South Georgia Conference on trial in 1891, his name was no longer Outlaw, but Outler. John (and/ or Gertrude) changed the name, making "Outler" sound more in harmony with his ministerial calling. Rev. John Outler served in the South Georgia Conference for nearly fifty years. His itinerating ministry (including four appointments as Presiding Elder) accounted for Albert's elementary and secondary education in Thomasville, Dawson, Savannah, and Americus (all in South Georgia). He was Albert's role model in ministry all the days of Albert's life. Albert's father was more than a role model; he was his son's friend. References made to his father in letters to and from his father reveal the intimacy of this relationship.

Albert honored his dad as one of the most educated men he ever knew. This, in spite of the fact that John Outler had gone only through the third grade. Frances (Fan) described her father's situation in these words:

"Papa had to grow up under circumstances that made the harshest demands upon an eager, ambitious child. He was sent to work in the mills in Macon when he was only nine years old. His own father had died, and Mr. Seago, his new stepfather, did not believe in wasting money on an able-bodied boy. There was no chance for schooling. Papa was self-taught—until Mama taught him in Sunday School and helped him with his studies to prepare himself for the ministry. Papa was an idealist and an optimist: he truly believed that, given the proper attitude and opportunity, man could raise himself to undreamed-of accomplishments. He also had a boundless sympathy for the underdog."[6]

John Outler was more than self-educated. He was Gertrude-educated. His wife motivated her husband to study, led him, pushed him. In the broadest sense *she* educated him. John Outler's mix of knowledge and vital piety gained him respect and positions of leadership in the South Georgia Conference. While "Brother John" excelled in his ministry, more than anything to Albert he was "Dad."

Albert's Siblings

Mother Outler's quest for education reached all members of her family, beginning with John, Jr., who was sixteen years old; Annie Elizabeth (nicknamed Annie Bess), who was fourteen; Jason, who was ten; and Fan who was six at the time of Albert's birth in 1908. John, Jr., was graduated from Young Harris College in 1911 and from Emory College in Oxford, Georgia, in 1914. He went on to become a pioneer in radio and television, serving as chairman of the National Association of Broadcasters and at his retirement was general manager of Radio Station WSB and WSB-TV in Atlanta.

The others followed in earning their college degrees and succeeding in their chosen fields. Annie Bess was graduated from Wesleyan College in Macon, Georgia, with accomplishments in piano, pipe organ, and professional concert piano. Her musical gifts and training gained her positions in colleges and churches throughout her life. Jason borrowed money from a banker in Dawson, Georgia, and attended Eastman Business College in Poughkeepsie, New York. During World War II Jason was assigned to high-level management in the War Shipping

Administration and then went on to become vice-president of the Strachan Shipping (steamship) Company in New York, where he remained until his retirement. Fan earned her A.B. degree at Wesleyan College, her M.A. in English Literature at Emory University, and her Ph.D. in the Division of the Humanities under acclaimed scholars of literature at the University of Chicago. She went on to become a celebrated teacher at the prestigious Westminster School for Girls in Atlanta. And then there was Albert whose involvements and accomplishments in ministry, scholarship, ecumenicity, and community service are legend. One has to conclude that the mix of genes and environment in the Outler family was extraordinary.

Not to Say That All Went Well

But this is not to say that *all* went well among the siblings. The reason for some of this tension came from the fact that Albert was born so much later than the others and was a sick baby. Fan wrote: "Because we were kept in such turmoil about Albert, the saying got norated [*sic*] around that Mama would kill all the well ones to make soup for the sick one. And he lost out early in the popularity contest in our family with all the siblings but me. When I went on the defensive for him, it was for life."[7] But Fan could not protect Albert twenty-four hours a day. One day Annie Bess became fed up with seeing her mother carry Albert around on a pillow. She proceeded to put infant Albert in the perambulator and pushed him to downtown Thomasville, where his father was pastor at the time, and sold him at the drugstore for a quarter. Little Albert was returned to the Outlers, but Annie Bess kept her quarter. It was not she who had welshed on the deal.[8]

Annie Bess's problem with Albert actually began the day and the way she heard the birth news. Fan described it this way:

"We did not realize how badly I would embarrass Annie Bess when I asked Miss Sarah Harley to let me go speak to her [Annie Bess] on a *most* important errand. When Miss Sallie Baker welcomed me at the door of the seventh grade, I announced in a voice of pride, 'Annie Bess, guess what? We've got a new baby brother!' Poor Annie Bess said that she could have died ten deaths. I was the only human in Thomasville, it seems, who hadn't known Albert was on the way. The custom then was to send young ones like me off on 'a visit,' and I had spent blissful months down the street at Grandma Bottoms' home. She was no kin, but I did not know that then. She had a loving daughter, 'Aunt' Mamie, who had devoted her life to taking care of her mother and her brother Amos, who was the town drunk (but who did not go to town to do his drinking) . . ."[9]

Fan, reflecting on her youth, recalled:

"My childhood seems brief in retrospect because from the hour my baby brother Albert Cook Outler was born in Thomasville, Georgia, November 17, 1908, I felt so responsible for him that I grew up fast. He was a sickly baby, but was blessed with an angelic disposition, and he filled my need for a constant companion to make up for the passing friendships and casual acquaintances imposed on a parsonage kid. I could push him in his 'perambulator' or read to him. He was entrusted to me on our first automobile ride. Our neighbor was Rev. George Matthews, and his son owned an open, one-seater Maxwell car with hand controls for the steering wheel. He took Albert and me to ride, and when the baby's embroidered cap blew off, I just stepped out to retrieve it and was knocked almost unconscious by the fall I suffered. Papa, summoned to carry me to Dr. McIntosh to be sure no bones were broken, was provoked to one of his rare exhibits of wrath. 'Didn't you have any more sense than stepping out of a moving car?' he stormed at me. 'But Papa, it wasn't but two notches from stopping!' I exclaimed. (I had watched the way the throttle was advanced or not [by notches] and *realized* that was the secret of driving this newfangled toy.)"[10]

Fan's First Pupil

Fan continues:

"He [Albert] was my first pupil, and I poured into teaching him all the love and devotion I was capable of bestowing. I required him to memorize all the lore I had achieved, and read him to sleep every night from the Bible. I would deliberately distort a quotation, and he would correct me as long as he was awake. If he left an outrageous misquotation unchallenged, I knew he was asleep. Because we had to stay fairly inactive [because of Albert's frailty] we played make-believe games around his bedroom. We ran a bank, where I was president and he was treasurer. That meant we made play money and conducted a thriving business refusing loans. I was J. C. Morrison and he was J. C. Copeland. We must have been paying unconscious tribute to the business acumen of our brother J. C. (Jason Curry Outler)."[11]

She went on to say: "Albert and I were so schooled in memorizing the words to whatever we loved that in 1951 when he and I hung over the top balcony at the Metropolitan Opera in New York (standing throughout its New York debut), we could sing *Die Fledermaus* from start to finish. This was true of all the Gilbert and Sullivan we had memorized and sung in the 30s! The Metropolitan Opera Co. came to Atlanta in 1910 and appeared every spring for years in the Old City Auditorium. When John earned his first money at *The Atlanta Journal,* he saw to it that I had seats at opera until I was out of college. So it was that we [Albert and Fan] were privileged to hear the grand opera and its great names: Enrico Caruso, Scotti, Geraldine Farrar, Mme. Ernestine Schumann-Heink, Feodor Chaliapin. The Atlanta productions were lavish and opulent, and the love affair of this city with the stars was the real thing. Tosca, La Bohème, Tannhauser, Madame Butterfly, Carmen, Trovatore, Pagliacci, Rigoletto, Lucia di Lammermoor were our favorites."[12]

With Fan, Albert's earliest books included *Little Women, Treasure Island, The Water Lilies, King of the Golden River, Aesop's Fables, Arabian Nights, Five Little Peppers and How They Grew, Rebecca of Sunnybrook Farm, Robin Hood, The Young Marooners, Marooners Island,* Milton's *Paradise Lost,* Dante's *Inferno.* And magazines: *Saturday Evening Post, St. Nicholas,* and the *Youth's Companion.*[13]

And then there was their reading of "the eleventh edition of The Encyclopedia Britannica (on India paper) and in 1974, fifty years later, when I [Fan] bought the Mortimer Adler version of The Britannica (called III), lo and behold! there was Albert among the contributors, author of the article on Doctrine and Dogma."[14]

Playing and Learning

Albert recalled how, when he was a tad of a boy, older brothers John and Jason came home from the war in Europe, where they had gone "to protect his future," and let him wear their helmets, which he did proudly. But most of his playing was done with

Fan who always seemed to have a way of making it a learning situation. When she taught Albert Latin, she made it a fun time. This ability followed her into her Latin classes at Westminster. For example, an observer of one of her Latin classes was amazed that Latin could be a game. "Ten students at the blackboard, the staccato of chalk, the sifting of dust from the board, the laughter of other students attentively watching from their seats, a contest clocked with a stopwatch, and suddenly—'Mary has conjugated the verb first!'"[15] Fan taught Albert how to "drive." She wrote: "Not being able to own one [a car] Albert and I sat in orange crates in the yard and steered with the churn dasher as we zoomed in our imaginary Stanley Steamer."[16]

Other games included "chess, archery, golf, roller skates, checkers, croquet, badmitton [sic], tennis, sledding, volleyball, jump rope, leap frog, blind man's bluff [sic], pin the tail on the donkey, antney over [sic], rook, old maid, horseshoes. Recreation at Young Harris [the family retreat in the mountains of North Georgia] consisted of: taking the cow 'Bangseye' to the pasture, going to bring her back, milking her, fetching the mail, fetching any errand for Mama, going to the mill, and climbing mountains. I was out of college before I ever had a deck of cards. It was considered improper for either Annie Bess or me to attend the harmless card parties in our small towns. Mama never relayed the invitations; she just declined for us!"[17]

Albert's First Teacher

In Albert's words: "Besides my parents, it was my older sister [Fan] who was my first teacher and probably the best one I ever had. My formal education was quite standard—which is to say, inferior. But my informal education was rich and rewarding."[18] He called Fan a true genius. She was a teacher in public and private schools, and taught Albert how to read and write Latin before he entered high school (actually *started* teaching him Latin before he entered the first grade!). Like her mother, she was a high-spirited person, as the following letter written to me on February 24, 1973, attests:

"I love and venerate my brother and look upon him as a forerunner cast into the lonely role of being fifty years ahead of his time, just as my minister-father was fifty years ahead of his time. I recall my father's attendance at every General Conference, from 1922 at Hot Springs until the earlier [as opposed to the 1968 Uniting Conference] Uniting General Conference of 1939, [a movement] embroiled in controversy that never lost its bitterness and has not yet subsided in rural pockets in the South. I have often wondered how these two men, father and son, whose combined ministries stretch from 1889 to 1973 [and beyond], were touched with an ambiance of charm, grace, and magnetism unexampled among their contemporaries and yet possessed of the ferocity of Uriel [one of the archangels of the Hebrew Midrash and apocryphal Scriptures. The name means 'the Light of God,' one who judges and forgives] in pointing a spear at what they considered unworthy of God's calling. Friend or foe bore them lifelong devotion or undying hostility; no one, to my knowledge, has ever yet paid one of us the anemic tribute of neutrality!

"It is all too easy to call us eccentrics.—It is equally easy to picture us as elitists. Except for the paradox of believing that all of us are equal as children of God in his boundless love, and the flat reality of my own senses after fifty years in the Atlanta schools (thirty in the public schools back when teaching was a calling almost as sacred as that of a minister, and twenty in *the* most posh private school in the South). I have the tragic and profound sorrow of feeling that education, as such, cannot solve all the problems it is beset with; nor can it be all things to all men; nor can all men be equal when most of us now seventy-plus had to pull ourselves by our bootstraps and wind up with a pension of fifty dollars a month! Papa never received more than $3600 a year (to my knowledge), though he was seven times a district superintendent (then called presiding elder); but on that, and borrowing, he sent five of us through college. After fifty years, with seven of those years to earn the M.A. at night, and three years for my doctorate at the University of Chicago under Hutchins and Clarence Faust, whom I could not then foresee would soon be running the twenty-five billion dollar *Fund For the Republic*!—It *had* to be Clarence Faust's class I walked out of when he put me to sleep with his mumbling lecture on Lovejoy's *Great Chain Of Being*! And I went out and sat on a park bench on the Midway and decided in the August sunshine that I wanted no more of the University if *he* was *it! So,* without the magic (it came later) of a Ph.D., I came back to the classroom where I have always been the happiest. The end of this long saga, is simply that (on the economic level) I came out at $7500—just twice Papa's maximum—with over $100,000 invested in my fifty years—at a minimum.

"These are thoughts I have not had time to organize. If I reread them, I should doubtless burn them. My point is too wordily made: we are equal only in God's prevenience and grace as his creatures, and most of the efforts we make to realize our greatest potential now turn out to be over-adrenaline, hyperactivity, or some other new name for a chemical imbalance that drove us to rise above the flock.

"That idiotic best-seller, J. L. Seagull, is cashing in at the moment on this Jesus-freak deal: *of* the flock, but always *above* it—what a rapturous, ego-warming notion! What a childish misreading of spiritual drive!

"From me [about Albert] you would get only loving reminiscence and awe I feel for all who truly walk with God, and don't need a sweatshirt to prove it.

"One of these bumper stickers on the back of a station-wagon load of car-pooled kids reads: "If you love Jesus, honk!" The lady in the car behind (stopped at an intersection) bore down on *her* horn to let her fervor be known. Whereupon, the mother driving her Country Squire load of kids, rolled down her window and yelled back, 'You damn fool, can't you see that the light is still red?!'—Whether it is true or not, it's going the rounds to give vent to the confusion between bumper stickers and sweatshirt folks and those who love him without being able to help themselves."

Both Fan and Albert shared a common inherited genius, a willingness to swim against the tide and a drive to speak the truth as experienced, no matter whom it offended. A prophet was in the making early in Albert's life. They also shared the habit of holding on to anything made of paper. Fan expressed this common habit in these words in a letter addressed to me dated August 29, 1979:

"It is devoutly hoped that this move and uprooting will be my last. After seventy-seven years of life lived in the full knowledge that we are promised no enduring habitation on this troubled earth, I still have some sort of irrational attachment to places in which I may have 'sojourned' as a comparative stranger, and a sense of totally irrational nostalgia for places in which I might not necessarily have had the happiest of experiences. Every uprooting had to be accepted as part of our lives when we were children in the 'itineracy.' We knew we had to move on a four-year basis, and took some sort of silly pride that our minister father was a 'four-year' preacher, and not one of those who had to move oftener. But nothing has ever reconciled me to the all-too-frequent relocations my life has known. One finally realizes that we are wayfaring strangers.

"Out of the eighty-plus boxes and crates required to bring us here in hot and humid May, we have as yet some twenty-five-plus stored in our tool shed, unpacked for lack of any more room in the house; and I am still, in hot and humid August, unable to cope with the physical effort of sorting out those boxes in the tool-house between my books and the family data. When the packers wearied of labelling the boxes, they just resorted to 'MISC.,' so that contents may be books or goodness-knows-what, though for some unknown reason, they managed to label clearly, if wrongly spelled, 'PIXTURES.' One box was labeled 'BAGS,' and when I opened it, expecting pocketbooks, it was an entire box of neatly folded grocery sacks! All this is to promise that as time goes by, and I feel more equal to it, I will try to sift out what I can lay hands on for your proposed records."

Albert kept letters that his parents kept, going back into the early 1900s. Plane tickets, boarding passes, itineraries, ticket stubs for plays, pictures of all sizes and shapes, thousands of letters. "File 13" was not his nor Fan's favorite filing place.

About Fan, a "Miss Chips" who had retired from the Westminster Schools whose fields were Latin, English, and journalism, Albert said: "I have been her protege; more than any other person in my life. Her interests, convictions about the intellectual life as a redemption from sentimentality and mindlessness, are as deep-rooted in me as my other moral values. To approve of something shoddy is as unthinkable to me as to approve of something indecent. And I got both of those from her."[19]

Mother Outler, Revisited

Behind Fan and Albert, as well as the other children, was a strong-willed mother, nicknamed by the children "The Little General." Albert's mother lived in the very fibre of his being. He

reminisced about her and his family in these words: "My brothers and sisters had been sent away to be with friends. One of the
bits of humor and folklore in the family has always been that,
when they got back, there was this little brother that had been
born, so to say, out of due season. I was [nearly] seven years
younger than the crop that had been born, sort of two years
apart."[20]

When pressed to say more about his birth, Outler said, "I
don't remember!" and then went on to tell the story of three
sisters who were vying with each other on how far back they
could remember. "One could remember when she was six; one
could remember when she was three; and Carrie remembered
when she was born because she was in the hospital and remembered her grandmother was there—her mother was off at the
Women's League of Voters!"[21]

That story typifies Outler's mother. He said, "She was a
pistol. Small. Heugenot extraction. They hadn't survived the wars
of religion without absorbing a certain resilience, but no bend-
ing. She was glad to serve in the itinerant system. And she would
go where sent, though she thought Bishop Will Ainsworth was
an idiot. She did not tell him so directly, but it was clear enough.
We moved into a parsonage at Cordele, and she went through the
parsonage and discovered that the mattresses were not quite suitable for us (bed bugs). She had them hauled out into the yard,
and she poured kerosene over them, set fire to them, and ordered
a new set of mattresses. She told the parsonage committee what
she had done—after the fact!

"It wasn't that she was at all self-concerned. She was feisty
and had a sense of worth and dignity, and then had an expectation of all of us that has made it impossible for any of us ever to
think that we have accomplished very much. Which always keeps
you aware of the fact that with a little more effort and care you
could have done a lot better. And I have lived through some of
the most extraordinary things that I know of—that have happened to a person with this background. And I cannot think of
any of them that mother would not have said, 'Now did you do
your very best?' And would have looked mildly incredulous if I
said I had! Which has had me stretched all my life because when
I see her next she is going to say, 'Did you do your very best?'
and she is not going to be content with a slack answer!"[22]

Reflections on Mother and Dad

In words spoken with the flavor of his Georgia accent, Outler continued to reflect the spirit of those about whom he talked:

"Mother and Dad were quite extraordinary people actually. Dad was this self-educated, wonderfully openhearted man. What I recall most clearly about him was the heartiness and dignity with which he moved through the world. Any and everywhere with people he was never obsequious. He grew up in the age of tyrant bishops—Candler, Will Ainsworth. He was never obsequious to rich or eminent men and women. Never condescending either.

"He was an awfully good preacher. A man before his time. Interested in foreign missions before the church committed itself to an active missionary program—in the Sunday School movement—his father died when he was in the third grade, and he had to drop out of school in order to help earn the family livelihood. Yet he taught himself. He read—and so when the Sunday School movement began, Dad was into that long before the Conference rallied around it, long before Bishop Atkins made it a cause in the Southern church. He served on the Sunday School Board.

"Ed F. Cook, from whom I get my middle name, was one of the patricians. He had gone to Vanderbilt, which was then like having gone to Yale. Dad and Cook were peers as well as colleagues. While I was out at Gordon in this little middle-Georgia town riding a circuit, Cook was at a church equivalent of what would be Highland Park [Dallas, Texas]. He pastored Mulberry Street in Macon, Georgia. Cook brought me into Macon to be the associate pastor at Mulberry Street, which is the mother church of Methodism in Georgia. He did so out of recognition that John Outler's son must have some talent, and he could put it to use.

"I was always proud of Dad for never being embarrassed that he had so little formal learning. And yet he was real pleased to have a son with a Yale Ph.D. This was remarkable to Dad. He took it in stride. Wasn't awfully impressed, but awfully proud. He was one of the most interesting men I knew amongst all the people with whom I had professional acquaintances."[23]

During an interview with H. Wayne Pipkin, Albert said, "In a way, my father was an old-fashioned, conservative Methodist preacher as far as his tastes and theology were concerned. But I can see now, in retrospect, that he was also a genuine reformer—both in the church and in the communities that he served—and I've come to appreciate this interesting mixture of theological conservatism and social vision and activism.

"For example, he was a pioneer in the Christian education movement long before it was a universal cause. And in the missionary movement and in the very early stages of Methodist labor and race relations, at a time when these were pretty far out.

"It was my father who taught me how to be a free and loyal Methodist. Free in a tight, connectional system; loyal to the system and yet independent of its power to repress.

"We lived under a series of very authoritarian bishops in Georgia—Bishop Candler and Bishop Ainsworth and the lot—with whom Dad was related, for he was sometimes Presiding Elder and at other times preacher in large city churches. And his relations with these bishops and the conference organization were almost always tense—in some sort of loyal opposition. He was, himself, never intimidated or subdued. And we lived in congregations that we loved—as I remember it—and who loved us—but whom mother kept out of our hair by insisting that the parsonage was *our home*."[24]

While "Aunt Mary" (a middle-aged Negro nanny) came every day to help Mother Outler in Albert's preschool days (he had pleasant memories of her), clearly the "presence" of his mother was felt in the very marrow of his bones. For instance, as he stood robed and ready to speak to the pope, the bishops, and the cardinals in St. Paul's Outside the Walls in Rome during Vatican II, his first words were: "I wish Mama could see me now!" (It takes little imagination to believe that she did!)

Mrs. Outler's Interview

Mrs. Outler described something of herself in an interview with Sara Singleton King, a reporter with the *Atlanta Journal*. It concerned a house in the mountains of Young Harris, Georgia, named "Trail's End," a place where Albert spent some of the quality times of his life. She said in the article: "This house, as well as the story behind it, is like Topsy, 'it just grew;' but behind it, like all other things worthwhile, it had to have a goal, aim or totem pole to work for.

"Our particular aim, or totem pole, was five children [Albert's wife Carla would say that this observation was a bit off the mark since Albert's birth, coming at a time that was a bit too late for parents to be considering another child, was a surprise] and as every sign and symbol on a totem pole means something to the tribe erecting it, so every dollar spent on this house that Hymen [the god of marriage in Grecian mythology] built meant something to us. But the scars of sacrifice have been healed by the years, and today, after twenty-seven years of stinting, saving a dollar here and a dollar there, we not only have the house that Hymen built, but a place for rest and recreation and a refuge for sick and sore hearts and weary bodies.

"All this requires an explanation. My husband is a minister. He began at the bottom, our first year's salary being $245, without the missionary appropriation which such salaries demand these days.

"In spite of our scarcity of funds, after that first year we managed somehow to get a few days' vacation with either his people or my own. But, as the children grew older, transportation as well as room became a problem.

"Fate at this time took a hand, at least that is what I would like to think now. At the time it really seemed a calamity.

"My husband had advanced, and his work was very exacting, with a large membership and all the work pertaining to one. We rarely went on any kind of a trip but what some member got sick and wanted his pastor. My husband would have gone back even to the poorest one, but somehow the poorer ones didn't get sick like the others, or, if they did, they were like us, accustomed to looking out for themselves. The year I speak of, my husband had a serious breakdown, and the little Scotch doctor, a member of no church at all, but a man whose sympathy and understanding made him one of the most beloved figures in the town—this Scotch looked at me and said, 'Take him some place where he can't get back, even if every member of his church dies.'

"That is how we happened to go to an isolated spot in the mountains of North Georgia, near the North Carolina line, and twenty-two miles from a railroad. In those days it took us eleven hours to travel those twenty-two miles. Today over a hard surfaced road, and in an automobile, it can be done in forty minutes.

"On that first trip, constant urging of a four-horse team was necessary, and the team reminded one of jackrabbits more than anything else. The road was nothing more than a trail, which passed over rocks so big that it took all the strength of the four underfed horses to pull us across, and was so steep that I wondered if it would be possible to stick long enough to get to the top.

"The driver was very busy with his hand brake and the four lines over his horses, but he had time to answer me in the vernacular of the mountains, when I asked him how far it was to Young Harris. He said, 'Wal, out thar, they say hits twenty-two miles, but you'll think it's forty, agin you git thar,' and I was perfectly willing to agree, after eleven hours of riding, that it was all of forty.

"We had been able to get board and lodging for our family for the huge sum, to us, of $60 for the entire month. Only those who have tried to take $60 out of a month's salary, which is needed to the last cent for food, clothes, music lessons, books, etc., will know how we accomplished this.

"Our visit to the mountains was pleasant and wholesome, with plain, but abundant food, cool nights, sweaters to snuggle after supper, and blankets to brag about to the folks back home. We wrote friends that we were sleeping under blankets, and they were so callous as to reply that they didn't care what we slept under, just so we didn't mention blankets to them.

"The time was drawing near for us to return home, and none of us wanted to go. I'd had a wild idea in my head for a long time, but I hesitated to speak of it, for I knew how my husband felt about the insurance he carried for our protection.

"However, the children's development and welfare were the paramount ideas in both our minds. The two oldest ones, then 10 and 12, were just like other children in their wants, and it seemed to me that if they could be satisfied with such wholesome diversions as mountain climbing, fishing, watching the sun rise and living close to nature, why not try to give them these things, why not let these things take the place of others which cost so much more? For instance, the oldest son spent hours developing a spring that has since furnished three families with water. Back in those early days he delighted in fashioning cups from grape leaves in which to bring us all clear, cool water to drink.

"One day, after a long climb, we were resting on the very hill which afterwards became ours. My husband said with a wistful look on his face, 'If we could have a shack in these hills to bring the children to during vacation, we'd save ourselves a lot of doctor bills, trouble and heartache, and have something to show for it in sane, sensible children.'

"Neither of us has had any patience with the old saying that 'preachers' children are the worst.' They are human beings and have all the ambitions, aspirations, weaknesses and human frailties that other people's children have. I once very cheerfully said as much to an old lady who was present when I had to reprove one of the children. She quoted the old saying about preachers' children, and I replied by telling her that, if this were true, it was probably because the preacher and his wife were so busy looking after visitors and other peoples' children that they had little time left in which to try to train their own.

"The idea of a shack in the mountains had come to me even before my husband gave voice to his own feelings in the matter. I felt that the time had come for me to speak my piece.

"'Would you be willing,' I asked him, 'to borrow the money on your life insurance to pay for an acre of ground?' He thought a while and said, 'Yes, I could do that, but where would we get the money to put up a shack and furnish it?'

"My ideas were working overtime at the moment, so I had an answer ready. 'Marriage fees,' I told him. Most preachers give these fees to their wives, which is appropriate and romantic. Some wives do one thing with them; some, another. My big idea was to save them as a building fund, and although it took a long time, these fees finally did blossom into our first shack. Some years were so lean that it looked as though no one loved another, for the fees were few and far between.

"Anyway, the seed was sown and the fund grew until my husband finally did borrow the money on his insurance to pay for the land and the lumber to start the house.

"I'm no architect, but I knew what I wanted in the way of room. So I drew up a plan for three bedrooms, a living room which could be dining room, too, a kitchen, and a pantry. The house was built on the side of a hill, so steep that there is plenty of space for rooms underneath the front. But the backside of the house has since that time had to be set in concrete to keep the sills from rotting on the ground. Nothing but a shack, but ours, to fight over, work for, and love!

"To pay for this shack, improve it, and keep it up, was our next objective. My husband had not stayed at the bottom [of pastoral appointments] by any means, and has received as good appointments as can be had at the hands of his church; but, as everyone ought to know, no minister receives a dollar that he does not have two places to put it.

"For ten years we kept the place as it was, adding furniture as was needed and as the marriage fees accumulated. We also bought two more acres of ground and set them out in apple trees. We then built another bedroom and sleeping porch.

"Sometimes we had to wait a whole year to buy this and that. For instance, we were living in a coast town during the World War, when the weddings were numerous, but not very remunerative. Most of them were Saturday night weddings that seemed to have been thought after the weekly pay envelope was drawn. Anyway, it required the whole of four years to pay for a fence. But that fence still endures.

"We have felt that the place was a trust and a means in our hands to help those less fortunate. We have carried people there, broken up from sorrow and bereavement, people suffering from various causes. Twice, when doctors have said, 'We've done all that we can do; nature and quiet must do the rest,' we've gathered up the broken bodies and gone to the hills—to the veritable fountain of youth.

"The only time we departed from our cut-and-dried rule of wedding fees or nothing was in 1930. My husband was a delegate to the General Conference in Dallas, Texas, and invited me to go; but I'm never happy in a crowd. So I begged off and asked instead to be given the amount that it would take to cover my expenses. This included the railroad fare going and coming, sleeping and dining cars, to say nothing of hotel bills and clothes suitable for the occasion.

"By this time another bee was buzzing in my head. For we had reached the stage where men have to take into account the infirmities of approaching age. Before many more years we would face superannuation, which in our church is one of those facts usually accepted in the most light as death and taxes. Most of us, like Mr. McCawber, are so sure that 'something will turn up' that very seldom do we make any provision against that saddest of all times. I, for one, did not intend that my husband and I should be wholly unprepared.

"The house was built of good oak lumber roughly and cheaply cut, and up until now had served its purpose; but for old age some comforts were needed, and what I did with the few hundred dollars that would have carried us to that western city and back, I'll be proud of all my life. Even with the thermometer down to six, as it was one winter we decided to run up for a visit, the house was cozy as our living room 375 miles farther south.

"The children have grown up, taken their places in the business and professional world with honor and credit. They make their annual pilgrimage to the place, each contributing something to its comfort and beauty: an outdoor fireplace, lawn or house furniture; books, for which in the rearrangement of the house plenty of room was provided. I had a rock fireplace built in the living room, with Bobby Burns's notable blessing inserted:

> "Some hae meat, and canna eat
> Some woud eat, that want it,
> But we hae meat, and we can eat
> And sae the Lord be thankit.

"One year I had a yen for a sun dial and lily pool, but it had been a lean season so far as weddings were concerned, and it was necessary to devise other ways and means. Being in the mountains it was not hard to find what we called 'pay dirt,' that is, a solid rock bottom for a pool.

"By maneuvering and building up the sides we soon had a pool fed by a spring, which furnishes all the oxygen for the fish, even when the pool freezes over. Planted with lilies, cattails, water poppies, and further embellished with a few figures used in around the pool, it is 'a thing of beauty and joy forever.' In the boggy overflow we have dozens of Japanese irises that are worth traveling miles to see. [I discovered upon a visit to that homesite that these irises still grow there and are dug up by neighbors and planted in their yards.]

"The problem of the sun dial was not so simple, since more scientific calculations were necessary if it were to serve the real purpose of a sun dial, and 'tell time.' But, as in most cases, where we want something badly enough to give up something else in its place, the sun dial was achieved. My husband had only two weddings that year, and both fees put together would not have paid for the pedestal. One of the fees I did not even keep, for when I looked at that bride, marrying a man of faith and no job (not a runaway match, either, but just a walk-over-to-the-preacher affair), I slid the $5 out of the license envelope and pressed it into her hand. Preachers and their wives cannot, for obvious reasons, indulge in wedding presents, but there have been a few times when I have felt that a man's estimate of the worth of his bride was more than he could afford. This was one of those times.

"But anyway, the sun dial was evolved from this and that, set perfectly by an army compass, and found to record the passing of the hours as accurately as a jeweled timepiece. On its face is the motto: 'Time takes all but memories.' We all feel that the hardships and sacrifices made to acquire a home so full of lovely memories are as nothing compared to its possession.

"We have in the course of time built ourselves a road and planted the grounds with shrubbery, much of this having been sent to us by people who at various times have been our guests. The latest addition to the house is in the form of double iron gates, which are set into rock pillars and make a very lovely entrance. It took the accumulation of two years' wedding fees to pay for these gates, but they are up at last, and all in all, we feel that old Hymen has done pretty well by a family that is making plans to spend the last days of a full and happy life at 'Trail's End,' which is the new name for our home.

"We are planning a new and lovelier sun dial which will bear the inscription:

> "Upon my face the hours of sun and shine are
>   read with ease,
> Within my heart the hours of stress and storm are hid,
> And only God can see the mark."

An Appalachian Hillbilly

Albert comments, "My childhood has two contrasting loci. One, from September to May in any given year, we lived in a parsonage in the South Georgia town or city where my father was a Methodist minister. And then, from June to the end of August

we lived in a little mountain valley high in the Georgia Appala-
chians where I could literally run free with the other hillbillies
and become one myself. To this day I have two alternating images that come from those years. The preacher's kid from Savannah or Americus or Macon or wherever, on the one hand, and the
hillbilly from Young Harris on the other. Here was the beginning
of a lifelong experience of living in more worlds than one at a
time."[25] [Albert was never known to live in "one world at a time"!]

Carla adds, "Young Harris was his real home. As a young
child (two or so), he had colitis. Mother Outler took him there.
She had no idea that he would survive. She nursed him back to
health. [It takes little imagination to understand how sickness
plagued Albert all the days of his life; he was born a sick baby.
That, plus the fact that he was the youngest of seven children
(two babies had died), and nearly seven years younger than the
one before him, ranked Albert high on the attention ladder for
his parents—and for Fan.] Every summer when school was out,
she [Mother Outler] took the family to Young Harris and returned to wherever Dad Outler was stationed just in time to
outfit the children for school—new shoes [especially]. Albert
remembered how they had outgrown the ones they wore in the
spring. Albert had very happy memories of the long summers—
the valley and the mountains."[26]

Albert's greatest pleasure came each year when, from June
until the end of August, he was climbing the mountains and
descending to the valleys around Young Harris. On a summer
afternoon he would shut his books, put on old clothes and walking shoes and slip out into a deer trail just to see where it might
lead. If time allowed, he would set his sights on the tallest mountain, 4,784 feet above sea level—Brasstown Bald. He hiked along
six miles or more of trails to reach its summit. From there he
absorbed the spectacular panoramic view of four states at a distance and up close the breathtaking foliage displays of oak, Lom-
bardy poplar, Pennsylvania maple, black locust, sycamore,
mountain ash, and pine against the background of a blue sky. In
the spring, wildflowers such as baby's breath, spirea, popcorn
spirea, and bridal wreath interspersed with trailing arbutus, wood-
bine trailing the hickory trees and wild clematis.[27] Everything
about these mountains seemed to unite in harmony that amused
and elated him. He was naturally inquisitive, serious about his

research into the life cycle of a butterfly or a frog or a fish, cheerful at his discovery, and elated when sharing his news with others. His world came alive with these marvels. When he told his story, there was a flash in his expression that vaguely suggested some strange inner power. He especially looked forward to spring, to the times that the hills came alive, not merely as the ground that held trees and flowers, but as some common life of which he was a part.

Albert was aware of this inner power himself, a curious ebbing force that came at times, whether in the woods or the pulpit, and filled him as the wind fills the sail. He called that power *God*.

The Ongoing Influence of Appalachia

The reader will note the influence of "Trail's End" throughout the life of Albert Outler. His sermons and lectures are chocked full of anecdotes and stories born in the mountains of North Georgia. Not knowing this background, his more sophisticated audiences were surprised to hear some of the "country" tales coming from the mouth of the church's number-one egghead. This incongruity accounted for much of Outler's humor, and for the good humor in others as they used Outler's stories. For instance, there was the time that the highly popular Southern Baptist preacher, Carlyle Marney, as the 1978 Peyton Lecturer at the Perkins School of Theology Ministers' Week, told this story:

"Once upon a time—twelve, fifteen years ago—I came here with some timidity to this Peyton Series. After the first lecture, your Albert Outler met me and said, 'You can't get there from here.' After the second lecture, dear Outler, always frank, if not exactly helpful, said: 'Why would you try to walk that tightrope between *via negativa* and *via negon* when there is a perfectly good bridge across Chalcedon.' Well, after the next lecture his comment was devastating. He said: 'You remind me of an old squirrel hunter I knew as a boy. He had St. Vidas Dance, but he always got meat because he shot all over the tree!'"

This high humor paved the way for Marney's closing comment: "In those days there were four Peyton sermons, and at the close of the fourth I had said, 'Friends, I shall have to stop here. For if I go further, I shall have to speak of resurrection which some days I don't believe at all.' In the hall outside Albertus Magnus met me: 'You shouldn't of said that.' And I, full of criticism said: 'Dear Albert, you are so damned smart. What should I have said?' And he, to my continuing enrichment, gave me great grace. I think of it all the time. Albert said: 'Whoever told you that you had to believe it every day?' And I said: 'When, then, my dear man, must I believe it?' He said: 'The day you die, or the day you die with someone you love very much you believe the resurrection of the dead.' This is so. Twelve, fifteen years later, I've died once or twice. I've watched my Daddy spit in death's eye and start on the long journey. And there are others. And so I believe the resurrection of the dead as the New Testament claims."

In this Carlyle Marney story one can see the influence of "home" in Outler's ministry. It gave to him an Appalachian Mountain "high" that lasted all the days of his life.

"Home" was a situation where there was a love far stronger than disagreements, a persuasion by truth that was stronger in its own way than any threatening and intimidating exercise of power, and there was a sense of belonging. "Home" quite naturally became Albert's metaphor for church.

2

Albert Becomes a Student, a Preacher, a Teacher

A Student

After his 1925 high school graduation in Americus, Georgia, where his father pastored, Albert did not want to go to Emory where his brothers went. Instead he chose Methodist-related Wofford College (Spartanburg, South Carolina). He arrived in plus-fours (slacks that fasten below the knees). This was Mother Outler's idea of what college men wore. *That* took some living down![28] It was that kind of experience that Outler did not want to recall when he returned to Wofford College in April 1985 to carry that graduating class on *his* sentimental journey. He said: "For whatever encouragement it may be to any of you here today, the record will show that I was no BMOC [Big Man on Campus] during my 'bright college years,' and was never included in the list of nominees of those 'most likely to succeed.' [According to records he was a success as a member of the Theta Chi Delta, a dramatic fraternity.] My quite modest record, however, did not prevent my getting what I have always been proud to call 'my Wofford education,' a cultural formation that has served me very well through the vicissitudes of a half century and more.

"That 'Wofford education' was an education that prepared me for nothing in particular. But it was an effective orientation for the continuing series of unexpected twists and turns in a whole life's work that began with a stint of school teaching in the backwoods of South Georgia, and that went on to include foregatherings with high domes in New Haven and Cambridge and with cardinals in Rome. More importantly, it taught me to understand my curiosity [about] the energy of learning and the powers of critical reason as the forming discipline of a civilized life. From home and here, I learned to love learning and wisdom above possessions and power, to prefer 'living well' to 'making a good living,' insofar as I ever had any such latter choice. My Wofford education helped give form and style to a basic code of Christian values that I had brought from home, but had never analyzed or tested. Here it became an ethical horizon for a conscience-guided self.

"You will realize, as I do of course, that I have never come close to this far horizon. Even so, here at Wofford [1925–1928] I was taught to aspire to such a goal, and to measure success and failure by its norms. My degree was an old-fashioned baccalaureate orientation in the heritage of Western culture and, eventually, I came to understand more clearly why they labeled the ceremony of its awarding a 'graduation' and a 'commencement.' For that is what it amounted to, rather than the *completion* of anything.

"These ideals of living for goodness' sake, that were focused for me here, were then promptly challenged by a series of unexpected exigencies that have provided the context for my life. First, there was the Great Depression and then World War II, followed by the upsurge of a confident secular moralism after World War II (labeled by President James Conant of Harvard as 'the religion of democracy'). At the peak of a moderately successful academic career, I suffered through the reckless wounding of American education in the '60s and the demoralizing defeat of America's leadership role in Vietnam from which we never have recovered. This was set back further in the OPEC crisis. And now we are witnesses together of the twilight of a Euro-centered world. Thus, in the '80s I am still trying to learn what I can from the latest changes in a world for which I have never been fully prepared: from the greying of the Hippies (who still have no shame for what they did to us) to the greening of the Yuppies (whose greed is so brazen as almost to veil its callousness).

"Very little of this history was prescripted as far as I could foresee (or can even now make good sense of, in retrospect). But it had to be reacted to as constructively as one could, and the extent to which I have been enabled to respond constructively was, in itself, a bonus from the sort of education I have had, in this place and in others. As one looks back over these past seven decades, they can be likened to the familiar glass that can be reckoned as half-full or half-empty, according to the expectations that one brings to the appraisal. In either case, it has been exciting and even rewarding in its way, a manifestation more of the grace of God in continuing his strange experiment with humanity than of any human merit or achievement on our own."[29]

While Albert might not have been in his words "a BMOC" (a typical self-deprecating comment), he was in those Wofford days full of big dreams, tempered by a sense of his own incongruities. For example, on April 12, 1926, in his *National Memory and Fellowship Book, dedicated to Keepers of Keepsakes* Albert wrote his nickname, "Dodunk," his ambition, "to be a bishop," and his happy thought, "I ain't much, but I sure try to be *that!*"

A Preacher

After receiving his A.B. degree with an English major from Wofford College in 1928, Albert was elected to Phi Beta Kappa. He got off to a running start in the church as his "workplace" when he was licensed to preach, approved as a local pastor, and admitted on probation in the South Georgia Conference in 1928. From November 12, 1928, until November 22, 1930, he served as junior preacher on the Baxley Circuit (pastored two small churches, Midway and Crosby's Chapel, under the supervision of Rev. E. A. Sanders, who pastored the other four churches on the circuit) in the piney woods of South Georgia.

Here is how Albert described this period of his life: "Now, one interesting interlude came between college and seminary. I'd finished college in three years, and wasn't quite old enough to go on to graduate school. And I wasn't quite sure about the ministry yet, so between 1928 and 1930 I went down to Appling County in South Georgia, deep in the Georgia piney woods, to serve as a principal of a rural junior high school and also as pastor of two

principal of a rural junior high school and also as pastor of two
country churches way out in the piney woods.

"It was a marvelous experience, total immersion in a folk
culture of southern Appalachia. And it was a marvelous discovery of myself. I learned that I loved both preaching and teaching.
And I think it was in this backwoods situation that I finally got
the foreshadowing of a career in which I could do both. This,
actually, is the way it worked out. Nobody ever planned it or
scripted it, as it did, in fact, develop.

"Now all this was the cocoon, the cultural and psychological
and social cocoon, of Georgia and southern traditions. It was a
self-contained, self-sufficient world. And it had in it all the future that I could project for myself at that time."[30]

A Teacher

With a more deliberate stroke of the pen Albert described this
transitional period in these words:

"Immediately after graduation I had the opportunity to test
my fledgling wings. The job was principal of a rural junior high
school in Appling County, Georgia, in the heart of the country
depicted in *Lamb in His Bosom* [a bestselling book that Albert
helped its novelist write]. There were two country churches thrown
in for weekend ministry. At school [Wofford], I had been keenly
interested in psychological problems, and soon after I came to
Baxley, I became acquainted with an interesting couple. Mrs. —
—'s condition challenged me to seek to find what abnormal
psychology could do to interpret and help a case of mental maladjustment and struggle, and she became my first 'patient.' Her
first book was the occupational therapy that helped pull her out
of the doldrums, and her second proclaimed her complete recovery. This naturally reinforced my interest in psychotherapy.

"Meanwhile, the work out in the country was causing acute
tension. The plain, uncultured backwoodsmen were not impressed
by tentative speculations about God and life, and I came to see
how fruitless is a preaching that ends lamely, with a 'perhaps,'
or a speculation, however dogmatically stated. Two years out
there gave me a love for the soil and the men who work it; I
learned that influencing human behavior was not a matter of
imparting knowledge but of moving human emotions, stirring up

loyalties that would then root themselves in habit and life. It was here that another crisis developed that involved an either/or decision, and the decision came, with great emotional stirrings, along the line of my second conversion: my destiny was to preach and teach religion."[31]

At nineteen Albert was too young to go to seminary, but not too young to teach school. He became principal of Dyal Junior High School, a consolidated rural school that went through the tenth grade. Each of the four teachers, who served under him, taught two grades. Along with being principal, Albert also taught all the subjects of the ninth and tenth grades. He was young enough for the girls to have a crush on him and old enough to threaten some of the boys. Or rather it could be that some boys might have been a threat to him. For instance, one boy by the name of Heyward Mixon, in Albert's ninth grade class, was twenty-one years old, two years older than his teacher! Due to the need of working on the farm, the lad was forced into a slower learning pace, but the point must be made that under Albert's tutelage, he was learning.[32]

In those early years of accepting responsibility, Albert revealed a genuine concern that the needs of his flock of students be met. In several instances he appealed to the school superintendent for help. One note concerning the condition of the school house read, "We need more desks." Another: "We need locks." Then a later note about the school house read, "Fair, but in need of desks and locks." Again another note reminded the superintendent in one word about the condition of the school. It simply read, "Poor!" Then the next month's report read, "The least said, the better!" After that month Albert never mentioned the matter, on paper![33] It was evident that Albert's priority was not to pacify his superintendent, but to persuade his boss to help his students, to make for them an environment conducive to study and learning.

A Junior Pastor

The fact that Albert ministered to the needs of his students while at the same time serving as a junior pastor for two small churches on the Baxley Circuit in the backwoods of South Georgia accounts for his oft-quoted statement: "Many Methodists have gone

further than I, but none started further back!"[34] In that situation
things happened for him that he never planned on.

Among other things, his destiny as a patristics scholar was
set. It happened in this manner, and told in his words: "On Saturday everybody went to town. So I could go to town and see all
my flock more efficiently than I could if I went around and
visited their separate farms. One fateful Sunday the pastor of the
town's Methodist church, Brother Shaw, decided that the Baptists had to be told off (and he told them off!) on the questions of
immersion and infant baptism. The Baptists weren't about to
take that lying down. So on the following Sunday (it would have
been a fifth Sunday; I can remember that in circuit-riding days
the four Sundays were normally for your regular responsibilities,
but you could take the fifth Sunday off if you wanted to flake it).
. . . the Baptist set this thing up for a Sunday night (people would
actually go to church on Sunday nights during those days).

"So we all went to the Baptist church. (It was bigger than the
Methodist.) I got there early in order to get a seat. It was crowded;
the atmosphere was electric. Presently the Baptist preacher came
in with a Bible (that was standard equipment), and a *big* concor-
dance (that was a little pretentious), and also a *Liddell and Scott*
Greek lexicon (the whole *big* one). Here was the most literature I
had ever seen in one Baptist arm in all my life! But this was not
enough because with him he brought the proprietor of the local
Greek restaurant, who was not a Baptist but Orthodox. There
was not an Orthodox church within two hundred miles of Baxley.
But never you mind. The regular rehearsal of the Baptists [be-
liefs regarding baptism] was gone through—and they were standard. The *Liddell and Scott* was opened up and expounded on.
We could have stood that much. We knew all the charges and
countercharges. (They had been rehearsed.) The real question
was variations on a theme.

"But then came the crushing blow: The Baptist pastor turned
to the Greek restaurant owner and said, 'Nick, what does *baptizein*
mean?' Nick in his ecumenical innocence said, 'Well, down at
the restaurant we use it to speak of washing the dishes.' That, of
course, struck home as a *coup de grace* because they came with
the question: 'How do you like to have your dishes washed, by
sprinkling or immersion?' And so we . . . lost that round. Brother
Shaw was so outraged by this kind of appeal to scholarship that

he gave me his mint set of the ante-Nicene Fathers because, said he, 'There was a man in there named Tertullian, and he is not sound on baptism either!'

"And so I got a free mint set of the ante-Nicene Fathers. That set became the nucleus of the library of a patristics scholar; and that set of books is still in my library at home."[35]

With a mix of those kinds of experiences one can see the validity of the 1987 statement Albert made in writing to a friend: "What I learned in my two years out at Midway and Crosby's Chapel prepared the way for a far richer experience at Candler than if I had gone there straight from college." His teaching at a public school providentially laid groundwork for future teaching occasions that, at the time, he never dreamed even slightly probable.

Albert was Admitted in Full Connection into the Conference, and his new appointment in the South Georgia Conference was made on the same day (November 23, 1930) by Bishop John Monroe Moore. He hooked his ordination up to John Wesley with these successions: Bishop Moore was ordained by Bishop Robert K. Hargrove in 1899, who was ordained by Bishop John Early in 1861, who was ordained by Bishop William McKendree in 1811, who was ordained by Bishop Asbury in 1784, who was ordained Superintendent by John Wesley.

Albert's move from the Baxley Circuit added to his pastoral experiences: "From Baxley I was moved up the state to a circuit [Pineview/Finleyson] in the cotton country, there to preach to landowners, some of whom were practicing virtual peonage. It was there that I tried my hand at reform and found out why the prophets accomplished so little, in the matter of tangible results. While serving this circuit, I entered the theological seminary, to carry on the two enterprises at the same time. I found at school almost no opportunity to carry on my study in psychotherapy. I wanted to be trained in a method of helping people in distress to find release and reintegration that would be more adequate than revivalism and at the same time more real than the glib futilities of religious education as I knew it. I had seen both tried in a variety of situations and fail to fulfill their bright promises.

"Failing to find what I wanted, I plunged into the conventional courses and gained what I now regard as an invaluable background in biblical literature, theology, and church history.

The chief service of my seminary days was to offer intellectual clarification about beliefs and problems that I had been holding suspended, waiting for a solution. From my professors I gained a new viewpoint of the social responsibility of Christianity that considerably broadened my horizon of interest and effort. On the side, and with unsystematic help from various sources, I worked at abnormal psychology and psychotherapy. Finally, over the protest of some of the more staid professors, I handed in a thesis on the subject, embodying all that I had learned from a rather meager experience and what I could get out of books."[36]

Albert served the Pineview/Finleyson Circuit from November 23, 1930, until November 22, 1931 (conferences were held in the fall). Carrying him from Baxley to Pineview was "Sir Galahad," his well-exercised Ford that had gone through many "second hands." Sir Galahad, the knight of the round table surnamed "the chaste," would have been proud to have had this well-utilized conglomerate of metal named after him. The machine carried one destined, not to capture the Holy Grail, but to be "captured" by the fascination and spirit of the *holy*.

Church As Workplace

After having followed Albert through college and into the pastorate and public education, his metaphor of church as "workplace" begins to take on meaning. One sees that "workplace" is not an antithesis for "home." Quite the contrary, they complement each other. He was at home in the workplace and worked when he was at home. That deep sense of belonging with those who loved him with God's caring love buoyed him in the workplace. It carried him into and through the next phase of his life's calling.

3

Albert Enters Two "Schools": Theology and Romance

Carlotta Grace Smith

Albert moved from Pineview/Finleyson to Gordon in the Macon District on November 22, 1931. Prior to his move to Gordon he had entered in the fall of 1930 Candler School of Theology at Emory University in Atlanta. At seminary he met lovely young Carlotta (Carla for short) Grace Smith, who was working in the seminary library. Carla, who has been mistaken for a southern belle, was not. She was born on April 14, 1910, in Flint, Michigan. With her mother she moved from Flint to Canada, where her mother married her stepfather. From there they moved to Newport, New York (near Utica). From there they went to Starkville, Mississippi, where she finished high school and attended Mississippi State College for Women for one year. Her family then moved to Birmingham, Alabama, where she registered at Birmingham Southern. There she finished her undergraduate work in two more years.

Her interest in becoming a librarian led her to the library school at Emory. One day as she was working in the reference library her friend, Margaret, came to her and said, "I've got somebody who wants to meet you." (Albert obviously had been studying more than books when he had come to the library.) A few meetings later and they were engaged. When Carla told her roommate that she was engaged to Albert, her roommate burst into tears and said, "I'll have to pack a missionary barrel for you every year!" She was very upset and felt Carla was doomed. She could see Carla on a four-point circuit in the backwoods of Georgia for the rest of her days.[37]

Carla's roommate was not the only one upset about the possibility of Carla's having to move into such environs. While vacationing with her parents in Birmingham, Albert wrote a series of letters to her. On December 26, 1930, he wrote: "Fan doesn't like Waycross [where his father was serving as pastor] at all. It's in the heart of the pine country, very flat, very swampy, not too many people, *only* swamp water and squalor. The towns are not pretty; the people, not refined; and when you get out into the country, as far as you can see, only scrub and pine trees, and palmetto scrub. The monotony is not lessened, either, by the farm dwellings, unpainted, ramshackle and dilapidated. All this depresses Fannie Belle intensely; and she is not at all pleasant about it. When I suggested to her that I probably would have to serve somewhere in this pine country and you would have to share it with me, she went up in smoke. The idea, she fumed, of that dear child, cultured and sensitive, tenderly reared and beautiful, having to live in such a place. I gently suggested that she was talking through her hat and that it was likely to give her a cold.

"But in my heart a terror struck: what if it were true, that you should hate the place we lived in? Don't you see, darling, you couldn't love me then. I can, with a stretching of my imagination, see how you could love me in a warm, comfortable parlor, in a fairly cosmopolitan city; but what about when we are in a little hick village, provincial and squalid? As for me, the pine trees and the scrub have gotten in my blood; and besides, people live here and nothing kin to humanity is alien to my thought and interest. I'd hate to make you unhappy, for, Carla, beloved, I love you so that I could even give you up before I'd ask you to live in a place or in such a way as would make you unhappy. Think of all these things even while you are merrymaking [Christmastime], for lives hang on its decision.

"Now for the reassuring thoughts: [1] Dad is sold on you. He likes your picture; he likes what I tell him of you; and when he knows and sees you personally, you'll find out what a dear he really is. [2] Aussi [Carla], Mother sends her sincerest Christmas greetings and says that if this is the *real* thing (you see, she knows about all the others, and it makes her just a bit suspicious) [earlier, Mother Outler had made Carla feel that she was not the *real thing* for Albert], she is willing to give her blessing and anything else we'll need to start off with.

"Finally, I am constantly being reassured because of the constancy, the urgency, the power of my love for you. It's a love that understands, that could forgive, that can and does rejoice, a love without shame, without fear. For the first time I love someone without the fear of losing that love; I love spontaneously, without the need of tricks or devices to keep the flame aglow."

Carla answered this letter in person and in reassuring tones. But from the following letter written by Albert on August 18, 1931, she must have wondered what on earth she was letting herself in for: "I have been pretty busy this morning. Besides my exercises, prayer, shaving, etc., I have been on a hunting expedition—for fleas! It was preeminently successful, and the world stands now the sad loser of *six* fleas. How would you like that?" There was no answer by letter of how she would like *that*. But it is highly likely that they later discussed *that*.

Carla's Romances

Carla had been writing three young men back home in Birmingham, and in her diaries anguished what to do about her dilemma. The answer that came was addressed in the last entry she made in her diary on September 13, 1931: "Back again, Little Diary, for the last time. You knew all my ravings were merely helping me find myself, didn't you? Well, having reached maturity, and having acquired a bit of knowledge, I have found the *one*. There's no mistake this time, no doubts or wonderings, no desire for other companionship while he is away.

"Goode came back for me in June, but the illusion is completely wiped out—and Billy, I neither know nor care where he is. I only hope he doesn't continue messing up his life. As far as Paul, that was unexplainable madness . . .

"And now rest in peace, little friend [diary]. Know, too, that I am happy because I have found the man of my dreams—and have dedicated my life to service."

A Man of Destiny

The man of her dreams was Albert Outler, and her "life to service" was a co-commitment with Albert that led to their divine destiny recorded in these writings. When she was not dating Albert while he was in Atlanta, she was writing him while he was at Pineview. On June 20, 1930, she prophetically wrote to him and vowed, "I really am going to take excellent care of you because you are really the most precious thing in the world to me, and you are invaluable to the thousands whom you are going to preach to and help in the next fifty years or so."

He agreed with her sense of destiny for him as he later, in August, 1930, wrote: "I had a very narrow squeak last night. Lightning struck an oak tree about twenty-five feet from the corner of the church [at Finleyson], just before service. We had a terrific storm and the people were excited and terrified. Somehow, I was no more afraid than I am right now as I write you; for I feel God has a destiny for me to fulfill, and he will keep me. That may be arrogance, but I feel like it is simple faith and trust in him. I'll tell you all about it later. We went ahead and had the service."

Later that week Albert wrote another letter stating: "The week's meeting has been preeminently successful. A very cautious estimate of the crowd last night was five hundred folks! Trucks, cars, buggies, wagons, and afoot. An old-fashioned meeting, in which you may have been interested, although I doubt if you would have enjoyed it. [This experience was far from Carla's urban Episcopalian tradition.] The best compliment of the week was given last night: 'Brother Outler, you have brought Wesley Chapel back up to where it *used to be!'*—high praise from a countryman." Not to take a thing away from Albert's preaching, but it is very possible that the lightning strike earlier in the week did not hurt the attendance. Carla's love for Albert absolved any problems that denominational differences might have offered. From the beginning Carla felt keenly a God-given destiny for Albert. And that she was part of it. *That* was her destiny.

The Impending Marriage

The three major concerns of Albert's life during these days were addressed in a paragraph written to Carla on July 8, 1931: his pastoring, his schooling, and his impending marriage.

[1. His pastoring] "This morning I went over to Finleyson, to the Baptist revival services. It was a good service, and I really enjoyed it. But the best surprise of the day was when I was coming away from the church: Who should drive up but Dad? Isn't he a dear? He came all the way from Waycross, to stay about three hours, just to see me and tell me not to worry, for he and Mother were back of me. He really doesn't understand my problem like you do, but he helped a lot. Of course, he asked all about you, and both he and Mother are extremely proud and delighted over you. What they really were afraid of was that we would simply fling reason to the winds and get married anyway, on nothing. He quite approves our present plans and said for us to go ahead, finish [2. his schooling] school at Emory, and if Scotland could be managed [graduate work at Edinburgh], well and good—if not, not to worry, but to work. So if you get your job—it's next June. If not, it's December. [3. his impending marriage] That doesn't give you much incentive to wish for you a job, but still I hope you get it. You are quite right—both of us will need a year of preparation for a life of wonder and joy, a taste of which we had last week."

Of the three concerns there was no doubt that Albert's impending marriage to Carla grasped him in a manner unparalleled in that moment. Before the ink dried on the previous letter (July 8), in a July 9, 1931, letter Albert wrote: "I have faced today the realization that I am, in spite of all the front I may put on, a curiously *dependent* and indecisive spirit. All my life I have had someone near to 'appreciate me,' to lean on, confide in. I have been horribly and perhaps incorrigibly 'spoiled.' And now, I have come to depend on you, lean on you for appreciation and inspiration. You have no idea what your letters mean to me. They make the day brighter and bearable. I myself don't know what would happen if you missed a day. Please write an extra one, so you can mail it on the day you are too busy to write. Every morning at 8:30 I go out to the mail-box and watch for the postman. As he comes over the hill, about a half a mile away, my heart quickens a little, and he comes to a stop, and grins as he hands me what he knows I've come after, and I hand him a letter to you. It has become quite a little ceremony, and a most pleasant one."

The Prophetic Spirit

The prophetic spirit possessing Albert [the priest represents the people to God; the prophet represents God to the people] came through loud and clear to Carla in two letters. On July 20, 1931, he wrote: "At the morning service I preached that sermon I told you of: 'But What Will You Do at the End of It All?,' from Jeremiah. Somehow, as I preached, I felt an inflow of prophetic power, and said things I would not have dared to say ordinarily. But I could see no effect. They listened respectfully; some said the conventional things politely; although I made a great effort, it probably got under nobody's skin."

Albert was learning early that self-judgment was nearly always poor judgment. He doubted the benefit of the message on his audience, but he never doubted the message. In another letter on July 31, 1931, he wrote: "Last night the crowd was equally as large as the night before, and the church was full of people. You would have been surprised, and possibly shocked, to hear your 'husband' [quotes added] preaching such a sulphur and brimstone sermon. But apparently it's the only kind that can penetrate the darkness of these people's brains and hearts. And you remember, too, that the prophets were a pretty fiery bunch." By this time Carla had seen enough happen in Albert's ministry that hardly would she have been shocked by these recent revelations.

The Soloist

However, she might have been taken aback by the news he put to her in a letter on July 21, 1931: "Then I went down to the church [Finleyson], and a group of the young people rearranged the church and made preparations for our choir, moving the piano and bringing chairs from a building a half a block away. It was then that I found I had to fill in a gap and sing a solo at the church service. Well, you know as well as I, that solo-singing is not one of my original endowments, but I selected Von Weber's 'My Jesus as Thou Wilt,' and sang as best I could." Carla neither encouraged nor discouraged Albert's solo singing. Her silence made its own witness.

A Puritan

Albert sensed a wedding of souls long before *the* wedding took place. In a letter dated August 11, 1931, he said: "Your letter, written from Rochester, came today. I'm glad you had such a pleasant trip up. Again, I am proud of you about the wine business. In truth, I believe you are as staunch a Puritan as I am; and I rejoice to know that you have the courage and the backbone to stand for something right. It means, dear, that you are winning your fight to be SOMEBODY, instead of a child whose individuality has not yet occurred to its family. Yes, you are worthy to be my wife, infinitely more worthy of me than I am of you! Sweet, you are going to be a wife of whom I am and will always be justly proud."

Freedom to Be

Albert had been very sure that this "Puritanism" was not forced on Carla. He wanted her to be herself in her upcoming role as parsonage wife and make her own decisions as to what was appropriate and what was not. In a letter dated June 23, 1931, he said: "A little note is creeping in your letters, sweet, that I hope I misinterpret. Your telling me of your temptation to buy a bathing suit in today's letter is a case in point. You said that you wanted it, but that you didn't buy it because it was too risque for a preacher's wife! You see what that means: 'of course, I would like to have had that bathing suit, but I am going to be a preacher's wife now. And I must deny myself these things in order to be a martyr to the cause.' You ought to be able to tell how that makes me feel, as though I were depriving you of things you wanted and felt would be all right if you just hadn't happened to the misfortune of falling in love with a preacher. Now I know that you didn't mean anything like that; but if you see a bathing suit, and it doesn't offend *your* taste and *your own innate standard* of propriety, why, buy it; that is, if you've got the cash. I want you to feel free as my wife, not cramped, and I certainly hope that it will be as much a process of gaining as it will be of depriving. I think I understand how you are situated. In your present atmosphere, everyone is reminding you of what sacrifices you will have to make. But please don't surrender to that spirit. I want you to love what you will have to do; and not do it as duty that you owe to me or to some superficial and mechanical standard that convention sets up for you."

Not only did Carla take Albert at his word. She bought the swim suit and entered a beauty contest! She described that eye-opening experience to him in a letter. He answered her and never mentioned the bathing suit or the beauty contest. The bathing suit "problem" never came up again.

Mother Outler and the New Bride-to-Be

While Albert was the man of Carla's dreams, in the initial stages of courtship Carla was not the woman for Albert in his mother's dreams. His mother had already picked out Agnes Highsmith, a high-spirited young woman who would have shoved Albert along, much as Mother Outler had done with her husband. Carla knew that she was no Agnes Highsmith, but she also knew that nobody's high spirit could match her committed spirit. She loved Albert and was totally committed to his calling, to his mission, to him. History records that Albert was propelled along quite adequately without pressure.

A converted Mother Outler is evidenced in this letter from Albert, dated June 14, 1931: "Guess what, today Mother was talking about us and this is what she said. She said that your mind seemed much older than you yourself were, for you grasped things mentally very quickly, and that you had a sanity and poise that she thought was perfectly wonderful. She further said that one good thing she had noted about you was that you retained your self-possession amid trying circumstances (I suppose that I constitute the trying circumstances) [Carla felt that the trying circumstances were between Mother Outler and herself], and that you were just the sort that I needed for a wife. Not only that (watch your head!), she said that John [Albert's dad] said that he really didn't understand how I had enough sense ever to pick out a girl like you for a wife. I haven't decided whether or not that was a compliment to you or a dig at me. You take it as a compliment. Now, make your best bow, and realize what an enormous hit you have made with my family. Who would have thought it! (A-hem!)." Before that time Carla had reason not to "have thought it."

Could Albert Make It in the Real World?

From Carla's family's side of this blossoming romance, Albert was not the man of their dreams for Carla, either. When Carla went home that first Christmas and excitedly showed them her engagement ring, her stepfather said, "It's all damn nonsense."[38] Carla felt that he was a bit awed by Albert. Her stepfather had no formal education and was superintendent of Bordens, a condensed milk company. Albert could converse about what Mr. Smith was doing, but Mr. Smith was at loss for words concerning what Albert was doing. He wasn't quite sure that Albert would make it in this real world.

It did not take long for an acceptance of this impending wedding, once both families recognized the fact that these two youngsters had their minds made up and that their commitment was genuine. Carla and Mother Outler became very good friends; and the Smiths took Albert in as one of their own.

While Carla and Mother Outler began to get along very well, Albert still had his *times* with his mother. He wrote Carla on September 23, 1931: "I don't know exactly whether or not I have been openly disinherited or not by my family, but I haven't had a line from a one of them since we left last Wednesday. I know none of them is seriously ill, or they would have wired me. I suppose Mother is determined that the breach shall be final. I hate it, for I do love her. But if she must feel I am an undutiful, reprobate son, there is nothing I can do about it. I will not be bullied nor badgered by anyone alive, and if she cannot realize that, then it is over as far as I am concerned." Whatever caused the rift in relations soon faded out of memory. Nothing was mentioned of it in later letters.

A Brief Respite

The mix of pastoring, romancing, and interfacing with families caused Albert to pause and take a time out by getting away from it all. But he never got away from Carla, and did not want to; he profoundly needed her. At times he lost himself in music. On December 26, 1930, he wrote, "This has been a quiet day, a day of peace and worship. I've done more praying than 'celebrating'—and now a quiet letter to you before Leopold Stokowski begins broadcasting a program of Bach and Handel."

On August 11, 1931, Albert wrote from Crooked River Club: "This is my last day here at Crooked River. I've had a good time, and time has mercifully flown by rather rapidly. But I still feel drowsy, lethargic, lazy. I'd rather just lie in bed than do anything else, and such a lack of pep and enthusiasm worries me, for by now I ought really be snapping out of it. I feel good; no more twitching nerves, no headaches, no stomach trouble. But no pep. I suppose that it will be a longer process than I imagined. I'm growing a little tired of being an invalid, albeit convalescent. The fishing has been a great sport, and I am really converted to it as a hobby. The water, too, casts a witching spell over me. More than ever now I want to go to sea, to feel a heaving deck under my feet, and the salt spray in my face. Some day again (with you), sweetheart!"

And then there were the times he escaped into golf. On November 20, 1931, he wrote: "Would you like to hear a big joke? Bond Fleming, golf manager, tonight invited me to play on one of the golf teams in a match at Druid Hills tomorrow afternoon. Luckily, nothing depends on victory. For it ought to be an awful flop. But I am going to play for the fun of it, and also for the experience of playing on one of the most exclusive courses in the South." Albert was right. His golfing was a flop. On the next day, November 21, Albert wrote: "The golf this afternoon was rotten, but I enjoyed it. I'm bringing my clubs with me for one or two afternoons, on the condition that you go around with me. That was the most fun I ever had golfing, even if I wasn't playing up to my best." Albert had again witnessed the miracle of recreation: the joy of living in his heart did not depend upon successes *out there*. His recreation succeeded if he could go back into the frays of life with that spirit. In most cases his recreation did just that for him.

The Pressures Were Taking Their Toll

Albert's letters to Carla by this time indicate a trend that lasted all the days of his life; life's pressures at times literally made him sick. In the summer of 1931 he wrote: "Darling, I am in a curious fix. Perhaps you have been able to tell from my letters a sense of strain and unnaturalness. The plain facts are that I'm still in danger of a nervous breakdown. And I haven't recovered by a long shot. You see, as long as I was in Atlanta I had you, and neither of us realized what a strengthening power you were in my life then. When I got home, there were Dad and Mother, both of whom I could confide in, and where I could be natural, and rest and relax thoroughly. I did make considerable improvement, and was feeling much better when I left; but, since I left Waycross I have been thrown under another strain: namely that of hearing everyone's troubles and woes, in a time when they are especially plentiful from all causes, and worse than that, it was my duty always to be sympathetic, understanding, helping, encouraging, giving.

"There was no one in whom I could confide that I was desperately weary; or who could understand why I wasn't brimming full of energy and enthusiasm? The result is that before I knew it, I was back in the fix I was that Monday night in Atlanta before you left me Tuesday. All day I have been away from everyone, reading my Bible, sleeping, praying, and singing as many beautiful songs as I could recall. All that has helped a lot, but I still feel like a small boy who just can swim, far away from the bank, and out of his depth. If only there were a hand to help, to uphold, a heart in whom I could confide. Even the face of God is obscured, and I grope in darkness to find him and secure his peace. I need you, my precious, to understand and help, to listen to my feelings and thoughts, to share with me these burdens."

One can easily see in this statement a troubled spirit in young Albert, which could have to some extent accounted for the heightened interest he felt in the new discipline of psychotherapy. We do know that when he entered Candler School of Theology, he went with a program in mind that included serious studies in that field.

Albert's Counselor

Albert experienced healing under Carla's care. Carla said that she would take care of Albert. Take care of him she did. In the best sense of the biblical tradition, she was his helpmate. While *he* was the professional counselor, *she* was his counselor. Albert carried the conversation on most subjects. The simple fact was that he knew more about the subjects. Carla would spend hours listening. But sometimes she would say in soft, genuinely kind, well-mannered tones: "But Albert, I think . . ." and would offer her differing opinion. And Albert listened. He valued her opinion and respected her as a friendly critic. For example, in a December 29, 1987, letter to Kenneth Kinghorn he wrote concerning an AFTE (A Fund for Theological Education) meeting he had recently attended: "Mrs. Outler raised a skeptical eyebrow at my report that I had managed to listen so intently and had not intervened even once." In many instances Outler's expressed thoughts were channelled to him by Carla. She was a research librarian and put information into his hands for him to digest and put out to others.

He listened to Carla. But he knew that he was listening to *more* than Carla. In a letter dated November 18, 1931, he said: "Your letter today was remarkable. I told you once that you had an unusual capacity for religion, and that you had the soul of a true mystic. My opinion is being born out amazingly. Every letter, almost every sentence, shows a new and deeper insight into the world of the spirit, and God. What an inspiration and help you are going to be. How clearly your intuitive mysticism will guide my rather impulsive rationalism. If you continue improving in thought and insight, I'll get you to write some sermons for me."

A Common Destiny

These letters from Albert to Carla and from Carla to Albert revealed in their hearts a common destiny. For nearly a year "Sir Galahad" had carried them in their pilgrimage of being captured by the holy. But a tired and worn-out "Sir Galahad" finally gave way to "Flying Ebony." "Sir Galahad" was still running, but not as sprightly as it once did. Albert wrote Carla on June 13, 1931, "Poor Galahad is no more ours. In his place there is a nice new shiny standard black Ford coupe, whose name will be 'Flying Ebony,' after the Kentucky Derby winner of a few years ago. That is, of course, if you approve the name." "Flying Ebony" took on a high polish, looked more fitting for his new bride, and how it did "fly," first between Pineview and Atlanta, and then between Atlanta and Gordon.

The Day of Matrimony

While riding high in their love for each other, Albert and Carla agonized over the date to set the wedding. Money was one factor, housing another, a possible move to a different church another, and where to have the wedding was another. Finally, they settled on December 18, 1931. At 2:00 P.M. in the School of Theology chapel at Emory University, Dad Outler read the vows. It seemed that everyone of the two hundred who received invitations (at a printing cost of $30) crowded into the chapel on that Saturday afternoon.

After their honeymoon at Young Harris, Albert and Carla settled into apartment six on Theology Row at Emory. Albert had prepared Carla for what it was like living on the Row in a letter dated December 3, 1931: "Believe me, it's cold over on the Row, even when you have good stoves. But honestly, I got a better sleep last night in a cold room with plenty of fresh air than I did the night before here in a warm building with just one window. I am sure we will get used to it; I'll learn how to make fires quick, so that you can get up within ten minutes after I do. How 'bout that?"

The two divided their time between living at the university and at Gordon where Albert had been pastoring since November 22. He had moved to Gordon on December 3, and had preached his first sermon there on December 6. So the New Year of 1932 presented the flock at Gordon with a new parsonage wife. What was the parsonage like? Carla described it this way: "We always had a garden. Albert enjoyed working in the soil, and having our own vegetables and fruit. I kept our freezer full. There was a garage, a kind of shanty. The plumbing was 'openly' arrived at. Beside the shanty was a chicken yard that you had to go through to get to the outhouse."[39]

Reflection and Healing

Retreats continued to offer Albert time for reflection and healing. In a letter from Blue Ridge, North Carolina, he wrote on June 20, 1932, "[I have been given the] opportunity to stop and think and rescue my life from its headlong restlessness. We live so fast and so furiously that our souls don't get the chance to catch up." And then he said something that carried him through-out his entire life: "There is no other way than the Cross. There is no easy way. But the hard way is not a gloomy way or a joyless way. It is one of simple living, sacred joys, and a deep abiding peace within." That statement is paraphrased in some of his last lectures in these words: "Following Christ leads not to Utopia but to Golgotha."[40]

His retreat at Blue Ridge was mixed with some recreation. The next day he wrote: "The Emory delegation played L.S.D. yesterday afternoon in basketball. Emory's team had never played, and there were two varsity men on the other team, and all of them experienced. Therefore, score: 24-1. You didn't know that I could play basketball, did you? Well, neither did I. But I played stationary guard, and shot our one and only point. Pure luck, and a lot of fun." When the time was right, it obviously did not take much success for Albert to have fun.

The Gardener

On May 6, 1934, from Gordon Albert wrote Carla, who was vacationing with her parents in Birmingham: "This has been a long, hard day, just as yesterday. Yesterday I worked in the garden all morning, went to Macon in the afternoon with Mr. Clint, and came back to work in the garden until eight o'clock. I set out fifty tomato plants, forty-five cabbage plants, and I have plowed every foot of the garden and now it is in good condition. I planted some more sweet corn, snap beans, lima beans, pole beans, and parsley, and have the rest of the ground in good condition. Don't scold, but I bought me a new plow, with a turning share, scrape and rake in addition to the scooters like I had on the other plow. With this rig, now that I have it in good shape, I can keep it that way. I've had two messes of greens and one of English peas. But I don't enjoy them half so much as when you are home to pick them and eat them with me. After the funeral, I came home and went to work in the chicken yard. I think I've demonstrated that care is the great thing with chick-ens. Okla didn't look after those hens properly; since I've been working with them a week, they have picked up steadily. Today I got an even *dozen* eggs. Then I borrowed Mr. Will's watering can and watered all your flower beds."

A Mule Investment

From the earliest of his adult days Albert was struggling to make ends meet financially. To ease his financial straits he gardened for his vegetables, raised chickens for his eggs, and invested in mules! On September 18, 1933, Albert, from his student pastorate in Gordon, wrote to Mr. Bruce Edmund in Baxley, where he began his preaching ministry: "Enclosed you will find a cashier's check for $200. This is all that we can spare at this time, but we hope it will be enough to help out. As I understand your plans, you are going to buy mules at Atlanta or elsewhere and sell them in Appling County and the surrounding territory. Well, I suggest that you buy as many mules as you can with this $200.00, and split the profits on them with Mrs. Outler, reserving a fair share for yourself for the time and effort on your part. If the returns are good, and we don't have any emergency which will demand money, we can reinvest the money with you.

"Of course, I believe you will use the utmost care and sound judgment throughout the whole undertaking. You can realize what a blow it would be to us to lose this money. With such a small salary, and with expenses that seem to be increasing, we would be hard hit. I mention this only because you know our situation so well. We are counting on you!"

Since there are no letters to the contrary (if there were, Albert would have kept them!), we may assume that Albert was not disappointed with his venture into the mule business.

Refereeing the Feud

Albert and Carla shared in ministry, when they were together and when they were apart. Early one Sunday morning he wrote her in Birmingham from Gordon; she was visiting her parents again. He expressed the excitement of the week in these words: "No sooner had you gotten out of town than the fun began popping. You knew of the feud between Mrs. Kate Brannan and Mrs. Pearl Strange. Well, they were both there. It broke into a blaze in the afternoon. Mrs. Brannan accused Mrs. Strange of "stealin'" a cake, a charge which, in this instance, was certainly unfounded. Mrs. Strange was, of course, furious and hurt and began threatening a church trial for slander. Well, to hear the tales of woe of those two fools and to go over town and check over the evidence to see which one was lying the worst took until late last night, and so when I got back, I went to bed. It is a disgraceful affair, and I don't know yet what consequences there will be. I have gotten Mrs. Brannan to agree to apologize and Mrs. Strange to accept the apology without bickering. But the story has travelled over town in various versions; and I don't know what the backlash will be. At any rate, I am sorry you missed it all."

On the following Tuesday morning, October 10, 1933, Albert wrote and mailed a hopeful conclusion to the "disgraceful affair": "Both Mrs. Brannan and Mrs. Strange were at church yesterday, and after church I practically forced them together and kept them there until Kate apologized and Pearl accepted it. So that spat is settled (at least, on the surface), and any possible damage to the church is averted. It was a ridiculous and disgraceful affair, and I am glad it is over. The strain of the row had me upset, and that was a second reason why the morning was so bad."

A Classroom Shocker

An excited Albert continued to write in a January 6, 1933, letter to Carla who was in Birmingham, Alabama: "I have a corking good subject for a term paper in the Reformation course. In an argument in class today I ventured the assertion that the Reformation did as much harm as good. The class was horrified, and Watkins [the professor] disagreed, but suggested I attempt to prove it in a term paper. I decided, however, that it would be unscientific to approach such a study with a definite bias. So I've landed on 'The Positive and Negative Results of the Protestant Reformation.' It ought to be a honey.

"Well, Shotgun [Carla], I must go to bed. It will be with thoughts of you, dreams of your tenderness and goodness. I love you, and to me you are the most precious thing in the world. Say 'hello' to the family, and 'meow' to Zade [the cat]."

Such class disturbances as mentioned in the previous letter classified Albert as an "upstart" to some. Was Albert a "smart alec"? Or was he just plain smart? Did Albert's abilities in some ways measure up to his ego? In a note to Carla, Albert, off the cuff, wrote a sentence about his Latin instructor: "He's a fine teacher, but he has a lot to learn." That sounds very much like one who thinks a bit highly of himself—until, upon reflecting, one remembers that this young man, tutored by his older sister Fan, was writing and speaking Latin while he was in grade school! Obviously others thought highly of Albert's capabilities. In another letter (date unclear) Outler wrote to Carla, "When I got back to my Latin class, I gave them [two students whom he tutored] a written review. Sarah made 98 and Catherine 85. They have made good progress, and I believe we can do better in future time." Albert never wrote Carla about how well he was doing in his studies of the Hebrew language; years later he mentioned in some correspondence how difficult the subject had been for him.

A Genius?

Was Albert a genius? He questioned himself in these matters. In an August 8, 1934, letter written to Carla he said: "The only thing is that I imagine myself a genius, and that I shall startle the world with brilliance, when as a matter of fact, I am but little above the average in the ministry, which is, as you know, bad enough. If I could be content with being what I am, by heredity, training, and background, I should be happy. But when I dream, and am not satisfied with dreaming, then come the 'blues.'" In these words Albert described his lifelong dilemma, that of a man with a powerful brain and a dauntless heart that could never settle for mediocrity.

A Time for Self-appraisal

Being a top-notch debater, Albert would argue a point anywhere, anytime, with anybody *except* Carla. Disagreements with her were too personal, and sometimes they hurt. On June 23, 1932, he wrote to her while she visited her parents: "Darling, I think your idea of a vacation has certain disadvantages. I am getting more and more lonely up here, and I'm missing you more and more than I ever thought I would. Strangely enough, I am seeing some of my errors in my attitude toward you. Perhaps I have been taking you for granted, allowing you to spoil me (a way of saying, 'I am demanding too much of you'); and perhaps the financial strain and specter which we've been under has been keeping me from being quite as considerate as I ought. Honestly, I'm sorry, and will try to do better further on."

A Broadening Religious Experience

Monday, June 12, 1933; 10:30 A.M., 1933 was one of the finest moments that Rev. John and Gertrude Outler ever experienced concerning two of their children, Frances (Fan) and Albert. During the same graduating exercises at Emory University, Frances was awarded her Master of Arts degree in the field of English and literature and Albert was graduated with a Bachelor of Divinity in the field of Psychology of Religion. Subsequently he was ordained elder in the South Georgia Conference under Bishop John M. Moore. Carla was a major contributor to much of the learning that went into earning that degree. He states: "During seminary days, I had married, and a new angle developed in my religious life. Being religious by yourself and among men is one thing; the intimacy of marriage, stripping away all pretense and reserve, is quite another. My wife was an Episcopalian, and so was I, only of the Methodist variety. Marriage has done a great thing for my religious life: it has objectified it to a certain degree and provided a lively forum in which to test ideas and conduct.

"Our [notice he said '*our*'] first appointment after graduation from seminary was to a small town [Gordon] in Middle Georgia. Here again I was worried by the wide gap that lay between the chill perfection of the religion of the seminary and the need and urgency of the religious problems of real people in real 'life-situations.' Here my work in psychotherapy, however crudely done, bore much fruit. This is no disparagement of our educational program or my sermons; it seems to me that they fit most naturally together. Three years among these plain people gave rise to considerable rethinking, brought a realness in prayer, hitherto undiscovered, and demonstrated the power of the Gospel of Christ, even in these times, to touch and change individuals and groups."[41]

Albert described this period of his life in these words: "The widening of my horizons came with a visit to the Georgia Pastors' School of Shelton Smith, who was heading up the new graduate department of religion at Duke. My upbringing had been conservative, theologically. College and Candler School of Theology had connected me to a typical branch of liberalism. Now Smith came to the Pastors' Schools—two in a row—talking about Barth, Kierkegaard, Reinhold Niebuhr. Smith was a professor of religious education to begin with, but then became greatly influenced by neo-orthodoxy, and that turned him into a student of American church history.

"Well, it was Smith who gave me the first real glimpse I'd ever had of the world of scholarship and theological inquiry way beyond the frontiers I had discovered or the boundaries I'd come up against. And I found all of this quite fascinating. He was also the first man to suggest that *I* had the makings of a scholar.

"From Smith's suggestions a plan formed in the family that I should go to Yale for graduate school."[42]

Disappointments

Outler developed the penchant early on in his ministry to regret having accepted some of his engagements, whether preaching, committee, conference, or classroom. He was always enthusiastic about going, but when he arrived, if things did not go well, he was "out of there"—in mind and heart if not physically. The following is a quote from a July 13, 1934, letter he wrote to Carla in Gordon while he was away preaching a "meeting":

"Another day is past, and I find myself wishing I were home again, with you and the work. This situation is far more unpleasant and difficult than I imagined: The preacher is densely elementary, but with it officious, vindictive, and disappointing. He is lazier than I am, and knows less! Then the people at Gibson present a problem, such as I have not even faced before. Wednesday, we had fifty-six, and about a dozen walked up and spoke to me; last night we had fifty-three, and after the benediction, they marched out of the church without so much as 'by your leave.' I am aware that my pride is involved, and if I can keep close enough to God, it will be a discipline and training for me. Pray for me, that I may have humility enough not to be humiliated, and strength enough not to be weakened."

Assistant Pastor

From Gordon Albert and Carla moved to the inner-city Mulberry Street Methodist Episcopal Church, South, in Macon, Georgia, on November 18, 1934, where he served as assistant pastor and education director with Rev. Cook until November 16, 1935. He enjoyed his stint as assistant pastor for these reasons: he could learn from the close association with a senior pastor who "had it all together." And the man with whom he was assigned to work was his father's good friend, and the one whose name was given to Albert *Cook* Outler. And he was serving in the largest Methodist Church in the Conference at that time. Albert brought to this fast-paced church his own fast pace. As the two energies met, Albert was flung into a whirlwind of activity that he never encountered on the circuit. This young natural-born workaholic was faced with more work than satisfied his taste. He had been on the job a little over a month at Mulberry Street when something had to give; and it was Albert. A doctor's prescribed rest turned him in the direction of the mountains of Young Harris.

In a January 28, 1935, letter, Hugh Quin, secretary of Mulberry Street Board of Stewards, wrote to Albert: "At the meeting of the Board of Stewards last Friday evening Dr. Cook told us of your having left for a rest of several weeks at Young Harris, Georgia. By formal motion you were granted a leave of absence for as long a time as was necessary to enable you to regain your strength. Your salary of course to continue right on. We purposely did not specify any particular time because, had we said four weeks, you would have been back here at the expiration of four weeks whether you were well or not. So we want you to stay as long as it is necessary for you to get in good shape again. You have nothing whatsoever now to worry about and should put all your thought and time on taking care of yourself and nursing yourself back to strength and health.

"Milton Richardson will look after your work, and you will not be cramped for finances. So we want you to cease worrying about things and get well again.

"You have greatly endeared yourself to the people of Mulberry and to the Official Board. We rejoice that we have you with us. With kindest regards to Mrs. Outler and trusting that you will rest and take things easy and be able within a month or so to be back with us at Mulberry."

Albert did what the doctor ordered. He rested. And while he did, the mail piled up. His obligations with programs other than those of Mulberry Street were still hanging over him. He began to respond to those commitments with this March 6, 1935, letter to Roy Gardner concerning preparations for a correspondence school: "I know you have been wondering why I haven't answered your letter of the sixteenth of last month. The fact is that I have been *hors de combat* for over a month, that is, until last week. Under the doctor's orders I took a five-week lay-off and spent all but a few days of that time up in the mountains at our home in Young Harris. All that time I was consuming a whole mass of such stuff as adrenaline and such to perk up my blood pressure and restore my 'spizzarinctum.' I am happy to be able to report that I am quite well and strong again. Indeed, I feel better than I have in four or five years. It was just a case of having burned the candle at both ends, until we were afforded to take time out and mold another candle. . . .

"Despite the fact that I have had only about a month of working time here, our work is moving along satisfactorily. I have a little bit of everything to do—preaching, prayer meeting now and then, visiting and the main responsibility for the program of Christian Education in the Church School. Lest your fears (which you expressed at Conference) that such an 'exalted' place would turn my head, let me confide to you that I have suffered terribly with nostalgia for the country circuit, with its far less complicated machinery and greater openness of heart. We are enjoying it greatly, but I just wanted you to know that I still have a warm place in my heart for my old job, and shall not be disappointed when they send me back out there with 'the boys.'"

When "Lights" Were Burning Low

On May 1, 1935, Albert wrote Carla, who was vacationing with her parents in Birmingham: "I was interested to hear the report of the Highland Methodist Service. You are indeed spoiled, for I am not as good a preacher as you seem to think. If I were, do you suppose some of the authorities would have known about it, instead of the kind-hearted people who are always nice to the preachers? When you realize that I am nearly twenty-seven, that

I have been in the Conference seven years, and in that time have gained no particularly important recognition from anyone except my parishioners, you see that your enthusiasm is like the mother who said, 'Everybody is out of step but my Johnnie.' Not that I crave recognition, for I had rather have had the warm love of our people and a happy home among them than any advancement or promotion that could come."

One can see in a later writing while a graduate student at Yale that Albert's light was burning low about this time. He said: "After the glamour wore away [of a large church in a large city], I began to perceive the difficulties in running a huge church, in which an overwhelming majority of the members were but very mildly interested in Christianity. Our church school was 'one of the most modern and best-equipped in the entire connection,' but the contrast between the amount of activity and results was disheartening. The total result of that year was disillusionment about the chances of the modern church to disentangle itself from 'the world' and thereby accomplish its mission. As Reinhold Niebuhr put it, what is possible in such situations is inadequate and what would be adequate was, apparently, quite impossible. And so I came to Yale!"[43]

The Quandary: Where to Go for a Ph.D.

As assistant pastor Albert was preparing himself to be a more effective pastor; but the role was not, in his mind, totally adequate. He felt that a Ph.D. would give him that edge he needed. He especially wanted to know more about psychotherapy, the fascinating new subject on the horizon in which he had been dabbling and that he felt offered insights into his future counseling ministry as a local pastor. At first Outler considered going to Edinburgh, Scotland, for further graduate work. And then, after considering the factors involved in such a move (a major one being financial), he decided that a school in the United States would be the necessary choice. His quandary was expressed in this April 1, 1935, letter to Professor W. A. Smart at Emory University:

"I am turning to you for advice in a rather crucial situation for me and my future. Carla and I are going away to school this year to work, for better or for worse, for the Ph.D. degree. Some of the reasons for this decision you may understand: The main one is that all my school life, I have wanted to go on through to the end, as far as technical preparation is concerned. The end I have in view, I suppose, is teaching in theological school, preferably in the South.

"The question before us right now is: 'which school shall it be, *Yale* or *Duke*?' This summer Dr. Shelton Smith visited our Pastors' School and appeared quite anxious for me to come to Duke and take a doctorate in religion, psychology and philosophy. Dr. McDougell is there in psychology, and Dr. Smith himself is a very keen man. It sounds like it would be a practical sort of discipline.

"On the other hand, the prestige of Yale is considerable, and that counts a great deal in academic circles. There I would major in church history with a minor in psychology, if possible. My two chief interests have been and still are the history and psychology of religion. I should like to be able to continue my interest in pastoral psychotherapy and be prepared to teach it, if the opportunity presented itself.

"Now, can you put yourself in my place, thinking about the future, and with the added experience and insight in these matters advise me which of the two schools would be [better] for me, and what a degree from Duke might reasonably mean in the future, or from Yale? The relative costs appear to be about the same with about the same opportunities for scholarship aid, etc. In other words, if you were dean of a theological school, how would you view the two degrees in value?

"I must be making a final decision soon, and will, therefore, appreciate a prompt answer giving your frank reaction to my questions. I would risk your judgment further than most anybody I know. Thank you very much."

The answer came back: "Yale." So Yale it was for Albert.

A Yale Ph.D. and an Intimidating Bishop

When Albert approached his bishop to talk about his very serious consideration of going to Yale, his spiritual leader went further than *discussing* the subject; he threw down the gauntlet and said, "If you go for a Ph.D., keep going. You will not receive an appointment in this conference." The bishop had already heard about how brilliant Albert was and felt that Albert would come out too educated for his own good or for the good of the church. Those muscle-flexing, intimidating, threatening words sounded strange coming from the mouth of a spiritual leader. Albert concluded: "I don't believe that this did anything more than stiffen my spine somewhat in the resolution to go through with our plans to go to Yale."[44]

Decisions! Decisions!

When Albert visited Yale to discuss with the administration the possibility of his attending there, his compulsion to bring the study of psychotherapy into his degree program almost torpedoed his plans for that school. Yale simply did not offer what he wanted, but he wanted to go to Yale.

A perspective of this moment in Albert's life is given by Leroy Howe: "The breadth and depth of Albert Outler's contributions as an ecumenist and as an historian of Methodism can obscure the fact that these areas of interest were not the ones of the greatest importance to him. What mattered most, instead, were the issues of pastoral theology and how they might best be addressed in a sustained dialogue with the theorists and practitioners of the modern psychotherapies. Early in his seminary student days at Candler School of Theology of Emory University, Outler developed the enthusiasm, which lasted a lifetime, for integrating the wisdom of the modern sciences of the *soul* with the classical Christian understanding of the *humanum* in its transcendent dimension. (It is both fateful and tragic that *psyche* continues to be rendered as "mind" in our society and that even the venerable American *Psyche-atric* Association continues to compound the confusion with its frequently revised manuals of *mental* disorders.) So taken was Outler with possibilities for integration that he wrote his Bachelor of Divinity thesis on the subject, sought eagerly in his pastoral practice for ways clergy might bring the insights of modern psychology to bear on their pastoral care and counseling, and finally opted for further graduate study expressly for the purpose of pursuing these issues further.

"Given the passion generating Outler's trek to Yale, it might seem curious that, once there, he pursued a course of study in historical theology instead. The reasons were pragmatic only: he had the resources only for a limited time of study for his Ph.D.; the faculty member who would be his principal advisor was on sabbatical during Outler's first year; and his background in classics, he was advised, would make it possible for him to complete a degree in historical theology before the money ran out! (One of Outler's most fetching stories of himself is with Carla, his young wife and most committed supporter, parked across the way from the Yale Divinity School complex on the day of registering for courses, debating their unanticipated situation in the front seat of their car, and his becoming an historical rather than a pastoral theologian as if in the blink of an eye.)"[45]

Carla Goes to New Haven

Albert brought to New Haven his B.D. degree from Emory University; Carla brought a need to work and unique qualifications for that work. In an August 7, 1935, letter to Dr. Andrew Keogh at Yale, she wrote: ". . . it is highly desirable, indeed, imperative, that I get employment to help out with our living expenses during the three years we plan to be there. If, therefore, there is any opening, for whole or part-time work, of any sort, I should like you to consider this as my application for the place.

"You may remember from our former correspondence my academic training. I have an A.B. from Birmingham-Southern College (1930), and took my A.B. in L.S. at the Library School of Emory University, Georgia (1931). I have had some valuable experiences since 1933 in library work: cataloging my husband's private library (800 volumes); directing the organization of a library in the small town where we formerly lived; doing supply work in the Public Library here. . . ."

They found her the job. Now she set about earning another degree.

Carla's P.H.T. Degree

Albert's limited funds were augmented by the unlimited energies of his working wife with her P.H.T. "degree." Albert described how Carla earned her P.H.T. while he was at Yale in this autobiographical letter that he wrote some years later: "You called for a little autobiography. Well, the tale is short and quickly told. I went from Mulberry Street in Macon to Yale and majored there under Calhoun, Bainton, and Macintosh. Actually I took my degree in the field of historical theology, which is the No-Man's Land between church history and systematic theology. I wrote my dissertation on Origin and then this job at Duke fell into my lap. Here I divide my time equally between the undergraduate department of religion and graduate courses in Historical Theology. We are just beginning to offer work for the Ph.D. here, and I have three candidates in my advanced course in the History of Doctrine. Carla got her degree at New Haven, too: P.H.T. That is a fairly common degree up here and stands for 'Putting Husband Through.' She worked as secretary in the American Schools of Oriental Research and then did all the stenographic work for the dissertation. So you see I'm just half the doctor, and she's the other half. We are enjoying the work here, although I cannot say that it is an easy place to make good friends quickly. In that respect it is something of a contrast between the Emory that you and I knew or, strange to say, even Yale. Now there is the account of our pilgrimage . . . ."[46]

Househusband Albert

While Albert was earning his Ph.D. and Carla her P.H.T., Albert was also learning how to do housework. Here is how he described it: "This is the end of a long hard day, divided between Social Psychology, Theology and German on the one hand and the usual routine duties here at the Home on the other. You can get the flavor of this letter more accurately if you hold in mind that I am dictating it to Carla while I do the weekly washing. You see, if she has assumed the masculine role of making a living, I suppose it only fair that I share partly the feminine job of doing some of the household chores. The bird who first decided that wringing out towels and sheets is feminine must have thought that nothing less than slaying a saber-toothed tiger barehanded was masculine."[47]

The Home

"Here at *the* Home" is not the same as "here at home." "The Home" is described in the following letter: "Carla is working for the American Schools of Oriental (Near East) Research, and we have an apartment in a Sailors' Home, where I work nights. I also have a men's Bible class, and with all that we are managing very well, until it comes to such items as getting the dissertation published, etc. But we are doing very well, considering, and we are enjoying all the new and rich opportunities that New England affords."[48]

When Albert said, "where I work nights," he was talking about a kind of work that he never imagined in his wildest dreams. In his words: "My work here at the Sailors' Home continues to provide lots of interesting experiences. I have gotten to the place where I can bounce a drunk or turn down a panhandler or talk to the other men on their own level and still keep order. When I remember how upset I was at the Weaver funeral, I laugh because now I think I could snap my fingers in his face and tell him to behave himself. Since May we have had two men to go crazy here in the house, and it was my job to handle them on both occasions. I got through with it all right, and both men are now committed to the state insane asylum. So you see that I am having a very varied life."[49] This "varied life" also included directing summer camps in New Hampshire (1936 and 1937).

The Yale Experience

Albert's life was equally as varied on the Yale campus. After his acceptance and move to New Haven on November 17, 1935, Albert's "balloon" was soaring. And never did burst. He loved working with Robert Calhoun, Roland Bainton, Erwin R. Goodenough, et al. The Yale experience changed Albert. It was in this setting that Albert first began to see the crying need of closer relations among separated and often rival denominations. He said, "This gave me the first exposure to the ecumenical movement. For in the period 1935–38 the preparations for both *Life and Work* at Oxford and *Faith and Order* in Edinburgh (in 1938), both precursors of the World Council of Churches, were proceeding, and both Bob Calhoun and Richard Niebuhr were involved in that, and they got their students involved. My teachers at Yale were Calhoun and Bainton and Goodenough. Calhoun's paper for Oxford was circulated within a very small group of students, and I helped redraft it and began to see for the first time what was going on in the ecumenical movement in its relatively early stages. The first conference on *Faith and Order* had been held at Lausanne [Switzerland] not quite ten years before in 1928."[50]

The Methodist Church

Outler was hard put to find something positive to say about The Methodist Episcopal Church in the Northeast. In a March 6, 1938, letter he wrote: "The church cannot in my judgment pronounce on economic and political problems, but it can and it must, it seems to me, define the rules of the game as it were, and particularly the spirit of concession and mutuality and in this sense referee between contending social forces. It seems to me that in New England the church has pretty well abdicated its proper function. The majority are dedicated to a ritualistic religion of sweetness and light that has no practical reference to the hard week-day problems of the people. The minority have gone stark crazy and are setting themselves up as authorities on economics, politics, and international relations with great positiveness and tragic ignorance."

A *Baptist* Preacher etc., etc.

Albert did not say how it was in the Baptist churches, but he had the opportunity to tell them how it was in his mind as he became a supply preacher in a Baptist church. In this ministry Albert practiced an ecumenism that went far beyond the mainstream ecumenists. This part of his history comes out in a July 16, 1936, letter to one of his former parishioners at Mulberry Street:

"Alibis lose their convincingness when repeated too often, and I am simply depending on the forgiving quality of friendship rather than an effort to 'explain' why I haven't answered your letter of March 11th before. I have found it very difficult even to make Mother understand the pressure and the pace of the work up here, especially toward the end of the year. I have worked my head off to get distinction in my courses, and while I am quite willing to grant you theoretically that grades do not mean anything, I know that actually it made a lot of difference to me and that it influenced my future opportunities here when the report card showed that the professors had broken down and given me As. So far they are the only tangible results I have of the year's work; yet there is no way to measure the intellectual enrichment that being at Yale and in New Haven have afforded. Since the end of the year's work (June 15th) I have been working at several small jobs which together have managed to take up all my time. My Bible class adjourns for the summer, and in order to make up for the prospective deficit as much as I could, I took a job as supply preacher in a *Baptist* church in Bridgeport. We go down on Sunday morning and come back after the services. Besides the financial help, it is being extremely good experience to get back to preaching regularly.

"In addition to that I have worked through a year's stack of *New York Times* and clipped out all items that seemed to be of interest and use to me and filed them for future reference. It may seem a light task, but actually it consumed the best part of three weeks. The only justification I can plead for spending so much time that way is that now I have a very valuable store of illustrations and human interest stories, book reviews and news items that will come in handy preaching and lecturing. Only the man who has groped vainly for the right illustration to clinch the presentation of a good idea knows just how much a file of distinctive and nonprofessional illustrations can mean. The rest of my time has been parceled out in language study and shorthand and typewriting. Note-taking has always been my chiefest pain in the neck because, writing longhand, I never could get enough of what the professor said without missing the overtones of the way he said it. As for the typewriting, I am just taking time out now to do what I should have been forced to do in the beginning, namely to learn the touch system. Hunt and peck were all right until I was forced to turn off an enormous mass of written stuff. I am giving these details of the past three months' work in part to prove that I haven't been loafing away the time and also because I am assuming that you may be interested to know how an earnest young man lapping at the Pierean spring fares. . . .

"The news about Mulberry is disquieting. I cannot believe that the old church will have to give up, and yet, I don't know what can be done to forestall the evil day. Perhaps with a rising stock market, astute traders like Gus Felton and Jim Porter may see their way clear to drive a hard bargain with the bond holders

and get the church out of hock. But even that seems a questionable way for a church to do business. I mean no disrespect to Dr.
Cook, but I do think that you will find a young man like Pierce
Harris will be able to rally the church around something else
than the call of duty (the tattered flag of an old order of preaching). The one hopeful thing to remember is that religious institutions are notorious for having more vitality and more latent power
for endurance than their appearance would ever lead one to suppose. I do not know whether it will be a good thing or not, but
the church will survive generations after the vital faith that gave
meaning to its work will have faded from its membership."

Albert's Yale Dissertation

All the aforementioned involvements were squeezed in between
Albert's research for his doctoral dissertation. In the process of
that research he discovered that his vision was far bigger than his
performance. And consequently discovered a change in the making. He said: "My dissertation was on *Revelation and Reason in
Origen and Tertullian* [the precise title was *The Problem of Faith
and Reason in Christian Theology As Illustrated in the Thought
of Origen*]. But before I got done, I had to drop Tertullian because Origen was quite enough."[51]

In referring to his doctoral thesis Outler wrote Ronk Buhman
on April 15, 1942: "Like the romantic innocent I have always
been, I choose a subject (thesis) which turns out to require French,
German, Latin and Greek besides English." Even after he had
reduced the scope of his thesis he strewed enough obstacles in
his pathway to ensure that the end result would convince any
reader that he had tackled a most difficult subject and had adequately revealed a scholar in the making.

The essence of this thesis is captured in Volume 8 of *The
Albert Outler Library* titled *Albert Outler, the Church Historian*
edited by Ted Campbell.

A Return Trip to His "Spiritual" Leader

While Albert anticipated going back into a South Georgia Conference pastorate, other options were becoming possibilities. This
letter written on November 24, 1937, to Carla from Columbus,

Georgia, lays out those options: "Last night, I finally faced up to Dad with the plain question as to what we might expect in the event we returned to the South Georgia Conference. He talked quite freely and said that we might rest assured in receiving a small station, paying at least $2000 or $2100, with parsonage. He mentioned places like Dawson, Cuthbert, and Cochran. Furthermore, he said he was confident that we could expect recognition and support for anything the Conference had, in the course of time. This was not his opinion alone, he said, but the general agreement of the Cabinet. Now, if that is the case, we are in a position to forget the future, don't you think? We can live and discharge our obligations on that salary in a very short time, and we can find a very happy and satisfying life in a place like Dawson and what would follow.

"We have now a three-way choice. Duke may offer something substantial and promising before May 1st. If not, Emory may have something to offer after May 1st, and after General Conference. If neither of these materializes, we will be well taken care of in the Conference. Therefore, unless something positively startling opens in the North, we can forget the possibility of having to live and work there the rest of our lives. Does that make the trip down worthwhile to you?

"This time I have missed you because I have wanted you here to talk over a lot of these things as they develop and get your characteristically practical slant on them. I think we have come a long way in the art of companionship (despite our silly and stupid quarrels). For we do understand and like to consider our common interests. I'll be glad when we can be together and talk all this over. And believe it or not, I'll be glad when we can get to work together again."

Carla and Albert got together and decided that they had better go ahead and take an appointment in the South Georgia Conference. That was the secure way to go. And, after all, that was their purpose for going to Yale in the first place. He went there to prepare himself for the ever-expanding challenges of the local church. Excitedly he appeared in conference with his bishop in 1937 and shared with him his work at Yale, where he would in 1938 receive his Ph.D. (specialization: patristics). This was the same bishop with whom he had spoken before going to Yale.

With his father and the entire Cabinet behind him, he was given to believe his future in the Conference was secure. It was then that his *spiritual* leader took the wind out of his sails; he would not even discuss with Albert an appointment. The "conversation" was one-way. Albert talked; the bishop listened and then laid down his edict: no appointment for Albert to a local church. Bishop Ainsworth had in his sights a great church world leader in the making—and did not recognize him. That fleeting thought that Albert wrote in his Wofford *Memory Book* about "being a bishop" did not apply to being like *that* bishop! He knew by experience what he was talking about when he called it "the age of dictator bishops." He saw in that instance a bishop wielding the kind of power that Outler avoided practicing all of his ministry as if it were a plague.

Outler talked about this time in his life in these words: "I went to Yale against the expressed wishes of my bishop, Bishop Ainsworth. He warned me that I would not be welcomed back in the South Georgia Conference with a Yale Ph.D.—that I'd be overeducated and not actually suited for the plans he had in mind for me. And that turned out to be the case.

"We went from New Haven back to South Georgia—back to Ainsworth—wanting to find a job preaching or teaching. But he proved faithful to his warning and so my first two ambitions, after Yale, were blocked. I was overeducated for a Methodist pastorate in South Georgia. As much as I felt he had blocked the career I had designed for myself, the career he accidentally made possible for me has been a very much richer and very much more fruitful one. So I'd have to say, 'Yes,' it was much better that I should have gone to Duke than that I should have gone either to a pastorate in South Georgia or have gone to Emory and settled back too quickly in the cocoon."[52]

Outler looked back on those days and said: "One's personal interaction with 'accidents' of history ['accidents' in this instance included a harsh rejection by a dictator bishop] may become meaningful. The meaning is perceived, recognized, appreciated, and then lived out. This is at least one way of the early stages of talking about a doctrine of providence in history and in personal life."[53] This instance dramatically illustrated an aspect of the irony of the nemesis of power: Ainsworth is remembered in this biography for the power he *tried* to wield over Albert.

One Eye on Becoming a Professor

Unwittingly this heavy-handed bishop initiated Outler's journey into the highest echelons of scholarship. Albert did not target greatness for himself; greatness targeted him as scholarship attracted his attention during his Yale days. While he was aiming for a local pastorate in the South Georgia Conference, he had one eye on becoming a professor if all else failed. "All else" did fail, and he ended up with a teaching position at Duke University.

A Meaningful Introduction

Friends from Yale helped to open the Duke door. In a November 6, 1937, letter to President Few of Duke, Liston Pope, Dean of Yale Divinity School, wrote: "One of my close friends, Mr. Albert C. Outler, will be in Durham on Wednesday, November 17, en route for a visit to his home in Georgia. He expects to receive his Ph.D. from Yale in June, and subsequently to teach, if possible, in the field of historical theology. I have suggested to him that he stop to see you as I think you will be interested in his capabilities, whether or not you can suggest any possible opening for him in one of our southern schools.

"In a number of years of graduate work, I have never known a graduate student in religion who would match Outler's ability. I recognize the extravagance of that statement, but his scholastic record lends its support. His record, incidentally, may be on file at Duke, as I understand that he was considered for the Gurney Kearns fellowship two years ago, prior to his decision to come to Yale. . . . His work at Yale has been top flight: in his preliminary examinations last spring, he made honors on half of them and high passes on the others. He is doing his dissertation this year, on the problem of faith and reason in Tertullian and Origen.

"I write to you because I believe that Outler has a splendid contribution to make to religious thought and scholarship, and I know you will be interested in anybody who can do that. He has the perspective and the qualifications for a life of genuine productivity, and is the sort of man I, for one, would like to see at Duke. . . .

"His personal qualifications are as excellent as his scholastic. He has several years of experience in the pastoral ministry, being

a member of the South Georgia Conference, in which his father is
a presiding elder. His wife, a charming person, comes from Birmingham. But I must desist from further description, lest you
think I am employing hyperbole or have lost my judgment."

A Follow-up Letter

Albert had his interview, arranged by Liston Pope, with President Few. He later followed his visit with this December 7,
1937, letter to President Few: "As you suggested in our recent
interview, I have asked Miss Hanson [about possible appoint-
ments] of the Bureau of Teaching Appointments here at Yale
and the estimates of my professors and certain others with whom
I have been associated. At the same time, I am following your
other suggestion and am arranging an interview with Professor
Branscomb within the next week or two. If there is anything else
you would like for me to do, or any other sort of reference you
think might be appropriate for me to furnish, please let me know.
I do not want to appear too aggressive, but at the same time, I
am frank to say that I hope you may be able to work something
out for me at Duke.

"We had a very enjoyable trip home. I had a short visit with
Dr. Snyder at Wofford and a very encouraging interview with
Dean Trimble at Emory. My father was glad to hear about my
interview with you and recalled his former associations with you
on the old Sunday School Board.

"Thank you again for a delightful interview, and for your
advice which has helped me to determine definitely that I shall
settle somewhere in the South for my life's work. And both my
wife and I would prefer it to be where the future of graduate
work in the South holds the greatest promise."

Albert's Interview by Harvie Branscomb

As was suggested by President Few, Albert was interviewed by
Harvie Branscomb, who on February 7, 1938, wrote to President
Few: "I spent this weekend at New Haven, where I had an op-
portunity to talk with the faculty members under whom Mr.
Outler is working and also of having dinner with Mrs. Outler and
him on Saturday evening. These impressions make me wish to

write a letter supplementary to the one about him that went to you several days ago.

"The Yale faculty speak of Outler in superlative terms. One of them said, 'One of the best men we have produced in twenty years.' Professor Calhoun was emphatic in believing that Outler will definitely make his mark. My own impression of him on further acquaintance was equally satisfactory. He has wide interests, speaks easily, and seems to have a good deal of common sense. I think he has an exaggerated idea of the severity of the Yale examinations and has taken them much too seriously. He has also been a little inclined to worry over not having an academic appointment. He seems to be the sort of person who needs a sense of security and permanent tenure for his best accomplishment. I believe, however, that we would run no risks in taking him on and am rather inclined to think that he has a definite promise of fine achievement."

Duke's Offer

President Few of Duke wrote in a February 22, 1938, letter to Albert: "I am glad now to find, as I had hoped when you were here last winter that I might find, an instructorship for you at a salary of twenty-five hundred dollars; and outlined tentatively something of the kind of work you might expect the first year. That is, you will recall, you would do some work with the undergraduates and offer one course open to the theological students. We shall be anxious to have you succeed and will do all we can to help you toward that end. After some two or three years here, you might keep in mind a leave for a year at the University of Edinburgh, as Professor Macintosh suggested in his letter to Professor Shelton Smith. I think if everything goes favorably that plan might be worked out.

"I realize that you are preoccupied with your tasks at Yale, and you can put aside next year's details here until you have cleared there. Meanwhile, do not take the examination too seriously. I have found from long observation that a man with a good record usually gets through in Ph.D. examinations, and elsewhere for that matter. If you will write me your acceptance I will attend to the necessary details here so that I hope you may then have a somewhat free mind in every direction."

Albert's Answer

On February 25, 1938, Albert wrote to President Few: "I am happy to accept the position which you have offered me in your letter on the twenty-second. My wife and I are both delighted with the prospect and challenge of a place at Duke. . . . The division of my work between undergraduates and the theological students appeals to me, at least for the first year. I shall be glad to follow your judgment as to the subjects and types of courses.

"Thank you for your encouraging words with respect to my work here. The dissertation is coming along nicely and, barring accident, will be ready for submission on schedule, May 1st. After that I shall be comparatively free for the month of May; at that time we can work out whatever details may be necessary. Meanwhile, I am entirely willing to leave all arrangements in your hands.

"Mrs. Outler and I will be in New Hampshire again this summer, where I am director of a boy's camp [YMCA's Camp Waldron and Andover]. The season begins June 24th and ends August 24th. We shall have plenty of time after that, I am sure, to get situated in Durham and ready for the year's tasks.

"Naturally, I will retain my connection with my own conference, and I hope that I may be free to do as much work in the church program as may not interfere with my teaching.

"Let me thank you again, Dr. Few, for your friendly interest in my situation and let me pledge to you my very best service and loyalty."

4

Albert Outler Enters the World of Scholarship

Duke called and in the fall of 1938, Albert was on his way in a totally new direction in ministry. His teaching ministry at Duke was in full swing in 1939, the same year that his father retired to Trail's End at Young Harris after nearly fifty years in the initerant ministry. (Albert transferred to the South Carolina Conference on November 16, 1941.) God took the decision of a petulant bishop who thought *he* was God and used it to bring to the church one of its most noted historical theologians.

"[At Duke] I got a university setting, a professional training—apprenticeship—and an ecumenical experience, all at the same time. Shelton Smith and Harvie Branscomb taught me what I needed to know about teaching, about university life, about university politics, about the relationship between the divinity school and the university and the undergraduate department of religion. And then they taught me more than I can ever quite remember about their fields and about mine. We used to have a luncheon arrangement every two or three days and talked about the world, so that became my second graduate education."[54]

One of the "fields" from which Outler learned was the internationally famous work done by Joseph B. Rhine in the field of parapsychology. Outler had studied about what Duke had been doing in this area of abnormal psychology since his days at Emory in the early 1930s. And now, as professor in the Divinity School, he was next door to where the experiments were taking place. He actually took part in the experiments through his niece Helen Outler (now Helen Lankford), daughter of his older brother Jason. Helen's parents had settled on Duke University for her because Albert was there and they knew that he would look after her for them. One of the first things Albert did was to get her to volunteer to work with Rhine's company of experimenters by throwing dice!

In this study of psychokinesis (the direct mental influence over a physical object or physical process) she informed her uncle Albert concerning the results of the experiments. They were that the size and weight of dice, number of dice per throw, and distance between subject and object all failed to show any regular relationship whatever. The results of her tests, and those sharing with her the dice-throwing, argued against a physical conception of the psychokinesis process, physical though the end effect itself must necessarily be. During his tenure at Duke, Outler did not depend upon any unique gift of extrasensory perception that he might have possessed to keep up with what was going with Rhine's experiments. He knew *whom* he could straightaway trust to get the facts for him, namely his niece.

A Pastor/Scholar

From the beginning of his scholarly pursuits Outler never forgot his pastoral roots. During his first year at Duke, Outler was immersed in a lecture on baptism, using Latin words to the confusion of many, when he paused and said, "Did I ever tell you about baptizing the two-hundred pound candidate in rural Georgia by immersion?" By the time he got through with *that* story he once again had full attention of his class on the subject of baptism. He would tell those kinds of stories in the classroom, in his words, "to keep them from yawning with their minds!" His motive in teaching was "to stretch their thinking and strengthen their commitment." An essential part of his meaning of teaching was "Love 'em and teach them and teach them to love learning and then let 'em go with whatever kind of launching impetus you can."[55]

Outler could not forget his pastoral roots because he continued to practice them. Students felt free to come to his office for counsel. And then there were those times he went to their homes to pastor them in times of crisis. These pastoral disciplines within the academic community started at Duke and continued throughout his teaching career.

While at Duke Albert began to be called upon to lead off-campus seminars. One such seminar was at Blueridge. In a letter to Carla on June 10, 1940, he wrote of this experience: "I was moved last night from the room we had over to 118, a room on the front. The advantage was offset by the fact that now I have a roommate, a very tiresome fellow, though infinitely benevolent, from Berea College. He 'just loves' to talk; and you know that while I talk too much in public, I love to have a chance in private to be clamlike or at least to mumble. But on the whole, things are going better, and I am making adjustments so that the week's experience won't be too much of an ordeal, although it will be far from a 'triumph.'" Albert also taught at the summer schools held at Lake Junaluska in 1940 and 1941.

The Need for a More Balanced Vacation

Later in the month, on June 20, Albert spoke eloquently of the part that Carla played in his life: "I know it's been a long while since I last wrote, and you've been mighty sweet about writing; but I've been very weary and thus counted on you to understand and forgive. For I think that I've thought of you more often and with a little more nostalgia than almost any time I can remember before. Everybody has been pleasant and helpful, and it has been a most interesting affair, but there has been no one like you with whom I can share my private impressions, etc., and no one who would give and receive caresses which would bind up all the little wounds of life. Your love, your self, all of it is very dear to me, little Boo; you've been a good wife and a grand comrade and this seems a cruelly long time to be separated from you. We did need a vacation from each other after that long and wearing spring with its anticlimax in moving, but I'm sure now that a week is quite long enough, and I hope that we shall have sense enough to remember this when we plan for our next summer."

Forums, Fun, and Games

An upbeat Albert wrote this letter on June 24, 1941: "The Assembly is steadily improving in interest and unity. The forum Saturday afternoon was not very 'forumish' (I had to do most of the talking), but they seemed more interested than they had the previous evening. Then we had a faculty vs. student ball-game: I got two hits out of four times up and no errors. At the banquet they called for a song and I taught them 'Dese bones—,' and they have gone for it like everything. Yesterday's sermon came off better than I had hoped. All I have left now is a forum this afternoon and the consecration service tonight."

Outler's Stand on War

As the rumblings of war could be heard across the world, Outler gave in an October 3, 1941, letter to Henry Danielwice what could be described as his "war" stand: "Now about your problem with respect to the war. Of course, it is not your problem alone, but that of countless thousands of young men like yourself, all of whom are caught up in the ghastly maelstrom of world revolution and war. Let us begin our analysis of the problem by recognizing the fact that very few of us, young or old (and I remind you that I have my registration card too and have waived ministerial exemption), do not hate war. The bloodthirsty boys, the swashbucklers, the militarists, are in the minority, I believe. The problem, therefore, does not center in the issue as to whether war is a good thing or bad. Any person with any degree of moral sensitivity acknowledges that war is bad, tragic. The question really boils down to what, under the circumstances, men are going to do when no one alternative presents itself as ideal, and where choices have to be made in terms of the greatest possible good and the least possible evil.

"Personally, I believe that the issues in this war are vast enough and clear enough, that with any reservations about the use of force, and the sense and blunders of Britain and America, men of God are going to unite in resisting the Nazi 'new order,' even though its alternative is by no means ideal. The surgeon has to decide how much pain to inflict and force to use in stopping the ravages of disease. The analogy does hold for war, because it is a disease, too. But in paresis, for example, they fight disease with disease because there is a greater and lesser evil when they can see it. All this adds up in my mind to this conclusion: All of us are involved in this great tragedy which the follies and sins of mankind have brought us to. 'Do not ask for whom the bell tolls; it tolls for thee,' and for many and for all sensitive and reasonable men, I feel. No one of us can afford, in good consciousness, to try to withdraw, 'to wait this one out,' or to try to live in a vacuum in the midst of the world's cyclone.

"The dread implication in this for me is that all of us must do something, the most effective, the most sacrificing, the most heroic, he can do, with the hope of contributing something, even microscopic, to the resolution of this great struggle in various degrees and on one side or the other, in various relations. I can certainly understand your aversion to fighting. Can you find something else, though, which you could do and which would be your full measure of devotion? For example, I have decided, if called, I am going to ask for service in the hospital corps or the ambulance service, or some form of rehabilitation that will involve sacrifice and service, but not require slaughter. This is not very logical, I know, but it is the nearest thing to a compromise I can find. The situation does not require that all of us do the same thing. Our involvement in the situation, however, requires that all of us find something to do which will be meaningful and not self-centered.

"This, of course, is no clear solution, though it seems to me there are no formulae which will dissolve the grounds of confusion and doubt. There was never a future more uncertain than ours and, hence, we walk by faith and not by sight. That faith, I believe, means that we must do the most constructive, the most unselfish, and the most self-denying thing we can at any given moment, trying always to see history in the long view. This certainly does not mean that I have any advice to give you or that I think that I know what you should do. You have a good mind and a sensitive conscience, and if we can't trust those, we have no other resources comparable."

A Baby Girl

More was happening at Duke than teaching, seminars, and digging into books. A little baby girl, born on September 4, 1941, was adopted by Albert and Carla. They named her Frances (after

Albert's sister Fan), but their pet name for her was Trudi. Trudi became a big part of Outler's life, not only when he was home, but when he was away leading seminars. Such was the case when he wrote Carla from Emory on May 30, 1942: "The days slip by, full of a lot of interesting things to do and people to see, but I'm very homesick and still pretty much fatigued. . . . 'Everybody' has asked about you and I've shown Trudi's picture to the people I thought would be properly appreciative. They have been, too! Lucy Quinn, Bro. Clary, Dr. Cook, etc. My roommate is Paul Quillian, pastor of a church in Houston, Texas, with 5,800 members. He's a fine fellow but with that typical successful-preacher stamp on him. On second-thought, he has it a good deal less than most."

More Counsel from Carla

After the seminar Albert went back up into the mountains of Young Harris. In a June 2, 1942, letter Carla wrote to Albert in that retreat setting: "If you and Fan will remember that you are adults now, and not spoiled children—and that the folks are getting old, and want some attention paid to them—and that they don't like for you two to get into these wild and furious arguments—and if you both will make a special effort to be diplomatic with Mother, and if you will make your bed, and keep your clothes picked up, and help her all you can—and really look for ways to help, then I think that having both of you there will be a joy and a pleasure. (That sounds like one of your sentences—it's long enough isn't it?)"

Taking Stock of His Situation

In a June 15, 1942, letter Albert wrote to Carla: "How this week has flown, and how happy I am for it because in just four more days (and a few hours), I'll be home; and will I be glad! The time here has been devoted to loafing, visiting with the folks, and very little else. I have done the sermon for Trinity and Raleigh (I think the same one will do for both) and today I worked out a first and rough draft of a syllabus for that introductory course in historical theology. I've decided that I must make a more positive, ingratiating approach to the whole business without lowering the standards or quality of the work at all. Perhaps during the summer I can reshape the other courses and have something tangible and well-organized for each one. I am feeling contrite over not having put my very best into all my teaching and I'm going to try to 'repent' of it for the coming years.

"Mother and Dad are well, although Mother continues to be in a very bad mood, unhappy and just a little martyred. Dad misses the harness and the fellowship which buoyed him up and he has to wrestle with boredom and irritation more than he ever has before. Fan is here in better than average form, but she and Mother are mutual strains. For all this, though, it's been an exceptionally happy week; and I believe my staying around has been good for me and perhaps for them, too."

In this response to Carla's letter nothing was mentioned about her earlier admonitions. Instead he casually discussed toward the end of his letter how the family relations actually came off, and suggested that his being around was a positive contribution to making those relations work. That was another indication that Albert listened carefully to Carla's words of counsel.

Albert stayed busy mending and maintaining his family relations. Meanwhile his academic star was rising. In a September 17, 1942, letter, Cecil G. Hefner said to Albert, "This summer I had a long talk with Dr. Hal Luccock at Union Seminary, and he has great respect and admiration for you. I want to tell you something which is off the record. He has an eye on you, and the School of Religion at Yale holds you in the highest esteem."

Helping around the House

In this October 24, 1942, letter to Carla, who was visiting her family in Homewood, Alabama, Albert said: "My, my, how self-righteous I feel tonight. I've cooked all my meals today, and now all the dishes are cleaned up and ready for more work tomorrow. It will seem routine to you, but I am proud that I have found that I can do [he lists the chores]— but doesn't it take an awful amount of time? I've so much less done than I planned and I know how you must feel when there are three of us instead of one. You deserve more help than I've given you, and I'm going to see if something can be done about it.

Writing

"Today I finally finished and sent off the manuscript to Dick Baker for *Motive,* and I also finished the outline for the chapter on the Reformation and sent it off to George Thomas. I had hoped to make a good beginning on the Duodecim paper [for the Duodecim Theological Discussion Group, a select assemblage of outstanding theologians], but haven't got very far yet. A synopsis of it has got to be sent off Sunday week, too.

The Explosion

"Things go along all right here. There's no news from Ruth, and I haven't seen any of 'the gang.' Sue comes over occasionally and asks about you and Trudi. We'll be happy to see you-all back. One little brackish incident happened yesterday over at school. I was asked to select two hymns for the service next Monday for Allan Booth, the secretary of the British Student Movement, who is visiting us over the weekend. One of the hymns was 'Glorious things of thee are spoken, / Zion, City of our God.' The tune is by Haydn, and Ed Broadhead proceeded to blow a fuse before me and the choir, refusing to play it because, as he says, it's the German National Anthem. We tried to argue with him, but he staged quite a show and finally I blew off. I fear dear Edward will never love me as well, but unless his skin is thicker than I think, he'll have cause to reflect upon his artistic temperament again. We shall have to patch it up in order to carry on the chapel program; but it seems to me a very distasteful task to indulge artistic temperament and hysterical superheated 'patriotism' at the same time."

War Involvement

Without embracing the War as "Christian," Outler realized he was implicated in the evil situation surrounding it and showed his loyalty to his nation's cause by teaching courses for Naval Reserve Chaplain candidates in the B-12 program that came to Duke. He said: "I did my military service there in the university teaching in the Navy B-12 program (War Advisory Service), and also in the churches—both with respect to crisis of the deepening involvement in the war and, also, in terms of their ecumenical relationships, because it was increasingly clear that divided and separated Christian churches were not able to mobilize themselves for the tasks of a nation at war and a nation in a very deep moral crisis."[56]

Job and Family

Later Albert wrote to Carla: "It is when you are gone that I realize what I cherish about you most: your making our home a friendly, understanding place, your patience when I'm edgy, your tenderness when I'm down, your energy and competence about the house and about Trudi, your adequacy and responsiveness when love rises beyond the commonplace (I confess that I am looking forward to Friday night as eagerly as if there had been no other nights). And it is when you are gone that I realize my own shortcomings as a husband: my desperate preoccupation with a job too big for me so that I can give you and Trudi only the fag-end of my energy and disposition. It would be too pretentious to promise to reform for there seems small chance that the pressure on me will let up. But if we can mutually understand and work at the job, it will help."

Chicago Comes Knocking

Early in his career Outler started getting inquiries from other seminaries feeling him out for a possible transfer. The following was Outler's response to Dean Colwell of the University of Chicago's Divinity School: "Your letter of February 2 raises, quite unexpectedly, an interesting and exciting possibility to which I have given very earnest and prayerful consideration in the last few days. I realize that your letter intends merely to explore one of many possibilities, but even to be considered for a position in such a school as yours is a very great honor and I feel quite flattered about it. At the same time, I have had to consider whether there is sufficient likelihood that, in case you should offer me a job, I would be willing to leave Duke and the prospects of my work here. Otherwise, it would hardly be candid on my part to accept your invitation to come to Chicago for exploratory conference.

"It is an extremely hard decision to try to make, as I am sure you will understand. The prestige, influence and resources of your Divinity School are, as everyone recognizes, quite extraordinary, and I am confident that under your leadership, the future will continue to add luster to the past glories of the school. On the other hand, Duke is at the beginning of a development in theological education in the South which may make a considerable contribution, in its own way, to the total progress of religion in America. If we lay hold wisely on our opportunities, it may very well be that the job one might do here will warrant the effort and sacrifice involved. I am not trying to argue the case; I am merely rehearsing for you some of the considerations I have been trying to weigh and evaluate.

"The upshot of it all is that, under the present circumstances, I feel sufficiently committed here at Duke, that it would hardly be fair for me to accept a trip to Chicago at your expense, since it seems fairly certain that, even if your decision were positive, mine would not be. I say this, believing that you will understand and appreciate my situation the more because you know and are interested in the South and its future development.

"Thank you again for your interest and invitation. I shall always be grateful for it."

Son David

Another interest entered the life of Albert Outler. A baby boy born on July 17, 1943 was adopted by Albert and Carla. They named him David. And now many of their experiences centered around Trudi and David.

Union Theological Seminary

Summer invitations to teach at other seminaries were easier for Outler to accept. In the summer of 1943 Albert Outler taught at Union Theological Seminary at Columbia University in New York City. He wrote to Carla in Birmingham: "Everything here is going along pretty well. There are twenty-five people in the class, and they are pretty well above the average I am accustomed to at Duke. So I'm having to tighten up a bit and pitch a little harder. It's interesting how you sense the increased tempo of life and thought in an atmosphere like this. . . . The chapel service went off pretty well, although I was too scared and self-conscious for it to be very inspiring."

More from Columbia University, written on August 4, 1943: "Have you seen the newspaper reports about Harlem? Well, Liston and a party from here were visiting Father Divine's 'heaven' in Harlem when the thing broke out. Luckily, no one of them was molested, but Liston says that there were some grim moments. I went over Monday morning and the place was an appalling shambles. Actually, it wasn't a 'race' riot, but well-informed observers say that it came near to being a general upheaval throughout the whole city. This is the nearest I've been to the boiling savagery that lies beneath the veneer of law and order in practically every city in America. And it is a frightening and ugly aspect.

"In addition to the steady chore of teaching, I've been working here in the library and feeling alternately good and bad over what there is to be done and my own shortcomings. And I've been nosing around the bookstores struggling with temptation. I may fall a wee-tiny bit—would you mind? [Outler invested every spare dollar he had in books; he was known to do this even when the dollar was clearly not there.] Everyone is surprised at my knowledge and interest in the Episcopal Church until I explain about you. [Before their marriage Carla was an Episcopalian.] And then they are surprised that I haven't been 're-ordained.' Last night was the best I've had here the whole summer. Liston and I went down to the Village and stumbled onto the most unusual and Bohemian restaurant I ever saw and got the best dinner I've had so far in New York (but, woe betide, it cost $1.50!). Then we went to see *Arsenic and Old Lace*. I had expected it to be gruesome and morbid; actually though, it was hilariously funny—light-footed, well-balanced. One of the characters, Aunt Abby, looked and acted alarmingly like Aunt Carl (she was the one who made the elderberry wine and put arsenic in it). "

Albert's letters always expressed deep love for Carla. Even light humor, as revealed in this 1943 fortune cookie clipping from a Chinese restaurant in New York City, never made light of their love: "Real love is when fellow rather have certain gal on mind than any other one on lap." Carla was always in his mind and heart.

VIP Transportation

It was no vacation for Outler during the fall of 1943 when he arrived by rail in Dallas, and from there went on to Denton via a means of transportation that even he, from the hills of Appalachia, had never experienced. He was the featured, fascinating, headliner speaker for a Texas Methodist Student Movement Conference held at Denton. Transport was hard to come by, and they had to settle for a flatbed truck covered with tarp. Paul Deats and his delegation from the University of Texas picked Outler up on a cold day in late November (around Thanksgiving). Hovering under the tarp and without heat they made their way from Dallas to Denton and back to Dallas. Those were the days before Outler's national prominence, but those huddled with him on that truck (including young theologian-to-be John Deschner) recognized their "fascinating headliner" for the conference was on his way to becoming a scholar of distinction.

Rev. John Outler Dies

On January 28, 1944, seventy-four-year-old John Outler died in Murphy, North Carolina, Cherokee County. Following the funeral service held at the Young Harris Chapel, the interment was at Old Union Cemetery in Young Harris on Sunday, January 30. This death impacted Albert's life greatly. Thirty-five years of the physical presence of a father's love were gone. And it hurt. But his father's love was not lost in his life. Gratitude prevailed as a result of losing one who had loved him. Thirteen years later Outler said in a 1957 class at Perkins School of Theology: "None of us were cared for by our parents as well as we might have been. But, to the degree that we are reasonably healthy, reasonably sane and are able to live reasonably fruitful lives, we evidence the fact that we have been loved. And for that love our rightful response is to be genuinely grateful."[57]

Outler's First Robe

An April 27, 1944, letter from C. Sylvester Green, Duke's adviser in Religious Activities, called forth an answer filled with typical Outlerian egg-headed wit. Against the backdrop of the years dating back to November 16, 1938, when Outler came to Duke, the students and professors had seen Outler on numerous occasions come to special formal services at Duke chapel without a robe. If he had worn one, it had to be borrowed because he did not have a robe. So when this letter from Green arrived, Outler read it with a cocked eye: "Following the last observance of communion on Maundy Thursday, we found a confusion in robes. We have one that does not belong to us, and we cannot find the robe that is ours.

"After checking all around it occurred to us that one of the Senior Ministers might have inadvertently picked up the wrong robe after the service. Will you be kind enough to check your own robe, if you used it that evening.

"Thanking you for your cooperation."

They were calling for him to check the robe that they knew he did not have! After six years of attending numerous formal services in Duke chapel with Outler that called for robes, professors and students knew he had not worn a robe; Outler knew that they knew that he had not worn a robe; Outler knew that they knew that he knew that he had not worn a robe. They were alerting Outler to something that all parties already knew. Why? Was it a joke on this upstart genius? Was it a not-so-subtle hint that he was out of sync with the high-church atmosphere of the Duke chapel? Whatever the reason for the letter from Green, Outler knew what could be behind it, and he also knew how to answer it. With the same air of "innocence" in which it was written, Outler wrote his answer to Green: "Thank you for your note about the robes. I can eliminate myself at once since I have no robe. I came to the chapel without one and I went away as I came. If, however, you all have an extra robe when the mix-up is finally resolved, I would be glad to have it for thus far the budget hasn't allowed for proper academic regalia for yours truly." The implication of the message plainly was that Outler was not paid a salary by Duke that allowed the purchase of a robe. And he was not so proud that he would not accept a robe if they gave him one, which in all likelihood warranted Duke giving him the robe that Outler carried to Yale when he went there the next year as professor.

More from Appalachia

On September 1, 1944, Albert (from Young Harris) wrote Carla, who was visiting her family in Birmingham: "As for me, I'm putting in some of the fanciest loafing you ever saw—and still loving it. Mother is being swell about it, even though it bewilders her some and cuts across her cherished routine. I sleep late and loll around the rest of the day, reading, daydreaming, or whatever. Yesterday I got up energy enough to hike up to Kirby Cove—and did I sleep last night! Tomorrow, I think I'll try Double Knobs and, maybe, Sunset. Then, next week, unless Mother makes a desperate objection, I'll see if I can take in Bald. Honestly, darling, this is as complete a vacation as I could possibly have at Gatlinburg or anywhere else. The only thing I can remember or imagine as better would be you and me at LeConte Lodge or on the Appalachian Trail. Some day, we'll do that again, too!

"Be sure to plead my cause with the folks persuasively. They'd rather have an absent son-in-law, recovering poise and vigor than one present who was still struggling to avoid the precipice, wouldn't they? And, although promises are rash, I think you'll have a nicer husband waiting for you when you come back than you had this past spring and summer."

He added at the end of his letter: "Dearest Trudi—Yesterday, I wandered in the forest and saw two lovely bushy-tailed squirrels, just like the ones who helped the lively little rabbit find his way home. There were other forest people there, too, and they told me to tell you and David 'hello' and to have a good time with Danny and Pappy and Aunt Carl and Greatgram! I wish I could be there with you, especially on your birthday, but I'll sing 'Happy Birthday' up here and I'll have your birthday present all ready and waiting for you when you come home. Be a good girl and help Mother take care of David. And, at night, before you go to sleep, 'plack-out' I'm singing you a nice song. Here are your kisses from—Your loving, Daddy."

More Than Duke Bargained for

When Duke Divinity School hired Outler, they got more than they bargained for. He taught subjects other than those that had to do with theology. Such was the case that fall day in 1944 when he found his class of students standing in front of the Duke chapel looking up at an airplane's aerobatic performance. It was an occasion set up just for them. John Oliphint, the brother of Outler's one-day-to-be-bishop student, Ben Oliphint, had returned home from World War II. John had piloted his P-51 fighter plane to Durham for a visit with Ben. As John returned to the field for his departure, he alerted Ben to the show that was to follow. Ben in turn alerted the students. John buzzed the campus and then proceeded to do his stunts. Outler came out to see what was going on and began to describe the aerobatics as they were taking place: the barrel roll, the aileron roll, the loop, the hammer head, the Split-S, the Cuban eight, etc. He knew them all. Ben reports that they returned to their classroom convinced that this man knew something about everything. Apocryphal stories about Outler began early in his teaching career.[58]

Faculty Jealousies

On September 26, 1944, Albert wrote Carla in Birmingham: "Things here [at the seminary] are getting off to a very good start. Harvie has taken hold and is doing a superb job of meeting issues squarely and ignoring the petty personal angles that usually tangle us all up. Last Wednesday, in the graduate faculty, Ken lost control of himself and became unsubtle, if not insulting, in an attack upon me for my part in Rogers' course last year. Thursday morning, Harvie called him and dressed him down. Upshot: Ken came down to see me that afternoon to apologize. We had a fairly long talk; in the course much of his bitterness came out. By setting the most invidious face on everything I did, he had produced a picture of my character as an arrogant, scheming, ruthless man who was being devilishly successful with his intriguing. He thinks, although he didn't put it so bluntly, that I am a mediocre person and scholar (he's right there, too) and, therefore, all these fantastic things which have been falling into my lap could not have happened without being engineered. When I told him what had happened, he then decided that Shelton must have been the snake in the grass. Luckily, I felt more sorrowful than angry, so I didn't lose my temper. At the end, Ken offered to shake hands and begin all over again. Naturally, I accepted his proffer. We shall see if we can keep this precarious cordiality alive for at least long enough for us to get gone from Durham."

From Duke to Yale

"Get gone from Durham." Those words indicated that Albert's mind was already on the move—from Duke to Yale. The actual move was to come a year later.

Prior to the move in June 1945, Albert, taking his vacation in Swan Quarter, North Carolina, wrote to Carla, who was vacationing with her parents in Birmingham: "It's just a week now since I set sail for my vacation and I think it's working out rather well. I'm still in the 'down phase,' half-stupid and draggy, but the sense of pressure has eased off and I'm getting adjusted to the new routine. Most of the time is spent lying around, either in bed or around the house—it's as near to a vegetable existence as you can imagine for me. The people here at the 'hotel' [boarding house] are very nice and have accepted me as one of them. Nobody is interested in the professor; it's nice to be amongst people who call me 'Mr.' without conscious effort. The regular cast of 'our boarding house' runs as follows: Miss Pearl Sadler, mistress and hostess (fat, amiable, and country); Belle, cook (a huge, globular Negress with a perpetual, toothless grin); a Mr. Cal Davis, crotchety bachelor in his seventies (reputedly the richest and one of the tightest men in Hyde County—but friendly withal); a Mrs. Gibbs (husband in service; she's secretary for the local draft board); two hitherto 'unclaimed blessings' named Roach and Cooper (half-or-less educated, but with the usual veneer of clothes and superficial manner); and I. (I forbear a characterization; you can supply it better.) The talk is incredibly trivial: the day's doings, what so-and-so said, 'who shot John.' In short, I have found a place as far from Duke and the Wranglers as one might hope to find.

"But, alas, it's also far from you and the children and I miss you all, etc."

Albert always ended his letters expressing much love to Carla and with a special note to Trudi and David.

From Swan Quarter Albert traveled to Young Harris and from there wrote Carla on August 12: "I wish I could see the children in their war paint. This summer's experience has been good for them and I'm glad that it is a mutually satisfactory arrangement for them to be with the folks [Carla's family]. Tell them both that I love them very much and that I'm proud of and pleased with them.

"I shall be working on my course plans and on my 'inaugural address' [for Yale]. And we must get settled as quickly as possible at New Haven so that I can 'get organized' for business. In short, I have to hit the ground running and I count on you not only to help, but also to understand. I shall stop short of nail-biting, I hope, and I'll try to be as relaxed as possible. You can help me in this mightily, and I know you will.

"These peace negotiations seem tragically prolonged. It seems possible now that the war may drag on for weeks or months and it will be a bitter anticlimax. And it may very well be that Russia's jumping at the very last minute is going to complicate the problems of peace far more than it has simplified the problems of war."

Professional Societies

Professional societies began to open to Outler while he was at Duke. Beginning in 1938 and lasting to the end of his days Outler was a member of the Duodecim Theological Discussion Group. In 1938 he also was invited to join the American Society of Church History, where he served terms as president and past president. In 1940 he was invited to join the American Theological Society, where he served as president and then as secretary.

Associate Professor

While at Duke Outler was promoted from instructor to assistant to associate professor. His dramatic move *up* in the scholar's world came with an invitation to bring his Yale Ph.D. back to Yale and teach. In a December 7, 1944, letter to sister Fan he wrote: "I've just come back [to Duke] from a series of conferences at Yale, making plans and arrangements for my joining the faculty of the Divinity School there next July. It was all very exciting and encouraging; everybody there was most cordial and helpful, and the program we agreed on is going to be far more manageable than the battery of things I have been trying to do here. More than ever, I am sure that my decision to have a fling at 'the big-time' is the right one, even if there does remain a real wrench-at-heart over the prospect of leaving the South, etc., etc.

"Carla is as excited over the whole business as I am, although she has more serious misgivings over the climate, the housing situation, and the notion of Trudi and David growing up with Nuymegger brogues and Yankee ways [Carla spoke out of her own earlier years as a Yankee]. But such things are endurable, and there will be many things about life in New Haven which we will all enjoy more than the situation here."[59]

Outler was offered a job at Yale in 1943 and turned it down. "But in 1944 the invitation was renewed and this time the struggle between prudence and vanity got solved in the usual way—vanity won. To become the Timothy Dwight Professor of Theology at Yale in succession to Douglas Clyde MacIntosh, and as colleague to Calhoun, Bainton, Goodenough, Niebuhr, Latourette and the whole galaxy!"[60] Reflecting, he said: "I never supposed that I should have gone. None of the things that have happened to me have ever seemed quite right for the kind of person I understand myself to be. All of these experiences were literally astonishing and surprising—and many of them, quite unprecedented. None of them has seemed to me to be a normal progression from what I was doing before."[61]

A New Member of the Faculty

This story is told by Dow Kirkpatrick, who was appointed as pastor and professor of religion and Bible at Young Harris, Georgia, in 1946, near the Outlers' Young Harris house: "Shortly after we returned from our year in England we were barely settled in before newly made British friends began to visit us. None was more interesting than Victor Murray, a Methodist layman who was head of a Congregational theological college at Cambridge University. He had come to North America on a lecture tour of universities—across the southern United States to the West Coast, returning to the East via Canadian universities.

"Eventually he arrived at Yale. Albert was a new member of the faculty there. The dean gave a luncheon for Professor Murray. As they were seated, to make opening conversation, the Yale dean asked the guest, 'Where else have you visited in the United States, Professor Murray?'

"He had a sense of humor. As a teaser he began, 'Well, I have been several days in Young Harris, Georgia.' Whereupon the entire room burst into loud and raucous laughter. They soon explained that Albert Outler had recently come. When he claimed his home was Young Harris, they kidded him by insisting no such place had ever been heard of nor known about! Yet it got first mention by their distinguished Cambridge visitor."

Upward and Outward Moves

When Outler made his quantum leap back to Yale on November 4, 1945, he first served as associate professor in theology and then in 1947 was promoted to full professor as the prestigious Timothy Dwight Professor of Theology, one of the University's oldest and most distinguished chairs. While at Yale he had two more summer stints of teaching at Union Theological Seminary.

Some of Outler's friends at Duke never did let him go. Whether their problems were theological, personal, or whatever, they wrote him seeking his counsel. Especially was this true with H. Shelton Smith, professor of American Religious Thought and director of graduate studies at Duke. Dozens of long and detailed letters between the two continued for years.

Outler established himself early on as one who could converse authoritatively on the subject of *your* choice. The backdrop of Yale helped to magnify for some that trait in him. A man named "Tom" wrote to Outler concerning a friend whom he had sent to meet and talk with Outler: "Dick came back completely floored and 'humble'—he kept using the latter word, though highly excited about the experience. Of course, I just tried to be nonchalant and kept telling him, 'What did I tell you?' Your broad interests and depth of information left him utterly bewildered. Of course I've for a long time simply labored under the accepted assumption that you know virtually everything, Albert, though in my utterly rational moments I say to myself that there must be a few gaps. But personally I'm not interested in searching them out."

Outler felt quite at home in the rarefied Yale atmosphere. Especially did Outler enjoy the matching of wits, a cross-fertilizing of minds that went on in Julian Hartt's office downstairs in the Stuart House during the noon lunch hour. Who were there? "That would have been Calhoun, who was next door; Richard Niebuhr, who was downstairs; David Napier; Hugh Hartshorne, from across the street—across the 'quad'; Ray Morris and then Bill Muehl and other people dropped in from time to time. It was a kind of almost continuous seminar in religion and culture and contemporary faith."[62]

Outler allowed his mind to be stretched in situations beyond his own theology. He said, "The matching experience was my life at Silliman College, down the hill. I was the only theologian in the college and so was in constant dialogue with people from the medical school and people from the graduate school—such as Richard Sewell—'Ditsy' Sewell. He was a Yankee who had discovered Faulkner. So I tried to explain Mississippi to him so he could understand Faulkner. Then he tried to interpret Faulkner to me so that I could understand the southern psyche seen from the outside.

"[And then there was] Gerald Wimsath, who was the 'new critic' in English literature; plus the university organist; the man in symbolic logic who worked out a demonstration of the ontological argument in logical symbols. These and others—all of them—Monday night after Monday night. They'd take out after the theologian to see if he was, in fact, as superstitious as they supposed he was."[63]

Outler was, indeed, a rare bird in their midst—in the classroom, in faculty debates, and at party time. "It's a silly thing, but my first Fellows meeting, at cocktail hour, all they had were martinis and things and so I asked the steward if he had some tomato juice. It was a minor crisis in his experience. He went off and brought back two small glasses and one small pitcher of tomato juice and then I went around, and kept on talking, finished it up, went back for some more and discovered that the *other* glass had been used and the tomato juice was all gone, so that there was one other nonalcoholic in the crowd who had not surfaced and I pointed that out. From then on we had options of fruit juice, martinis, Scotch and whatnot and everybody was happy. And a lot of people who had drunk martinis and aperitifs because there were no options found that they preferred grape juice, tomato juice, apricot, etc."[64]

Religion in Higher Education

Speaking of his Yale years Outler said, "Those were the crucial years, when we didn't know if tax-supported and secular education was going to wipe out religion or relegate it to the margin or to theological schools and seminaries. And I think it was fairly important, in the decade between 1945 and 1955, that a great many religiously oriented educators worked at this job of religion in higher education—not merely the study of religion but the study of religion in every one of the humanities and the physical sciences! And I was in the thick of that, with the Hazen Foundation and the Danforth Foundation.

"Out of this came the departments of religion, for example, at Princeton, at the University of North Carolina, at Iowa. A new attitude developed toward religion in a great many places. I went, for example, to Amherst and to Southwestern at Memphis, to Reed [Portland, Oregon], to the University of Michigan, to all sorts of places. Talking at Stanford, talking to faculty about religion as a humane discipline and about the fundamental obligation of educators to make it possible for a person in the course of a humane education to study religion. This, now, I think, is in jeopardy once more, but at least formally and culturally speaking, it has become a commonplace. It was very far from a commonplace when we started in 1945. And so I think *that* was probably the main extracurricular endeavor and achievement of my six years at Yale."[65]

Tynshene

Though Outler was foremost a pastor/lecturer for his students, a glance at the major off-campus lectures listed at the end of this book reveals a momentum toward a catholic influence in the church's history. As busy as he was, he made room for Young Harris. In 1946 he joined in partnership with sister Fan and purchased their own cottage there. Because of his schedule, the details of the transaction and upkeep were left up to her. On January 21, 1946, she wrote: "I also agree that we do not project any extensive improvement program, but within the year, we shall be compelled to patch the leaking roof to the extent of safeguarding the house itself or stand to lose in the long run. I got Jack to patch with slate shingles about four square feet of the worst leak that showed up in my stay at Young Harris, and am now making arrangements to obtain a good quality roll roofing which will serve and yet will not be too steep an outlay. More of that later, but Jack will help wonderfully by being our patch-boy on minor emergencies. I found the storm had broken out a window pane in one bedroom, drove to Hiawassee to buy a new pane and putty, and Jack and I installed it ourselves. Little by little, whatever we do short of absolutely expert installation we'll be well advised to do ourselves. This is an opinion based not on my egotism but my estimate of the shortage of know-how in our mountain bailiwick available for our employ!

"Mama seems to be wearying a great deal, but that is perfectly understandable for her age and the hell's brew of weather we had. My visit was very pleasant, and she seemed to enjoy my being there. I worked on a crosscut saw and used a double-bit axe and a 'go devil' under Jack's mountaineer tutelage and felt very proud of the stack of logs we piled on the back porch. Officially, the day I reached Young Harris, the Ranger reading of the thermometer on Bald Mountain was *five* below *zero*. Brother, it was thirteen [degrees] two days of that same week, and then warmed up!"

In an undated letter Fan wrote concerning the name of their common investment: "For name—I offer (in Gaelic) *Tigh-an-Sithein,* anglicized to sound and spelling as *Tynshene,* and there is your 'Hilltop House' with the added auspicious factor of 'being presided over by beneficent Little People,' '*the Sheen*' being as near as we can sound '*Sithein*,' their correct Gaelic name." With Outler's full agreement from then on it was Tynshene.

Drastic Changes!

Drastic changes were taking place in Outler's life during the forties, *viz.,* the adoption of their children, the war, his move from Duke to Yale, purchasing Tynshene, etc. The grief events that affected him the most were the illness and death of his dad. And then in the late forties another testing time came with caring for his mother's needs. In a January 9, 1949, letter to sister Fan he wrote: "Thank you very much for your letters keeping us abreast of the development there in Atlanta and the establishment of Mother at Mrs. Little's. It is by all odds the best step we could have taken, and I am delighted that Mother was willing to cooperate in the new arrangement. It will be interesting to see what really competent medical care and diet will do for her now after the years in which she has been unwilling to accept such treatment. And it will be a considerably easier matter for you to stop by there occasionally than it was either to get to Murphy or to worry in the interim of how she was getting along.

"As you know, I have been contributing either twenty or twenty-five dollars a month to Mother's care ever since Dad died. Previously to that, I had been paying from fifteen to twenty dollars a month to Dad and Mother in payment of the loan they advanced me during graduate school days. What with our new house and the cost of living, our budget is well-nigh stretched to its limit, and I don't see how in the immediate future we can add much more than the twenty-five dollars a month already provided in it. I don't know what the situation is with John or Jason [his two older brothers], and suppose you are in something of the same fix that I am, and hence will not be able to add to what you have already been doing. All of this suggests to me that we ought to try to finance Mother's care out of her bond, and also probably from the proceeds of the sale of Trail's End. There is a lump in heart and throat when I mention selling Trail's End and yet, under the circumstances, it seems to me not only the best thing to do, but practically a necessity. One of the provisions of Dad's will was that it was to be sold to care for Mother if it should come to that. [While there was a lump in heart and throat, it was not as large a lump as it would have been earlier. For now there was only the land of Trail's End. The house had burned around the time they joined the Yale faculty.] Somehow or other we can make Tynshene do for our purposes, since it is unlikely that either of us would be able to maintain a double establishment as we have been trying to do.

"Naturally, I should want to see Trail's End sold, if at all, for a really good price, as I should think that on the market now that should be possible. Mother naturally thinks in terms of the Rustins, and I have no objection to selling to them, but I would want to be sure that it is really a competitive price, and not another sentimental gesture. With the proceeds we ought to be able, with what we are now contributing, to finance Mother's care under the present arrangement for the period of at least three years. Beyond that, none of us can see, and I think none of us need plan at the present moment."

Death of Mother Outler

Mother Outler died in her eightieth year on August 15, 1950. Her funeral service was held at Sharp Memorial with E. L. Adams and her pastor, Dow Kirkpatrick, officiating. She was interred alongside her husband in Old Union Cemetery at Young Harris. Albert's grief not only included the loss of his mother but also Trail's End (which by this time had taken on a second name, Eagles' Nest, and goes by that name with the people of Young Harris today). Trail's End had been sold as Albert anticipated.

But Albert and Fan still had Tynshene, a cabin in the mountains that never became a part of his life. The purchase was Fan's idea, and she wanted him to be her partner. But Tynshene never really caught on with Albert. His distance from it had to do with more than miles. A look at the commitments on his calendar put Tynshene far, far away. Finally, when it became too much of a burden for Fan to keep up, she wrote him on June 12, 1951, and asked him to sign with her the warranty deed conveying Tynshene to Punch (Miss Thelma Bond). She said: "I intend to reimburse you the investments you made originally in my behalf, as well as for your share of the roof, if you will be indulgent as to the time element and let me repay you on installments."

The mountains of North Georgia now were mostly memories for Albert. However, as long as health would permit, in his future road travels through North Georgia he would return to Young Harris, climb to the place where Trail's End once stood, stand on the desolate grounds of broken down stone fences where the old iron gate once stood and the level ground where once there was a spring giving forth a clear pool of water. There he relived those days of yesteryears. Daffodil bulbs continued to reproduce and bloom into flowers that reminded him of the life that once was. He stood where his roots lived in every marrow of his bones.

Leaping the Wall

Things worked out very well for Outler at Yale. But he began to feel alienated from the local church, which had been so much a part of his life. He was called to be a pastor, but his life was going down a path that he did not intend to take. The church and the university were two totally different experiences. He felt that he had to leap a wall in order to get from one to the other.

In order to remedy that, he accepted an appointment (1947–1949) to serve as pastor of a small urban church about fifteen miles from Yale at the little silversmithing town of Wallingford, Connecticut. Albert and Carla lived at Wallingford and he commuted to teach at the divinity school. Outler said, "There was not a single college graduate in my congregation; they were artisans, and wonderful people. But, this business of ministering to a congregation like that, and then going to Silliman [College] on Monday evening and then teaching the next week at the divinity school, and being involved with the Kent and Hazen and Danforth Foundations—it was a wonderful sort of spread across almost every dimension and every shade of the spectrum, from very ordinary to very extraordinary relationships."[66]

About that appointment he wrote in an April 3, 1948, letter to Robert Wicks: "This is proving an extremely interesting and valuable experiment in connecting the teaching of systematic theology with the weekly responsibility of pastoral care and preaching to a congregation of about one hundred and fifty people. But it means that I can do no barnstorming, or take on any outside engagements for the period I shall be out there. According to our present plans this will be for one more year."

Serving as a professor and a pastor never broke down the wall between the two institutions. He still had to leap the wall. But the experience served him by keeping him in touch with the church that he loved so much. And it helped him to understand how it was possible for the university and the church to work together for the common experience of knowledge *and* vital piety.

Leaving Yale for Perkins

An attack of ambivalence caused Outler to suffer through another major job crisis. Not that there was a problem at Yale. The problem came from a craving to return to the South at a place where he might really make a difference.

On January 23, 1951, Carla, from New Haven, wrote to Albert who was lecturing at Stanford University in Palo Alto, California: "It seems too cruel to tempt you to SMU. You have a charming letter from Dean Hawk. I wish I could evaluate why we hate to leave here. Is it the prestige of Yale, and is the resulting tension worth the prestige? Well, we'll spend the next few weeks going over the pros and cons.

"I can't imagine you not pulling the Stanford mess out of the hole [the 'hole' of non-interest in religion]; for your own sake, I hope you do. Bless your heart!"

Outler spoke of his Yale days as the zenith of a theologian's dream, but those old vibes came alive, calling him back to the southern regions of the United States. He enjoyed his days at Yale, but Perkins offered the right challenge at *that* time. He was ready to move. But he was not ready for the misunderstanding that developed during this transition. The following letter, written in longhand and corrected in the same manner that he gave all his sermons and lectures, was never mailed. It is included here in order to show how deeply Outler felt about how his well-planned exit had gone awry: "Dear [Dean] Liston,

"It was natural enough that you should have replied to the criticism implied in my letter of resignation by citing 'the record.' Your account of the case, in respect of the main points which you chose to stress, is accurate and fair. Moreover, considering the purposes for which it was written, it has just the right note of imperturbable justice and decanal self-righteousness.

"Nevertheless, since it glosses over the only crucial point of my complaint, I should like to amplify 'the record' for the benefit of any who might be interested. In my letter of resignation I said plainly that 'I have been honored [by Yale] far beyond my due' and expressed my gratitude for all your generosity hitherto. But in regard to this last, terminal episode, there is something more to be said than you have set down as 'the record.'

"When I talked with you [in] February about my interest in SMU's invitation, I asked quite specifically if I might consider it in terms of 1952. You stated definitely that I might; and that you would *prefer* my staying on through 1951–52, even if I should leave at the end of it. As you say, I knew—or ought to have known—that this was an expression of your personal opinion, with no official force behind it. I accept the point implied here, for I know, and greatly approve, the Yale Divinity School tradition of administration by consultation. But, you also knew that I was going ahead on the basis of your 'personal opinion' and that all my discussions with SMU were predicated upon it. Moreover, I consulted the following members of the faculty: Bob Calhoun, Julian Hartt, Richard Niebuhr (the men most closely related to my work and most directly affected by the decision I had to make), and also Ken Latourette, David McLennan, Paul Schubert, Raymond Morris, Davie Napier, Frank Young, and Ken Underwood, Seymour Smith . . . . This seems to me to be a representative group of my colleagues and the ones with whom I have had the closest personal ties. In talking to each one, I made a special point of speaking of my plan to stay on through 1951–52, even if I should decide to go in '52. Not a single one of these men raised any objection to that plan and several of them spoke of it with definite approval. During a period of *seven weeks,* in which I talked to you about my problem at least twice (including the very pleasant lunch at Mory's) nothing was said by you or anyone else that gave me the slightest indication that there was any opposition whatever to the plan. And so, I went ahead, trusting that your personal opinion, plus those of the others I have named, amounted to an effective, firm agreement, as has been the case in so many other consultations which were finally confirmed officially by the Board of Permanent Officers. Meanwhile, I asked the people at SMU to go ahead with their arrangements for '51–'52, since I would not be interested in coming to them, in any case, until 1952.

"Then, on Saturday night, April 31, I telephoned you about my trip to Nashville, and during the conversation you asked me, rather testily I thought, to reach a decision as quickly as possible, since, if I were going, you would want to move quickly to arrange for my replacement. To me, this was a thunderclap. For then I realized, all too late, that I had been trusting personal assurances which institutional interests might easily override. I told you over the phone how much store I set by my plan of staying on at least another year and how badly it would scramble my negotiations with SMU; your reply was that you had to look out for Yale Divinity School. To me, that was an entirely unforeseen *reversal of position*—and a most ominous one!

"On Wednesday, April 11, I announced to you my decision to go, and I expressed once more my strong desire to have it arranged so that I could get my quarter's leave (you will remember I offered to add a seminar to my winter and spring teaching load), help complete the half-dozen dissertations that were ripe for finishing, and give you time to make a leisurely canvass of the situation for my replacement. You expressed your judgment that it would be wise for me to leave at the end of *this* year, and you reported that it was the *unanimous* opinion of our colleagues to whom you had talked (including how many of the ones to whom *I* had *also* talked?) that, if I were going, I ought to go at once. You offered to present 'my case,' together with my arguments for staying on, to the Board of Permanent Officers the following Tuesday. But you did not say then that you favored it or would push it with the Board! It was on this note that the interview was terminated.

"I went home, genuinely dismayed and distraught. All along, I had been counting on the firmness of personal assurances and now I had crashed head-on into the interests of the institution. And the worst of it was that I could see how naive I had been in assuming that your previous personal opinion and those of eleven other colleagues would suffice when the chips were down. This is what I meant to convey to you in my expression of chagrin at having neglected to observe, in the practice, the distinction between personal and institutional ethics. (I always mention it in my lectures and presume that you do, too.)

"Well, there I was with my well-laid plan knocked into a cocked hat! I debated for three unhappy hours if I should wait for the outcome of the Board meeting or if I should take the matter out of your hands at once. Suppose the Board should agree that I might stay on; after you expressed your opinion that I should leave and your report of the unanimity of opinion among your consultants, my situation would have been embarrassed, and if the Board should officially judge it wiser for me to leave, my situation would then be quite intolerable! I knew that legally I might refuse to resign until the Spring of '52, but that would have been a shabby way to behave, and I never really considered it. Moreover, it occurred to me that the people at SMU might have completed their plans for '51–'52 or were in the process of doing so—and then I would be in the soup for sure!

"Finally, in great perturbation, I telephoned Merrimon [dean of Perkins], and in thirty minutes, the matter was settled! It was a hasty thing to do; but if there was a better way to do it, I could not—and cannot yet—see it. I don't know how the Board might have acted if I had waited for them. And I don't believe I really want to know! When I phoned you late on that night, you said that you had changed your mind again somewhat and were now more favorable to my proposal and would back it in the Board meeting. But *then* it was too late! Your account of what happened after that is substantially the same as my own.

"I am still well content with my decision and the grounds on which it was made. I no longer protest against the judgment that if I am to go, it were wiser that I go quickly. But if we are to have a full record of this ungraceful exit of mine from the community I have loved and served and been greatly honored by, I want to include this report of my naivete and disillusionment. If last February you, or anyone else, had given me the slightest inkling of the possibility that the affair might have turned out as it has, I could have discussed it all along with SMU on a very different basis; and the transition, if it had come to that, would then have been smoother and happier for *all* concerned. *This* is the point—the *only* point—I have been concerned about, since here, and here only, is the focus of the bitterness and disappointment to which I gave voice—perhaps unwisely—in my letter of resignation.

"Your letter makes me out as having acted quite unreasonably in the whole affair. I could have accepted that characterization with some feeble grace if only you had not made it out [that] your own role [was] one consistently reasonable and objectively wise. The plain fact is that neither of us has managed this business very well, although you've certainly made a better showing in it than I.

"The great preponderance of my memories and my feelings about Yale Divinity School and Yale are filled with deep gratitude and great pleasure. These six years have been exciting and rewarding beyond my ambitions or dreams. The good things so outweigh the bad that I would very much like to hope that we can wall off this and all the other discontents and prevent their leaving a permanent scar. It was hard enough to bring myself to the choice of leaving Yale at all, and I had so counted on being able to hold on to many of my ties here, both personal and academic. If this hope has now been spoiled by what has happened, I shall be the more bereft. Has it happened? Need it happen?

"In concluding what I would like to be my last word about all this, I want most of all to thank you for your good wishes that 'I find the pot of gold.' I do believe that we will be happy in Dallas and that I shall get . . ." [end of letter]. A much shorter version of this letter was sent to Dean Liston Pope. But Outler's displeasure came across adequately loud and clear in the account of affairs that he did send to the dean.

The Dean's Acknowledgment

The dean acknowledged receiving the letter of resignation plus the letter of clarification written by Outler and responded in this May 2, 1951, letter: "So be it. I am very glad to have your letter of April 30, with its clarification of your own actions and decisions in regard to the transfer to SMU. I am genuinely sorry that misunderstanding and unhappiness were allowed to enter into our negotiations. I am afraid the plain fact is that the negotiations were considerably overextended, and came to resemble a 'war of nerves.' Your friends and colleagues here were disappointed and unhappy to hear in the first place that you were considering whether you would leave us, and the prolonged discussion and indecision on the question did nobody any good. For nearly eight weeks, the question of your decision was one of the principal topics of discussion among your colleagues, and it was out of this discussion that the sentiment clearly emerged that you should make a clean break if you decided to leave Yale.

"You need have no apprehension about the continuation of your many friendships here. I have heard many expressions of regret, but none of anger. If our own long friendship cannot survive this entire matter, it is a more fragile thing than I have ever held it to be."

Colleagues at Yale did question the soundness of Outler's thinking, leaving the most prestigious chair of Yale Divinity School for a "nonstatus" professorship at Perkins School of Theology. For Outler it was not primarily a matter of *his wanting* to leave, but a matter of the nudging of the Spirit, beginning from the time he left the South. Here is how he described the matter: "I was very much at home at Yale; I still am. [He was invited back in 1975 to give the Nathaniel W. Taylor Lectures.] But not at home in the region—in the sense that the university and the divinity school and the churches are almost hermetically sealed-off compartments. [He missed his workplace and home, the church.] And this meant that you had to vault a wall whenever you went from the university to the church and then back again. This is not what I had contracted for in my own sense of vocation, either academically or ministerially. I thought it was possible in the South—and it was. So, I kept on thinking about what would be the way in which a person could serve there, i.e., either serve the South from Yale or come back South to work. I couldn't quite go back to Duke. I *could,* but it wouldn't have been quite the same.

"Meanwhile, Harvie Branscomb [with whom Albert had worked at Duke] had gone to Vanderbilt. And there was no opening at Emory. That was the place I really wanted, but there was no vacancy there. So this job at Southern Methodist University turned up. Merrimon Cuninggim, whom I had known at Yale and was then at Claremont, and I worked out a deal with Umphrey Lee here at Southern Methodist University that Merrimon would come as Dean, and I would come as professor of theology; and between us we would start a new school. . . . The Perkins money had come, but this present quadrangle had not yet opened. So, Merrimon came from the West Coast and I came from New Haven, and we met here in 1951 to start what was to become the 'New Perkins' at SMU."[67]

A New Perkins

A large part of that "New Perkins" was to come in the racial integration of Perkins. By letter and by sending me his essay, *Perkins Led the Way,* published in 1994, Merrimon Cuninggim confirmed himself and Outler as the team, not tandem but "harnessed side by side," which came to Perkins with one common goal, to integrate Perkins and ultimately SMU. Cuninggim wrote: "I accepted Lee's invitation [to come as Dean] in January, 1951. Though it would be midsummer before I was to begin my duties, Lee encouraged me to get one or two able people to come along with me, if I were to have time to give to it. I told him I would try with one, my good friend Albert Outler, already full Professor of Theology at Yale. [During those days Cuninggim often addressed Albert in his letters' salutations as "Dear Owl."] One of the arguments I sought was to say, 'Al, as Southerners we'll have a great chance to work on desegregation; Lee says we can admit Negroes as regular students right away.' It was one of the reasons he and Carla decided to come. If he and I had known that, when the chips were down, some of the Church leaders would not support that interpretation, and some of the University leaders would counsel turning back, we might have stayed where we were."[68] Had the two known that much of their SMU support was shaky, it might have been that Cuninggim would have stayed where he was, but judging from the letters of Outler, he was "biting at the bits" to get back somewhere in the South; he would have moved somewhere. His readiness to move somewhere south shows in the fact that he waited five years, until January 20, 1950, before transferring, under bureaucratic pressure, his ministerial conference membership to the New York Conference. This was only a year before he moved to Dallas.

BMOC Outler

A door to an uncertain future had opened for Outler at Southern Methodist University. And he walked through it with the understanding that Providence had always worked this way in his life. While he was inclined to go south, he did not *ask* to leave so much as he was *sent* to go. Go he did. From the day he landed at Perkins (August 1, 1951) things began to change on and off campus. There was no doubt in anybody's mind that, unlike his comment about not being the Big Man on Campus (BMOC) while in undergraduate school at Wofford, Albert Outler was *the* BMOC upon his arrival at Perkins. The image had been thrust upon him by the powers-that-be. He knew what he was coming to when he came to Perkins.

He had read the school catalogue and knew who were on the faculty, and they were *not* Niebuhr, Paul Tillich, Karl Barth, or Emil Brunner, et al. With the urging of Cuninggim, President Umphrey Lee had prearranged through outgoing Dean Hawk to obtain Outler. Outler's modesty would not permit him to admit that he was Perkins' hired "big gun." But it would have been an insult to his intelligence to think that he did not have a strong inkling of the position he would have at Perkins School of Theology. The ones who hired him knew what the title "full professor" implied. So when he arrived on campus in 1951 he was in the fullest sense a *full* professor.

The "Fullest" of Full Professors

Outler's particular gifts and graces were utilized and recognized through some of the activities that he was called upon to perform, such as chairing the newly dean-appointed Admissions Committee of five faculty members with the new Dean Cuninggim a member *ex officio* (this move took admissions out of the hands of the dean solely and set standards so that every candidate would not necessarily be admitted[69]); in 1959 chairing the first committee that gave the first report for the Graduate School toward a doctoral-level degree, the Ph.D. in Religious Studies;[70] in 1961 becoming the first faculty member to be elected a member of the SMU Faculty Senate;[71] chairing the SMU Graduate Council of the Humanities, 1960–1963;[72] chairing the committee to develop the Master Plan for the university, 1962; chairing the Theological Study Commission of the United Methodist Church reporting to the September 27, 1969, Perkins faculty meeting what was to be brought before the 1972 General Conference;[73] bringing many honors to SMU and particularly Perkins through his many ecumenical involvements.[74]

Still Sure

On July 13, 1952, Outler wrote: "Carla and I are still as sure as before that this was the right decision. We greatly enjoyed Yale and New Haven, and it was fun being Dwight Professor. But Yale was made and needed only to be kept up—and although that was an appalling challenge, it wasn't really what I needed to satisfy my inner yen to be building something that wasn't there before. You remember I left Duke when I became convinced that the powers-that-were (and still are?) had agreed on letting the Divinity School develop on provincial administrative lines. I may have made a bad guess, but I believe we've a chance here at Perkins to build something a lot better than we found—and that in a region where there is enormous vitality and promise for the future. We've a new dean, and in five years we will have a new faculty."[75]

The New Faculty

During the Cuninggim years of remaking Perkins, Outler had a hefty hand in recruiting the new professors. That was part of the deal they made in coming to Perkins as a team. Some were Outler's earlier students at Yale: Herndon Wagers, John Deschner, Richey Hogg, et al. Others whom he especially welcomed were Douglas Jackson, Joe Allen, Van Harvey, et al. And then there were the mavericks—Schubert Ogden, Edward Hobbs, and Joe Matthews—who were praised highly by Outler at the time they were hired for the contributions he felt they would make toward a broader education of the Perkins students. His praise came, not in the context of his approval of the men's brash characteristics, but in what he felt was best for the seminary. As did Cuninggim, he wanted a diverse faculty who would give the students a more diverse educational background and give him some minds a notch above the average with whom he could dialogue.

John Deschner gave Outler full credit for hiring him and Schubert Ogden in one fell swoop and then lining them up with himself in teaching systematic theology. When Outler called the three of them together to decide how they would work out a triad approach to teaching theology, he permitted them to choose first which to emphasize in their teaching: Father, Son, or Holy Spirit. Ogden jumped on Father; Deschner quickly chose Son; and Outler had what was left. That suited him fine since the Holy Spirit *is* God. Outler also got the two young theologians to agree to sitting in on each others' classes, forcing the trio into lengthy dialogues outside the classroom.

In the long haul Outler felt Ogden proved himself to be an exceptionally gifted scholar: "Mr. Ogden has named the program of post-liberal theology, of which he himself is the most brilliant exponent, *neo-classical theism*."[76] He left no written comment about Matthews. But about Hobbs he declared in a January 4, 1956, letter to Claude Welch of Yale: "As for Hobbs, you can have him without a fight from us! He *is* a vivid person and an exciting teacher but he is also doctrinaire and undisciplined, with prejudices which he communicates to his students and makes into party cries. He has been here now three and one-half years and has neither finished his dissertation at Chicago nor written anything else of substantial worth. He is a very versatile man and a fair-going sophisticate. His first impression to both his students and his colleagues is slightly terrific—but he does not wear well save with a small coterie of disciples and cronies. In short, he has been a serious disappointment to us here."

What was Outler up to in this role of, on the one hand, exposing students to these professors' sometimes rude (and sometimes crude) demeanors and then, on the other hand, trying to help repair the shattered minds and shaken faith left in their wake? He wanted students to learn to *think* for themselves, and through that agonizing process come to a deepening of their faith, not in a professor's teachings, not in one's own thinking, but in God. *That* was a large part of what Outler considered an adequate theological education.

In speaking to the shapes of these disarrayed lives suffering from the lingering effects of unsolicited shock treatments, Outler had a standard comment: "The first five years out of seminary will tell if the seminary education *took.*" It would in his mind take that long for the shock to wear off, for the students to assimilate the whole picture of where *they* stood in their faith, and whether, indeed, their calling was to serve the local church as pastors. Among the reasons one might choose a vocation other than the pastorate would be this one: If during that five-year period a student mimicked the firebrand professor in the student's pastorate, it was highly likely that the student would not make the grade as a pastor. Some imitators proved Outler right. They soon fizzled out.

Scholarship Overemphasized?

One particular criticism of Perkins had to do with what some called an overemphasis on training scholars. Outler's answer to them carried an attractively stylish bite: "Over the years it has been complained of Perkins that we overemphasize scholarship—as if that charge could not easily be disproved by examination of any half dozen Perkins graduates you can pick up *anywhere!*"[77]

Outsmarting the Professor

Outler's mix of knowledge and vital piety and good humor made him popular among the student body. He recounted the time that he was going over a paper in which the young man was struggling mightily, though unavailingly, with a fairly tricky idea. The idea was belabored this way and that, and then in the middle of one page, without punctuation and quite deliberately to see whether the professor was reading the paper, he inserted this question between the lines: "Are you still with me, Doc?" Outler scribbled in the margin: "Yes, but I don't know where you are headed!"

Whether one was a student or scholar, Outler was not going to let anyone who thought himself a thinker out-think him. If one felt he had outwitted the old master, time would tell that the debater's time would have been better spent time wondering what the professor was saying when he dropped the conversation just as the challenger thought he was ahead. It was smart to try to win in a battle of wits with Outler, but never smart to believe one did.

Richard Heitzenrater recalls such an attempt to outsmart Albert: "I heard the story of some students at Perkins in one year's class of United Methodist Constitutional History, who either were astounded or exasperated at [Outler's] ability to answer any and all questions on any subject, no matter how trivial, decided to trip him up, checked with some previous students, decided on the most trivial thing they could think of: types of barbed wire used in frontier Texas; raised the question in the context of a lecture on Methodism on the frontier. Outler launched into an excursis on history and typology of barbed wire on the frontier, with names of different styles of barbs, inventors of each, dates of use, reasons for the different designs, etc.

"I was not in that class, but did audit a class with him my first term as a professor at Perkins; the lectures were absolutely astounding in the density of their content and gave me writer's cramp every time, trying to write down the stream of names, issues, insights, pithy comments, interpretive views, clever witticisms. Very early on I noticed that very few students were taking many notes—most were simply captivated by the learning, the experiences, and the humor of this passionate student and leader of the church.

"It turns out that they may have known something that I did not at that point. For later I discovered that he perhaps unwittingly shared one quality with [Duke Wesley expert] Frank Baker, who is still called 'easy B Baker' by some of his former undergraduate students at Duke, especially the basketball players who knew where they could get a grade that would help their quest for athletic eligibility. I think sometimes scholar/teachers give the students the benefit of the doubt and assume that they are really working as hard as they can, but without the benefit of long experience. Albert's rationale was a bit different, however. He said one time that he would never fail a student because he didn't want to stand in the way of the student's call to ministry (a sensitivity that not all of us instructors share).

". . . In fact it was my experience that nearly every conversation, public or private, with Dr. Outler was a virtual seminar, sprinkled with recollections of ideas and events, names of historical and contemporary thinkers, titles of books that should be read and those that should be avoided."[78]

Grades and Grading

The comment about Outler not wanting his grading "to stand in the way of the student's call to ministry" was typical of the mind and heart of the man. He had recognized in his ministry those who barely passed his classes and yet made the grade as pastors in the local church. When pressed by his students to explain how he reached his conclusions as to the proper grades to give students, Outler gave his classes in Contemporary Theology (1969–1970) a prepared lecture on the subject of grading that took up the entire period. He went to great lengths to describe the parameters. The taped lecture began, "I do set a good deal of store by spelling. You are called to preach the Word, and spell it right!" That comment elicited a nervous laughter (hereafter called "NL") that came unsolicited throughout his lecture. Their ears perked up because they knew now that what they had asked for they were going to get. The following excerpts illustrate some of the complexities built into his system of grading:

"There are misunderstandings of this business of academic grades that corrupt its positive intentions and effects. [A major misunderstanding] is: 'A grade is a value judgment on a person.' It is not. It is a value judgment on a performance, a public performance that is appraised by public norms. Note: I do not say, 'Objective.' *This* ['objective'] I do not understand. But 'public' I do understand.

"Grades are arbitrary and are inconsistencies given by various professors, and grades are imprecise. And this is so. This is why our numbers systems are absurd. There are discrepancies and yet there are more conscientious grades given than you would ever expect. And grades are more educated than they have been— if all you want to know is 'what did I get?' 'And how much more did I get than somebody else that did less than I did and I know that he did less than I did? And he is not as smart as I am. But he did something nice for the professor.' *That* happens so rarely as to be negligible. (NL)

"The point is: What is your alternative? Not to be graded? Let me tell you what I want: a mix of four publicly accessible factors: (1) information, (2) methodology, (3) creative insights, (4) technical perfection. When I get papers that are miswritten, there is a reflex—I get stabbed here and so I stab the paper in revenge with annotations. (NL)

"When you split an infinitive simply out of ruthlessness (NL), not because it has some kind of syntactical function, but because you cannot stand to put an adverb before the 'to,' I put 'ouch' in the margin. (NL) And this is an honest cry of the heart. (NL)

"So that I could say, 'Well done, good and faithful servant,' would I point to a performance that is better than good but not as good as best? Which is to say, 'B.' Given a 'B' base, 85, you move up the scale, always working with a quadratic equation by increments of one, two, three, or four factors in abundance or superabundance. 'B+' is a 'B' plus one factor or one or two fractions of factors. 'A–' is a 'B+' to full factors or some permutation. 'A' is a 'B' plus three and 'A+' is a 'B' plus all four—all in superabundance. I keep my 100s for performances that are distinctly better than I could do myself on the same assignment. (NL) This means that it is perfectly possible, but it is rare. (NL)

"Now it works out the same way on the downside. My 'B–s' always get corrupted by sentiment, [which is] an earnest C+ and a floppy 'B–.' A 'B–' creates a moral ambiguity in my mind, partly out of pastoral concern. And there are more 'B–s' on my record that I will have to account for in limbo or in purgatory than I would like to think. 'C+' is unfailingly honest. 'D' is for a good job that should be done over. 'F' is for a job that hasn't been done. A grade is satisfactory when it records your optimum performance."[79]

These searching inquiries into the subject of grading revealed as much about how the mind of Outler worked as it did about the student's graded paper. One thing this convoluted lecture did do for the students was to motivate them to do their best. The highly intellectualized message was delivered with the fervor of an evangelist. The egghead humor delighted his audience, but it did not allay their fears of what he might do to and with their papers when grading time rolled around. They did not have the foggiest idea of how he would grade their papers. But there was no doubt that the papers would be graded.

Outler the PR Person

When Outler was not teaching and grading students, he was upgrading the social/racial situation on and about the campus. As dean, Cuninggim would be the administrator of the social/ racial change, finding suitable students and staying closely in contact with them in the process. Outler would be the public relations person, not in title but in action. Cuninggim's role was to jump into the hot water of social change; Outler's role was to make efforts to cool down the water. As readers will note in the reading of the papers in *The Albert Outler Library,*[80] Outler was convinced that Christian social change must come by persuasion, not coercion. That conviction accounted for his going into the businesses near the Southern Methodist University campus and parleying with the owners concerning the admission of blacks into their places of business. But in these instances it was not a strict "parley" because Outler did not look upon them as the enemy. To him they and he had a common goal. And that was the way he presented the matter. Outler had a unique, southern dignified charm (as his sister Fan described him earlier in this book), which helped considerably in getting his point across to the store owners. Being from Georgia, *South* Georgia at that, he sounded more like a southerner than they did! The rest of the story is history.

From the success in public relations that Outler had in dealing with these integration problems, he quickly gained a reputation with the media and concerned laity as the one to contact whenever a row was created by some disturbing event that had to do with the seminary. When a maverick professor would speak his mind, indicating to the supporting laity that there was not much mind there to speak of, a credible Outler would come to the school's rescue. The irate supporters would quiet down, not because Outler had vindicated the actions of the runaway professor, but simply out of respect for Albert C. Outler.

A Supreme Test of Public Relations

Outler spent part of his credibility at the time that some SMU supporters prevailed upon J. J. Perkins, a benefactor of the seminary from Wichita Falls, Texas, to go before the SMU Board of Trustees and have their three-year-old interracial policy rescinded. Dean Cuninggim, in response to this most delicate situation, called on his highly credible negotiator Outler. He was to attempt to convince Bishop Paul Martin to prevail upon Mr. Perkins from the vantage point of the great good that a black presence was bringing to the campus, the community, and the entire world. In his November 17, 1953, letter to Bishop Martin, the one whose friendship had influenced Mr. and Mrs. Perkins to finance the building of the new Perkins, Outler wrote: "Ordinarily, I would never intrude on your busy schedule or into the overall issues of administrative policy in the University and our School of Theology. But it seems plain that we are now involved in an urgent and momentous crisis in the life of our School, and I feel sure that you will be interested in considering as much responsible testimony in the case as possible. And since your influence on the outcome seems likely to be decisive, I feel free to share with you my very real alarm and deep concern over our situation here."

After elaborating in a most endearing and convincing manner the good reasons for continuing the policy (there was no *good* reason for discontinuing it), Outler summed up his plea with these words: "I have written you in great candor and concern, for it seems clear to me that this is an issue of extraordinary delicacy and moment. Furthermore, I have every confidence that you and the Committee will succeed in finding the way to a constructive, Christian answer to the problem. I've no desire to meddle, but if there is any way I can be of any service in any part of the business, I am at your command. May God grant us all the spirit of wisdom, and love in such a time of decision."

Bishop Martin thanked Outler for his good sense, informed him that he would meet privately with Mr. Perkins prior to the meeting of the committee, and agreed with Outler that, in the vein of Outler's letter to him, a right, just, and peaceful conclusion must come of the affair. Bishop Martin had the meeting with Mr. Perkins, and the potential explosion was defused before it could be ignited in a committee meeting of trustees.

Mountain Retreats a Thing of the Past

The move to Dallas removed Outler farther from his Young Harris roots in North Georgia. In about the same time frame, both Fan and Albert found themselves in similar circumstances; the usefulness of their mountain retreats was a thing of the past. This November 22, 1955, letter to Fan indicates that both had accepted the inevitable: "We were all genuinely and deeply touched by your letter and the accompanying Prudential policy. There is *no* obligation on you—either legal or moral—to 'recompense' me for our common loss in Tynshene or Trail's End. Certainly I neither regret nor begrudge the money I put into either venture—and certainly do not hold you to blame for their going awry. They both were, as you rightly say, ill-starred, and there was *no* reasonable way of keeping them within the framework of our present and prospective living schemes. And much as we both regret their loss, it is much better to remember the happy times we had there—these memories are ours for good!—and go on from here as best we can. It begins to be increasingly clear that if Carla and I are to have a summer place, it will have to be somewhere in a day's reach of Dallas—and the prospects of our being able to swing such a deal before the kids are through college are quite dim. In any case, we couldn't have put either Tynshene or Trail's End to good use from here. Nor could you, in your circumstances. The one constructive outcome I could see from the sale of Trail's End is if you will put the entire proceeds of the sale into some safe escrow or trust arrangement so that money won't be available or tempting for any use short of dire emergency in the near future or after you are no longer teaching, in the far future."

With their North Georgia mountain retreats gone, when the workload became too heavy, Albert and Carla would make their way to the Davis Mountains in southwest Texas to walk once again the hills and breath the fresh mountain air. About those experiences Albert said, "It takes considerable conversion when you can live in a place as flat as this [Dallas]. Then you get to the Davis Mountains where you can see for forty miles and you say, '*That* is the way Texas should have been built!'"[81]

Ministries Beyond Perkins

With all his involvements with teaching, counseling, peacemaking, Outler still had time for ministries beyond his duties at Perkins. Beginning in 1952, Outler launched headlong into the workings of the church: local, national, and international (his appetite for such church involvement was whetted at Yale; but now he got action—and plenty of it). He served in the North Texas Conference (to which he transferred on December 1, 1951) successively as chairman of the Board of Social Concerns, and the Board of Ordained Ministry (1958–1970). And he served six times as a delegate to the General and Jurisdictional Conferences (1960–1976; the called sixth General Conference he attended was a special session held in 1966 in Chicago to consider the Methodist/EUB merger). He was the preacher at the Uniting Conference in 1968. As chairman of the Doctrinal Study Commission (1968–1972), he brought to the floor of the 1972 General Conference the Doctrinal Statement that remains the basic document with which the United Methodist Church perennially works.

New Horizons

New horizons were now visible on the campus of the university. During the 1953 Ministers Week, the Dallas community came to hear this newly heralded voice at McFarland Auditorium on the campus of Southern Methodist University. A thunderous ovation greeted the speaker as he concluded his lecture.

Still applauding, prominent Methodist clergyman Marshall Steel turned to the then Southern Methodist University president, Umphrey Lee, and whispered, "Why are we clapping? I didn't understand what he said. Did you?"

President Lee answered, "I didn't either, but I am glad to have a man like that on our side, aren't you?"[82]

The subject of those 1953 lectures was "Psychotherapy and the Christian Message," a subject so far out at the time that a local paper reported it as a talk on "Cycle Therapy."

Helen Parmley of the *Dallas Morning News* summed up the man Outler in these words: "Since coming to SMU's 'side' in 1951, Dr. Outler has been a harbinger of social and religious trends and changes."[83]

A BMOC on Other Campuses

Outler was BMOC on the campuses he visited. The influence of Outler as recounted by collegian Bill Smith could be told by many. Bill said: "Outler came to Oklahoma City University, our Methodist University in Oklahoma, and spoke to the student body. I was so enthralled by what he said that I followed him around to the different classes he attended. He came to the biology lab, jumped upon the counter and said, 'Well, you all are obviously involved deeply with science. Let's visit a few minutes about the relationship between science and religion.' He let go with the best description of the relationship of science and religion that you have ever heard. And there I stood, taking no notes and with no tape recorder. And it was all gone. I was so frustrated I did not know what to do. I wrote Dr. Outler and told him that I would like to talk with him. I went in and told him what his speech at OCU meant to me. And that I didn't take notes nor had a tape recorder. He said, 'Oh, I know I have the manuscript somewhere. But here is what I said . . .' And he began to give me the information exactly as he had said it before. I was enthralled. When he got through, I walked out totally frustrated; I had heard this subject expounded again. And again, I had taken no notes and did not have a tape recorder!"

Bill Smith identified with the Perkins student who once came by Wanda Smith, Outler's secretary, as he walked out of Outler's office and said, "Mrs. Smith, one thing Dr. Outler *doesn't* understand is stupidity." Outler understood many subjects, but not stupidity!

Wanda Smith says that Outler looked on his genius as normal, never talked down to anyone, but, rather, believed everyone comprehended at his capacity. He was, in her words, the only true genius she had ever known.

Those out in the boondocks of this southern region attest that this Outlerian influence brought a fresh new breath of life for the local churches as well as for the seminary and the university. Appreciation for the man and his accomplishments came from all corners of the Southwest. The churches of the Texas Conference, under the leadership of Outler's "first student at Duke, Finis Crutchfield" (first student to come into the classroom to greet Outler), honored his name by raising for Southern Methodist

University more than a million dollars to finance the Albert C. Outler Chair in Wesley Studies at Perkins.

Beyond the Spoken and the Written Word

Outler's influence went beyond the spoken word and the written word. His mind and heart were captured by activities in which he never received his due credit. To D. C. S. Jackson of Charles Scribner's & Sons, Outler wrote this October 15, 1954, letter: "I am immensely pleased with *Protestant Christianity*. As you know, I was a member of the committee that conceived and supervised the project and have been interested in every stage of its development. There has been an urgent need for a really good book which surveyed and interpreted the larger sweep of Protestantism than the denominational histories ever do and now it is clear that Welch and Dillenberger have amply met the need. At last we have a book we can put in the hands of students and laymen which is at once scholarly, ecumenical and highly relevant to the concern most of us have to see the positive and constructive essence of Protestantism, and to evaluate its place and function in the contemporary world."

Flogging a Tired Horse Uphill

In the following June 13, 1955, letter to President Wright of Columbus College, Outler compared his efforts to meet all his obligations as "flogging a tired horse uphill." He described this self-induced time-out upon himself in these words: "I still feel bitterly disappointed that my poor health has made it necessary to cancel my visit with you and the South Carolina Pastors' School. I had been looking forward to it for a whole year and was counting heavily on this opportunity to renew some very deeply cherished friendships I have there in South Carolina; but I have been flogging a tired horse uphill a bit too long now—and the Doctor and Mrs. Outler finally laid down the law—I have to clear out the summer and submit to a regimen of rest and injections. The latter are a nuisance; the former an unaccustomed pleasure! I have hopes that by the end of summer I shall be pretty nearly sound again. Please be sure to give my love—and my regrets—to all my friends. Tell 'em not to forget me and not let this miscarriage of our plans discourage them from making some opportunity in the future for another visit."

The Additions of a Neurotic

Along with his working in many facets of the church's activities Outler maintained his steady diet of giving major lectures across the continent and other parts of the world. And, as always, felt the pressure of those obligations. He had cause to identify with the neurotic described in his December 13, 1955, letter to Paul Derring: "Have you heard the wheeze which distinguishes between a psychotic and a neurotic? The psychotic adds up 2 and 2 and is calmly prepared to insist that the proper sum is 5; the neurotic adds 2 and 2 and gets 4 all right—but he cannot bear that it should be so! I have kept my calendar straight but somewhere along the line October has gotten awfully close and I am still very far from being ready with my Richards Lectures. If you have any reassuring words to the effect that the boys at Charlottesville neither expect nor would be prepared for a Copernican Revolution in theology, they would be most welcome." Outler's full calendar kept adding up to "4," and he could hardly bear to have it so!

The Man and the World Council of Churches

Outler brought his Methodist tradition to the World Council of Churches and the traditions of world churches to his Methodist connections. As vice-chairman of the Ecumenical Affairs Commission (1964–1968), he was able to bring firsthand to the annual conferences his vast ecumenical experiences that began with his research studies with professors at Yale and continued with his election as a delegate to the 1952 Third World Conference on Faith and Order in Lund, Sweden, and as a delegate and vice-chairman at the 1963 Fourth World Conference held in Montreal, Canada, where his working "faith and order" peaked with the submission of the report of the Theological Study Commission.

Frustrations often arose out of these ecumenical meetings. Outler came from the 1956 meeting at the Ecumenical Institute in Celigny, Switzerland, somewhat perturbed and disillusioned: "The seminar is going pretty well—but I'm afraid it is not the most profitable use of my summer I could have made, and so I'm beginning to begrudge it more than is good for my usual 'all-out investments.' Moreover, the ecumenical movement at close range is as unimpressive as the bureaucracy of the Methodist Church. And, finally [the truth came out], I'm homesick!"

"The rest of Sunday and today have been put in on my lecture on Methodism. Few of these people know anything about Methodism and are already certain that it is not significant theologically. So I've had to recast the lecture I had planned and start a few steps further back than I would have otherwise. I've finally got it done, but I have my doubts whether it's worth trying to break the prejudices of Europeans about Americans. They are simply sure that we are all activists and unable to manage the deep waters of theology or truly to appreciate European culture. And half of what they cherish as culture is an opiate to dull their discomforts and their class stratifications. As of now, at least, I have just about had my fill of Europe. It is, as Sarte says of man, *une passion inutile!*" [useless suffering]

From a meeting in Milano he wrote: "The meetings at Herrenalb were something of a disappointment. The place is a typical resort town—and Germans resorting are not their most attractive. The arrangements for the meetings were rather slipshod, and the meetings themselves—although interesting and sometimes exciting—were frustrating. We touched on a dozen big problems and dug into none. And I don't like Visser 't Hooft, the General Secretary of the WCC [World Council of Churches]! He fancies himself something of a Protestant pope—and once I had to tell him off. But it was worth doing—and I'm glad I had the experience."

From Copenhagen Outler wrote: "The Conference ended Friday night with a dinner party, with the Bishop of Copenhagen, a few more professors, and some of the corniest speeches and toasts I've ever heard—or heard of. Actually, the theological discussions we had didn't get the project of Tradition and Traditions very far forward; and the plans they have arrived at for next year don't seem to me to be very promising. But it became increasingly clear that, without any ill-will toward us, they were simply not interested in the American point of view and did not propose to take it into account in their own planning. This is still another aspect of the European sensitiveness toward its own rather shabby situation and the threat of having Americans as equal partners in a domain where they have reigned supreme for centuries. Moreover, they are used to, or interested in, theological *conversation;* but not in theological dueling. So the party was to make everybody happy: wine and toasts, innumerable 'skols' [an exclamation pledging health in drinking] to each and all. But my Frigidaire had turned on—and now at least one group of Europeans know what a stiff and stuffy American is like. Sorry—but this pervasive anti-American attitude has turned me into an anti-European, and really doubtful about the ecumenical movement for the first time in my life."

In spite of his misgivings about some people and their self-serving attitudes, Outler's ecumenical drive shifted into high gear. He went on to become a delegate to the 1957 North American Conference on Faith and Order at Oberlin College, at which time he gave the plenary address and served as chairman of the North American Section of the Faith and Order Study Commission on Tradition and Traditions (1953–1963). He was a delegate to the 1963 Third Assembly of the World Council of Churches in New Delhi, India, where he and Leslie Newbiggen did the principal drafting for the statement on the nature of the church. He was also a delegate to the 1968 Fourth Assembly at Uppsala. He was a member of the American Catholic Historical Association and served as president beginning in 1960. From 1962–1965 he was a delegated-observer to the Second Vatican Council. He served as a member of the Academic Council for the Ecumenical Institute for Advanced Theological Studies in Jerusalem (1965–1967), as a member of the 1965–1981 Bilateral Conversations (Methodist-Roman Catholic), and as a member of the Board of Directors of the *National Catholic Reporter* (1973–1983). In July and August 1961, Outler taught at the Union College School of Theology of British Columbia.

Another one of his out-of-class involvements was the World Methodist Council. At the 1966 WMC conference in London, he gave the plenary address. He was a lecturer at the 1981 World Methodist Conference in Honolulu, served on the Executive Committee (1976–1982), gave the 1974 plenary address on evangelism; and gave lectures at the Oxford Institute on Methodist Theology (1962, 1982, 1987).

Also a part of his extra curricular activities was his election as a Fellow, beginning in 1968, of the American Academy of

Arts and Sciences and a member of the Academy of Senior
Professionals at Eckerd College, beginning in 1986. In 1974 he
was invited to become a member of the Texas Institute of Letters. A glance at Outler's lectures and professional appointments
and offices at the end of this book reveals a man stretched beyond the expectations of an ordinary person.

Visiting Senior Fellow, Princeton

A major off-campus commitment came in 1956–1957 when Outler
was invited to Princeton as the Visiting Senior Fellow, Council
of Humanities. Letters between Albert and Carla during that period inadvertently offer autobiographical insights into his life.
Some of those comments are from the following letters:

A Shy Man?

September 27, 1956: "Princeton goes Yale one better in following the custom of not speaking to strangers and expecting everybody to go about his own business. In a way, I welcome it, for I
am a shy man (guffaws from the unknowing!), and also I'm
going to need all the privacy and time I can get. But a letter from
you and the children is different—so remember how much I
enjoy and cherish them."

Supercilious Attitudes

September 29, 1956: "This afternoon there was a 'reception'
for the Graduate Department of Religion in the library—and
we had a nice time of it. But interestingly enough, the department here is not rated very highly by the other departments,
and already I've run into what seemed to me rather supercil-
ious attitudes. You know what that does to me—and it did! All
the more reason, then, to be well armed from now on for every
foreseeable fray. The uncomfortable thing about it is that my
impression of the graduate students is not as favorable as I had
hoped. They seemed not only cautious and timid—which is
natural enough for a first meeting (and they *did* seem unprepared for a hearty and informal procedure), but even a little
sluggish. I hope that all this proves deceptive, for you know my

horror at having religion rated near the bottom of the academic ladder!"

The "Lift" of Memories

December 18, 1956: "Wednesday night I gave the address at the Student Christian Association Christmas banquet—about 200 students. It went *pretty* well, about as well as anything I've done here—except I had no lift; they had no lift; and we all needed more Christmas spirit than any of us apparently felt."

That "lift" came on the same day when he wrote another letter in which he reminisced: "Imagine—a quarter of a century! And how many lovely memories I have, still heartwarming through the years. That first wonderful week at Young Harris, our theolog apartment on Theology Row, the excitement of doing the dissertation together, 'at homes' on Lamond and in Tuscaloosa Forest, the Appalachian Trail, Trudi and David's first years on Englewood, hamburger, fries, and corn-boilings out on 'The Hill,' your visit to New York, that hike together among the Grand Tetons (and that night in the motel at Fort Collins!), the rodeos and state fairs and, best of all as it seems to me now, our wonderful "second honeymoon" last month! The list could go on and on—and maybe we're getting to reminiscences. I'd love to hear you rehearse the years—and relive them with you. We might make this a sort of project for our times alone this Christmas—and get some perspective on the hurry and pressure of the days! On balance it has been a good quarter century—and an instructive background for us both as we start into the next. We aren't likely to finish out another quarter century together, so let's take to heart the blessings and the lessons of our past to make the years left to us rich in understanding and happiness!" Outler did live another quarter century, however, plus almost eight years.

Stage Fright

January 12, 1957: "The Aquinas lecture is finally done —and I hope it goes better than the first one did. The fact is that I had a case of stage fright yesterday—although there was no logical reason for it. It goes to show, I suppose, that I'm still intimidated by the Ivy League atmosphere. This afternoon I got a start on the Scott Lectures. As usual, it turns out that they are going to take more reworking than I had thought—and so I've got my work cut out for me for the rest of the week, what with the Aquinas lecture tomorrow, the seminar on Thursday and a session with Jacques Maritain on Thursday night."

Austin Presbyterian Seminary

January 23, 1957: "In between times—and at odd moments—I keep turning over the question about Austin [Outler had been invited to join the faculty at Austin Presbyterian Seminary]. In many ways, it is an extraordinary opportunity—both a pioneering venture and yet also a chance to restrict my field of operations. On the other hand, I find the prospect of pulling up stakes and setting them down again a rather formidable thing. I'm tired of moving and of striking out in new directions. If I could only be certain that it *is* worthwhile to stay on at Perkins and running out my string there. I'd be grateful for some more of your comments—even to the same effect as before—and any report of your impressions of how this thing would look to the people at SMU."

Austin or Perkins?

In her answer Carla described how it looked to Dean Merrimon Cuninggim: "I finally got a chance to talk to Merry tonight, and we really had a good talk. He said, 'I can't say this to Albert; but if he leaves us, it will leave us in a terrible mess.' He honestly feels that Perkins needs you, especially if it continues to go forward at the rate it has been progressing." She further stated in a January 27, 1957, letter: "Bless your heart! I can well imagine your letdown, and the emptiness of having to think this through by yourself. You know, you have fooled me, as you do others, in seeming so self-assured—so that I have felt it impertinent (some exceptions, I'll admit) to offer suggestions or opinions. How little we really know about other people. Or maybe I say that because I feel as if I'm not really known. Oh my, this is getting complicated."

A Rolling Stone

A January 28, 1957, letter from Albert stated: "Most of our time was spent on 'my problem.' He [Shelton] heard me out, but was quite positive in his judgment that I should stay on at Perkins—even if I should personally prefer to go to Austin. His main points were two and both hinge on 'the eyes of the theological world.' They would, he thinks, jump to the conclusion that something was wrong with Perkins. And they would raise the question as to whether I am a rolling stone. The last point doesn't phase me much—for I am a rolling stone and have never pretended to be otherwise. But the first point hits home—and so brings the matter back to an even balance. At bottom, I think my real difficulty is my feeling that SMU is not going to become a good university as a whole in my lifetime—and that the unusual achievements at Perkins in the last few years and the next will finally run into the 'ceiling' of our being yoked with a mediocre university. But then Texas is no great shakes, either—and I'd have taken my satisfactions from the seminary growing to its full capacity. Tomorrow, I'm to have lunch with George Thomas—and will get his slants. Then when I get Nelson's reply, I'll go into an 'existential huddle' and cast the die. Meanwhile, any word from you, commenting further on your feelings and foresight will help more than you can probably realize. Tonight, I went over to the Thomases with the grad students in religion for a gabfest. A pleasant evening with some hearty discussion, in which I got too much involved, as usual. By hindsight, now, I envy you of your ability to sit and listen!"

The Need to Be Appreciated

Albert wrote Carla on January 30, 1957: "Yesterday I talked to George Thomas and Paul Ramsey about the Decision. And they both, independently, had the feeling that the job at Perkins is much too far from being done to make it a neutral matter whether I leave or stay. So that adds two more small weights on *that* side of the scale. Your letter today, and the word from Sterling [vice president of Southern Methodist University], were also *much* appreciated. It seems so odd to me that my friends, at least, don't realize that the thing I most need—or want, at least—is to be needed and 'appreciated.' It is the only appeal that almost invariably gets me—and most of the things I do are motivated by this more than anything else of which I am conscious. It's immature, I know, but there it is. I ought to have a clear and unwavering sense of my 'vocation,' etc., but I don't. There was a time when I felt I was needed at Perkins, but not 'appreciated,' except by Merry. Now, I feel less needed and not much more appreciated, except again by a very small circle of personal friends. But this ought not be the final feeling that sways the final cast of the dice. Now *another* invitation has come—from Penn State—to be the University Professor of Religion, in their new program. Now, that really *would* be a job, with $12,500 and perquisites. Interested?"

Time to Pray

February 1, 1957: "'Tis the end of a long day here in my 'cell'— not stirring out except for meals, and that only to the refectory. There was no incentive to go abroad, either, for the weather has varied from snow to sleet to rain and now back to sleet (as I gather from the noise on the windows!). And I've had every incentive to stay in and plug, for the mound of work goes down very slowly. But I did manage—after three false passages—to get the review of Dave's book done. This makes five book reviews since I came back [from the Christmas holidays at Dallas], along with other things. And you know how I *have* to read a book in order to review it.

"Yesterday, I had a really wonderful letter from Merry [Dean Cuninggim]. He's really an extraordinary person—and he keeps on growing and developing month by month. He wants me to stay and thinks I've still a job to do at Perkins. But he knows that it is, in part, a sort of thankless job and he realizes as clearly as I do that the University is going to be very slow to move forward even toward the first rank. As for my own teeterings, I keep thinking that Austin would be a good deal less stressful—and that if I *were* cut off from a lot of 'contacts' by the move, it might not be a bad thing. This year has confirmed my love for privacy and isolation. There's only a part of me that wants to be lionized—and I've no high regard for that part—*most of the time*. And yet I am beginning to believe that I matter at least some to the future of Perkins— and that constitutes a considerable obligation. As soon as Nelson's reply comes, I'll go sit for an afternoon in the chapel—and decide! Pray for me to have wisdom—for us both!"

The Decision Made

February 3, 1957: "I've just folded and sealed the letters to the folks at Austin saying that I am going to stay on at Perkins. Perhaps you can understand a little why I feel sad about it all— for this was an unprecedented opportunity, and I would have enjoyed it and been enriched by it. But the timing was wrong: either too late or too soon; I don't rightly know which. But when I came right down to it, it was plain that, save for the Austin people, nobody agreed with me that I ought to go—and all my own inertia was on the side of staying put. I wish I didn't feel that the Austin crowd will feel sadder about the decision than the SMU people—our *real* friends excepted—would feel glad if they knew about it. Anyway, it's *done*—and I feel I've made the right choice, all things considered, and the fact that I don't feel very happy over it is of no great consequence in the long run.

Penn State, Too!

"Naturally, I've turned down the Penn State offer, too—for it, too, was ill-timed. If either of these two had come two or three years ago, I'd have taken one or the other. And if things should begin to go badly at Perkins, I'll wish for an 'out' and there won't be one. So we must work and pray for victory at Perkins, for that's where we are set for a while.

"You can tell Merry and Sterling about the decision—and tell Merry that I'll be writing him toward the end of the week, for he's now embroiled in Ministers' Week, and I've quite a string of chores myself: lunch on Monday at the Institute for Advanced Study, my first seminar in the new semester Tuesday, a lecture at Drew on Wednesday, another to the WSCS [Women's Society of Christian Service] here on Thursday, and a visit to the OUP [Oxford University Press] folks on Friday.

Prefers to Be Liked

"Perhaps I should comment that when you tell Merry and Sterling that you needn't mention my ambivalent feelings—and that it might help if you'd try a bit to interpret me and my real 'ambitions' to them. Do they know I'd rather be liked than admired, to 'belong' than to lead, to be one of the boys than to be put up for show? And does Merry know how much I want, and need, a *good* halftime secretary? And is this last incompatible with the rest? And does *every*body know that I *hate asking* for things—*any*thing? Childish? Yes, I suppose—but!"

The Need to Relax

February 15, 1957: "There's no use exhorting you to get more rest, for more rest means time taken from something that's got to be done. And it's no comfort to point out that you are sharing the dilemma that has dogged me all my life: I not only prefer to loaf; I've got *gifts* for it! And yet always there is something that *seems,* at least, to be laid on me which has to be done. Meanwhile, all my friends give me the helpful counsel to relax and the unhelpful accusation that if I managed better, I wouldn't have any of these difficulties."

Get Busy and Relax!

The counsel of Outler's friends to relax was on target. But it was his friends who gave him the invitations that caused the tension! In a letter from Princeton dated February 6, 1957, he wrote: "Things have begun to 'move' again—even though I still feel pokey and inwardly subdued. Sunday afternoon I went over to the W. D. Davies' for tea, and Sunday night I spoke to the young adults at the Methodist Church. Monday I had lunch with a great Byzantine scholar, Glanville Downey, over at the Institute of Advanced Study. At lunch I sat next to Robert Oppenheimer, the director. He is an amazing man—and they have a fabulous setup over there: everything geared directly and unreservedly to the scholar's needs and interests. Yesterday, I had my first session of the new seminar—with *twelve* students, instead of the four or five that George said I would *surely* have *this* time. In a way, of course, I'm flattered but more seriously, I'm *dismayed,* for it means extra work which will have to be taken away from the project. Now, today, I'm off to Drew, for a discussion with the faculty about curriculum and an address to the whole University tonight. The dean, Barney Anderson, is a wonderful guy and I couldn't refuse his invitation—at first just to visit, then a little talk, then a full dress convocation! But it will be fun, I hope."

Faculty Selection

February 20, 1957: "The next best thing was a letter from Merry—full of understanding and insight, and with just enough news to excite my curiosity, but not satisfy it. It seems that there was a very earnest session of the Trustees' Committee on the School of Theology during Ministers' Week, in which they raised many questions about our policy on faculty selection, appointments and assignments. At least some of the trustees had never supposed that it was the faculty's business to set personnel policy or to play the decisive role in choosing new faculty. This led to some deep-going analysis of what we are really about as a seminary and university—and Merry seems to think that the overall result was constructive and enabling. But I can imagine that we haven't heard the end of this business. They did approve the three new appointments: Grady Hardin, a bright young preacher from Houston in preaching; Floyd Curl, an ex-D.S. from Southwest Texas in Martin's place; and Joe Allen, from Yale in Ethics. The last was cooked up, you may remember, at the Morrises last Thanksgiving—and I'm very pleased."

A Sounding Board That Talked

Somewhere along the way Carla took Albert at his word—he asked for a "sounding board." And she became his sounding board that talked when asked about "stands" he had taken. Her reactions to his reactions to events influenced him greatly. In this role she became a prophetess for a prophet. She very seldom spoke out in contradiction of him. And when she did, she got his attention! And triggered a reaction, as revealed in his following March 4, 1957, letter to her:

"I read, with the greatest interest, your passages on self-analysis and appraisal in yesterday's letter. Obviously, I think that this sort of thing is terribly important if we are to understand ourselves and each other—and to change, at least a little. I think you are getting somewhere, and it seems to me you hit the nail

on the head when you underscored the phrase: '*I'm passive.*'
You are and I am not—and neither of us quite likes the opposite
trait. You tend to *let* things *happen* and hope for the best. I tend
to make 'em happen, on the assumption that if I don't, the worst,
or at least worse, *will* happen. I've tried too hard to make you an
activist-on-your-own, and you have fought too hard to stay passive. But what can we *do* about this? If I were a little less a
protestor and you were a little less passive, it would help, and if I
could let you be passive without wanting to leave you alone—
and you could let me protest without wishing you were somewhere else, this, too, would help. But it *is* a problem, and we
need to keep on trying to understand it, more deeply, more fully,
more frankly. I hope you'll feel moved to write me more about
yourself—and me, too; for in this atmosphere of detachment and
loneliness, we may be more open to change than when we are
together."

Declined Invitations

March 20, 1957: "Merry called Sunday night (or was it Saturday) with a most attractive invitation to speak at a conference at
Perkins just after the Ayers. I was sorely tempted to accept but
just couldn't see the time between now and then when I could
get anything credible ready. Woe is me—and us, I guess."

March 23, 1957: "Yesterday was cut up a bit—a lunch with
Glanville Downey at the Institute and, in the evening, a dinner at
the Nassau Tavern with Roy Lee and, afterwards, his public
lecture—the one I refused to do. He did pretty well, but I was
glad I'd turned the thing down—for the committee running the
program are highly critical young men, applying ruthless standards of perfection to others that they could not afford to have
applied to themselves—so ruthlessly. But the dinner was superb,
and so I came out of that deal with a slight profit.

"I had a note from Willis [Willis Tate, president of SMU]
last week, and in it he spoke of 'exciting new developments in
the program of the Graduate School' and wants to have a talk
while I'm home. So, please help me to remember to call his
secretary first thing Monday and set a date. The two crucial
things about our graduate school are: (1) a dean and (2) money.
Curiously, there's a part of me that wishes Willis would ask *me*

to be the dean, for I've a fear he won't get a 'better man'—and if he takes one of the men off the present [Arts and Sciences] faculty, we'll be stuck at substandard level. But the better part of me says, 'God forbid'—for this year's experience has suggested to me that I *could* have been a scholar, and would rather be one than anything else. And I feel pretty sure I am safe on this score."

This had to be a "curious" experience for Albert, to be tempted with the idea of being a dean. But it was no more than a temptation. He never sought the office of dean, and his desire to be a scholar came to be fulfilled in experiences that he never dreamed at that time would come to be.

Eccentric Academics

March 24, 1957: "I'm just back from one of the oddest evenings I've spent thus far in Princeton. It was a dinner party at the Harold Cherniss-es—he's a great specialist in Greek philosophy and one of the most eccentric academics among a carefully selected lot of eccentrics at the Institute. The other guests included the head of the Murkel Foundation—like the Hazen Foundation, but interested in medical education—and the scholar who is writing the history of the Institute. It was, in a polite way, a thoroughly disorderly conversation about education, with nobody really listening to anybody else and everybody talking at cross-purposes. It's interesting to see this sort of intellectual demoralization at 'the top' of the American educational heap. It makes me a little more content with the confusion so manifest a little further down the ladder.

"Last night, I took part in the Sabbath Service of the Hillel Foundation—Rabbi Levy and about sixty Jewish students. I talked briefly with them about Maimonides and Aquinas—and they were so surprised that a Christian theologian should know anything about their greatest theologian that they didn't mind the fact that I obviously don't know very much about him. It was, on the whole, the best response I have gotten from any of my 'appearances' here at Princeton.

"I'm glad the McCreless dinner went well and hope the Library show did, too. Save for my cinema excursion, everything here is *strictly* routine. But, strangely enough, I'm enjoying all but the 'too-muchness' of it. I'm learning a lot and getting a lot of things clarified—and a good deal of ammunition for future skirmishes."

Serendipitous interludes amidst studies gave Outler the balance his life needed. In a letter dated March 30, 1957, he wrote: "I'm just back from the first movie I've seen here all year. Some of the boys came in around nine [PM] and offered to take me along to the late show of Olivier's 'Richard III.' I was pretty bushed with Chalcedon, so I went along with them—and it was very good. Now I can unwind my mind in bed with majestic free-verse and vivid medieval colors instead of more balancings and distinctions between ουσια, φυσισ and υποστασισ."

Graduate School Program

April 20, 1957: "Keep in touch with Merry so you can keep me apprised of any developments in the graduate school program. Despite Sterling's reassurance and Merry's confidence, I've still some active fear that they'll make some irrevocable commitments which will cripple the possibility of really good work in graduate religion. They could do it without realizing what they had done!"

Outler's fears proved unfounded. Upon his return to Dallas, he plunged headlong into the Graduate School business. And was as pleased as perfectionist Outler could be pleased.

Self-doubt

May 17, 1957: "The lecture is over and done, thank goodness, and I've been recovering from it—and trying to pull things together for this final lap. It was something midway between a flop and a triumph. Everybody was 'nice' and Mike Oates was satisfied. But I don't think anyone was greatly impressed, and I wasn't either. Reflecting on this experience has helped me understand a little better my inner attitude toward places like Princeton and Yale. In a community like this, only the *really* first-rate is deeply and sincerely cherished. What I can do is pretty good—and sometimes nearly first rate, but not really, not ever. And I have a strong aversion to being unable to measure up to what is really cherished instead of being tolerated. It is true, of course, that not many of the people here are really first rate, either—but the good second raters have made their peace with the situation and bask in the reflected light that comes from the overall excellence of the place. I can't settle for that happily—so I need to be in a setting where I'm as good as the best, and this is pretty nearly the case at SMU. For all my occasional discontent and critical reactions, it's a better place for me than Yale was or this would be. This is a useful lesson to have learned."

Despite this self-depreciation, in 1994 veteran Princeton librarian Bill Harris told me that Outler impacted the Princeton campus with an endowed intelligence and ethos unmatched by other visiting professors who have come and gone through the years.

Juggling the Balls

Outler's last letter from Princeton before returning home, dated June 2, 1957, reflects his eagerness to get home: "The end of the last full week here—and just a full week before I'll be home, with you and the children! I'm thoroughly impatient to be off, and tense as a fiddle string about all that needs doing—and what will go undone—before Wednesday at 1:40 P.M., when I catch the Toonerville Trolley for the last time. Any way I can figure it, it's going to be another of those tight squeezes where I juggle the balls right down to train time—and then lie back and try to recover my orientation for the next episode. I certainly can't claim any real effectiveness at self-management—though I do manage to keep a good many balls in the air, and, save for the tension, I'm in pretty good shape after the long grind.

"People have been calling up or dropping in off and on for the past three days and nights—always with a problem on their hands. Yesterday I had lunch with Mike Oates at the Nassau Club (the inner Citadel of old Princeton) and we talked over the year and his great projected work on Plato and Aristotle. We don't see eye to eye on many things of classical philosophy, but he can take it as well as dish it out. He asked me if I would like to come back to Princeton on the faculty, and was genuinely puzzled when I told him I didn't think so. Besides, that whole question has become academic because in the course of the year my lack of wholehearted and enthusiastic approval of the graduate program has piqued George Thomas, who is fearfully sensitive about 'his' department and takes lack of approval as positive opposition. It's not the kind of setting in which I could fit easily. But it's been a wonderful year for the thing I came to do!"

Proving Himself

Outler returned from Princeton and then he was gone again. From Montreat on August 23, 1957, he wrote Carla commending her on a statement she had made back home in defending one of his "stands": "It's more of a boost than you can realize, maybe, to have someone *really* in your corner. I get more *admiration* than I need, or is good for me. But I need somebody to explain me to other people when I can't, and toot my horn instead of doing it myself. Maybe I wouldn't get the compulsion to prove myself so strongly if I'd already made the grade with someone who could turn in a report when it was called for. So thanks a million, darling. This new sense I have of you is a bit amazing—and wonderful."

A Busy Man

The peeks into Outler's personal life that these letters from Princeton provide reveal at times an anxious man and always a busy one. His life emulated in many ways the man John Wesley, who was introduced to him in the late 1950s as a serious subject to study. In a January 7, 1959, letter to Robert Beach, librarian at Union Theological Seminary in New York, Outler wrote: "Do you remember a couple of summers ago when we talked briefly about a Wesley project that I hoped would develop finally into a new, critical edition of Wesley's works? Well, the latter stage of the business hasn't come much closer, but a preliminary step has been taken—and I wonder if you'd be willing to help me with it. The Editorial Board of the prospective *A Library of Protestant Thought* has assigned to me the volume on Wesley. The original proposal was that Wesley be included in a volume along with other leaders in the Evangelical Revival (Whitefield, Fletcher, Simeon, Wilberforce, et al.). But I have insisted that if Wesley is to be understood properly, he must have a volume to himself. The board has now agreed to this, and this raises the question as to what should go into such a volume.

"If you wanted to exhibit John Wesley as a significant theologian—both to non-Methodists and to Methodists—what would you choose from out of all his writings? The usual image of Wesley is of the great evangelist, of the founder of Methodism, of one who with his brother gave evangelical Christianity a new thrust and a new seriousness. But was he not also a theologian—albeit more by Providence than his own express design? I see him as occupying a unique place in the evolution of Protestantism, as achieving a notable synthesis of both the Catholic and Reformed traditions, of finding a middle way between antinomianism and moralism, between universalism and double predestinarianism, etc., etc. Obviously, you wouldn't have to agree with my particular thesis in order to agree that Wesley is a sufficiently significant theologian in the history of Protestant thought to deserve a presentation of him as such." Unknown to Outler at the time, he was innocently embarking upon a long journey that would gain him the fame of a preeminent John Wesley scholar.

Wofford Calls for Counsel

Outler felt that whoever tinkered with John Wesley's life and works should be a scholar; anyone who tinkered with any aspect of higher learning should be a scholar or at least show promise and respect for scholarship. This aspect of Outler's character was displayed in this November 19, 1957, letter to Wofford's Francis Cunningham: "For a couple of weeks now, I've been trying to find the time to answer your letter of October 29th. But one week I was at Cincinnati at the Christian Education conference—and last week I was in bed all week with the 'flu.'

"The fact that you are considering Grady Hardin, Sterling Wheeler and Joe Quillian [for college president] is encouraging to me as a Wofford alumnus—and a little disturbing as a member of the SMU faculty. It means that you've got your sights high and clear—but it would mean a serious loss to us if you managed to get any one of them.

"They are, all three, absolutely first-class men—in character, personality, Christian commitment and ability. I'd be glad to serve under any one of them as my dean or president—and you'd be fortunate to have any one of them at Wofford. Now, as far as the differences between them go, I'd put it this way. Grady is the best preacher of the trio—and the most closely identified with the parish ministry and the inner life of the Methodist Church. Joseph Quillian [brought on the Perkins faculty in 1954–1955 as professor in homiletics and worship] is the best scholar of the three—actually, the only one with a Ph.D.—and he would be able to lead the faculty to its optimum output while not losing touch with the Church. Sterling is the best administrator of the lot—with an uncanny gift of leadership, morale building and public relations. He is a good enough scholar to command the respect of the faculty and good enough churchman to help both college and church in their mutual relationships.

"If I were ranking them in any order of preference—and this would be both arbitrary and very close—I'd put Wheeler first, by a very narrow margin; then Quillian, and, again by a very narrow margin, Hardin. But as I said, we can't afford to lose any one of them from the exciting challenge and opportunity we have before us here—and I'd have mixed loyalties if I were drawn into the picture to counsel any one of them, in case you asked him.

"But these men represent the pattern I earnestly hope you'll hold to in your search for Wofford's next president. He should be a churchman—and I think, a minister. He should be a *scholar*—for Wofford's quality depends upon this quality of the intellectual atmosphere engendered in the campus community, and the president is a crucial factor in this 'weather-making.' And he should be a good administrator. Remember what it was that made 'Heinia' a great president—and that made Wofford a really remarkable school in his time—and look for its equivalence in the new and changed circumstances of these days."

And a Time to Rest

In keeping with Ecclesiastes 3:1, "To everything there is a season, and a time to every purpose under the heaven," workaholic Outler once again needed his time of rest. And as usual, it always came at a time he had planned to be accomplishing a needed work, as the following July 18, 1958, letter to Kenneth Brown, executive director of The Danforth Foundation, indicates: "Your letter of June 25th was heartening and helpful—just when I needed it most. I felt deeply chagrined to have become a cropper and let you down, and I was keenly disappointed to miss the Teacher's Conference. It was the show in the summer's round that I was looking forward to most eagerly, for that's a great bunch you'll have there. But it's a comfort to know that you've gotten Harold Bosley to do the job, for that assures the job *well* done!

"Ever since the Doc and Merrimon lowered the boom, I've been a real good boy and am putting in full time on this new project of bed, board and books (the 10-foot shelf of those I'd promised myself to read 'someday'!). I've no energy to be aggressive and no immediate pressures—a quite unique experience. Come September, we add up the score card once again and see how the prospects shape up for next year. But it seems unlikely that I've got anything the matter with me—physically, that is—that three months rest won't cure. Who has?"

Dean Joe Quillian

The academic year 1959–1960 was Merrimon Cuninggim's final year as dean of Perkins School of Theology. The transition from Cuninggim to Quillian went very smoothly. And Outler could not have been happier over the selection of Quillian, his student from Yale days and now a colleague and friend. Herndon Wagers, Outler's pick to come to Perkins, was chosen to be the faculty person responsible for consulting with SMU's President Tate, to chair the faculty search committee, and to secure recommendations from the faculty.[84] Insiders saw Outler's influence work throughout the entire selection process. Quillian was pleased to have Outler on the faculty and, for starters, saw to it that Outler was elected a member of the SMU Faculty Senate (the first Perkins faculty member to hold this university office).[85]

The following sentence from a paragraph of an August 1, 1960, letter to John Taylor presents Outler's evaluation of Quillian's first days on the job as dean: "Things are going along well hereabouts—with no particular news that I've heard that seems unusual. Dean Quillian is taking hold very well, indeed—and the new faculty appointments (Littell, Carney, and Ward) are amongst the best we've made."

Outler, Dean of Perkins?

The closest time Outler came to being a dean was when *Newsweek* misreported it in their last issue of January 1968. Outler received this pulling-a-leg message from J. Robert Nelson: "Having just read *Newsweek* I am delighted to learn of your new title. May you have a long and fruitful administration! What's Joe going to do? I know you will be glad to be relieved of the burden of teaching."

Outler answered in a February 8, 1968, letter: "I shuddered and flinched at the *Newsweek* goof; I knew it would set people off on pleasantries that aren't at all funny to either Joe or me. I am not now, nor ever have been dean—of Perkins or anything else!—and Joe still has his hands on our tiller here, one of the best deans I ever had, or know about. As for 'the burden of teaching,' that is the only business in my cluttered and misspent life where 'the yoke is easy and the burden is light.'" It is interesting to note that the humor-at-self was totally missing in Outler in this stage of awareness of the event. He was too close to the distressing state of affairs. Later, as time removed him from the existential moment, he could laugh at this journalistic blunder where he (and Joe) were the butt of the joke.

A New Dean; New Challenges

The glory days for Outler at Perkins were the years he served with Dean Cuninggim. He knew he was important to the school under Cuninggim, but with a new dean coming he was not sure. He was hoping his presence would continue to count for some good. As Cuninggim packed to leave to become director of the Danforth Foundation (July 1960), Outler cancelled a trip in order to remain on campus to prepare for the coming of a new dean. He made every effort to assure his ex-student/colleague, Joe Quillian, that great days were ahead under Joe's leadership.

Outler was out of the city on May 3, 1961, when a convocation honoring the new dean was held. He was, however, a major part of the occasion anyway as he left a paper to be read in his absence. Here is a May 5, 1961, letter written to him by Richey Hogg, who organized the special event: "How grateful we all are to you for the magnificent paper you prepared for the May 3 convocation recognizing Joseph D. Quillian, Jr., Dean. We all regret that you could not be here to deliver your own paper and to participate in that occasion, the structure and execution of which was so much a product of your own thought and vision. At the same time, we are all thankful that you could write the paper which now becomes part of the permanent record of this day and of this institution. May I add, too, that Schubert [Ogden] did a first-rate job in delivering the paper. Everyone has spoken with the highest appreciation of your contribution. This event marks one more advancing step in the forward march of SMU. For the thrust and direction of that march, this institution owes you a debt the full dimensions of which, I believe, will become clear only after the passing of several decades. For that larger contribution, as well as this immediate one, our heartfelt thanks." The reader will note that Outler was in the minds of his colleagues at Perkins the highest on the totem pole at this point in his history at the school.

The Troubleshooter

By the time Quillian had arrived on the scene as dean (he was already on the faculty as professor of homiletics and worship), Outler was well established as the Perkins troubleshooter. He was sorely missed by Quillian when, just two years into his administration (October 1971), while Outler was out of the country, Professor Harville Hendrix in his "Church and World" class showed films of explicit sex acts, both heterosexual and homosexual. It was designed "to enable the seminarian to conceive of the world as the essential stage for God's mission and to prepare him to formulate principles and techniques appropriate for developing an effective ministry."[86] Helen Parmley, longtime religion editor of the *Dallas Morning News,* on November 2, 1971, wrote that whether the films were obscene or educational was in the "eye of the beholder." Some in the class beheld obscenity; others claimed that it was the most educational experience they had ever had. They wanted to see more! Some who heard about it saw through its ill-conceived projection and set out to stop it.

Wanda Smith, Outler's secretary, wrote Outler concerning the reaction of some to this bombshell which was heard around the world. As far as is known, Outler was silent about the matter. He did not carry the conversation forward in a letter to Wanda. One can only guess what his reaction might have been had he been in the city. But he was there for the next explosion, which was captured on film and seen in newspapers around the world. This time it was Claude Evans, the university chaplain, dancing down the aisle with a young woman, a member of the choir who was clad in what were then called "hot pants," very tight-fitting short shorts. In short order Outler was on the telephone mollifying the critics— neither condemning nor condoning Evans' bizarre efforts to portray worship. Evans, pleased with his creative art forms, invited the media in to take the pictures. Albert persuaded critics that only one campus official was involved; that his act did not have the blessing of the university; and that while it took place in Perkins chapel, it was not Perkins-sponsored; and that he (Albert) would not soon take up the dance routine in his own efforts at leading worship. *That* was an inconceivable sight for those who knew Outler. His good humor was redemptive in this situation and others that had been and were to come.

An Invitation from Duke

Quality of scholarship was foremost in Outler's mind when faculty members were being considered; that was also the foremost concern in a January 8, 1959, letter to Outler from Duke Divinity School's Dean Robert Cushman: "It is a good deal more than common pleasure that I am able to invite you to consider an appointment to the faculty of Duke University Divinity School as Professor of Theology. This invitation comes after proper and full consultation of the University. The appointment would be effective September 1, 1959. It will, of course, carry with it responsibility for instruction at the graduate level, and you would be expected to take your full place in the support of that program. In addition, it is expected that you will teach three of the six hours of required work in Systematic Theology for students in the B.D. course. I contemplate teaching the other three hours.

"I realize that this proposal must startle you with its abruptness and directness. We have a future unfolding before us in the Divinity School and Graduate Program in Religion of Duke University in which we feel you can play a significant role. We are prepared to make precise and specific proposals in the way of terms and to fully articulate the position and its responsibilities, but before doing so, I would like to have personal conversation with you in the next few days.

"I am planning on being in Kansas City February 9–12, and it is my proposal to call you by phone when I arrive in Kansas City to arrange for a personal interview at some place which we can commonly agree upon. I greatly hope that you will think favorably enough of this initial approach to converse with me more fully about details. I will be in touch with you. Warmest greetings to Carla and the children."

The Quandary

Outler answered with this February 5, 1959, letter: "As you can well imagine, this last week has been spent in considerable turmoil of mind and spirit. Decisions never come easy for me, and *this* one is so critical that I'm having a rough time of it. Everything is still considerably in flux, but the whole weight of my reflection, prayer and 'disinterested counsel' is so clearly on one side of the balance that I feel I ought to let you know how matters stand, and then let you decide if it is still worth your while—and Duke's money—for me to come over on the 13th.

"You know why the invitation to Duke is so attractive and important. The chief attraction, to put it simply, is *you* and Shelton and the program you have developed in the Graduate School. As a whole, Duke is a better university than SMU and, under your leadership, the Divinity School is going to be one of the best in the country. Carla and I have happy memories of our years in Durham [and a few unhappy ones as Outler's letters leaving Duke for Yale are recalled], and we both feel that we would be happy to finish out our works and days in those parts. We know that you would deal generously with us and that we would find a stimulating association in the University community. If there were no basic countervailing demands and duties here, the decision would be easy.

"But, there are such counterbalances, and they add up to a rather clear sense of vocational responsibility. Let me suggest what some of them are.

"Four years ago, it looked as if we weren't going to make it here at SMU—or at least, that it was going to be more trouble than it was worth. Even then I turned down opportunities to go back to the Northeast, but I think I would have gone to Duke or Vanderbilt if there had been an opening. Since that time, we have turned a real corner, both at Perkins and in the University. But we are not so far past the 'breakthrough' to make it certain that this place can consolidate its gains—and if some of us pull out now, it could well have a disproportionate effect. I'm not posing as an indispensable man (*and all that!*) but it seems fairly clear that my leaving at this time would unsettle the plans of several of my colleagues to stay on in face of equally attractive offers to them. I could spell this out, but I'm sure you'll be able to understand without that.

"In the second place, SMU has just committed itself to the development of a good graduate department of religion, and Stuart Henry and I have been working on the blueprint for it. President Tate has invited me to take the chairmanship of the Department, and although I'm not eager to do that, I still have some obligations to whoever is going to implement this blueprint I've helped to draw up. If I pull out now, this particular program will be set back at least a while, and I'd be unhappy to be responsible for that.

"Third, although I greatly appreciate your offer to take care of my sabbatical leave at full pay, I've begun to have some serious misgivings about that, too. Anyway you look at it (or, any way I've been able to look at it) it would be preferential treatment and could make trouble for us down the way. Theological faculties are sensitive plants, and although my friends would rejoice at my good fortune, there could be other consequences not so pleasant [Outler's presence had been known to trigger jealousies among some faculty members]. We had some trouble on this line here in the early years—and I don't want it to happen again, ever.

"Fourth, the family would be upset by a move just now. There's no problem about Carla, of course; she adjusts wonderfully. But Dave and Trudi are at a stage where uprooting them could well be serious. Dave is not going to be able to go to college—and that means he's got to find the sort of work he can and likes to do, in ranching, farming or something to do with the outdoors. This section is a better bet for that than Durham. But it is really Trudi who would be scarred. She's a senior in high school, in love with a nice boy (her first really big affair!) and they are planning to get married after their sophomore years in college. The thought of moving from Dallas makes her literally ill—and this naturally weighs on Carla and me.

"Finally, I've come to feel that a man at my stage of things ought not to move again unless there is a very strong impera- tive—either to leave the place he's *at,* or to go strike out in a new direction after a Ulysses-like vision of the Isles of the Blessed. Duke, Yale and SMU—that's about enough for any but a rolling stone. Petry has always believed I was restless and opportunistic. He's wrong about the latter, but he *was* right about the restless- ness (earlier I thought of it as 'chasing rainbows'). I'm either more lethargic now or else wiser (at my age the two may be the same thing), and the thought of continuing here and subsiding more and more into the routines of study and writing looks posi- tively tolerable. And by the same token, the thought of moving again—save under the duress of a catastrophe here—seems a very formidable undertaking.

"I'm not trying to convince you that I'm right, and I'm not quite sure that the die is cast. But I feel that you and Shelton have a right to know how I'm thinking and the highly probable outcome of our weighing and balancing act (Carla's and mine). I told you that I'd come to Durham to talk things over—and I will, still. But since it already seems quite unlikely that I will feel free to accept your invitation—however generous and gracious— wouldn't it be easier all the way around if we canceled the trip and you started working on your alternate plans right away?

"You will know better than anyone else, except Shelton, what this letter has cost me emotionally. I'd love to work with you; I'm deeply involved and committed here. Duke is already a good school; SMU is making strides toward excellence and needs all the help she can get. The move to Duke would offer more of a certain sort of security [the reader will remember this comment when years later Outler discovered there was no office space for him at Perkins] and a magnificent opportunity! To stay is a good deal more risky (financially, politically, etc., etc.)—but also a magnificent opportunity! But I'm *here,* and I can't find a really convincing justification to leave.

"Ministers' Week is here, and after my junket to Edmonton— to the Golden Jubilee of the University of Alberta—there'll be no leisure between now and the 13th. Please make your decision in the light of this candid, all-cards-on-the-table-face-up summary of my situation. If you agree that we'd best drop it here, quietly, then just cancel that ticket. If you and Shelton won't feel I've done right by the decision without a visit, be sure to have the ticket here when I return from Canada.

"Meanwhile, try to understand the evident struggle I've been making to be responsible in this affair—to my friends, my vocation, my family and the larger enterprise of theological education. Please share this letter with Shelton and Alma—and with it, my sincere affection for them and for you all."

Ball Bounced Back to Outler

Outler had put the ball in Dean Cushman's court to stop the conversation or to continue it. Dean Cushman attempted to bounce the ball back in this February 10 letter to Outler: "I have been pondering your letter and have been doing so in company with Shelton during the past two or three days.

"In the first place, your letter is convincing up to a point. I am sensible of the personal and family intricacies that perplex and distress you. I cannot believe that these, however, are decisive. I do sympathize with your animal indisposition to undertake the physical difficulties of another transition. Furthermore, I can well believe that you are very deep in your responsibilities to the younger colleagues of the school, but I cannot wholly agree that this binds you inalterably for the future, and the future is now.

"In particular, the point which I would like to discuss with you is whether having corralled all the theological talent of Methodism in one institution is the most assured way of playing fair with the advancement of theological education, especially in the Methodist tradition, across the nation. In short, I am not sure that your responsibility is exclusively with Southern Methodist University. I think I say this with rather complete objectivity. [An acknowledgment that Outler was wooing the best of the young theologians to come to Perkins was turned into an indictment for doing so.]

"In short, I think you had better come on to Duke and examine the issue from this standpoint as well as that. After all, there are two perspectives at least upon any decision, especially one of this moment.

"If you are inclined, in the light of these comments, still to dissent, then let me say regretfully we shall accept your own decision not to come. I might add that Barbara shares the sentiments of this letter."

Making the Decision

Dean Cushman stopped the conversation with this less-than-subtle authoritarian approach. The idea that anyone could look at anything with "*complete* objectivity" must have flipped Outler. But it was what Outler needed in order to make the decision (as hard as it was) easier. Outler's response in a February 13th letter reveals how Dean Cushman's letter resulted in favor of his remaining at Perkins: "This is not an easy letter to write. My decision was reached in a real agony of spirit, but it is as honest and responsible a choice as I could make. There is no use in reviewing my arguments and the inner gropings and the final tipping of the scales. The sum of it all was that I do not feel free to leave SMU at this stage of the game. Nobody is indispensable—anywhere. I know that. But, over against this is the fact that I have undischarged commitments here, involving a sizable number of other people, and I'd be responsible if there were untoward consequences from my pulling out. I haven't actually *finished* many jobs in my career, and I feel obligated to see this one through at least a little further—and, probably, 'from here on out.' I only wish it didn't involve saying 'No' to you and Shelton, for you are two of the people I'd rather please than almost anybody in the world.

"Once the answer came as clear as this one did [once Outler read Dean Cushman's letter] there was no use in coming to Durham to try to persuade you of it. It would not only have wasted your money but it would have harrowed all our feelings. It wouldn't have been right to 'bargain' about a matter as deeply personal as this, and I've carefully refrained from making this business a public affair at this end of the line. The only thing I can do is to ask you to try to believe that I've tried desperately to make this a responsible decision, before God and all the claims involved that I could assay.

"You may be right that it is 'unfair' for us to have 'corralled all the theological talent of Methodism'—allowing for this as a gracious hyperbole! We certainly haven't had a deliberate plan to corner the market. I'd be *willing*—though not *happy*—to have you take one of these 'youngsters.' (Ogden, Deschner, Harvey, Wagers and Shipley is the order in which I would rate them as to caliber and promise—but it's a close cluster.) Indeed, I think you'd have a good chance of getting one, for you've got a better budget than we'll have for several years to come. What is more, any one of them would make an excellent man for you, both in the Divinity School and the Graduate School. But, as you will understand, I'm not going to urge any of this on you, for *we* don't feel 'overstaffed' with our present load. Remember, you kept Mac Ritchey when we did our darndest and, from some faint clues he has thrown out, I'm afraid you are going to get Stuart Henry.

"Arthur Kale has just come by, and we had a good talk. He seems a perceptive sort, and he opened up the question, so I told him something of 'the outside' of my deliberations. He'll tell you more about it, he says, when he gets back.

"You know that I am fearful of saying 'No' to my friends. And if you know that, you'll know what this whole business has cost me. And if you and Shelton know *that,* it may be that you'll accept what I realize you are not likely to approve of. In any case, believe me, as I am grateful to you, very fond of you and quietly confident that you'll know how to go on from here."

Time Out!

During those hyperactive years it was common from time to time for Outler to be forced by his doctor into a mode of rest and healing. In a January 20, 1960, response to John Newton Thomas of Union Theological Seminary, Outler wrote: "I was acutely embarrassed to have to renege on my Davidson engagement. The doctor is trying a composite treatment of hectoring and reassuring me. He fusses about my schedule and 'load'; he takes some pleasure, it seems to me, in finding symptomatic warrant for putting me in the sack. My private hunch is that he is tired, too, and figures that if he can't rest, at least some of his friends are made to. On the other hand, he seems reasonably candid in his assurance that these angina symptoms are merely episodic and premonitory—and that better men than I, with worse tickers, have lived on to break even on their annuities. I am feeling better now and am planning to turn in a standard spring semester's job of work. In February I am doing the McNutt Lectures at Louisville." This meant that he was heading back into a work load that only a workaholic could manage—until the doctor came calling again.

Feeling Better While Working on the LPT's John Wesley

Outler's work on his John Wesley volume resembled more like play in his attitude. *That* was the kind of medicine he needed. In the midst of his overall busyness was a man having fun. Well into the preparation stage, Outler wrote this paragraph in a January 26, 1960, letter to Dr. John Dillenberger concerning his proposed Wesley volume of *A Library of Protestant Thought:* "I'm still having as much fun as a bee in a jam-pot, soaking up stuff and running down clues and leads, pinching off shaky hypotheses and getting the general feeling that the basic picture really is substantiated by the accumulating evidence. But it does go slowly, and now tomorrow I have to break off for a round of denominational and ecumenical shindigs for the next two weeks. Then—back to the jam-pot!"

While Dillenberger was the one who chaired the work on *A Library of Protestant Thought*, Marian Pauck (née Hausner), the publisher's editor assigned to the project, kept it going until she left Oxford University Press. Here are her words: "I first met Albert in 1952 when he was teaching at Union Theological Seminary (of which I am an alumna) for a summer term. At the time I was working for Reinhold Niebuhr as an editorial secretary at *Christianity and Crisis.* A few years later, I became an assistant editor of religion books at the Oxford Press in New York. Albert or 'Al,' as he was called by his friends and colleagues, was very outgoing and warmhearted from the beginning. He referred to himself as a 'Georgia cracker,' and the southern lilt of his speech captivated the ear of this native New Yorker.

"At the time of our first meeting Al was teaching at Yale Divinity School, but he was seriously considering a call to the Perkins School of Theology in Dallas, Texas. He felt an obligation to communicate a sophisticated understanding of the Christian Gospel as well as of the Christian tradition (as he viewed it from his church historical perspective) to his brothers in the South. He and his lovely wife, Carla, and I met several times over the summer, at lunch time, and at dinner. At those meetings I sometimes shared anecdotes about Paul Tillich and Reinhold Niebuhr (my teachers) and Al, in turn, spoke often of his colleagues, e.g., Calhoun, H. R. Niebuhr, Roland Bainton, and Liston Pope, who were also at Union that summer. These colleagues, Al said, were in a stratosphere so far above him that he felt that no matter how talented he himself might be or how hard he worked, he would remain 'in their shadow.' For this reason also he looked upon the call to Perkins with considerable enthusiasm.

"What seemed to so many of us in the Northeast 'a step down' for Al ultimately proved to be a great opportunity for him. Carla, also a southerner [Carla, in fact, was from the north; but few realized this; her speech became 'southern' through the years], was blessedly able to adjust to new surroundings in the blink of an eye. They were a well-matched pair, very happy in their marriage, and faithful to one another. Carla's steadiness was a feature upon which the more anxious, frenetic Al depended.

"In the fall of 1954 I accepted an invitation to work at the Oxford University Press in New York, and was soon eagerly searching for authors not only in the Northeast but everywhere in the United States. In 1957 one of my teachers, John Dillenberger, came to the press in order to discuss his idea for publishing the second half of *The Library of Christian Classics.* We issued a contract and named the new series *A Library of Protestant Thought.* Albert Outler became a leading member of the Editorial Board. At our semiannual meetings there were long and intense discussions among the members of the board in their effort to define the list and to match the perfect editor of each proposed book. Albert and another member of the board frequently engaged in slightly quarrelsome and long-winded exchanges, which amused some of us and tried the patience of the rest. The first volume which was published in the series was, of course, the volume on John Wesley, which Albert edited and for which he wrote an introduction. I treasure the dedication he wrote in my copy of said volume. Two further volumes were published, but after my departure from the Oxford University Press in 1963 interest in the series diminished and the remaining volumes were not published.

"I miss the long and interesting conversations Al and I had in the years before my marriage. He and I would always have a special evening alone and eat lobster in a wonderful restaurant on Broadway. Had I been wiser then I would have taped them. So often he would say, 'Why, bless your heart,' in that southern gentlemanly way that was truly gallant. Albert was a man whose sensitivity was perhaps greater than was good for him, but it enabled him to reach out to others in a truly pastoral way and to help others in need. I am not sure he ever overcame his feeling of 'living under the shadow' of men like Tillich, Niebuhr and Pauck, but that is a private realm into which even the most astute biographer might have difficulty entering."

Casting His Own Shadow

While serving "in the shadows" of the theological giants, Outler was beginning to cast his own shadow from the light of truth that found its way to him as he was doing his own many things. In his own words, he bounced about like "a cat on a hot tin roof." One of the important projects he landed on in the 1960s was the *John Wesley* volume of *The Library of Protestant Thought* in which his Introduction described Wesley as a man of "serene strenuousness." That was a truthful description of Wesley—and of Outler himself!

The *John Wesley* volume was the precursor of Outler's annotations in the four-volume set of Wesley's sermons in the new *Works of John Wesley* published by Abingdon. His research for this initial volume revealed Wesley as a theologian (via his sermons and notes) to be taken seriously by the whole church. Outler dedicated his life to spreading that word.

First Taste of Frank Baker

It was during the time that the LPT's *John Wesley* manuscript was being reviewed by various editors that Outler got his first taste of Frank Baker. In the opening paragraph of a January 19, 1962, letter to Dr. John Dillenberger, Outler wrote: "The logjam is beginning to break up. Claude's report came through (favorable and helpful). Ray Morris has sent a three-page letter, with manuscript to follow. It, too, is favorable and helpful. Today, I got twelve pages of comment from Frank Baker on the Introduction alone, with more to follow! Much of it is chitchat, some of it is nitpicking, some of it *very* helpful—and we can all be grateful to have this kind of help from a real twenty-four carat Wesley specialist. It goes deep against his grain to see an American—and a nonspecialist at that—do a book like this on Wesley. His criticisms reflect this, but where they are helpful they are *very* helpful, and I can take the back of his hand in order to get the advantage of his erudition. He's a real deathwatch beetle on bibliography and texts—and so typical an English Methodist that you would think he was mimicking them!" In no way did this involvement resemble a jam-pot relishment. Rather, from that time on—on through the Wesley sermons project that was to come years later—Baker became more like a bee in Outler's bonnet!

The Second Oxford Institute

In the summer of 1962 Outler spoke at the Second Oxford Institute held at Lincoln College, Oxford. His involvement with the Oxford Institute came about in this manner: During the earlier years of Outler's tenure at Yale, back home at Young Harris, Dow Kirkpatrick had been appointed in 1946 as pastor to Outler's mother (Kirkpatrick had earlier served as pastor of Outler's brother John and sister Fan at St. Mark in Atlanta). Having watched the meteoric rise of Outler's prominence in the world of scholarship from his close association with Outler's family, Kirkpatrick had an acquaintance with Outler's accomplishments that few possessed. This allowed Kirkpatrick to have a ready answer when the occasion arose for a qualified *American* theologian to address the Oxford Institute.

But first a look at the Institute: As a 1946–1947 recipient of the Pilling Fellowship for study overseas, Kirkpatrick came to know Reginald (Rex) Kissack, who was pastor of the Wesley Memorial Church in Oxford. These two discussed the need of a center at Oxford University where international persons could gather, live, study, and worship together. At the time individuals over the globe were giving a lifetime doing theology under the Wesleyan banner with no place nor possibility to know and interact with each other. World War II was over, and international travel was once again a possibility.

Kirkpatrick states that the proposed center would serve two purposes: "It would give the World Methodist Movement a larger agenda than that of simply dedicating shrines. And it would correct the imbalance which sees Aldersgate as the birthplace of Methodism. Oxford would be recognized as equally vital as a place of its birth. [Having both sites would help Methodists remain] faithful to Wesley's balance of vital piety with sound learning."[87] Before World War II the World Methodist Movement was no more than a conference every ten years (comprised mainly of speeches) with meetings alternating among the United States, Canada, and Great Britain. Postwar efforts to revive the organization were begun by "Bishop Ivan Lee Holt, Elmer Clark and Oscar Olson. Through informal conversations, among themselves and British colleagues they got it going again. A conference was held in the United States, but the primary beginning was at a World Methodist Conference held in Oxford in 1951.

"I was asked to sound out the idea in the United States of a 'living memorial' by the establishment of a Center at Oxford for world Methodists. Rex would do the same in Britain. I presented the vision of such a center to Holt, Clark and Olson. I also visited some seminaries.

"In those days it was common to hear United States Methodists say, 'The British are much more theological than we.' I said, 'No, they just handle the English language with such facility it sounds like they know more than we do!' But the real reason for this evaluation came from the way persons were chosen to make major speeches at World Methodist Conferences. When the subjects were assigned to member churches, the British chose the person best suited for that topic. We have a list of dignitaries who have expense accounts. So we matched assignments and availability. Often the person doesn't do justice to the subject.

"'We have superior theological minds in the United States, but they never get a hearing on the World Methodist platform,' I said to Elmer Clark. He replied, 'Like who?' 'Albert Outler,' I responded along with other names. 'Oh, but Outler is not a member of the World Methodist Council,' Elmer shot back to me. 'That is precisely my point,' I said, 'you're running an *Old Boy's Club*. That's why a theological institute is needed.'

"Eventually, in 1958, the First Oxford Institute was held. The theme of the Second Institute (1962) was 'The Doctrine of

the Church.' Albert gave the opening lecture, 'Do Methodists
Have a Doctrine of the Church?' In his typical breezy and attractive style he began, 'the answer *yes* says too much; *no* says too
little . . . . In the beginning the people called Methodists had no
distinctive doctrine of the church—for the very simple reason
that they had no intention of becoming one.' (quote taken from
his lecture: Abingdon Press, 1964, pp. 11–12)

"He [Outler] was to be a member of subsequent Institutes.
At the Seventh he chaired the Working Group on Wesley Studies
and read a paper to the plenary, 'The Future Of Wesley Studies.'
At the eighth he did a paper titled 'Methodists in Search of
Consensus.' The papers of this Institute were published after his
death. The volume is dedicated 'To the Memory of Albert Cook
Outler.'"[88]

Almost Did Not Make It

It is interesting to note how close Outler came to *not* attending
Vatican II as an observer. While attending the Second Oxford
Institute he wrote a July 19, 1962, letter to Carla from Lincoln
College at Oxford, and casually dropped this sentence: "I've
been invited to be one of the three Methodist representatives at
the Second Vatican Council (which would amount to from two
to six months next year and the year following). This is another
exciting and exotic adventure, but I don't think I'll do it—don't
see how I can."

The Vatican II invitation was not even mentioned in a July
31, 1962, letter from Paris, where Outler was attending a WCC
meeting. The following comments reveal that his mind was elsewhere: "The [Faith and Order Commission] Working Committee
has started off rather peaceably and well. We have an enormous
agenda, planning for the Montreal Conference—and thereafter.
In this connection the oddest things keep on happening to me.
Without consultation, the chairman (the Lord Bishop of Bristol,
whose whiskers I have tweaked in times past) appointed me
chairman of the subcommittee on the program for the conference, as distinguished from the mechanics and business affairs—
with some very hard-eyed characters to deal with, like Wingren
of Sweden, who deeply disapproves of our Traditions project.
Then, to add to the confusion, the Geneva secretariat, have brought

a proposal that Tomkins should be chairman of the Montreal Conference and that D'Espine and I be the two vice-chairmen— and that I give one of the four public addresses at the Confer- ence. I shall try to get this modified, in one direction or another, but I find it altogether inexplicable as to how such a thing should have happened and am both intrigued, and inevitably, flattered."

Vatican II

Outler was making history while teaching history wherever he went. But Vatican II (1962–1965) gave him front-page billing on the biggest stage in history that he ever played on. Even there he was teaching the Romans *their* history.

Ordinary experiences found Albert teaching. On one of the afternoon walks of Bishop Bill Cannon and Albert on the streets of Rome during Vatican II, Bishop Cannon said to Outler: "Albert, what about that chain of hotels here? He must have been a wealthy man. Everywhere you turn around there is an *Albergo* hotel." Outler with a wrinkled brow bordering on squeamishness said, "Bill, that *is* the Italian name for 'hotel'!"[89]

During one session Outler thought he had a heart attack and stayed in the hospital for a week, which proved to be time well spent. With restored energy he kept round-the-clock engagements with Catholic groups from across the world, with fellow observ- ers, and with mixed groups. It did not take long for the Roman Catholics to do with Outler what he was doing with them—ob- serving him as he moved among them and their history with ease.

Ecumenical Institute at Tantur

Out of the weekly meetings with the secretariat arose the desire for a continuation of the meetings after the Council. Professor Skydsgaard presented this as a proposal in one of their audiences with Pope Paul VI, and the eventual consequence was the Ecu- menical Institute at Tantur. At this writing (1998) Rev. Thomas F. Stransky, CSP, the Roman Catholic who knew Albert and Carla better than any other Roman Catholic during the Vatican II years, is the rector of the Institute. Outler not only played a vital part in conceiving this new ecumenical venture on the part of the Roman Catholics, but also in instituting it. Under the leadership of Theodore M. Hesburgh, then president of Notre Dame, Outler worked to make this dream a reality. These are Hesburgh's words: "When I was trying to put together the Ecumenical Institute For Advanced Theological Studies in Jerusalem, Al Outler was one of the best of the five Protestant members of our advisory council. He was always practical, open minded, and ready to help.

"We met here and there around the world, and I can't remember a meeting that he missed. He was always there and always helpful. What is even more, he had a very practical side to him, and he never gave me advice that was impossible to follow or ill directed. I am deeply grateful to him for all of the help he gave me at that time."[90]

Roman Catholic/Protestant "Revival"

After Vatican II Outler was as busy dealing with ecumenical ramifications of the council as he was when attending the sessions. Outler invited Fr. Thomas F. Stransky, in conjunction with the participating universities, to lecture at the University of Texas at Austin, Southern Methodist University at Dallas, and Rice University at Houston. And then, during their last time together in the mid-1980s, Stransky and Outler co-preached a "revival" or mission to Catholics/Protestants in Corpus Christi, Texas. The evening services alternated between the Catholic and Anglican cathedrals. A spacious home on Padre Island was provided for the two "evangelists." Stransky cooked their breakfasts while Outler "cooked" up details on the high cholesterol content of eggs, the grams of fat in bacon and sausage, the calcium content of milk, and the percentage of fiber in the various cereals offered.

A Lamentation on Behalf of Roman Catholics

While Hesburgh initially intended to speak only for himself in this final note, he ended by including all ecumenically-minded Roman Catholics: "In a larger context, I always considered Al a very good friend and a very helpful person in every way possible. He was in and out of Notre Dame a great deal. If my memory does not deceive me [and it did not], I think we gave him an honorary doctorate on the occasion of Vatican Council Two and a Half, as the conference was called. Al was an extraordinary person, open-minded and yet firmly founded in principle. *We* have certainly missed him."[91]

(While more will be said about Vatican II and Faith and Order in Part 2, Chapter 6, of this book, a greater detailed look at these involvements may be found in Volume 7, "The Ecumenical Churchman," in *The Albert Outler Library*.)

Faith and Order of the World Council of Churches

Outler took a short time-out from Vatican II when in 1963 he attended the Faith and Order Conference at Montreal. He performed there with the same level of intellectual energy he had unleashed upon Vatican II. The Rev. Dr. John A. Newton, presently (1997) warden of John Wesley's Chapel in Broadmead, Bristol, says: "In 1963, at the Montreal Faith and Order Conference, I saw a good deal of Dr. Outler, being in the same small study group as himself. I had experience of the extraordinary range of his knowledge and of the power of his mind. After one hot evening session, a number of us were drinking cold drinks and talking informally. John Robinson's controversial book, *Honest to God,* had recently appeared, and the discussion turned to the issue of theism and philosophical arguments for belief in God. Dr. Harold Roberts, whose specialty was Philosophy of Religion, was propounding an argument with which Dr. Outler disagreed. It was not long before he had Dr. Roberts on the ropes, and, in the judgment of those present, by far the better of the argument."[92]

Young Harris Commencement Address

Among the dozens of speaking engagements received and accepted by Outler following on the heels of Vatican II, none was more welcome than the one from Young Harris College, where he gave the commencement address on June 7, 1970. The 'Eagles' Nest,' the name given by the students to the location of the Outler summer home, was a mere stone's throw from where he spoke. The old mountain cabin was gone but not the memories. The school honored Outler with a doctor's degree. But his greatest privilege came when he walked again that hill where Trail's

End once stood. It was for him another one of those sad/glad experiences.

The Development of Catholic Christianity

Flushed with his recent Vatican II notoriety, Outler returned home to Dallas ready to do something bold regarding catholic (universal) Christianity. That intention he developed at Vatican II. And he wanted more than Methodists and Roman Catholics to be involved in whatever was to be. So early in the summer of 1966 he and Perkins New Testament scholar Bill Farmer came up with the idea of starting a seminar on the development of Catholic Christianity. A special sort of cooperation between the practitioners of New Testament studies and church history was needed. These seminars were to answer that need. Scholars from other disciplines who had an interest in this relationship were invited to participate. They meet semiannually at the various institutions whose scholars are participants.

I was the guest of Bill Farmer at one of their seminars during the fall of 1995. The event, which was held at the University of Dallas (Roman Catholic), followed the same format it has followed since its 1966 inception: The seminar is preceded by an informal coffee hour, after which the seminar opens about 5:00 with brief papers from the responders (the main paper had been mailed earlier to each participant). Then opportunity is given for the author of the major paper to respond to the responses. Dinner is usually at 6:00, after which there is extended opportunity for general discussion of the major paper. In that evening's activities were found those who still refer to Outler as their mentor.

Out of this ecumenical array of scholars, whose specialty was to zero in on Christianity in the second century, came forth in the spring of 1981 the scholarly journal *The Second Century: A Journal of Early Christian Studies.* Growing with a wider scope and circulation, the journal in 1993 was absorbed into the *Journal of Early Christian Studies (Journal of the North American Patristic Society).* Its first editor was Church of Christ historian, Everett Ferguson, who in the first issue of the "new" *Journal of Early Christian Studies* said about the group's then-deceased elder mentor Outler: "Outler was lively and called forth life in others. His own grand conceptions put material in a large frame of reference and enabled others to see new relationships between points that might otherwise have remained disjoined."[93]

A New Perspective on the Church of Christ

The gathering of these scholars of second-century Christianity that I attended proved to be more ecumenical than the self-proclaimed ecumenical groups. Out of the twenty-one Roman Catholics, Baptists, Episcopalians, Presbyterians, Methodists, et al., present, four were Church of Christ theologians. Earlier Outler had opened the door for the Church of Christ scholars. He had lectured at their schools and was highly respected by them as a historical theologian.[94] Here is what Outler had to say in a September 4, 1985, letter to Walter Underwood about his new "discovery" of these folks: "All along, I have known what everybody else has known: that they are 'fundamentalists,' separatists—and contentious. But I had supposed that this carried with it the rest of the fundamentalist syndrome: obscurantists, pietists, mystics, sentimentalists, steeped in 'heart religion' and all that. At Abilene, at that conference I . . . got a new perspective on them. They are not especially pious or mystical or even sentimentalists; they spoke more often of John Locke and the 18th-century Scottish philosophers than of Luther or Calvin or the pietists and the mystics. They are, however, 'matter-of-fact supernaturalists' without embarrassment. Thus, with frankly biblicist premises, (plenary inspiration, literalist interpretation, etc.), they draw quite logical conclusions that 'the modern mind' finds startling (to say the least) but which *they* can take for granted, since their conclusions ('anti-organ,' for example) follow from their premises. Their 'style' in planning and staging the conference was as matter-of-fact and businesslike as a stockholders' meeting—and far less laden with cant than an SMU Board of Trustees' meeting."

Especially did Outler appreciate the gifts and graces of Church of Christ historian, Everett Ferguson, who became the chairman of the Editorial Board of *The Second Century.*

Under That Man's Spell

Bill Farmer told how he, in a typical professor's independent stance, first saw Outler when he (Farmer) arrived on the Perkins campus for the academic year 1959–1960 as New Testament professor. Farmer saw a group of persons standing in a tight circle, some looking over others' shoulders. Inside that circle of people was a slight-statured man whose talking had the whole group mesmerized. Farmer swore then that he would never fall under that man's spell.

As Farmer later looked, from the spectators' gallery at St. Peter's in Vatican City, upon Outler sitting in the front row of the observers' tribunal close to the delegated Roman bishops, cardinals, and the Pope, he thought: "This man is out of the ordinary, unusual, very different." For Farmer, Outler became more than a colleague. He became a mentor and, in a real sense, a pastor.

The Duodecim Theological Discussion Group

"This man is out of the ordinary, unusual, very different." Members of the Duodecim Theological Discussion Group also felt that way about Outler even when he was not present with them. Julian Hartt in a May 24, 1971, letter to Outler said: "You were keenly missed at the recent sessions of Duodecim. We had good discussions—there is lots of life in the company!—but at several points we had cheerfully to admit than your learning and lively wit would have lifted the conversation to a point measurably higher up the slope."

The Emory Offer

The quandary Outler had regarding a move to Austin Presbyterian Seminary (he never took the Penn State offer seriously and the one from Duke by Dean Cushman served only to strain relationships) was replayed all over again when his alma mater, Emory, set in the very midst of his Georgia roots, offered him full professorship in 1973. This was by far the most exciting offer he ever had—back home with unparalleled credentials, nearer to remaining family members, working with old friends, etc. But the calendar was against the move. Had this challenge come back in the 1960s, the situation would have been far different. Or would it? Recall that Perkins School of Theology had financed his involvement with Vatican II, and that carried on from 1962 to 1965. And he did have Wanda Smith, the best assistant he ever had, working with him on the Wesley Works. Whatever the case, he made the decision to stick with Perkins.

From James T. Laney, dean of Candler School of Theology at Emory, Outler received this September 25, 1973, letter: "Needless to say, we at Emory are keenly disappointed in your decision to remain at Perkins. At the same time we honor and respect your reasons. I just wish the year were 1968 rather than 1973, and maybe the situation would be different!

"Despite the outcome, I am grateful for our conversations and the privilege of getting to know you better personally. Your graciousness in all of our dealings; your thoroughness and care in reaching your decision—these have been most impressive to me.

"It is important to Christians everywhere that the years ahead be richly productive for you. I hope they will be personally rewarding as well in the Perkins setting."

Bishop William R. "Bill" Cannon, recent Emory dean, wrote Outler this October 8, 1973, letter concerning the matter: "I had been away, so I had not heard about the decision relative to Emory. Though I regret it terribly, I can understand your position and I support you in it. I can appreciate the terrible burden of moving at this stage of the game. I can see too the hesitancy in giving up such a good secretary and strong assistant. If Carla supports you in this, then the decision must be the right one, because the two of you together, with the guidance of the Holy Spirit, could not be wrong."

Ending on a High Note

Outler climaxed his active full-time teaching career with a stellar lecturing performance during the February 1974 Ministers' Week in McFarland Auditorium at Southern Methodist University. Comments and letters came from many in that audience. This March 19, 1974, letter from Ed Matthews to Outler is typical of the expressions that came from many who heard him on that occasion: "I doubt if your 'fan mail' has subsided to any lesser amount than it was a few weeks ago immediately following Ministers' Week, when I should have written—all of us pouring out our gratitude to you for what you mean to so many of us.

"Yet, I add my words to those countless ones, and repeat what many will have already said. But I feel that I must say that among the many, many things you mean to me, you have most of all personified that 'third alternative' with which you describe Mr. Wesley. (I have long since recognized this quality in you; your term 'third alternative' for Mr. Wesley just verbalized what so many of us feel about you.)

"Since I first became personally acquainted with you, when you came to Arkansas in 1956 as our State Methodist Student Movement speaker, in the midst of a day of efforts to tie labels on theologians, which has changed only in the sense of digging up a new set of labels today, you have for us all stood above those 'labels,' just being a 'simple Bible lovin' Christian,' as I once heard you answer a student wanting to know how you would label yourself. You have stood, and stand, as one who can listen to and speak with, add to and take from, most any position one might choose to espouse, and neither be gravely threatening nor threatened, careful not to tactlessly offend, nor compromise away your deep commitments. But mostly you stand as one pointing to that 'third alternative,' which is no cheap syncretism, yet calls forth the best from us all . . . namely calling us all to be more serious in the matter of being responsible to the Holy Spirit who regularly wants to deal with us about such 'positions' we zero in on.

"It is this matter of being open, honest with self, trying to grow, that has taught me much, and to you I am deeply indebted, for charting such a course.

"Well, I didn't mean to launch into all this . . . which must seem like platitudes to you . . . but for me such thoughts have been a light to keep me 'keeping on,' squaring up on Scripture, tradition, faith, and reason, and hammering out an image of church and morality that weathers all change."

Research Professor

The church remained Outler's "home" and "workplace" as he transitioned into official retirement from Perkins on June 1, 1974, at which time he was appointed Research Professor of Theology, Emeritus, at Perkins for a five-year period. (He retired from the North Texas Annual Conference in 1978.) In this capacity Outler remained on campus, making himself available for counseling graduate students, faculty members, and administrators. He taught at least one course each year while spending most of his time working with the help of his secretary, Wanda Smith, on the editing of the Wesley sermons.

The Wesley Sermons Project

Curiously, along the way, and as a historian of Christian doctrine, Outler "discovered" the patriarch of his own denomination, John Wesley, as an interesting theologian in his own right, but even more relevant as a synthesizer of much of the best in the whole of the Christian tradition. But Wesley was not careful with footnoting his sources. Outler was moved to do something for Wesley that Wesley did not do for himself. And that was to edit a new, critical *footnoted* edition of Wesley's *Works.*

Outler described what he brought to this monumental scholarly venture and what he hoped it would uniquely achieve: "Substantively my reputation will have to stand or fall with my lifelong teaching and research in the history of Christian thought (represented mostly by articles in 'learned' journals and chapters in symposia of various kinds) [plus the posthumously published nine-volume *The Albert Outler Library*]. All of this (plus my lifelong vocation in psychotherapy) has been background for the work I'm trying to finish, somewhat desperately now: a critical edition of John Wesley's *Sermons.* The LPT [*Library of Protestant Thought*] *Wesley* volume is a sample of this project—but by now, though, it seems embarrassingly *thin.* The distinctive contribution I'm trying to make now is to exhibit Wesley against his *ecumenical sources*—in contrast to the conventional studies of his career as 'founder of Methodism.'"[95]

Project Launched

Outler urged such a project on Dean Merrimon Cuninggim and the SMU authorities. A "Wesley Works Project" was actually launched, along somewhat different lines, and has resulted thus far in fifteen volumes out of a planned total of thirty-two. Outler dropped out of the larger project, frustrated by its tilt from its intended ecumenical orientation to a denominational affair. However, with the expert assistance of Wanda Smith, Kate Warnick, Page Thomas and his librarian-wife, Carla, he painstakingly

labored as unit editor of the four volumes of Wesley's *Sermons.*
To show the scope of the project: in the first volume alone there
are 324 footnotes in the Introduction and 3,910 footnotes in the
sermons themselves. Close to forty of Wesley's sources are left
for future researchers to dig up or stumble onto.

Poring Over Wesley's Quotes

Outler spent thousands of hours over a period of twenty years
poring over unfootnoted quotations Wesley made in substandard
handwriting. Outler's major research was done in the famous
reading room of the British Museum, where they have in their
collection every book published in Great Britain. He also found
Dr. Williams' Library a helpful source. And then there were the
official archives of British Methodism at John Rylands University Library in Manchester, the archives at Wesley's City Road
Chapel, Richmond Theological College (Surrey), Oxford
University's Bodleian Library, Wesley College (Bristol) and the
St. John's College library at Cambridge University, as well as
other universities in Europe and America.

The Rev. Dr. John A. Newton, presently (1997) the warden
of John Wesley's Chapel at Broadmead, Bristol ("The New Room
in the Horse Fair," the oldest Methodist building in the world,
dating from 1739), shares some of his experiences with Outler
during those research days in England: "I first met Dr. Outler in
the summer of 1959, as near as I can recall, when I was teaching
as a junior tutor at Richmond College, Surrey. The college library
included a room housing John Wesley's own library, or a major
part of it. The collection included first editions of Wesley's own
writings, corrected and annotated in his own hand. In the absence of autograph copies of many of these works, these books
were the nearest scholars could get to Wesley's original manuscripts. Dr. Outler spent several days working hard at these texts,
and noting Wesley's corrections.

"Our principal, Dr. Harold Roberts, gave me the pleasurable
task of looking after Dr. Outler—giving him coffee, taking him
for a walk when he needed some fresh air, and so on. The college gardens had a great variety of plants and shrubs, and Dr.
Outler paused at one bed, and pointing to a flower, said, 'Say,
John, do you know the name of that one?' I replied, 'I'm sorry,

Doctor, I don't.' He then—not boastfully but out of sheer interest—reeled off the botanical name of every plant in the large
bed! I mention this, because it exemplifies his immense intellectual curiosity and the great range of his knowledge. I think he
was the nearest person to a polymath [very and diversely learned]
I have ever encountered.

"From 1965 to 1972, I was Tutor in Church History and
Librarian at Wesley College, Bristol. I'm afraid I forget the year,
but I think it would have been about 1969 or 1970, when Dr.
Outler came to the college to work on the few manuscript sermons of Wesley in our collection. They were mostly early ones,
from his Oxford days. I went up into the gallery of the Library,
where he was working, to see if he had found what he needed
there. He then paid me the compliment of asking for help with a
brief note at the end of one of the sermons, which read: 'St. H.'
He was working on the assumption that it may have been a date,
and asked me, 'What d'you make of it, John? Is it 'St. Hugh' or
'St. Henry' or what?' Off the top of my head, and diffidently, I
said to him, 'Do you think it might be Stanton Harcourt, Doctor?' That was one of the Oxfordshire parishes where the young
Wesley preached—i.e., the reference was to a place rather than a
dating by the saint's day. He exclaimed—half with pleasure, half
with annoyance that he had not thought of that, 'You've got it,
John, you've got it!' It was a very small triumph for me, but I
was gratified that I had been able to assist him, in however
minuscule a way.

"During that same visit to Bristol, he asked to see Kingswood
School, originally founded for the sons of Wesley's preachers,
and now situated in Bath. I drove him over, and we were met by
a rather pompous senior member of the school staff. Before I
could introduce Dr. Outler properly, the senior master launched
into a lecture on the history of John Wesley, early Methodism
and Kingswood School, for the benefit of this American visitor I
had brought over. Outler took it all, with a seraphic smile on his
face, and never enlightened the lecturer, and nor did I."[96]

On one occasion while working in the basement of Epworth
House, Outler was shown the courtesies of the place. The curator
locked him in the room and would come by every so often to see
how things were going. Outler said: "In those intervals I could
go about looking at what stuff they've got there. While I was

rummaging around to see what they had that they knew they had and what they had that they didn't know they had, I found a box inside one of the safes. I opened the safe and found inside a cigar box. And inside the cigar box, to my very great astonishment, was the Field Bible. This has since been remedied because I could not keep it to myself—that this sacred icon that represents linkage between Mr. Wesley's personal authority and the personal authority of the Conference reposed for part of the past in a cigar box in the basement of City Road.[97] When I pointed out this incongruity, they went and fixed it up. And now it has a kind of monstrance in which it sits up and looks nice and pretty. But at least the relationship to *religio et eruditio et tobacco* has been changed."[98]

Inner Workings

Concerning the inner workings of the Wesley Works Project Bishop Cannon said: "When Outler began the Wesley Works, they had Bob Cushman, Joe Quillian, and me presiding in rotation. The main editors were Frank Baker at Duke and Albert Outler at Perkins. Cushman [the Duke dean] defended Baker vehemently; Quillian defended Outler vehemently. Finally, they came to me and said: 'You do all the sessions.'" This freed the four men to engage in vigorous exchanges as they worked on the project. Cannon continued, "Albert reminded me of Samuel Johnson in the eighteenth century. He did so much of what he did through consultation and a vigorous theological aggressiveness."

At times these heated exchanges spilled over into conferences where a dignified and respectful decorum normally prevailed. Richard Heitzenrater recalls: "I still had no hint of the depth of this competition two years later when, in the midst of the WMHS [World Methodist Historical Society] conference in Bristol, after Baker admitted that he had made a mistake in an earlier comment in the discussion, Outler, with a smile, quickly blurted out, "So much for infallibility!"[99]

Outler felt he had to be aggressive in his dealings with Frank Baker. And he remained aggressive in his editing the sermons. But he had a difficult time accepting that they were ready for publication. In his earlier days of scholarship, dilettante Outler turned out documents for publication at a record pace. He cranked out the manuscript *Who Trusts in God* in six weeks (note the number of publications in the bibliography). In his later years the tendency toward perfection outpaced the tendency toward expeditiousness; he had a difficult time letting go. In his editing of the sermons, Outler did all the introductions and footnotes while he had students looking up and verifying scripture. But when it came to ordering the sermons, things began to go in circles and led to no conclusions. First he put the sermons in the chronological order in which they were written. Then he decided to arrange them by their subjects in alphabetical order (as generally in the Jackson edition of ordering the sermons). Later he decided once again to rearrange the sermons chronologically.

While this reordering was being considered, the drafts of the introductions and prefaces were redrafted by Outler as many as four times. And all of this typing went on before the days of the computer. Meanwhile, in the estimation of some of those closest to the project, the papers were not improvements over earlier versions.

Another factor in this time-lengthening process was the on-going disagreements between the two elderly Wesley scholars, Outler and Baker. If either had a conviction at some point, the other often had a stronger one in another direction. Copy text editor Baker furnished the copy texts for Outler, who at times disagreed with Baker's decisions concerning the texts offered.

With these rumblings in the background Outler took the texts supplied to him by Baker and proceeded with his editing, sometimes taking liberties with the texts supplied to him by Baker; e.g., some of the texts did not have sermon titles, the reason being that Wesley himself did not title those particular sermons. He simply let stand the Scripture texts in the place of titles. In those cases Outler proceeded to title the sermons himself. The sermon on Hebrews 5:4, e.g., was usually known as "The Ministerial Office" or the Korah sermon. Outler changed this to "Prophets and Priests." "The Rich Man and Lazarus" became "Dives and Lazarus," etc. Most of this labor by Outler took place in the "salt mines," his little hideaway office in the basement of Bridwell Library.

Richard Heitzenrater was caught in the middle of ongoing disagreements between Outler and Baker. He recalled, "I consider myself a student of both. Baker, the antiquarian scholar who demanded that every detail of the eighteenth century be correct, was my dissertation advisor. Outler's office next to mine in the Bridwell Library was the place [where] I learned that, if those details were not in some way understood as being relevant to the twentieth century, they were not much more than historical trivia. Outler [would] call me wondering if Baker really meant such and such (code language for 'please tell him that I will bend only this far, so I don't have to put it in writing')."[100]

Heitzenrater continued: "The actual number of strong disagreements between Baker and Outler on the copy text was fairly small. The acrimony was based in a dispute over the basic approach to textual styling that occurred at the beginning. Outler for a more modern, open style; Baker for a more antiquarian, formal style. The board went with Baker, and Outler never quite got over it. In any dispute over matters relating to Wesley, Baker was seen by almost everyone as the longtime expert and Outler the newcomer (rightly so, in most cases). But Baker carried this position of power over into matter of opinion, and this rankled Outler."[101]

A glance over the shoulder at Outler's history of dealing with those who attempted to exert power over him in a condescending manner reveals a man who did not take to such goings-on lightly. His natural bent was to kick the traces. Which he did. Hard.

While Outler had Heitzenrater to help him deal with Baker in the last days of the editing process, he had Patrick Henry to be the nitpicker finding errors in his editing of all the sermons—from the first through the last. Henry said, "Albert and I are likely the only two people in the world who have meticulously read every word of every sermon that John Wesley preached."[102] Outler had been a friend of the Henry family for many years, making this a welcome chore for the young scholar. But it also proved to be a difficult task for Henry. In the years past it fell to Outler to advise young Patrick to go to Christ's Church, Oxford, where John Wesley went to school. And then when Patrick returned to the states to consider graduate study in patristics, Outler said, "You *must* go to Yale and study under Jaroslav Pelikan."[103]

But to Henry's relief, that imperious approach was not used by Outler with him or with the Wesley Sermons Committee when Outler *suggested* that Henry be the reader and editor of Outler's editing of the sermons. Out of friendship and respect for

Outler, Patrick Henry accepted the challenge of reassuring the publisher that every "i" was dotted and "t" crossed in the sermons. Here was a young scholar given the task of over and over having to show this surrogate father in the faith (who happened to be one of the world's premier scholars) where he had made some mistakes. Henry developed the fine art of correcting Outler without offending him, which was not easy to do. One thing Henry learned about Outler during those twenty years of working together on the Wesley sermons was that Outler "could tell you what to do, but he could also listen."[104]

Much relief for Outler came from Page Thomas, who worked as Outler's research assistant and did the bibliography, from secretary Wanda Smith, who worked with Outler on the project from December 1, 1963, until he "retired" again in March 1980; and from Carla, who entered corrections on the galleys sent back to the publisher.

The Pain of Working Relationships

The extended period of hard labor doing research was easy in comparison to the pain inflicted upon him in his working relationships with Frank Baker and a committee whose members talked and talked but to Outler's thinking did little to show they knew what they were talking about.

Outler forewarned Quillian, as the first president of the Board of Directors of the project, in a February 25, 1969, letter that problems with Baker could very easily arise and informed Quillian that those working conditions would be intolerable. Here are Outler's words: "About this business of the Wesley Works Project, I'm more and more inclined to concentrate on being the unit editor of the *Sermons*—and, if needed, one of the other *theological* units (like the *Appeals* or *Original Sin*)—and let the business of editorial supervision go. There's no use in having an Editor-in-Chief *and* an Editorial Board (especially the Editorial Board we have)—and Frank would like being Editor-in-Chief as much as Bob [Cushman] would like having him so. The only stipulation that I would make is that I will be unprepared to have Baker overrule me (or any other competent unit editor) *arbitrarily* on matters of editorial *judgment* and he *is* inclined to be arbitrary, especially on trivia that finally get to be important."

A Stroke of Genius

It was a stroke of genius on Quillian's part when he, in the school year 1977–1978, brought to the Perkins faculty Richard Heitzenrater, trained under the tutelage of Frank Baker. Heitzenrater was hired to teach church history and Methodist studies, but it was no small matter for Quillian to have him also assist Outler with the Wesley sermons. So important was Heitzenrater's help to Outler that his first term was spent assisting Outler with footnotes, etc., which speeded up the editing process considerably. This close relationship allowed Heitzenrater to be eased into the role of mediator between Baker and Outler. Heitzenrater did not solve the problem between Baker and Outler, but his presence allowed the project to continue to the end.

The Problem Persisted

But the problem persisted. And then on October 15, 1979, Outler wrote to Quillian: "It turns out—as I suspected all along, but rather more so than I had imagined—that Frank's self-understanding as 'Editor-in-Chief' is literal and very nearly absolute. Wanda and I knocked ourselves out this past mid-August to get 1,500 pages (vol. 1) to him—*after* they had been revised in light of many useful 'corrections' and 'suggestions' from both Patrick Henry III and Dick Heitzenrater (as competent a pair of nitpickers as you could nominate!). I knew that the work would have to be 'styled' for the compositor (that's standard procedure); I knew that it could bear further refinement. What I wasn't prepared for, however, was the *level* of the hassling that began immediately and that looks now as if it might stretch out over a long, unhappy—and fruitless—future. For example, I'd agonized [for fifteen years] over the 'ordering' of the sermons . . . and had come to a conclusion that is less than perfect but somewhat more defensible than any previous ordering. Frank responded quickly by suggesting 'a *minor* change,' but it involved a major misunderstanding of the rationale I had already set out in the Preface and Introduction (and that both Henry and Heitzenrater had found persuasive). I was assured that I would have the final decision— but we then took two exchanges of letters and a long telephone discussion (debate, actually) before he could bring himself to let my order stand (and even then he hoped that I would see the light before he sent the thing on).

"The point is not whether my ordering is right *or* wrong, but whether we are going to hassle over every jot and tittle that strikes Frank as questionable in the whole unit. Another example, shall we use a hyphen in 'Wesley-studies' or not—or, is my contrast between 'the Edwardian *Homilies*' and the Elizabethan ones bibliographically correct? Since Wesley never used the phrase 'native Americans,' should *I* use it? Etc., etc. Last week, he brought along a seven-page, single-spaced memorandum on the first 150 pages (the Introduction)—*without the footnotes!*—150 pages out of 1,000. And we spent nearly four hours sorting out the wheat from the chaff—with my agreeing with him on every point I could and a few I wish I hadn't.

"Again, the point is not that I object to careful and minute criticism. Indeed, I welcome it and have urged Frank simply to proceed with all non-substantive revisions, including some that strike me as faintly ridiculous and crotchety. But a quick calculation suggests that this could go on and on, for more years than either of us has to count on. Thus, if Frank proposes to edit the *whole* project after this fashion, it's obvious that it is simply not going to get done—ever.

"He *is* an expert in many respects of Wesley-studies—incomparably better than I at many levels. I need and count on his help at 'styling' and on many points of fact and evidence. If we were both ten or twenty years younger, I might even relish some of these picayunish debates. But we *aren't* younger, and the debates *are* picayunish. His and my relationships need not concern you—or any of the others. The point is that they highlight this large problem: of his determination to edit the whole project, jots *and* tittles, and as if his own limited general education and experience were normative for each jot and tittle (e.g., we had another brief hassle over the punctuation of the Greek interrogation point; it took a checkout of a raft of lexicons to settle the point, and my feeling is that he's still unconvinced inside!).

"If this sounds ungrateful for the really priceless help he has been and can be to the Wesley Works Project, or that I'm appealing for help on my side of the counterproductive wranglings, then I've not made my real point. The '*real* point' is that the whole project may be endangered by this sort of thing and that the future of the cause of Wesley-studies in general is a rightful concern of those no longer responsible for *this* edition. It is in these terms that I bother you with these comments—since I'm morally certain that you've already got something like them in your own mind.

"The crucial problem is twofold: first, Frank's self-conceived role as 'Editor-in-Chief' (viz., as actual editor of every page of every unit); and, second, his honest conviction that he is the only fully competent Wesley scholar in the world who can carry this edition through to its proper end. This means, among other things, that Frank is out to discredit all *former* editors and editions—and this is bound to create serious confusion among readers who still have access to Jackson, Sugden, Curnock and Telford. Nothing but trouble can come from such triumphalist conception. One of the basic rules in *good* editing is: 'always acknowledge your debts to your predecessors'!

"This one-man band concept of editorship is what Ray Morris foresaw early on—and it was one of his reasons for getting out. This is what Cushman *wanted*—and that's when *I* got out. The original idea was collegial in its essence; what has evolved is collegial in only a *pro forma* sense. I realize that this complaint can be interpreted as churlish—and even jealous. Cushman thought so, and that spoiled a lifelong friendship. [The "spoiling" likely began when Outler rebutted Cushman's insistence that Outler return to Duke.] Private affairs quite aside, though, there are the stark questions of time and cost-benefits involved. How long will it take Frank to edit Wesley the way he wants to? Will he really get the *Bibliography* done (the *one* thing he really can do better than any of the rest of us)? How long can he hold to so heavy a pace and overload? How long can the expectations already raised about a 'new edition' of Wesley' be put off without serious harm to the larger cause? Already, quick-and-easy schemes for new Wesley publications are springing up like mushrooms, and Ron Patterson [Abingdon's editor working with the Project] is not going to bide his time forever. By the same token, how long will the present Board of Directors (and Editorial Board) continue intact? Cushman and Baker shaped the project to their vision of it, but now Bob's off the stage, with Langford to follow—and after that . . . ! Oxford's interest in and commitment to the project have weakened—now that Colin Roberts and Henry Chadwick have moved on—and I've no heart to shore them up (as a member of their editorial board) as things stand now and as the future looms.

"Again, this is *not* an 'intervention' on my own behalf; I've already made my partial peace with a foreseeable anticlimax to an overblown career. It is the much larger cause that concerns me, with its wider ramifications in contemporary theology and ecumenism. *This* is what I would hope that the Board of Directors would recognize and face up to. Moreover, I've no unsolicited 'solutions'; that would seem even more self-serving than this letter already must seem. But, it is demonstrable that serious interest in Wesley-studies *is* growing (in circles where we had no right to expect response twenty years ago), and it really would be too bad, strategically, for the new Wesley edition to inhibit this interest and not foster it."

'The Cause' in Jeopardy

A behind-the-scenes stepping on Outler's traces got to be more than he could handle when it finally came to the publishing of the fourth volume of the Wesley Works. In a March 28, 1985, letter to one of Abingdon's editors Outler said: "I am told [that] Mr. Gifford has a revised manuscript of Volume 3 that I have not seen and will not see until the postman brings the galleys, with an invariably 'tight schedule' which I will then be supposed to meet. That will mean that I will bear responsibility for all its flaws and glitches, without ever having had the chance to deal with them and with no chance to explain them to whatever critical readers may ever see the volumes.

"But, and this is why I write you now with real embarrassment, it is bound to sound as if it is only my vanity that has been bruised from having been 'used' so brazenly by self-serving people. Actually, it is now 'the cause' that is in jeopardy, since Volume 4 has most of the '*new*' sermons, with explanations about the ones hitherto mistakenly attributed to John Wesley. Thus, I have come to the reluctant decision that, unless I am allowed to participate in the final revisions of Volume 4 (supposing I am around by then), I will be forced to deny permission to have my parts of it published.

"I shall be saying this same thing to Professor Baker and to Dean Kirby with scant hope of being comprehended. They have had me over a barrel for so long that they have come to take this posture for granted. Now, however, I am prepared to 'plant my foot' (as Wesley often said) and withdraw from the project.

"This is the unhappiest development in the whole of my career (which has had its share of encounters with strong-minded men and women and such give-and-take). But 'Wesley's cause' cannot be well served by me unless I have some autonomy in the service—and this has been an alien notion in this project since Dr. Baker took it over.

"Thanks for the shoulder, and towel. If you think I am wrong or overreacting, I would be glad to have your counsel as to a wiser and more constructive procedure. If you find any sympathy for my dilemma, I would be grateful for your help. In any case, all the best to you and yours in your work."

Outler's Dilemma Expressed to James Kirby

James Kirby, who succeeded Quillian as dean of Perkins School of Theology, also succeeded Quillian as the president of the Wesley Sermons Project's Board of Directors. And heard from Outler about his bouts with Frank Baker *before* Kirby arrived in Dallas, via this June 19, 1980, letter: "The occasion for this rather ridiculous and time-wasting letter [referring to Baker's enclosed letter] is a single point of difference between me and Prof. Baker as to editorial method in my new edition of Wesley's *Sermons,* of which he is editor-in-*chief!* In my preface I have made the suggestion that since, in his quotations from the Psalms Wesley habitually preferred the BCP [*Book of Common Prayer*] Psalter, unless otherwise indicated, as by 'AV' [Authorized Version]. Prof. Baker had written three pages in support of his contrary view since we had already agreed, in 1973, to use the AV as 'norm.' We are now irrevocably committed to footnoting every reference to the Psalms that is *not* from the AV. This will add on a great many 'BCP' annotations in the notes that, in my view, are unnecessary (and expensive and cumbersome). But his further, and personal, point was that I was defying 'the agreement of 1973' which now, apparently, has the form of the laws of the Medes and Persians. Hence, the enclosed reply."

[At this point Outler goes into detail explaining "the unedifying tensions that have characterized our efforts to work together since 1965."]

"I hope it goes without saying that I would not bother you with minutiae like this if I didn't think it useful for you to know, somewhat more concretely, why my job with the *Sermons* has been prolonged and complicated rather more than it might have otherwise. What has made it worse is that Prof. Baker has been consistently supported in his role as Editor-in-Chief by the Board of Directors and the Editorial Board. Under anything like normal circumstances, I would have thrown up my assignment as unit editor of the *Sermons,* and I have often wanted to, since it has been like a heavy millstone around my neck, in terms of other interests in my career. But I am earnestly committed to the larger cause of a new kind of Wesley Studies and it may be that this new edition of the *Sermons* will contribute something to that larger cause. No part of the job has been very easy—and the circumstances under which I have had to work have been less than optimal.

"There is nothing I am asking of you, except to try to understand the problem thus illustrated: of a *modus cooperandi* between a historian of Christian thought (trying to place Wesley within that history) and a Wesleyan specialist with incomparable expertise in his specialty, but with limited interests in the broader theological issues that are at stake.

"This calls for no reply and no specific action. Just have it in mind as you continue your work with the Project."

After Kirby's arrival at Perkins as dean, the pressures continued for Outler to get the *Sermons* completed on schedule. Kirby's relations with Outler were on the blink the day he set foot on the Perkins campus. Kirby had allowed events to build on Quillian's efforts to oust Outler from his Smith Hall office and, from Outler's understanding, lay claim on the seminary's behalf to Outler's *Wesley Sermons* papers. But Kirby's most vocal displeasure had to do with Outler's completion of the *Wesley Sermons.* At one point a disturbed Kirby "told Outler that, unless the material was turned in within four months, he [Kirby] was pulling the flag down on the project."[105] While Outler bristled at the threatening tone of Kirby's confrontation, he made no effort to keep Kirby from "pulling the flag down" on his twenty years of hard labor. When reasoning returned to Kirby, he approached Heitzenrater and entreated the young scholar to persuade Outler to hand over his work for Heitzenrater to do the final editing. Heitzenrater, without using threats, persuaded Outler to let him have the notebooks with the understanding that Outler would still be working on them as long as they were doing final editing, including through the galley stage. That agreement between Outler and Heitzenrater broke the logjam.

We now know that, in spite of all these problematic relationships, the Wesley *Sermons* are edited and published, and the "Wesley cause" has been well served because of it. Heitzenrater put it this way: "Here were two strong personalities [Baker and Outler], two strong scholars (but with different goals and different expertise on the same subject)—when they were forced to make contact, it was like the coming together of two powerful electromagnets with the same polarity—if too close, sparks and damage; if controlled distance, great energy and motion; in the long run, the project has benefited tremendously from the energy; and few have even known about, much less seen, the sparks."[106]

Vainglory never figured in Outler's recall of the inner workings of the Wesley *Sermons* project. He recalled no glory for himself or Baker or anybody else. He was the first to say, if there is any glory, it goes to God.

The Publication

The Wesley *Sermons* project was first accepted for publishing by Oxford University Press, only to be derailed; next came a rejection by Abingdon under Publisher Proctor; and then the *Sermons* appeared with the imprint of the Abingdon Press under Publisher Feaster. After the project came to a halt in Oxford's hands, it took some doing to get it back on track with Abingdon Press. On October 14, 1982, Outler called me in Longview, Texas, concerning his Wesley *Sermons* project's cancellation by Oxford University Press. Twenty years of his life were going down the drain, and he felt as if he were going down with them.

I volunteered to call Bishop Crutchfield, who at the time was in Oklahoma. I arranged for Bishop Crutchfield to be at the Outlers' home in Dallas on Saturday, October 16, for a 9:00–10:00 A.M. meeting. While Outler had proved himself a first-rate negotiator for the seminary in dealing with *others,* he would never undertake negotiating on his own behalf. It was typical of Outler in those situations *not* to initiate the talking; I, noting a nod from Outler, proceeded to relate the situation to Bishop Crutchfield, who listened and then got further facts from Outler by asking questions. He then called Abingdon Publisher Proctor in Nashville and explained the situation to Proctor. In fewer than ten minutes, Bishop Crutchfield hung up the phone, came back into the living room and said, "It is done."

Outler and I thought that meant the Wesley *Sermons* would be published. It did not. All it amounted to was that the conversation at that time was over. What it did do was set off a major hassle in Abingdon's Publishing Committee. Outler called Ron Patterson, Editorial Director and Book Editor for Abingdon, to check on matters and to ask for Ron's support. Meanwhile Ewing Werlein, chairman of the Board of the Methodist Publishing House, had talked with Outler and was totally committed to the project. When Bob Feaster came on board as the publisher of The Methodist Publishing House in the fall of 1983, it was practically a "done deal."[107] Then the publishing committee voted *for* the project. Though Feaster was the publisher, he gives these others credit for getting Abingdon Press committed to the project. Book Editor Patterson not only was charged with seeing that the delicately footnoted Wesley *Sermons* papers handed to him were properly edited for the final galleys, he also had to play the role of counselor/mediator between the two scholars.

The Presentation of the Wesley Sermons

At the General Conference session held on May 5, 1984 (commemorating 200 years of American Methodism), a leather-bound Volume I of the Wesley *Sermons* was presented to some of its key players. The chair of the Conference recognized the new publisher of the United Methodist Publishing House, Robert Feaster, who in turn introduced UMPH's book editor, Ronald Patterson, who presented a leather-bound Volume 1 of the Wesley *Sermons* to James Kirby, president of the Wesley Works Board of Directors. Patterson then presented a leather-bound volume to Frank Baker. UMPH's board chair, Ewing Werlein, made the final presentation of a leather-bound Volume 1 to the editor of the Wesley *Sermons,* Albert Outler. *That* presentation triggered a rousing standing ovation on the part of the delegates and visitors.

Professor Emeritus

Officially Outler's title of Research Professor in Theology was intended to cease on May 31, 1979. In an April 1979 letter to Bishop William C. Martin, Outler wrote: "On May 31st, I become *emeritus,* the current translation of which here is 'out of sight, out of mind.'" From that point on he was Professor Emeritus in Church History and Theology.

As these days lengthened, they deteriorated from "good" to "worse," hardly touching "bad." Outler's last days at Yale had a last-minute communication glitch that marred his departure. But the results of that misunderstanding were readily overcome. At the very minimum, common grace prevailed between the dean of Yale and Outler. Not so with his departure from Perkins, which, from Outler's standpoint, was distasteful. Nobody was on-site to get the true story of how once-good friends became alienated. One of the first signals that something was wrong came in a telephone call from Dean Quillian to me in Longview, Texas. Quillian, in a most exercised, exasperated manner, broached me in order to get me to "help get Al out of his study," which at that time was in the vault of Bridwell Library. The dean needed the space, and he said that Outler wouldn't budge. (Quillian had just left Outler's study following a heated exchange about the matter.) I responded with a statement indicating that I would prefer not to become involved with this dispute, suggesting that the two men could surely come to a meeting of the minds on how to make that transition.

Outler put forth his account of what happened on that occasion in a November 28, 1979, letter to Bill Scales, a Texas Conference pastor: "As you know by now, our well-intentioned plan [to purchase the personal Outler library for Bridwell Library] has backfired and must be abandoned. On the 20th, Dean Quillian came charging into the study [the vault study], very angry, and bluntly charged me with an attempt to 'pull off an end-run' around *his* authority—to direct all matters involving Perkins' money or even money for Perkins. He is obsessed with this notion of authority and resentful of anything that he construes as a challenge to him. I wasn't prepared to accept such a charge, and so I am sorry to report that our relations have come to the point of serious rupture.

"Among other things, he made the point that I may have no other alternative except to stay on here, on whatever terms that he may provide. These 'terms' begin with a move out of my present situation in Bridwell Library, to an office study in Smith Hall, *without a secretary.* One of the comments was that no dean at any other place would have a place for me, what with my age and health. I mention this as an illustration of the intensity of his feelings—and yet his insensitivity toward mine. He may be right about no other alternative. We shall see about that. Even so, we will do this reluctantly, since Mrs. Outler and I would have preferred to stay on in Dallas. For one thing, selling our house here and buying another elsewhere, at this time, would amount to a substantial loss (and a great deal of fruitless bother).

"The prudent and gracious way forward, then, is for you and your committee to drop this particular project about my books and future, and press on with the larger project of the Chair and its program. One way or another, Dean Quillian and I will work out our present estrangement or turn to whatever alternative providence may discover for us. The Chair of Wesley Studies and the program that we all hope will develop around it is the crucial cause to which you are committed, both with this dean and with his successor. My own hope and prayer is that *that cause* will succeed and bear much fruit, on a time scale that will far outlast the personal concerns of any of us. I take seriously the motto in Westminster Abbey about God's burying his workmen, but his continuing to oversee and provide for his work!"

While no human can judge what Providence does or does not do in the process of redemption, what is seen "through a glass darkly" concerning this Quillian/Outler affair is this: the Outler library books problem was resolved. I, unaware of any misunderstanding pertaining to Outler's personal library (that was never mentioned in my telephone conversation with Quillian), talked with Ruby and Wayne Crisman, members of Longview First United Methodist Church, about the matter. They in turn gave $70,000 to the Texas Annual Conference to purchase the personal library of Outler for the Bridwell Library.

Southern Methodist University President Shields honored the Crismans with a dinner. From all outward appearances both Dean Quillian and Outler were very pleased that their strained relations no longer existed. But the idea presented by Quillian that Outler would be unwanted by any other dean (because of age and health) served only to make Outler realize that he was unwanted by this dean.

Cause of the Rift

The following February 11, 1974, letter from Quillian to Outler suggests the finest of relationships: "I do not need to add much in writing to what I have said to you verbally concerning Ministers' Week, but I do want to say the gist of it on paper.

"This the best Ministers' Week we have ever had, it seems to me. Many things went into it, but outstanding for us all were your lectures. As I commented to you, the ovation was genuinely for you, but it also was for Mr. Wesley and for the renewal of hope that the brethren sensed, feeling that they now have the prospect of some handles for the doing of theology in a vital and meaningful way.

"I was enormously proud of you as colleague, representative of Perkins, spokesman to and for the church, and as the friend I hold in such a special esteem and affection."

Something happened to change that relationship. It was known that Dean Quillian was "running" for bishop (prior to the 1980 Jurisdictional Conference at Lincoln, Nebraska). It was during that time frame that the relations between the two men began to go sour. From this point on it was a tragic experience in the lives of both men and for the seminary.

Word first came out across the Southwest Texas Conference [Dean Quillian was a member of the North Texas Conference] that Outler was not supporting Dean Quillian as a proposed candidate for the episcopacy in the 1980 South Central Jurisdictional Conference. Federal Judge Tom Reavely of Austin, Texas/ Washington D.C. recalls that, on a flight from Lincoln to Dallas following the Jurisdictional Conference, Dean Quillian expressed his feelings to Reavely. Quillian felt that Outler worked against him in the election. "But," Judge Reavely later reported, "that is not the way it was. Outler had been approached by delegates across the Jurisdiction and told that support for Quillian was not there—that supporting him would hurt him in the long run. Albert talked with me about the matter. It was his decision simply not to take a position in the election."

Further Clarification

Further clarification comes in a March 23, 1976, letter from Outler to Jack Heacock: "Up until a few days ago I was opposed to Joe Quillian's being elected bishop because I thought we needed him here (where his *overall* influence for good exceeds that of most bishops) more than the UMC needed him—and because I thought *he* understood his vocation in those terms. But, as the situation here has developed, it becomes clearer and clearer that he 'wants out' of this deanship and that there are influential people in the administration and Board of Governors willing to speed him on his way. This is tragic—for Quillian stands next to Luther Weigle amongst the best deans I've known in America (and that will add up to a couple or three dozen!).

"This being so, I'm now prepared to see him elected bishop (and to help him, as far as I can)—for his alternative (i.e., to return to teaching) would be a mite shy of the ideal. And this means that I hope your efforts in the Southwest Texas delegation (and elsewhere) bear fruit. It also means that I'd be glad to be 'let in' on whatever you know about the present state of the Quillian cause—and, obviously, in strict confidence on my part, too, for I've not talked to Joe about this and do not aim to, until I know more nearly what 'the score' really is."

This word of Outler's final willingness to support Quillian either never got to Quillian, or it got to him too late. In Quillian's mind the damage was done. His sources pegged Outler as a big cause of his loss of support. There is no evidence in the correspondence that Outler ever realized Quillian was fed this information about Albert's assumed lack of support. Nor is there any evidence to indicate that the two men ever talked about the election.

Lost Zeal

Quillian, who once vigorously defended Outler in his Wesley *Sermons* debates with Baker, lost his zeal about the time that Outler was, in Quillian's thinking, without zeal in helping elect

Quillian a bishop. How much, if at all, bruised feelings played in Quillian's dealings with Outler from that point on is not known. But this is known: Through a dean's directive Outler was forced to give up the larger vault study in the Bridwell Library for a much smaller one in Smith Hall before September 1980. That directive by Quillian to move Outler was made only a few weeks following the conference. This suggests that the personal disappointment that Quillian felt concerning what he considered his Outler-engineered defeat triggered his efforts to move Outler. Assuming that Quillian's decision to move Outler out of his vault study in Bridwell Library answered a legitimate need for space, his adversarial approach to Outler plus Outler's gifted ability to stand his own ground hardly helped accomplish a smooth transition.

The Dispute over Ownership of the Wesley *Sermons* Papers

Quillian's assumption that Outler was working against his episcopal election started well before the Jurisdictional Conference and likely was a motivating factor in Quillian's frontal attack assertion via a February 20, 1980, letter to Outler. In the letter Quillian stated that the Wesley *Sermons* papers were the legal property of Perkins School of Theology. Outler responded to Quillian in a letter dated February 28, 1980: "On page 2, paragraph 3a., you say: '*All* of the papers and working apparatus developed in the work pertaining to the Wesley Works Editorial Project would, I think, clearly belong *to* Perkins School of Theology.' If this could be construed to mean that this material, culled or even xeroxed, would fittingly belong *at* Perkins, since they were largely developed there, there would be no difficulty for me. Since there is to be an ongoing program of Wesley Studies at SMU, I would *want* my papers and notes where they might continue to support that program in any way they could. Nor could it require a decanal directive that I share the results of my studies with other interested and qualified students: what else have I been doing for forty years?

"But if you mean that *all* my papers (personal correspondence, etc.) and *all* the working apparatus' of this project (bibliographical and lexical notes, etc., etc.) *already* belong to Perkins' campus, I would *have* to leave *all* of this material behind—then obviously, I would have to demur, not only on grounds of an alienation of personal rights but on the grounds of the clear principles and precedents of academic freedom and propriety. I would much prefer not even to open this case for argument here, since I would far rather continue on the assumption that even a modicum of goodwill and good faith can solve this problem to almost everybody's mutual satisfaction, in some other way than legal contestation. But it is urgent that the crucial point be clear: The originals of my research materials in the Wesley *Sermons* project are as securely my own as are the materials left from the LPT *Wesley,* or my Vatican papers and files [some of which are still confidential], or any of the successive drafts of all those lectures, here and there, which are still only half-finished because of my preoccupation with this *Sermons*-unit for fifteen years. Others are welcome to their use—this goes without saying—but not to their alienation.

"I hope you realize how utterly distasteful it is for me to be writing this sort of letter in this tone and style. In forty-five years of academic life, I have always found such problems working themselves out in accordance with the *mores* and *ethos* of academia and not exposed to legal adversary proceedings. Carla and I are at least as anxious as anybody else for a 'graceful exit' here—and 'peace at last.' My paramount concern, from first to last, is and has been the promotion of the larger and longer cause of Wesley Studies here—and with as much productivity in research and writing as may be left in the time there may be to work, here or elsewhere. This is why I feel threatened, *on this one point,* by what purports to be a legally enforceable claim to what I have always regarded as my own private property. The problem is that the document is open to two possible constructions by you and your successor: a friendly and positive one and the other, hostile and adversary.

"My hope and prayer is that both of you will find the friendly construction the more reasonable one, for all parties involved. Otherwise, Carla and I need to know where we stand—to plan accordingly. This would mean that there really would be no 'peace at the last' and that would be as needless a miscarriage of good intentions (and an immense investment of labor and love on both sides) as I can really imagine."

Needless to say, Quillian's challenge as to the Wesley papers' ownership would hardly motivate Outler to work the next few months for Quillian's episcopal election. And would certainly be enough to cause Outler to take the position that he did take. And that was, as Judge Reavely stated, simply to take no position, which could have easily been taken by Quillian as a "statement" against.

Given the natural bent of Outler to rebut forcefully anyone who revealed a condescending attitude in making demands of him, the end of this once amicable relationship was inevitable. Outler turned his attention toward the new dean, and Quillian, thoroughly disgusted with "the whole mess," headed for the hills of Washington state in 1980.

Quillian's Final Directive

Within days of the aforementioned challenge to Outler concerning the Wesley papers, the following directive went from Quillian to Outler in a February 20, 1980, letter: "The two offices that you will occupy in Smith Hall are committed to you through May of 1982 at no rental charge. This is done with the approval of the Provost. The reason for the commitment to May 31, 1982, extending a year into the tenure of my successor as dean is simply because the arrangement for 1981–1982 would have to be made before he takes office. Your occupancy of the offices beyond May of 1982 will be entirely a matter to be decided between my successor and you, with the period that I have indicated neither constituting a mandatory terminus nor implying an option to extend."

The New Dean

When Dean Kirby arrived on the scene after Quillian left in 1980, he, without the baggage of Quillian's injured feelings and with the need to establish his own leadership style, permitted circumstances to move Outler expeditiously out of his study space in Smith Hall well before the May 1982 arrangement agreed upon by Quillian and the University Provost. In a September 29, 1997, letter to me, Kirby (now a professor at Perkins) said: "When I arrived at SMU in 1981, faculty and staff of the School of

Theology were occupying offices in the basement of Smith Hall. We, in fact, were using the entire floor and compensating the University out of our budget for the space. Albert Outler had two rooms which had been given when he moved from Bridwell Library. As you said, Joe Quillian had made that decision before I arrived. I don't recall the date, but sometimes during the regular school year I was notified by the head of the Physical Plant that Smith Hall was scheduled for renovation and we would have to vacate by the end of the spring semester. Shortly after that, Student Life notified me that after the building was finished, it would be fully utilized by students."

When this straightforward message was relayed to Outler (with no modifications allowing for Outler's office space), Outler set into motion his final move from the Perkins campus. He left Smith Hall in 1981 (not 1982 as Quillian had mentioned). For all practical purposes Outler's on-campus activities ceased at the time he moved from Smith Hall.

No Office Space

In a span of a few months Outler was moved from the Bridwell vault office to the much smaller Smith Hall office under Quillian, and from the Smith Hall office to no office under Kirby. The church outside the walls of the seminary just simply could make no sense of it. The people out in the boondocks saw Outler in the light of SMU chancellor and former president Dr. Willis Tate, who said at Outler's 1974 retirement luncheon: "I must testify what great eminence this man has brought to this university. Wherever I travel around this country and around the world, and I am identified with SMU, people always say, 'That is where Albert Outler is.' And when they say it, I walk a little taller."

The official Perkins position was "no space for Outler." Bill Scales chaired the Texas Conference committee charged with raising one million dollars for The Albert Outler Chair of Wesley Studies for Perkins School of Theology. Albert's good name "earned" the one million dollars for Perkins. In an April 4, 1978, letter, Scales expressed another position that a multitude of people across the church shared: ". . . it would be criminal to let a person of your stature leave the SMU campus

FOR ANY REASON. I will say at least that much at the proper time and with the proper persons. Let me know whatever else any of us could do."

Outside Initiatives Nonproductive

In a January 4, 1982, letter to Judge Tom Reavley, Outler wrote of his feelings about the whole matter: "I am more grateful for your interest in my 'leftover career' than I know quite how to say. But the more I have reflected on the situation here, the more I am inclined to counsel caution against your doing much more, lest Dean Kirby, John Deschner, Jim Ward and my other colleagues be able to construe it as 'pressure' that they would have to resist, on principle. There is no want of goodwill here; it is simply their (regretful?) judgment that my case [the Wesley project] is not 'exceptional' enough to warrant exceptional treatment—and they are determined to avoid a precedent that they cannot sustain. That, clearly, was the signal that Kirby was sending to George Ricker [in a November 24, 1981, letter to Ricker, pastor of University United Methodist Church in Austin, Texas]. It explains both the interest *and* the reluctances of John Deschner, Charles Prothro, *et al.* What is more, I see their point, given their premise that 'equal treatment for all' is more important than 'optimum productivity for everyone.' You and I know other places with other *mores;* SMU is not yet ready for comparison with them. Thus, it could well be counterproductive to prod this new administration; even a nudge could be misinterpreted, since they are not quite certain that *I* am not behind these various unwelcome initiatives 'from outside.' Now that I think of it, this may have been the reason that the Meadows Foundation decided that their single-grant-in-aid of my Wesley project be handled by a local church rather than through the seminary. And it is being managed through Oak Lawn Methodist Church, in a separate account in their budget for a congregational 'Institute for Wesley Studies.'

"Their business manager has handled requisitions for payments to the various people who have helped me in various projects. It is important to me that you, of all people, *not* misinterpret these musings on *sic transit gloria mundi,* as self-pity. Far from it. I have already had the most extraordinary career of anyone I know of, with comparable gifts and graces [a typical Outler understatement when talking about himself]; and, at bottom, there is a solid sense of thankfulness and peace. I do regret that there will be no proper 'harvest' of it all; there is, however, no profit in dwelling on what might have been."

That regret subsided somewhat when later in 1988 I published some of Outler's edited sermons with Abingdon Press. I then apprised him, while visiting him in the spring of 1989, of a plan to publish eight books that would compose *The Albert Outler Library*. He readily agreed to it, which was a surprise since he was normally reluctant to permit unperfected documents to be published. Those books are being published posthumously by Bristol House, Ltd. Carla's comments suffice: "Albert would be so pleased."

Related to all this, in a February 12, 1985, letter to Pastor Wayne Odom, Outler wrote: "You will know that the contributions to the Oak Lawn Wesley Studies Institute have come from various sources, and that the present sum is within sight of being used up within a year or two. This prospect was brought to the attention of Jim Moore, the new pastor of St. Luke's (Houston) by our mutual friend, Bob Parrott. Moore was interested and St. Luke's has a 'discretionary fund' that, as it turns out, includes such projects as ours. The fund's executive committee has approved an initial allocation of $2,500 and that is the source and purpose of the enclosed check—from St. Luke's to Oak Lawn."

Disposition of the Wesley Sermons Papers

Quillian cranked up the procedure of closing down Outler's office space. And Kirby made no attempt to stop the turning of events that made it happen. The same thing occurred concerning the ownership of the Wesley *Sermons* papers. Following is Kirby's response in his September 29, 1997, letter to me concerning the matter: "I had no conversations with Professor Outler about the ownership of the papers related to the Wesley *Sermons*. I do remember discussions about ownership of materials related to the project [the sermons were a part of that project] in the Wesley Works Project Board of Directors, but they were about the larger issue of preserving and making them available to scholars. The project would, in my judgment, have the strongest claim to anything related to their publications [this included Outler's papers on the sermons]."

This was the same conviction of Quillian as dean and as president of the Board of Directors of the project. The message came loud and clear to Outler that both men felt that his Wesley *Sermons* (a major part of the overall project) papers did not belong to him. Outler was convinced that both were wrong. And, for Outler, the atmosphere in which all this took place was not friendly.

The Matter Settled

Page one of *Circular 1—Copyright Basics,* published in March 1992 (two and one-half years following Outler's death), under "Who Can Claim Copyright?" states: "Copyright protection subsists from the time the work is created in fixed form, that is, it is an incident of the process of authorship. The copyright in the work of authorship IMMEDIATELY [in caps in the document] becomes the property of the author who created it." Simply put, regardless of where the money comes from to support the scholar's works, the papers belong to the scholar. Outler, well versed in the history of jurisprudence, knew this and acted out of that understanding as *he* allowed *his* papers to be placed in the archives of Bridwell Library at Perkins School of Theology.

Here is the way *he* worked through this sticky situation: In conference with me, Outler discussed the matter and mentioned three other seminaries as possible recipients. It was in this conversation that I strongly urged him not to do that but to allow his papers to be stored in the Bridwell archives. Outler then asked me to negotiate with Bridwell librarian Robert Maloy about getting his papers into the archives. Having an intermediary negotiate on his behalf concerning *his* papers further accentuated the fact that the papers belonged to Outler. Maloy graciously received the papers into the archives. They are as Outler wanted; they are *at* the library without belonging *to* the library. Kirby discovered this fact just days prior to his September 29, 1997, letter to me and said: "I did check with Page Thomas [Bridwell librarian] who told me that the Bridwell Library does not own the Outler material related to the *Sermons.*"

This arrangement protects the understanding and will of Outler as expressed in paragraphs of the following April 22, 1988, letter to me: "On the eve of our departure from Dallas, it may be important for me to restate to you my understanding (and Carla's) of the terms of the grateful trust under which we are asking you to continue to serve as custodian, trustee and executor of the personal papers, books, offprints, and personalia that we are turning over to your care and keeping (plus the other materials from my files that you already have in your possession). We do this on the long-honored assumption in academic practice that by right and by law, all these materials are now, and always have been, my own rightful possessions, as produced by me or as having been my private acquisitions. None of this has required, or had, any institution, board of directors or project (as, e.g., the *Wesley Works Project*) since none of it has ever belonged to any of them. I write in these quasi-legalistic terms only because of any possible challenges to the question of my original domain of and responsibility for the materials and their disposition. In short, they are mine to dispose of, and I gratefully leave them in your care for their most useful service—including more storage for such stuff that seem of no especial use at the time [over 1,500 volumes remain stored with me, waiting for the *kairos* to come for their disposal].

"I would much rather speak of my gratitude to you and Doris for your willingness and generosity in all the constructive initiatives that you have already taken to aid and support my work, especially in these last difficult years. I am also deeply grateful to Bridwell Library (and its librarian, Dr. Robert Maloy) for its willingness to receive the large fraction of my books, papers, memorabilia, etc., and to create and conserve them in what Dr. Maloy has chosen to speak of as 'The Outler Archive.' When the last round of these materials here at home is collected and transported to Bridwell (scheduled for April 28), I shall consider my side of my agreement with SMU as having been discharged. The materials that were involved in the generous Crisman bequests [the Longview, Texas, family who gave the money to the Texas Annual Conference to purchase the Outler Library] will have been delivered to Prof. Heitzenrater, for his program in Wesley and Methodist studies, but not as a concession as to their proprietorship by Perkins or by the Board of Directors of the Wesley

Works project. I have every confidence in Prof. Heitzenrater's understanding of this intent and in his wisdom and discretion in their use."

Lon Morris College in Jacksonville, Texas, and Wiley College in Marshall, Texas, have received any books from Outler's personal library that Bridwell could not use. Presently 250 boxes of Outler papers, personalia, and memorabilia are in the Bridwell archives. In time the seven filing cabinets of papers and letters and over 200 audio tapes that were sent to me following Outler's death will go into the Bridwell archives. The upshot of all this is that Outler owned the papers and granted them to be stored in the Bridwell archives. In a letter to me Outler said, "They are now in your hands to do as you can or are able to do." As legal custodian of those and other materials, I am working with a most cooperative library staff toward making all the papers, personalia, and audio and video tapes available to students and scholars via the Bridwell Library. In time custodial care will be *legally* transferred to the Library's Archives Director. In this procedure Outler's papers were *his; he* put them in my custodial care; I in turn will that custodial care to be given to Bridwell Library. They will forever be *his papers* in the custodial care of others. The papers have what Outler did not have regarding them— 'peace at last' in serving as resources for scholars and students alike, as Outler had envisioned.

Research Professor

When President Jon Fleming invited Outler to serve as Research Professor at Texas Wesleyan College in Fort Worth, Texas (1983–1984), Outler accepted, thinking that his time and talents could contribute in that setting something worthwhile in the life of the church. In a May 2, 1983, letter to Judge Tom Reavley, Outler wrote: "The people at TWC have worked out an appointment for me there as 'Research Professor,' with quite flexible arrangements as to my 'duties' and quite generous arrangements as to secretarial and research assistance. We will live on here, of course—now that we have the garage turned into a library—and I will commute to Fort Worth occasionally for conferences, consultations, and an occasional lecture. Mainly, though, they seem as eager as I for me to get on with study, research, and writing.

Most of all, it will give an academic *pied-a-terre,* now that I have none anymore at SMU. Carla and I are quite pleased with the prospects."

What started out as an "upper" for Outler, where he received an honorary Doctor of Science degree on May 11, 1984, turned into a "downer" at Texas Wesleyan College. Judge Tom Reavley received this February 15, 1985, letter from Outler: "The TWC story was an incredible mess. Jon [the president] set the stage for it with his grandiose notions of transforming a long-time bush league college into a Cowtown 'Rice.' He hastened his demise by his wheeling-dealing with Fort Worth philanthropists. He even convinced me that the transfiguration could have been brought off and that I could help with it!

"Meanwhile, the Central Texas Conference preachers (led by Sidney Roberts and Barry Bailey) had taken umbrage at Jon's 'flashy lifestyle' (although they live well, too!), and when he fired his financial officer, she turned on him with a disclosure of private files and with charges of mishandling the college's accounts. I saw enough to think that 'carelessness' could have been proved, but *not* malfeasance! Nevertheless, this brought in the University Senate [the United Methodist accrediting agency] (the real villains of the piece). Their investigating committee came to Fort Worth with what Durwood Fleming swears were foregone conclusions (and he was on the Senate himself, to no avail). The result was a 'confidential admonition' to Jon, which was promptly leaked by his enemies to the *Star-Telegram,* followed by an unprecedented sentence of two years probation with a threat of suspension thereafter. The faculty then panicked and shot itself in the foot by voting nonconfidence in their president and demanding that the trustees fire him. He had enough support on the board to block this, but in so untenable a position, his only honorable recourse was resignation. It was, in effect, a lynching.

"Somewhat incidentally in the melee, I got shot down, as a half-innocent bystander. I had been caught up in Jon's vision of helping upscale TWC in some such fashion as we had upscaled Perkins thirty years ago. And so I went about my teaching and consulting (and commuting) without salary but with support from the college for a research assistant and a part-time secretary. What is more, we could have succeeded (at least part way) but for the hubbub and the lynching. As it is, except for the financial loss, being out of that scene is a good thing since the association was becoming an embarrassment in the academic world.

"Upshot: after six decades on one campus or another, here I am now at home, without an academic *pied-a-terre* anywhere. Still, such is the gracious providence of God, 'the sun also rises.' With nothing to do at SMU, I have more to do elsewhere and otherwise than we can say grace over. The chief casualty in it all has come from the desertion of my *Protestant* 'liberal' friends (my Roman Catholic liberal friends still stand steadfast). It turns out that I was wrong supposing that an ecumenical Christian can move at will across old lines of division. The postliberal age (which I had hoped would continue to cherish the liberal *spirit*) may become an illiberal age (he that is not with us is against us—*anathema sit*!!).

"Actually, I have got to get on with the chores—and with the discoveries that 'where one is' is far less important than what one is up to."

What Outler Was Up To

It was about this time that Albert and Carla began to consider moving out of the Dallas area. The desertion of his Protestant "liberal" friends, along with what he considered a campaign to get him off the Perkins campus (compounded by the experience of being "shot down" as an innocent bystander at Texas Wesleyan) made a relocation farther south most attractive. During this general time frame a final move was in the making that included plans to accommodate their needs to and through the end of their lives.

His Greatest Teacher Died

The single most penetrating grief that Outler experienced came with the news that his sister Fan had died on February 15, 1984. That loss caused him to experience once again the truth that, when one who loved him died, a part of him died, too. And yet it was the depth of his gratitude to God for Fan that conquered the grief. To Father Peter Gorday, her priest who officiated at her funeral at St. Luke's Episcopal Church in Atlanta, Albert wrote: "Life has been unduly hectic the past two weeks for Mrs. Outler and me and there has been no leisure in which we could 'stop' and come to terms with our grief. Or to write you a proper letter of gratitude for your truly pastoral and priestly offices in my sister Frances' funeral. In every way the funeral was an experience of grace—and you helped make it: you and Marie Sims, and those pallbearers, and that 'honor guard' of Frances' former students. *We* had known that Frances was a rare and special person; we had not known how many others knew that as well."

Outler had thought about finitude, had taught about finitude, had philosophized about finitude. But when this one whom he loved so much died, he deeply felt his own finitude. And the gift of the Eternal Life of Love—Heaven!

Unbelievable!

Outler's horizon broadened to what some would describe as "beyond the horizon." Students, friends, and family could not believe it when in 1987 they heard that he had accepted through his niece Helen Lankford an invitation for a free reading from Dallas psychic Dan Fry. Their first thoughts were of the occult—divination, incantation, magical formulae out of a reading of the stars, etc. And they were right in their concern. But Outler went not as a believer. Outler was a Wesleyan scholar who strove to be open-minded toward the experiences of Wesley whose life was greatly influenced in earlier years by "Old Jeffrey," the noisy Epworth rectory ghost. But Outler's interest went in directions other than the *poltergeist*.

The study of psychic phenomena (a branch of psychology) had been an interest of Outler's since his days of study at Emory where he studied psychotherapy and abnormal psychology. And then there were his studies with Dr. Rhine at Duke University while he taught at the Divinity School in the late 1930s and early 1940s. His letters spell out how he had many conferences with Dr. Rhine and his colleagues at Duke concerning the studies of parapsychical phenomena. It was vintage Outler; if others knew it, he wanted to know it, too. After all, parapsychology is to religion what biology is to medicine. Or physics to engineering. And he did come to know what they knew about parasychology's branches of extrasensory perception, clairvoyance, telepathy, and precognition, as well as the second basic type of parapsychical process of psychokinesis.

When Outler moved to Yale in the mid-1940s, he lost contact with these experts in the field of parapsychology. Then when he was invited to meet a psychic in Dallas, he jumped at the opportunity to have an evening of talking about a subject that interested him very much. In his visit with psychic Fry, Outler got a reading all right—of what *he* went there to find out: How much did Fry know about what he (Outler) knew? It was testing time for psychic Fry. But this was a test that Fry could neither pass nor fail. Outler simply wanted the man to be himself: the psychic. Only from that perspective could Outler learn what the man was about.

Back to Wofford College

The following paragraph from a November 3, 1987, letter written by James R. Hackney reveals how one man reaped the benefit of Outler's popularity: "I graduated from Wofford in 1957 and entered Yale Divinity School that fall. One of my first classes was taught by Dean Colin Williams on the theology of John Wesley. It was a seminar with about twenty students. During the first class meeting all of the students were introducing themselves and telling where they had gone to college. As I heard the colleges announced I was sure that some mistake had been made in admitting me in the first place. Brown, Harvard, Penn, Duke were mentioned. When I said that I had gone to Wofford, one of the others asked me, 'What is a Wofford?' Dean Williams picked up your book on the theology of John Wesley and proclaimed, 'Wofford is Dr. Outler's college.' You saved me and empowered me to realize that my academic background is a fine one." Wofford meant a great deal to Outler; Outler meant a great deal to Wofford.

Outler often talked about "the joy of learning and how to learn almost anything he wanted to learn" that came to him out of his Wofford experience. For that reason it was a very special honor to be named their "outstanding alumnus" for 1988. When he received his award, he said that it was almost as good as a "naturalization certificate"!

Still Behind the Scenes

Outler served as delegate to six General Conferences of the United Methodist Church and worked on the scene on those occasions to keep the United Methodist Church reformed, evangelical and catholic and grounded in a Wesleyan theology. With those involvements as a delegate behind him Outler remained active behind the scenes for the remaining days of his life. That behind-the-scenes activity continued as he was preparing for the move to Bradenton, and was the inspiring counsel behind the Houston Declaration, a hue and cry heard from across the United Methodist Church at the General Conference of 1988. This event came at a time when a fad to supplant the historic Trinitarian formula with "Creator, Redeemer, and Sustainer" was being promoted by some as better than Scripture.

Bill Hinson, pastor of First United Methodist Church, Houston, Texas, relates this history: "More than any other person Albert Outler is responsible for that massive intervention at the General Conference of 1988. Albert called me one afternoon and talked with me about his distress concerning what was happening to the concept of the Trinity. A functional modelism was making a serious effort to replace trinitarian relational language. I shall never forget his words to me. He said, 'Bill, if we get careless about the Trinity in this generation, we will be Unitarians in the next generation.' His brilliant insight and his deep concern were at the core of our calling for the massive meeting here in Houston that issued the Houston Declaration. Many of our radical feminists are very surprised to learn where the Houston Declaration came from. They somehow thought that those of us who still call God 'Father' just got together one day and wanted to express our sexist ways. Some still cannot understand how one can be a champion of equality and still refuse to usurp the place of Jesus Christ."

Outler fought for reforms in the church (denominational and catholic) right up to his death. Those reform processes that he started many years ago continue in the life of the church in ways and moments that present day (whatever "present day" may come in any future) participants will never know. And that is as Outler had hoped—it was not he but his message that transformed, and as a result reformed church institutions.

Left Out of the Loop

It is known across the church that Outler left the Perkins campus with a sense of being left out. When Bill Scales, on behalf of the Texas Annual Conference, during Ministers' Week, February 1985, at SMU's McFarland Auditorium, formally presented the Albert C. Outler Chair in Wesley Studies, complete with a one million dollar endowment, to SMU President L. Donald Shields, Albert Outler, who lived just minutes away, was not there as a part of the program. When my wife and I asked Albert the next day at a lunch meeting why he was not there for the presentation, his answer was, "I was not invited."

Amends for this public oversight were made by the university in the form of an honorary Doctor of Humane Letters (May 17, 1986), conferred on Outler by President Donald Shields and Board Trustee Chairman Edwin Cox. The following excerpt from the presentation made by John Deschner captures historical facts of Outler's contributions to the university: "Resigning the prestigious Timothy Dwight Chair at Yale University, this strategy-minded Southerner helped SMU create in the heartland of southwestern United Methodism a theology school of national rank and reputation. And because theology is not an end in itself, because 'faith seeks understanding,' because a theology school needs a university, he also dreamed, prodded, designed, wrote and spoke SMU toward a vision of humane scholarship and teaching as the center of its academic mission. As guiding spirit of the University's Master Plan Commission in 1962–1963; as author of its remarkable statement on 'The Idea of SMU as a University'; as inventor of SMU's University College whose successor, the 'Common Educational Experience,' continues to this day; as an instigator of SMU's first tier of doctoral programs; as adviser to presidents and as academic conscience in crises and celebration, Albert Cook Outler stands as a faculty leader of decisive influence in SMU's third quarter century."

A paragraph out of a 1989 letter to me went to the core of the truth from Outler's perspective concerning those ambiguous moments of his life: "In any case, you may understand more clearly the circumstances which finally led us to feel neither welcome nor unwelcome on the SMU campus but simply cut 'out of the loop.' Given those circumstances, the least unacceptable alternative was to flee the place in as quiet and dignified an operation as we could manage. Clearly, this was also agreeable with Dean Kirby and President Pye [of the University]; from the first public 'announcement' [of the Outlers leaving the area] till now, there has been no word from either of them (or reported comment). Moreover, there has been no acknowledgment of any sort about the books [Outler's personal library] and papers that left Lakehurst Avenue [their Dallas home] for Bridwell Library or the collection of records designated for the Music School. We have presumed that Page Thomas took care of this [he was right; Page did], but none of his administrative superiors has signified their receipt. We take this less as a sign of 'hostility' than of indifference; at the least, though, it was another of those anticlimaxes that remind us of the differences between what the place has become in comparison with what it was in 'the glory days.'"

With his academic turf gone Outler soon turned his mind toward the inevitable—a real retirement.

5

Albert Outler Enters *Real* Retirement

The Move to Florida

While Outler retired from Perkins School of Theology in 1977, he did not retire from work. As research professor and then emeritus professor of Perkins, he continued to lecture (see lectures listed at the end of this book). But psychologically and existentially Outler's final retirement came with his physical move to Bradenton, Florida, a move graced with the help of Bishop Earl Hunt. Outler accepted the fact that the "rolling stone" had finally come to a stopping place. Texas friends who visited with the Outlers in Florida were made to realize that divine Providence was caring for the Outlers properly; they fitted perfectly into that retirement community. Ultimately grace reconciled the mixed motives and emotions of this messenger, called and sent by God. He knew and radiated an inward peace, the gift of grace, amidst the evils of the world, which too often he saw reflected in the power-play machinations of some in the church, the "home" and "workplace" he loved.

Outler described that *kairos* of his life in these words: "This is not to swap the earnest life for thumb-twiddling, but to redefine my calling within the limits of what I can still do—even though at a snail's pace. As long as God's grace bestirs, I mean to go on studying and writing—with an agenda that will outlast by a good deal my life (else what *is* heaven for?)"[108]

Outpouring of Love

Some of that peace came in knowing a love from the community he was leaving. The distasteful circumstances that surrounded Outler's move from Perkins in no way reflected the spirit of some of Outler's faculty friends, the university, or the Dallas community. Outler's friends in the Dallas area were many. Prior to his leaving Dallas, on April 22, 1988, persons from the Catholic Diocese of Dallas, the Greater Community of Churches, the Isthmus Institute, Northaven United Methodist Church (where Carla was a member), Southern Methodist University, The Thanksgiving Square Foundation, and the United Methodist Church packed the Fellowship Hall of First United Methodist Church in downtown Dallas to honor Outler with a celebration banquet. A videotaped "This Is Your Life" program narrated by Howard Grimes and speeches by faculty colleague Schubert Ogden and Dallas City Councilman Craig Holcomb highlighted the program. Such an outpouring of love, appreciation, and support caused Outler to leave Dallas with ambivalent feelings.

A Sad-Glad Note

But it did not take long for the matters of the move at hand to relegate this baggage of ambivalence to a lesser place of awareness in the back of his mind. From all accounts the Outlers' move to Bradenton, Florida, from the outset to the "settling in" was one of the best moves they ever made. In this January 26, 1988, letter to Judge Tom Reavley, Outler wrote: "A sad-glad note to end on. The 'sad' news is that when you come to Fort Worth in May, Carla and I will be on our way (or on the verge) to Florida, and *real* retirement. The glad news is that we have found a promising 'life-care center' there that we can afford and that allows for 'independent living,' 'infirmary care,' and 'nursing care' all in one establishment and under one roof. Carla is actually looking forward to it, and so am I: all the viable alternatives that we have canvassed are not as adequate. Most of what we will miss in these parts are our friends and loved ones (and the children are being very understanding and supportive), and there will still be the mail and maybe some occasional path crossings. But the crux of the matter is being as 'intentional' about retirement as one can be."

A Glad Note

Outler received a glad note written August l, 1988, from one he knew fifty years before. A hearty laugh of remembrance came to him as he read of these accounts from his friend, Robert C. Clark, Sr.: "I have just read the article by Rev. George E. Clary, Jr., in the last issue of the *Wesleyan Christian Advocate* titled 'Notes On Georgia Methodist History.' If you have read the article you will know that your Dad's ministry is mentioned. Because of his assignment to the church at Thomasville you were born there in 1908. I was born in 1907 at Ochlocknee. Your Dad was my Dad's Presiding Elder part of the time that Dad was a pastor in the South Georgia Conference.

"We moved to the C. R. Jenkins farm at Baxley in 1917; we were there, and members of the Melton Chapel Methodist Church, when you were assigned the 'Junior Preacher' of the Baxley Circuit, working under Rev. E. A. Sanders. Either that year or the next year you were supposed to go across the Altamaha River one Sunday night to preach at a church at 'Jones Cross Roads,' and asked me to go along with you. I went and we had a good service, I thought. When the service was over, we were invited to go for a visit to old Mr. Jones' home. I think we ate supper there, but whether we did or not, we were entertained by several daughters of the family, and, let me add this, I sorta believe one of those belles set her cap for you, and you ignored the threat!

"One thing I remember about the service is the fact that you preached from Moffatt's translation of the New Testament.

"Something I remember about the trip over there and back home is the fact, especially on the return trip, that you, in driving that little Ford roadster, almost 'let her fly.'"

A 'Settling-In' Mode

An October 13, 1988, letter to Judge Reavley revealed an Outler in the "settling-in" mode: "The situation here is all that we had hoped for in some respects and a good deal less in others (which is only to say that life *is* a mixed bag anywhere, but that the mixes are different, here and there). We have comfortable living quarters and a splendid seventh-floor balcony overlook to a tidal creek and river, with forested suburbs beyond. I have a secluded study with stuffed book shelves along three walls, with a pleasant view out of my 'window wall'—plus a big desk and a 'judge's chair' in the middle of the room! [This was his last workplace for the church.] It is a godsend to me but an anomaly for the 'management,' who have a whole set of stereotypes about 'the care and feeding of old folks' (and a lot of 'experience' to justify their reflex impulses to condescension). They have never had a card-carrying egghead in their midst before, and this is the first community in which I have ever lived without at least one other egghead on the roster. It is a useful exercise in accommodation. I tell you all this because you will be able to understand how curiously *positive* all this has turned out to be for us.

"Carla has found a real home here with some of the really friendly women (who outnumber the men in the community, ten to one!). And this has been a big plus for us both. As for me, there has also been a clear gain in the swap from my role in the later years in Dallas (as *persona non grata* with the new people at SMU and Perkins) to a refreshingly *new* role as *persona incognita* in Bradenton. The summer has been even more productive than I actually expected, and our prospects brighten for a more comfortable seclusion from here on out. The unpleasant parts of that ill-fated Wesley project are now behind me; the *Sermons* unit will now have to make its way in the ecumenical world on its own.

"The United Methodist Church has absolved us (i.e., our Doctrinal Commission) from any further guidance in the church, with its new 'doctrinal statement.' The new one is better than it might have been (and nearly was), but despite all the protestations about 'continuity,' the St. Louis Statement is a differently conceived document than the one we produced in 1972. Now the 'United' Methodists have a confession of faith (actually two!) and have had that bad old phrase, 'doctrinal pluralism,' placed under solemn interdict by episcopal decree. [Bishop Tuell had earlier written and received helpful insights from Outler in preparing his episcopal address. And then he triggered an irony in that address as he closed the door on pluralism, to the cheers of a General Conference, even as he received insight from the one who had earlier opened the door of pluralism.] This, too, therefore, is a closed chapter in my book. I still wish SMU well, but sense a different orientation there now (especially at Perkins)."[109]

The January 26th letter ended with this quote: "Newman said it for us:

> '. . . when the busy world is hushed and the
> fever of life is over and our work is done.
> Then in thy mercy grant us a safe lodging, a
> quiet rest and peace at the last.'"

Died with His Boots on

It may be said without exaggerating that Outler "died with his boots on." It became obvious to those nearest him that all was not well at Lake Junaluska during his last visit there. He came to speak to the United Methodist Church Historical Society. On the day before he was to deliver his address on July 3, 1989, he called to cancel an invitation that he had accepted to visit in the home of Bishop and Mrs. Earl Hunt. He confessed to feeling not up to par. But on the day he gave his address[110] those who stood and cheered were convinced that he outdid himself. Those who knew him the best recognized symptoms of a failing heart that nitroglycerin tablets could no longer jump start. Carla said: "I can remember that, after one of the Junaluska lectures, they were having a question-and-answer period. I remember thinking he did not look too good. And he said, 'I can't go on anymore.' He almost did not make it through the session. And we came back here [Bradenton]. I could tell that he looked tired. I was surprised when he said that he could not go on—because that was not like Albert."

Outler promptly wrote all of those with whom he had scheduled engagements and said, "I'm hangin' 'em up."

Outler suffered a stroke on August 20, 1989, and died September 1, in Bradenton. A memorial service was held in the Asbury Towers Chapel in Bradenton with H. Hasbrouck Hughes, Jr., bishop of the Florida Conference, giving the memorial address and assisted by Rev. Gary W. Buhl and Rev. Dr. Jiles E. Kirkland.

Another memorial service was held in Dallas on Thursday afternoon, September 7, with Outler's family and approximately a thousand of his friends in attendance at Highland Park United Methodist Church, adjacent to the Southern Methodist University campus. Realizing Dean Kirby was not included in Outler's Memorial Service program, a person from the seminary (not Kirby) contacted Carla, urging that the dean be a part of the memorial service. The reason: it would not "look good for the seminary" if the dean were left out. Carla contacted me with her mid-grief crisis. I assured her that Dr. Outler's colleagues and friends knew of the positive image that he had brought to the seminary through the years and that they would respect Dr. Outler's desires concerning his memorial service. Carla chose to stay with what Dr. "O" wanted.

Dean Kirby attended the memorial service at Highland Park United Methodist Church and participated as a congregant. As it turned out, Albert's good friend and colleague, John Deschner, represented the seminary well in his excellent message on that occasion. And it is history that Outler's papers, tapes, memorabilia, and personalia now reside at Perkins' Bridwell Library for use by scholars and students in their study. In the world of scholars and the church catholic, Outler continues to bring credibility to Perkins School of Theology, *his* school that he helped in its new beginning in 1952.

Choirs from the United Methodist churches of Highland Park, First Dallas, and Lovers Lane sang the Sanctus and Agnus Dei from Gabriel Fauré's *Requiem.* (Outler had said, "Fauré's *Requiem* ends, not like the usual requiem, but with the hymn of the angels welcoming the soul into Paradise." Reflecting on that, he added, "That's what I would want at my funeral!")[111] Leading in the service were Bishop Bruce Blake of the Dallas Episcopal Area; Dr. Leighton Farrell, pastor of Highland Park United Methodist Church; Dr. John Deschner, professor at Perkins School of Theology; and I. I said in my remarks: "[Outler] preached grace with grace. His preaching was more than *his* preaching—God touched his life with grace, and he touched our lives with the same as he preached. His 'asides' reflected a wit that elicited a joyful delight in his hearers. Even his 'uhs' seemed filled with great theological content. He chuckled at himself when he described his sermons as 'plain truth for plain people by an egghead.'

"He was a busy, busy man with many irons in the fire. In his own words, his was the ordeal of a happy dilettante. He likened himself to a dog walking on his hind legs, rather pleased with himself that he could do it at all!

"It bothered Dr. 'O' when something was not as it ought to be. And he rattled many institutional cages with his candid comments. But you never doubted his great love for the church, the seminary, the community. Never! Because he loved, he judged. That was his style, and was right up to the very end. His latest efforts to make mid-course corrections of the doctrinal directions of the church came at Lake Junaluska this summer—straight talk spoken in love.

"When you knew his faith, you knew the man. If the hours could be added up that Albert Outler has talked about the Rule of Grace to those of us here today, what would the total be? And think of that quality of time spent. That quality, grace, was present when he talked with you. And you never got enough of his word on God's Rule of Grace. He was so absorbed in the subject. And now he knows the grace of glory in a dimension that even the greatness of his earth-bound mind could never comprehend. I can see him now in God's heaven say through that Outlerian smile: 'Now this is all right!' And it is all right for him and for you, the family, as you share with each other those private and intimate memories of Dr. 'O' as husband, father, and grandfather."

John Deschner said, borrowing from Archbishop of Canterbury William Temple's epitaph in Canterbury Cathedral, "Remember in Christ Albert Outler. With Albert Outler, we found John Wesley coming alive, not in Wesley's language but in our language . . . the truest thing that this post-Freudian can say about himself is that 'God is my friend!' . . . Ultimately, Albert expects nothing that he has said or done to make sense except Christ as his center . . . His life is a witness to us of how Christ's life can take form among us today . . ."[112]

The struggles of the world and within the church he loved so much continue. But as for Albert Outler, he had "fought a good fight, had finished his course, had kept the faith" (2 Timothy 4:7). The people concluded the memorial service by standing and singing "A Mighty Fortress Is Our God," a bulwark that never failed Outler and would not fail them. This was a *kairos* of celebration, a *kairos* of victory.

Many remembrances came from across the church:

Inner Spiritual Aristocracy

Lutheran theologian Martin Marty described Outler's manners and style as those of a "courtly person. He could be intensely personable, but he had a little bit of an inner-spiritual aristocracy. He could gab as much as I and be noisy. But if there were thirty people on the stage and he spoke, he was the one you remembered."[113]

Incomparable Teacher

Dr. W. A. Criswell, pastor emeritus of Dallas' First Baptist Church, said that while he and Outler were "at opposite ends of the theological spectrum," Dr. Outler had "gone out of his way to be my friend. He was a tremendous theologian, one of the most gifted representatives of the Christian faith in all of Christendom. I wish that all professors in all our schools were as devoted to the Spirit of Christ as was this incomparable teacher at Southern Methodist University."[114]

On a Desert Island

Past president of Notre Dame, Theodore M. Hesburgh, said, "If I had to spend some time on a desert island [with a friend], Al Outler would constitute my first choice."[115]

He Drank Deeply of the Total Gospel

"[From the office of DePaul University] Monsignor Jack Egan, who was ecumenical before ecumenism was allowed among Catholics, remarked, 'Never did I meet a man who had drunk so deeply of the meaning of the total gospel and the implication for him and for his world, which he loved so much. It can honestly be said of him that we shall not see his like again, and we shall be the poorer for it." [116]

A Photographic Retrospective

Albert and Carla Outler

Left: Outler's niece Helen Lankford at the Outler family's mountain home at Young Harris, Georgia.

Right: "Aunt Mary" at the Outler's Young Harris home.

Right: John ("Dad") and Gertrude ("Little General") Outler.

Left: Sister Fan and Albert in 1939.

Carla and Albert *(left; back row)* at Gordon, Georgia, with a
Sunday school class.

Outler speaking at the close of Vatican II in the Basilica of
St. Paul's Outside the Walls with Pope Paul VI in the audience
(December 12, 1965).

Joint Roman Catholic/Methodist Commission which met in
November 1979 at St. Simons Island, Georgia. *(Left to right):*
Bishop William R. Cannon, Mgr. Charles Moeller, Canon Richard
Stuart, Bishop J. Francis Stafford, Rev. A. Raymond George,
Father Cuthbert Rand, Father Edward Malatesta, Bishop James M.
Ault, Dr. Ira Gallaway, Mgr. William Purdy, Dr. Albert C. Outler.

Outler and A. M. Alchin, Canon of Canterbury (November 19, 1984).

Outler autographing Volume 1 of *The Works of John Wesley.*

Above: Outler and Elton Trueblood. *Below:* Dalai Lama and Outler at Thanksgiving Square, Dallas.

Outler and evangelist Edmund Robb at the 1976 General
Conference in Portland, Oregon.

Albert Outler and Martin Marty. (The two men in the middle are unidentified.)

Bob and Doris Parrott; Carla and Albert Outler at the Outler's home in Bradenton, Florida (1989).

PART 2

The Story of a Dilettante

Introduction to Part 2

In the February 3, 1960, issue of *The Christian Century,* Albert Outler wrote of himself in an article entitled "Ordeal of a Happy Dilettante." It is important to know what Outler had in his mind when he spoke of himself as a "dilettante" and "opportunist." By *dilettante* he meant the gifted amateur with so many different interests that he could never become a full-fledged master in any one of them. The interesting offset to this "defect" is that he was welcomed into the company of real masters in many fields (theology, church history, psychology of religion, etc.—as his election to the American Academy of Arts and Sciences would indicate). Three of his honorary degrees were in divinity; one was in law; the others were in humane letters.

Seizing Opportunities

Outler's connotation of the term *opportunist* was a wry reference to a principle, based on a notion of providence by which he lived all his life with evident poise and satisfaction. Outler had few memories of taking any initiative in the matter of career or self-promotion. In the old Methodist phrase, he was "a man under appointment," reacting to initiatives of others where he was involved and seizing opportunities as they came along. All the scenarios he wrote for himself seemed to be rewritten by circumstances, with many frustrations and not a few disastrous setbacks and disappointments. He professed to be unyielding at one point: he had an aversion to administrative or executive responsibility. His students remember how he hated to have to grade them and how much he loved to evaluate their performance in class and to read and annotate with red ink in the margins of their work. He professed to have no gifts or tastes for disposing of other people's affairs, *ex officio*. This attitude, which was expressed later in his career, was the opposite of his much earlier whim at Wofford to become a bishop. His letters indicate that there was a time that his fancy was tickled at the possibility of *being called on* to become a dean. He wasn't. And he fell easily into the conviction that it finally was best for the university and for him. This tied in neatly with his "opportunist" idea of providence. His opportunities came in areas commensurate with his personality and temperament.

A Connoisseur

In the complexity of his many-faceted personality, Outler described himself as "a *happy* dilettante." Martin Marty, in a later issue of *The Christian Century* (1984), felt that the description had an inappropriate connotation of the aesthete, which without a doubt Outler *was*. Marty suggested that the concept of connoisseur (as of fine wines) better described Outler. Those who knew Outler would agree with Marty's description. For indeed he was the connoisseur of many flavors of life, who not only enjoyed the "tastes," but also enjoyed describing the tastes in abstract and/or picture words to any who inquired and to some who didn't.

But *connoisseur* was not a word that Outler *could* use in referring to himself because it was a term reserved for the highfalutin rare birds in the aviary of life. He simply *could not* apply the word to himself. To him an amateur *dilettante* was a lowfalutin way of saying the same thing. Recall his oft-quoted self-description: "A dog walking on his hind legs, rather pleased with himself that he can manage it at all." As delicate a self-effacing as one will ever hear, which in itself proves Marty right. Outler was also a connoisseur of *fine* words.

At Home with the Subject of *Your Choice*

For Outler, living was an art to be contributed to as well as appreciated. He brought the eye of the critic to whatever he did and savored all his involvements. Whatever the subject he chose to speak on or write about, when the performance was completed, his audience realized that he knew what he was talking or writing about. Even an audience of experts in the field of inquiry felt that he was one, too. This was true from jurisprudence to gardening and whatever fell in between. Concerning the science of law, Attorney Floyd M. Kocher in a January 4, 1957, letter wrote Outler: "For several weeks, since studying your first chapter of *Studies in Jurisprudence, Natural Law and Natural Rights,* I had determined to write this particular letter of commendation. I have been tremendously pleased and edified by your treatment of Martin Luther, Hugo Grotius and Samuel Pufendorf, also with others.

"In the *Time* magazine of June 1956, introducing Paul Tillich of Harvard, the statement appeared, 'One of the surprises of the century is the Renaissance of Protestant Theology.' Not until I studied your formulae concerning the motif of the Protestant theology, did I feel that I had an appreciation of the matter. Yours was superb and I personally approve.

"Your theological participation in *Studies in Jurisprudence,* together with the philosophers, indicates conclusively that you are seeing this we call Existence, WHOLE.

"I have spent much of the past summer with Tillich's *Systematic Theology. Time* magazine rates him as our #1 intellectual. I am placing you on the same plateau."

Gardeners Mr. and Mrs. William A. Liddell would have placed Outler on the agricultural plateau of that field's best scholars. In a March 3, 1953, letter to them he wrote: "I was greatly interested in the herbicide report—so far as I can tell, little or nothing has been done along these lines in these parts, namely perhaps, because we grow few, if any, peas and beans in large commercial lots. I have asked a seed-supply man to look up the prospects of getting some IPC just for fooling around with. So far, however, my chief—and not fully solved—problem is soil texture and alkalinity. Krilium is the most effective soil conditioner I have tried (among four different kinds), but it takes so much to alter the crumb structure of the soil far enough down to make any difference. I have discovered that if you mellow the top three or four inches of soil, but go no deeper, the practical effect is something like that of a shallow hardpan. As for alkalinity, I have run into the serious difficulty here that enough aluminum sulphate to reduce the pH down to 6.5 leaves so much free aluminum in the soil as to make it toxic to feeder roots. Actually, I managed to kill off one flat of tomato seedlings with that treatment.

"As for fertilizer, I am learning new tricks in this department that will interest you even if they are not directly applicable in your soil and situation. The main nutrient deficiency is available nitrogen. I have been using foliar urea sprays, but now I have found that Dupont makes a thing called Nu-Green, which is pelleted synthetic urea, 40% nitrogen fully soluble and yet not deliquescent as ordinary USP urea is. With triphosphate and this Nu-Green, I get a much cheaper and highly concentrated fertilizer for this soil than anything else available. This is a real advantage because ammonia sulphate, which is clearly the next best shot for nitrogen for alkaline soils, has a definite deflocculating effect upon the clay."

Expanding further on Outler's interest in things agricultural, Robert Young told this story: "My daughter Rebecca went to Hillcrest High in Dallas in the early seventies. Her friend Julie Parrish lived next door to the Outlers. Julie was at our house and said, 'Dr. Outler is *something* at SMU, but Mother says he knows more about roses than anyone she knows!'"

Outler's is the story of a dilettante with varied interests, one considered expert (when he would not claim such credit) by many in those fields of inquiry. Following are seven broad areas where his scholarly skills are recognized and appreciated:

As a Historical Theologian (Patristics)

As a Sports Enthusiast

As a Psychotherapist

As an Arts and Sciences Person

As a Methodist

As an Ecumenist

As a Community Person

6

As a Historical Theologian (Patristics)

A Dramatic Shift In Direction

Outler's journey into historical theology took a circuitous route. In his words: "I came to Yale (in September of 1935) with what I thought was an interesting program. I wanted to study *pastoral psychology*—not just psychology of religion, or pastoral care, or systematic theology, but all three together as a theoretical perspective on the pastoral office in the modern world. There was this fantasy I had about the pastor's theological groundings for his distinctive tasks: (1) diagnosis of the human situation; (2) some sort of *evangel* in that situation; (3) effective procedures in therapy and *paideusis* [from the Greek meaning *rearing, training, education*]; (4) prognosis as to the human options; and (5) the responsible exercise of the 'power of the keys,' viz., the pastor's responsibility for ethical judgments in human affairs. Professor Hartshorne wasted no time at all in disposing of my fantasy. No such academic discipline existed, he said, nor was likely to. I was trying to conflate too broad a spectrum of inquiries into a single program that would be unmanageable, pedagogically.

"My alternative was to switch to the curriculum in *historical theology* (a discipline which has *also* turned out to be pedagogically unmanageable), and on the side I had two exciting years of moonlighting over in the Institute of Human Relations (of blessed memory). Since then I have dabbled in most of the accredited disciplines of theology (systematic, philosophical, moral) with a few sallies into the so-called practical fields: psychotherapy, social action, theology and culture, liturgical innovation (which nowadays need be only the resuscitation of one of the *old* liturgies). My career in ecumenism has always had an avowed pastoral concern, viz., the liberation of pastors from their sectarian blinkers. And, now for the past fifteen years, my preoccupation with John Wesley has had a similar motivation—ever since my discovery of him as a pastoral theologian, largely misperceived by Methodists and largely ignored by others."[117] It is interesting to note that Outler came to this latter comment about John Wesley being a pastoral theologian while he (Outler) was *being* a historical theologian.

A New Awakening

You could hear the excitement in his voice as he said, "At Yale [where he received his Ph.D. in 1938], the whole world—in both space and time—began to open up for me for the first time in my life, literally. I began to be aware of the global situation of Christianity. Kenneth Latourette [Yale professor of Missions and Oriental History] was, even then, working at the business of his seven-volume *History of the Expansion of Christianity.* I became aware of the ways in which Christianity and culture have always been in interaction, and I began to reflect upon the constancy and recapitulatory character of basic theological problems. The problems that I had thought were new and crucial began to show up in the second century and the third century and the fifth century, the thirteenth century, the sixteenth century, eighteenth century. And so the basic notion of continuity and the identity of Christianity through all of its crises and changes began to form, and the perspective that has actually dominated my historiographical life and work took shape there and under those influences."[118]

Atmospheres

Historical theologian Outler wrote these autobiographical statements in the February 3, 1960, article in *The Christian Century*:

"For a long time now I have been convinced that one of the hidden causes of our current confusion is the often unrecognized hiatus in our consciousness between the Christian present and the Christian past. The Enlightenment and its theology caused a deep, near-fatal breach of continuity between contemporary Christianity and historic Christianity. The consequences of this are all around us, in the unhistorical and sometimes antihistorical developments in Christian thought. How can this breach be healed? How can a man be a modern Christian, one who has assimilated the theological impact of the 19th century, and still claim his full share of the whole of the Christian heritage? I have been puzzling over these questions a long time. Alongside a hundred practical ventures of one sort or another the one constant and continuing project I can see in my distracted labors has been the effort to recouple the past and the present—and to persuade others that it must be done or at the very least attempted. To explain how I got started on such a project and what has happened to it in the past decade I have to go back to the beginning of my theological career.

"Speaking in terms of atmospheres rather than dates, I was born and reared in the 18th century—in a parsonage home of warm, vital piety and in a college still devoted to a classical curriculum. My years at seminary and in the pastorate (1928–1935) marked a brief but exciting passage into and through the 19th century. My conversion to liberalism came in the years of the Great Depression—at the very time when the first effective critiques of liberal theology were being noticed in this country. It now seems long ago and far away, but that conversion left with me two significant residues that I still cherish: the liberal temper and the social gospel.

"It was not until my years in the Yale graduate school (1935–38) that I was thrust boldly into the 20th century—this in the course of a degree in historical theology. There I first read Barth and Irenaeus, concurrently. I was 'all shook up' by A. J. Ayer's *Language, Truth, and Logic;* Reinhold Niebuhr's *Moral Man and Immoral Society;* and T. S. Eliot's 'The Wasteland.' At Yale I first heard of Kierkegaard and existentialism, and I actually *met* Paul Tillich. I took seminars in the Institute of Human Relations and wrote a dissertation on Origen that was passed by Robert Calhoun, Roland Bainton and Erwin Goodenough. What a jumble it all was—and what an adventure! If I spread too wide and too thin, at least I gained a range of insights and outlook that I would not even now exchange for a narrower specialization.

"In this swift journey through three 'centuries' I discovered for myself the radical tension between the Enlightenment and the relatively continuous Christian tradition down to the end of the 18th century. The 19th century stood—and still stands—as a sort of gap between my own theological childhood and maturity. I had pondered the previous breaks in the history of the church—the transplantation from Jewish to Greek soil, the transition from an illicit to an established religion, the passage from the ancient to the medieval world, the upheaval of the Reformation and so on. In each of these instances the further development of Christianity depended on the way the transition was handled or mishandled. It seemed to follow, therefore, that one of the specific and fundamental tasks of 20th-century Christianity was to deal with the 19th century. As a matter of fact, this has been the strongest impulse in those theologies which have dominated this century thus far. In Barth, Niebuhr and others I saw a variegated pattern of protest and assimilation; in others such as Tillich and Bultmann there was an equally variegated pattern of assimilation and protest. Similar configurations appear in the new biblical theology and in the theological work of the ecumenical movement.

"In the field of church history and the history of doctrine, however, no such progress is apparent. Contemporary Christian historians have been caught in a bind between their historiography and their theology. Time was when the first Christian historian, Eusebius, could follow the simple maxim that history was the stage on which the struggle between God and the devil was being acted out. But it has now come to pass that the modern historian is committed to the contrary maxim: God does not intervene in history—no appeal to divine action or causality will serve as an historical explanation. But what happens to *church* history when God is left out of it?

"And yet we cannot escape our own church history, whatever it is. We do not do so even if we attempt a leap of faith directly from the present moment to the New Testament—seeking to hear God's Word, so to say, from out of time. The fact is that we hear what we hear with the perception produced by our own histories, and these affect what we hear and what we do in response. Nor is it better to select one or another segment of Christian history, such as the first or the fifth or the 16th century, and make that the norm for our own. Both these approaches ignore the question of the identity and the continuity of the Christian community and its message throughout the total historical experience of that community. But this is the question that has to be solved if we are to deal with any major instance of discontinuity.

"Grandiose as it may be, and ill equipped for it as I am, I came to believe that this inquiry into the continuity of historic Christianity was my theological vocation. This has meant a double effort to comprehend the Christian tradition in its historic continuity and the modern world in its intellectual and spiritual ambiguities. [Origen, Gregory of Nyssa, and Clement of Alexandria shaped Outler's thinking as much as or more than any others.] I have of course sought to merit the respect of my fellow historians and to speak to the condition of my fellow moderns. But I've had no illusions that I could master such a job, even by my own standards of excellence. It was bound to make a man a dilettante. A perfectionist in my shoes would have gone down in despair."

This statement lifts an eyebrow on those who knew Outler and takes some explaining because he *was* a perfectionist in some areas. When it came to producing a paper or a book for publication, especially in his later years, he could hardly let it go to press, such was the pressure that every "t" must be crossed and "i" dotted in grammar and meaning. He never called the papers published in *The Albert Outler Library* "manuscripts." They were for him "notes" not fit for publishing by *him*. Somebody else was allowed by him to publish them. But *he* would never consider submitting them for publication *himself*. Yet, as he stated in this article, a perfectionist in his shoes, trying to fit all the pieces of ancient Christian history into a pattern with modern intellectual and spiritual ambiguities with any idea that he or she might pull it off, would have gone down in despair. He was not a perfectionist in this instance because he knew he was not God. Only God has all the answers concerning the *true* picture of history. Outler was *perfectly* willing to accept his limitations when it came to being a *perfect* historical theologian. In no way did this acknowledgment keep him from the struggle of *being* perfect in his efforts, with the knowledge that this perfection would ever happen in fact. As Outler continued:

"The master image of the 19th century—man redeeming himself and his society—has been shattered beyond easy repair. Zealous as I was in that iconoclasm I have come to think that we must now attend to the other face of Christian man— his original righteousness and the basic health that God sustains even in his rebellious and sinful children. This idea has shaped my work on the relations between psychotherapy and the Christian message. But every shift in anthropology entails a readjustment in soteriology: a modern doctrine of the Savior of modern sinners. Again, if a modern man is to witness to Jesus Christ as *his* Lord and Savior, what sort of language, derived from what noetic categories, can he rightly use to celebrate his new life with God in Christ? Finally, how can he learn to think of himself in real relation with all other Christians 'in this world and the next'? These are some of the 'new' questions which I have seen emerging in the last few years and which I expect to see influencing the shape of theological things to come. At any rate they are the questions which have exercised my mind for the past decade, accounting for whatever changes have occurred.

"I have already mentioned the fact that Christology has come to confront us again as if it were almost a new question. Along with many others I have spent the past ten years exploring this maze and mystery—trying to rehearse its history and reformulate its import in modern terms. The gist of my conclusions thus far can be scantily summarized in five theses: (1) the Definition of Chalcedon, understood in context, is still the basic text for a valid, modern Christology; (2) since Chalcedon, 'orthodox' Christology—East and West—has failed to maintain a proper doctrine of the full and real humanity of Jesus Christ; (3) the Protestant stress on the work and corresponding de-emphasis on the person of Christ is a misunderstanding; (4) Enlightenment Christology was the function of Enlightenment anthropology and hence is now as archaic as its scholastic counterpart; (5) modern personality theory is a major new resource for the interpretation of the biblical and Chalcedonian witnesses to the Man of God's own choosing. I would like to see a modern restatement of the two-natures doctrine that would move from our knowledge of the agent of our salvation to an understanding of the act of our salvation, to that faith-acting-in-love which is the Christian life.

"Ten years ago, as I can see by my lecture notes, I was still belaboring traditional phrases—rational and irrational, natural and supernatural, transcendent and immanent, finite and infinite—as metaphors about God and the world. Aided by biblical theologians I have come to see that this split-level language does not ring true in terms of the Bible or Christian experience. I have come to believe that it is better to begin with the fact that God is *always* present and acting, whether 'known' or not. Then one can speak of the two different ways that he is present: either in his mystery or his manifestation. God-Mysterious is utterly ineffable; God-Manifest is actually knowable, but only when, where and as he chooses to reveal himself. We are aware of God-Mysterious—and this awareness is as primitive as our awareness of motion, causality or self. We are also grasped by the presence of God-Manifest, and this supplies the data of religious knowledge. In neither case is God at our disposal.

"Thus faith and reason are not two different ramps or two different levels of reality. Rather, they are two different responses to the two different modes of God's presence and action. Faith cannot verify itself; reason cannot originate its data. Our language-games—of worship and theology—must reflect these two dimensions of experience. The language of worship adores God-Mysterious, confesses God-Manifest, and speaks of repentance, forgiveness and new being. It is therefore essentially doxological and confessional. It confesses, without rational proof that the supreme manifestation of God-Mysterious is Jesus Christ—in manifest fullness and not merely as symbol.

"The language of theology is both like and unlike the language of worship. Theology is reflection upon the reality of worship and an explication of it. As such it is a rational affair—receiving its data as given, testing its methodology, trying to make sense—faith seeking to understand. The function of theology is to guide the dialogue between faith and understanding and to prevent either from excluding the other. Significantly new and somewhat unexpected resources for developing these notions are being provided for us in the work of those linguistic analysts who are exploring the meaning of theological explanations.

"The happy dilettante, who believes in justification by faith *and* hope, prays to be judged by his intention as well as by his performance. He is as much concerned with what he can see as needful as with what he himself can provide. If I could choose my own epitaph, I would want it to speak of one who was sustained in a rather strenuous career by the vision of a Christian theology that gives history its full due; that makes way for the future without having to murder the past; that begins and ends with the self-manifestation of God's Mystery in our flesh and history; that binds itself to Scripture but also claims scriptural authority for a rational hermeneutic; that opposes human pride and speaks of God's healing grace without despising or exalting the creature; that unites justice and mercy without resorting either to legalism or to antinomianism; that organizes the Christian life by the power of grace and the means of grace; that celebrates our redemption by the invincible love of God which is in Christ Jesus our Lord—in sum a theology that does justice to the reality it reflects upon. It is enough for any man to believe that he has been called to labor in some such task as this, for he cannot doubt that whether it is given him to plant, to water or to harvest, God will give the increase."[119]

History and theology were inseparable in Outler's mind. He derided those who prided themselves on their theology and ignored history. He once said, "There are those who know little about Luther or Calvin and even less about Christianity before the Reformation—because they knew in advance of studying it that there wasn't anything you needed to know about Christianity. When you know what you don't need to know, you have a very interesting license for ignorance."[120]

Theology Via Sermons

The previous statements describe Outler the historical theologian. Outler described in answers to my queries on how his theology reached his hearers through his sermons: "Theology is the attempt to make credible and persuasive the experiences of faith and love, of hearing the Word. You hear the Word from the text in these circumstances. Then you try to make sense out of it. You enlist the people in their reflections upon the Word—not upon your words. I don't ask people to hear what I say and accept it verbatim. I ask them to hear what I say and then take the problem at their own particular levels. It is a question of: here I am; there you are; and there you are [he looked at different ones in the room as he said this] and here is the Word. What does it say to you? What are you going to do about it?

"So this means that every theological enterprise (including the sermon) arises out of living faith in participation with the living faith of the living church. And instead of being the directive of the church's thought, *it is a reflection of the church's heart and mind.* If this is the case, it cannot be systematized in a neat and complete fashion beyond which you cannot go. I have told you about my friend Nels Ferré who wrote his theology back in the 1940s and spent the rest of his life defending it.

"From this I have concluded that theology is perennial, unavoidable, but also in the nature of the case not a completable undertaking. And that means that what I have tried to do is to formulate whatever insights I am given, and in the formulation comes the discovery of new horizons of insight, inquiry, and understanding. I cannot fully express the understanding that I have. So I do the best that I can. So then when I am through, I wonder why I can't say this over again. Because if I can say it over again, I can alter the perspective a little and that will help somebody see from a more lucid angle.

"This means, not that I am changing my mind, as much as I am trying to discover what the mind of Christ is to that situation, and how to communicate this to people, not so that they will say, 'Ah, I see now what you mean,' but that they will say, 'Ah, I see now what I can understand in my own way.'

"This is why I have managed to do pretty well preaching with a manuscript and without illustrations. Both of these methods work against you in any normal congregation. And yet the compensation for it is that I am not trying to fix a point in anybody's mind. I'm trying to start a process of reflection of insight within their hearts and minds. And they supply the illustrations. They hear the thing from the manuscript, and then they turn it into some kind of spontaneous process for themselves. That is a view of preaching I don't propose as a paradigm, but that is what I have been doing.

"I had begun to wonder about it because people had begun to comment on it. But I have to have a manuscript. I have to read a text. And I never know when, as I am going on, that an 'aside' will strike. In some ways that has either added to or provided the dimension of surprise, of humor, and illumination. I remember Willis Tate [president of SMU] once saying that it wasn't half as good to sit far back in McFarland auditorium [at SMU] as when he could sit up close because if he missed the 'asides,' the rest of the thing wasn't all that good!"

Apropos of Outler's comment on Nels Ferré, a contributing factor to Outler's commitment *not* to write a systematic theology came from his studying John Wesley and realizing that Wesley's quadrilateral—Scripture, tradition, reason, and experience—with its emphasis on a *doing* theology rather that a *having done* systematic theology, made more sense than any system he could devise in any particular time and place. Outler noted that a systematician, in efforts to conceptualize the mysteries of faith, sometimes tends to say "absolutely" when one means "on the whole," "totally" when one means "generally," and "precisely" when one means "nearly."[121] This much we do know—just as Wesley before him, Outler altered his alterations with any new symbols that had to do with the mysterious Word of Life. His words pointed to the Word.

A Faith Proclamation

These statements by Outler showed that he allowed his faith proclamation (kerygmatic preaching) to make full use of history and dogma. His preaching brought a balance of both in a manner that permitted them to be the carriers of the gospel that they were. He saw in history divine providence at work in the human condition (estrangement from others, God, and self). He saw history with a destiny not yet clearly laid out, but with an end determined by God in spite of what seemed like humankind's determination to destroy itself. That view of history transformed dogma (creeds and other statements *about* God and all things that have to do with God) into a living Word *of* God. Thus, Outler preached in theological terms the truth of God. In the previous paragraphs he told about the unorthodox formation of his sermons. They *sounded* more theological than most sermons largely because they had something theologically sound to say. Like Wesley before him, Outler preached doctrinal sermons.

The Vehicle of the Proclamation

A closer look reveals that he was not proclaiming a historical theology or a dogmatic theology so much as he was presenting his deep beliefs and experiences of faith via the vehicle with which he was best suited, viz., the theological jargon, with "asides" giving them the lift they needed in the preaching moment. This accounts for the fact that no preacher can preach like Outler simply because one reads well Outler's sermons. Yet a reading of Outler's sermons does provide a wealth of material to preach. To try to imitate his Georgia drawl would be disastrous. Outler once said, "Sometimes I get such doubtful compliments as 'you don't sound like a theologian.'" And then he mentioned the DePauw coed's comment: "That's the best lecture I ever heard in a grits and gravy accent."[122]

A Baptism by Immersion

While teaching historical theology, Outler often referred to his own history in those "grits and gravy" settings. He told this story to his students: "In my first circuit [1927], during my first revival—I was fresh out of college; I was twenty—the superintendent of a rural junior high school and pastor of two Methodist churches, and the only person in the whole of Appling County School System with a B.A. degree. In the first membership class was a high school girl who wanted to be baptized. It turns out she wanted to be immersed. So I explained to her that she would not need to be. And she explained to me that she would need to be! She had been converted and would not settle for [what she considered to be] an anticlimax. She did not want to die in baptism. She wanted to be drowned! So I tried to explain to her, and she tried to explain to me. So I got out the *Discipline.* It said she had the selection of modes. I had not been to seminary then. I don't know what good it would have done if I had! And then there was no *friendly* Baptist preacher around from whom I could learn anything. So she was immersed.

"But if I were teaching in a Baptist seminary, I would make very sure that students learned early that when you baptize people in a running stream, you always do it upstream. I do not know why I did not think of that. I understood the principle of hydraulics. But you don't convert physics and metaphysics on a thing like this. And she was the most fairly immersed of the membership class. When she came up against the front of the current, she was not only immersed outside—her sinuses were flushed. Moreover, she was a sizable girl. And I just barely got her up. It made an indelible mark on my memory. For her, baptism was a sign of her conversion."[123] And it also was a sign of a young pastor's willingness to do what the situation called for, even if he was not at that time ordained to do it.

Summary

The reading of Outler's sermons and lectures reveal the heart of the man. Since "reflection of the church's heart and mind" was his definition of preaching, it would follow that *his* teaching and preaching reflected Christ's heart and mind through the church of which he was a part. This suggests that, to know Outler, one has to know his Christ.

All his days academician Outler worked hard as a disciplined teacher who expected and required the same of both students and colleagues. As a scintillating teacher in command of a great sweep of church history and doctrine, Outler applied the past to the present. With squinted eyes, he peered into the future with his knowledge and piety (faith). And more often than not he saw most things clearly.

7

As a Sports Enthusiast

W here in the midst of Outler's many activities do you put his interest in sports? A letter written by him to Carla on October 11, 1956, suggests that this is the place: right after the chapter, "As a Historical Theologian." With sports being so totally foreign to the average egghead community, its place here accentuates the dilettante aspect of Outler's makeup. He said: "This is the main news since I wrote last. Since then I've done some bibliographical chores in the library, outlined Chapter Two, and watched *three* World Series games! How about that? The two Dodger victories were great fun, for even if I am not for the Dodgers in the National League, I'm for almost anybody against the Yankees. I feel just a mite guilty taking time out for such lowbrow recreation; only a very small group of the graduate students come to the TV room for the games and *no* professors! But I do find my drive faltering after a long stretch here at the desk, or on the books. And as for the eyes of the eggheads, I'm coming to find a certain zest in cocking my snoot at them. And all along I thought I was an egghead!"

Indeed Outler was an egghead, even in his involvement with sports. Things like the field judge placing the football almost at random on any of the downs generally shy of ten yards bugged him. A foot either way did not seem to matter to anyone on the field or in the stands. But if the players or the judges felt the ball was fairly close to an advance of ten yards, then a precise measurement to a quarter of an inch had to be made. Outler found humor in how precisely a ball would be placed on one play and how imprecisely it might be placed on the next. He enjoyed more aspects of the game than most spectators.

Baseball

Involvement in intramural sports continued from boyhood through undergraduate and graduate schools and into his days on the faculty. Writing to Carla from Union Theological Seminary in New York, where he was teaching in 1945, Outler said: "This letter is being written under some difficulty, for I've 'gone and done it again.' Yesterday, in a softball game, I snagged a high fast one right in the left eye, and the broken glass did a nasty job. But, thanks be to God, there's no serious nor permanent damage; the only result is some discomfort and the inconvenience of having to work with only one eye and that without glasses."

After he could no longer participate in the more physical sports, Outler continued to share vicariously in the action and play them in his mind. Once in a classroom at Perkins School of Theology, a student asked Outler at the beginning of a class who would win the World Series that year. Outler laid aside his class notes and proceeded to pick his winner based on the batting averages of the players (he named them—all of them on both sides), the records of the pitchers (he gave those—all of them), defensive characteristics of both sides (listing them). And then compared them to World Series teams of years gone by (giving statistics, etc.). While the class did not learn much about Systematic Theology on that day, they did experience systematic thinking at its best—in sports!

Fish and Fishing

In his early years Outler enjoyed the sport of fishing. In his later years he did more armchair fishing than actual fishing. For him fishing meant more than putting a hook or lure in the water. It included the study of fish. On one occasion in 1959 he came to preach a Sunday morning service for me in Whitehouse,

Texas. We had a twenty-gallon aquarium with numerous types of tropical fish swimming about. Without prompting, Outler proceeded to name kingdom, phylum, and subphylum of each kind of fish. His interest in fish went far beyond wetting a hook and putting meat on the table—though it did include that aspect of the sport, too.

On that same trip to Whitehouse, following Outler's sermon a farmer in his overalls came up to Outler and said in a very helpful sympathetic voice: "You don't *have to* teach. You have the makin's of a durn good preacher"!

Along with stamp collecting and photography (especially of churches and church art and sculpture), sports were his hobbies. His encyclopedic knowledge of baseball, golf, football, basketball, etc., revealed an informed mind that functioned at an accelerated rate whether at work or play.

8

As a Psychotherapist

Theological Anthropology

Outler, in all of his scholarly meanderings, was a theologian. He made this clear in the following declaration: "First and last, I am a theologian; a dilettante, maybe, but a *theological* dilettante! And my liveliest intellectual curiosity throughout the years has been focused on the question of Christian faith and secular wisdom. Hence, my interest in patristics, where Platonism was appropriated and transformed by the Christians in construction of the Christian doctrine of *God*. And [I have an] interest in medieval scholasticism, when the newly discovered Aristotle helped Christians develop a doctrine of nature that supported the Christian doctrine of grace, in a fashion that could rightly be called 'scientific' then and now. And finally [I am] interested in modern psychology, which is the humanistic distillate of the modern life sciences and behavioral sciences. At stake is a Christian doctrine of human nature that can match the biblical revelation of the fullness of the stature of humanity perfected in Jesus Christ and the critical self-understanding of modern man as to his place before God and in nature. For there can be little doubt that the overwhelming dominant issue of our time is the problem about human beings themselves—

our nature, identity, possibilities and destiny. From the Christian point of view, [we have] the urgent and open enterprise of what we might call a *theological* anthropology to lay alongside the secularized anthropologies which are being developed in such great profusion by our psychologists and philosophers."[124]

He wrote, "Psychotherapy, as a strictly empirical discipline, cannot tell us what we are—and ought not tell us we are *nothing but*. Neither can it supply a vigorous description of existence as a whole."[125] But Outler used it in a manner that enriched existence as it was played out in the moment. This ability gave him a unique edge as an observer at Vatican II. He commented on the third Session's discussion of religious liberty: "In this ruckus, as in others, it was instructive to watch the onset of the liberal's panic-syndrome and the cynics' vindication-complex. The first of these is somewhat similar to a manic-depression pattern, with mood-swings that range from soaring hopes of total victory to panic-fears of total defeat, with vivid bitterness toward the villains held responsible for so dire an insecurity."[126]

Outler, from his Emory days on, applied the truths of psychotherapy alongside theological anthropologies grounded in revelatory truths of scripture. He saw each discipline drawing strength from the other, each uniquely contributing to a broader evaluation of the human situation.

Epistemological Limitations of Psychologies

One of Outler's largest contributions to understanding the many shoots from the trunk of psychology is the up-front epistemological limitations that they carry concerning the human quandary as a whole: "For seven years at Duke, I lived as neighbor and colleague to Joseph B. Rhine, and so have had something of a ringside seat at the contest over the data and interpretation of ESP and of telekinesis. The problem never was whether there is something 'real' in the alleged data of parapsychology, but rather whether and how it can be quantified and made a matter of verifiable and manageable public knowledge (i.e., to allow for precise and regular predictions). [1] All the parapsychologists have ever achieved—according to the general verdict of their academic peers—is the sort of gross statistical generalizations like those of insurance actuaries: important for any calculations of percentages; negligible for individual case procedures.

"My dog-eared copy of Sir Charles Sherrington's *Man on His Nature* (his Gifford lectures of 1937–38) is mute witness to a lifelong interest in psycho-neurobiology; and it was in graduate school that I first discovered Hughlings Jackson and his distinctions between the successive levels of neural stimulus-responsiveness—from spinal ganglia to the granulated frontal cortex of human brains. Two years with Clark Hull and Skinner illustrate the difference between the professional and the amateur scientist. None of this, of course, has made me a scientist, in any strict sense. I'm no qualified judge of the speculations now being bruited about in the current psychological investigations. [2] But it has taught me a sturdy skepticism as to any claims that he made in the name of experimental science as to what is known or knowable about an identifiable personal agent in neural activity of any sort and on any level."

Pastoral Vocational Interests

"My own first glimpses of this new frontier run back into the mists of pre-history (i.e., before there was a movement—and not many pioneers). It was in my seminary days—when B.D. theses were required! My own academic major was theology (historical theology at that), but my vocational interests were pastoral (they still are, in a curious, frustrated way) [Outler had little sympathy for those 'pastors' who were 'incomprehensible on Sunday and invisible the rest of the week'[127]]; and so I asked myself what I could do for a thesis that would focus on the pastoral office—and also garner the smatterings of my widely scattered interest. And so I proposed to the faculty committee a topic with a 180 degree angle: 'The Use of Psychotherapy in Pastoral Work.' And what was even more preposterous was that they solemnly accepted the project— partly because it had not been preempted (to their knowledge or mine) in 1932, partly because they didn't know enough about it to know just how preposterous it was, and also partly because we were very fond of each other and they believed that it might be a useful lesson in the delicate balance between curiosity and foolhardiness!

"I mention this as evidence for my own partial identification with the Pastoral Care Movement, before there was one—and as the beginning of my marginal involvement in it ever since. My Yale Ph.D. was in patristics, but on the side, I also managed a sizable chunk of the residence requirements for a graduate degree in psychology (in the Institute of Human Relations), and then later (when I'd returned to Yale on the faculty) a series of seminars at the William Allenson White Institute of Psychiatry in New York. Twice I came within a hair of going whole hog into medicine (or, alternatively, a Ph.D. in 'clinical psychology')—on the premise that I would still defend, viz., that scientific psychiatry is the paradigm for any fully respectable specialization. My decision, in each case, therefore, was a vote for the *generalist* conception of the pastoral office and, for myself at least, a judgment that pastoral care as a paramedical *specialization* would always be something of a professional anomaly. How I got to be neither a doctor nor a pastor nor any other one 'thing' is another story that we can ignore for our purposes here."[128]

Writing the "Wedding Ceremony"

Among the many "things" that Outler did regarding psychotherapy and the Christian faith, foremost is that he wrote the "wedding ceremony" that brought these two disciplines together: "The Christian gospel is a joyous word from God to man in the depths of his existence. It speaks of the origins and the ends of human life, of God as ground and sustaining power of existence, of man under God's command and blessing, of man in quandary and sin, of God in Christ reconciling the world unto himself, of the Holy Spirit making for a community of truly matured and fulfilled persons. It is a word of man's reliance on God, of man's hope in God, of God's imperative that we should love him devotedly and our neighbors mutually. It is God's word by which he has ordered life from the beginning in faithfulness, has redeemed it in love and will so order it to his gracious end that men should be both righteous and blessed. The gospel is a call to repentance and faith, new life and Christian maturity. It is a divine promise of reconciliation in a new fullness of life. It is an invitation of the Holy Spirit to life in the body of Christ, the beloved community of faith and grace, in which there spring up the spontaneous impulses to thanksgiving and worship and service to God, whose grace is the power of our goodness, whose service is our perfect freedom.

"What is called for—and what seems to me clearly possible—is a *division of labor*, on the one hand, and *a synthesis of goals* on the other. The professional therapist cannot do the work of the Christian minister, nor can the minister replace the therapist. But both could do their proper work within the same assumptions and goals derived from a basic Christian faith and commitment. The time is fully ripe for those psychotherapists who are devout believers in God—there are a few, and in good standing, too—to undertake the exploration of the issues in their field in the light of their faith. The believing physician must show that his science concretes his faith as his faith supplies ultimate meaning to his science. And on the other side, the well-furnished Christian minister must enlist in the arduous enterprise of really learning from the psychotherapists and appropriating all possible aid from them in understanding himself and his task more adequately. Together in joint projects, the believing physician and the well-furnished minister may widen and enrich their service to God and their fellows far beyond what we have known from either in the past."[129]

The Forensic *and* Clinical Metaphors

Outler recognized an unconscious wedding of the two disciplines (before they were disciplines!) by John Wesley: "Wesley was forced by grace to open his heart to his hearers—to seek them on their terms, rather than flinging the gospel to them like brickbats of faith."[130] Then Outler consciously allowed psychotherapeutic insights to open up theological insights that had been lying dormant in the Holy Bible for over 2,000 years. While affirming the forensic metaphor of the courtroom scene as a scripturally valid way of talking about our guilt "position *before* God," it is far from the only way that the Bible talks about our relationship with him. It also has a message for us moderns that has nothing to do with the courtroom scene, a scene that has been devalued by a social cynicism of the modern justice system. "Once upon a time 'law and order' had a metaphysical reference. Now it is only a tainted euphemism for the coercive power of those who have the police and taxing powers on their side. This domestication of the law and its agents is the real solvent that has washed out the moral cement that held Western society together, however tenuously. And with it went all the traditional notions about *guilt*—guilt before God and divine justice and right."[131]

"Suppose, then, we let the forensic, courtroom metaphor go and turn, as so many have, to therapeutic and clinical metaphors. What then? This is a clear advance, in many ways, and is much to be welcomed and incorporated into our pastoral theory and practice. But there is no avoiding the fact that *therapy*, in any and all its images, means nothing more than amelioration—not complete and real fulfillment. Therapy is the reduction of this symptom or that, the curing of this malady or that. It does not and cannot mean the resolution of our ultimate concerns. It cannot fend off death. Its best good news is never better than a comparative judgment that our frustrations are not as dreadful as they might have been.

"Thus, beyond the courtroom and the clinic, the human hunger for happiness still reaches out in an intuition that there is and must be some sovereign power of caring that is neither a bloodless category nor a wishful dream. The good news that we really need to hear is that 'God so loved the world that he gave of himself that the world [we!] might not perish [in some void of thwarted dreams], but have *life* in *all* its human potential.' There is nothing forensic in the old text; it reaches above and beyond any sort of clinical model.

"There is, therefore, real *gospel* in the message of God's love in Christ—'the power of God and the wisdom of God.' 'You,' said St. Paul, 'are in Christ Jesus by God's act, for God has made him *our* wisdom; he is our righteousness; in him we are consecrated and set free (1 Corinthians 1:24, 30, NEB). There is nothing forensic here." [132] This is found to be so in the majority of the New Testament scriptures.

"This is not to reject or even diminish the living truth in the grand articles of justification, pardon, regeneration, reconciliation, and so on. It is only to stress, more than our traditions usually have done, the fact that our Christian hope rests in God's calling us to participate in his goodness, which is the primordial and ultimate ground of our true happiness—to participate both in the human *potential* and in the divine *actuality*."[133]

A Teacher of Pastoral Psychology

Outler, prior to his retirement from full-time teaching at Perkins at the end of the 1973–74 academic year, was approached by Leroy Howe, who "suggested to Outler that he might consider offering a course on pastoral theology that would afford an occasion for summing up his reflections on the discipline which had been of interest to him for over forty years. With enthusiasm he [Outler] agreed to teach a course entitled 'The History and Theology of Pastoral Care,' during the fall semester, 1973. Dr. Harville Hendrix, then a member of the Perkins faculty in pastoral care and now a well-known therapist, author, and lecturer in his own right, shared some of the teaching responsibilities with Outler in the course. Outler's lectures had a broader impact than they might have had otherwise, for they were delivered over closed circuit television to which students in other institutions beyond Southern Methodist University had access. Restoration of the videotapes of his and Dr. Hendrix's lectures is currently under way at the Outler Archives of Perkins' Bridwell Library. Evaluation of the course itself was positive, and in some quarters bordered on what Outler termed the 'embarrassingly glowing.'

"Outler's lectures for this course provide an unusually close look into the way he typically taught his classes, mixing magisterial historical overviews with insightful comments on contemporary issues, garnished with good humor and conveyed with uncannily apt turns of phrase. Read in context of his earlier discussions, these lectures offer more than a glimpse into how Outler's thinking matured over several decades. But in this editor's [Howe's] judgment, they have their importance not so much for what they reveal about their author, but for what they contribute to the discipline of pastoral psychology itself. For they bring impressively to fruition a perspective which insists that neither pastoral care nor psychotherapy can be well served without theoretical reflection committed to seeing the *humanum* in its fullness, that is, in relation to its transcendent origin, environment, and destiny.

"The reflections Outler here offers set pastoral care on a firm foundation, make plain the continuing relevance of psychodynamic psychotherapies to pastoral care and counseling (and in the process show the silliness of a variety of still popular technique-driven approaches to healing), outline an agenda for future discussion between healers from the pastoral and the clinical disciplines, and proffer a theology of the Christian life which contains within itself norms capable of guiding both ministers of pastoral care and counseling and psychotherapists alike."[134] Assuming that Howe's statements are true (when one sees the taped lectures he refers to, assumptions turn to facts!), the video images and sounds will bring Outler "alive" for many years to come in keeping these two disciplines in sync.

An "Intrusion" into Union's Affairs

Outler's interest in the two disciplines working in sync lasted all the days of his life. In a November 27, 1981, letter to Professor Ann Ulanov in the Program of Psychiatry and Religion at Union Theological Seminary in New York Outler wrote: "It was shocking (and a mite incredible) to hear from you the proposal that your program in 'Psychiatry and Religion' be discontinued in favor of a radically diminished substitute. Ordinarily, I would hesitate to do more in response than to deplore this in private, since I know (and generally approve) the 'law' in Academe against 'outside interference' in curricular and budget affairs. If the case were reversed, none of us here would welcome (or heed) gratuitous advice from an outsider as to how we should run 'our business.'

"But my professional and personal ties with Union run deep and far back—longtime friendships and collaborations with both faculty and students over the years. Moreover, and along with other theological educators of my generation, I have fine old traditions of regarding Union's outstanding record of contributions to the American (and world) scene with admiration and gratitude. In times past you have helped us all with your pioneering and with your concern for academic standards, and you've helped me immensely in the hospitable use of your incomparable library!

"I am, therefore, emboldened to break the rule and to send you and your committee a very earnest appeal to ponder, very carefully indeed, the wider, long-range effects, of any such discontinuation of what has been one of Union's glories. I know about budget crunches; the fiscal woes of seminaries are grim all over. But why sacrifice your leadership in an important area of theology and psychotherapy that runs back, as I know well, to the days of David Roberts. Back in the late forties, when Dave and I began the dialogue between theologians and psychiatrists in America, the reaction was largely cool and uncomprehending. Now, as we all know, the climate of dialogue and collaboration between the two fields has become much more hospitable.

"But this is also to say that *now* is exactly the *wrong time* to cancel one of the programs that has done so much to effect this important climactic change. In my judgment, this would mean a serious loss to your own students (which is, I grant you, *your* business). But it would also mean a serious loss to the rest of us out here, who stand to profit from your leadership (as we have in the past). Such a discontinuance would amount to a public statement that Union has backed away from its traditional role of probing the horizons of inquiry that lie between psychiatry and theology (as nonidentical wisdoms about life). The consequences of such a 'statement' would be deplorable. The notion that a few courses in pastoral care and counseling could replace your present program without a drastic loss will seem quite incredible to your professional colleagues elsewhere.

"The program in Psychiatry and Religion has been one of your stronger points over the years. Why weaken it *now?* And *for* what? I realize that in times of retrenchment, the questions of priorities become urgent and struggles for survival tend to blur an institution's concerns for its extramural responsibilities. I hope, therefore, that this hesitant intrusion of mine will be understood as a respectful testimony to the fact that your program in Psychiatry and Religion is widely regarded as highly important and as a value judgment to the effect that its discontinuance would widely be regarded as both retrograde and regrettable."

The Outcome

Professor Ulanov answered in a December 4 letter: "You will be glad to hear that the Program in Psychiatry and Religion survived the challenge in the Curriculum Committee and was no part of any recommendation to cut faculty positions to meet the budget constraints facing the Seminary. We want very much to thank you for your own warm and good-hearted and very useful contributions to this happy outcome."

In this instance Outler had counseled (and challenged) the best of the counselors. And won the day for this, one of many of *his* interests. He helped keep alive an ongoing conversation between two disciplines for whom he had *the Word*. The *humanum* foundation in Jesus Christ that Outler laid out remains a bridge over which pastoral care and psychotherapy advocates may walk freely and learn from each other as they share insights in passing.

9

As an Arts and Sciences Person

As a Fellow of the American Academy of Arts and Sciences and the blue ribbon Society for Art, Religion, and Culture, Outler identified with a community of persons who valued highly aesthetics and the adventures of the mind. Concerning the latter he said, "It was founded by Paul Tillich over two decades ago, and still has an impressive roster of outstanding artists, social scientists, philosophers, theologians, and public figures. Don't ask me how I got to be a Fellow; I never understood it either."[135] But they understood that *they* needed him on *their* roster. And he enjoyed being in their company. For him these were interests akin to his own. His devotion to beauty and good taste and good thoughts came out of the divinely influenced nature of the man.

Bach, the Fifth Evangelist

A deep appreciation of poetry and music flowed from Outler's lectures and sermons. At times his conclusions rang with poetry or poetic prayers that resembled something out of Bach. He said: "Bach was the fifth evangelist. He told the story of Jesus in his music as Matthew, Mark, Luke, and John did in the gospels. He was the last of the great aesthetic geniuses in Western culture to have a global sense of goodness, beauty, and truth—the last with a genius level of technical competence, of lyrical beauty, of a genuinely heavenly vision of what is glory. When he lets all of these talents go, you have something in music that the rest of Western music strives toward but doesn't achieve. There is no part of Bach, including the secular music, including occasional music, that isn't touched with genius and from which one cannot keep studying and appreciating. Nearest thing to this is Beethoven's *Last Quartet*, the *String Quartets*. There you have the agonizing sense of tragedy redeemed by beauty.

"In Bach you have the sense of human dependency upon the grace of God. But not this titanic struggle against fate. Bach has a sense of providence with which he must struggle, and in which he must receive and use his gifts. Beethoven has a sense of fate with which he has to struggle. So that in a certain sense I find that Bach's music is more nearly inexhaustible. I listen to it and I listen to it, and it seems to me that this is what Christian faith and aesthetic genius do together. Beethoven was formerly a professing Christian; but you do not get a New Testament sense of awareness of and communion with God. Bach seems to me not to have said the 'last word,' but to have made a kind of aesthetic achievement that the rest of Western music has to, not imitate, but take as its benchmark."

Bruebeck

"In popular folk music Bruebeck is important because there you have the peculiar combination of spontaneity in jazz with the discipline of classical and contemporary music. When Bruebeck starts, he is either playing jazz or he is jazzing up the classical tradition. As the Spirit begins to work, you get something that transcends both. I can live with every part of the heritage though. . . . Vivaldi's *Four Seasons* . . . I have a new recording of it that is just wonderful. One of my favorites is Fauré's *Requiem,* which ends, not with the normal *Requiem,* but with the hymn of the angels welcoming the soul into Paradise. That's the one I want done at my funeral"[136] This was sung at his memorial service.

A Music Critic

On February 20, 1957, Albert wrote to Carla: "I'm just back from a piano concert by Eduard Steverman, a man of whom I had never heard until he was wrung in as a replacement for Solomon, who has canceled his American tour because of illness. It was, alas, only a fair program and only moderately well-done. A Schnabel he ain't! But the last half of the program was the Diabelli Variations of Beethoven, which I had never heard before, and this made it definitely worthwhile."

Just seven days later Albert wrote Carla from Princeton: "Today was devoted to the seminar—and tonight another concert. [He had been to a concert the night before.] It was the Vienna Octet—the top desk men from the Vienna Philharmonic playing some of the quintet and sextet chamber music of Brahms and Mozart. The music was not very heavy, but the performance was superb! And that reminds me—yesterday I went into Sam Goody's to see if they had a copy of the Landowska record of four Mozart sonatas. It came out in December and got rave reviews. I had assumed that I could pick up one any time I got around to it, but at Goody's they said that the masters have been damaged and there may be no more copies available. Would you be willing to call up several of the record shops and music stores in Dallas to see if they have any copies left? It is an RCA Victor record: #LM6044 (2-LPs 12"). If you find one, latch onto it and I'll square up with you, come April; for it's to be a collector's item; we'd better grab it, if there is one to be grabbed."

The record was purchased and added to a music library that furnished classical music entertainment for his neighbors. His living room was a "boom box" before its time. His collection, consisting of hundreds of records, was given to the School of Music at Southern Methodist University at the time he moved to Bradenton.

Music influenced Outler's preaching and lecturing while the music itself may never have been mentioned at all. Musicians from Bach to Bruebeck gave rest to his soul when he had nothing to say (hours were spent in silent listening), and gave soul to what he had to say when he stood behind a lectern or pulpit.

The Isthmus Institute

Outler's interest in science equaled his interest in the arts. During his days as Research Professor of Theology, Emeritus, at Perkins in the 1970s, he found relief from the extraordinarily tense and intense scholarly effort of editing the Wesley *Sermons* by helping found and direct (on the Board of Directors) the Isthmus Institute in Dallas. The metaphor of a narrow strip of land between two oceans suggests the vision of convergencies between science as one body of knowledge/experiences and religion as the other body of knowledge/experiences. The metaphor recognizes their separateness, but suggests an easier commerce between the two across the isthmus.

He immersed himself in the discussions of these uncommonly erudite and professional persons committed to exploring the relations between science and religion at the frontiers of both disciplines. He lived to see the day when science lifted its old veto of religion moving into the areas of motivations and action; whereas theologians now have a whole new realm of questions for the scientists to concentrate on and seek to find answers. He saw scientists and theologians supplying agenda for each other. In response to Nobel Laureate Sir John Eccles' thesis that "there is a moral responsibility stemming from free will from the ability of your mind to work on the brain,"[137] Outler brought their mind-boggling thoughts about the mind down to earth with this question: "Could it be that the brain is the mind's computer, and the mind is the brain's programmer?"[138]

Where did Outler rank among this group characterized by wide knowledge of their respective disciplines? Interest questionnaires sent to Isthmus Institute members asking them to grade the speakers (Outler was included as one of the twelve speakers, four of whom were Nobel laureates, for the years 1982, 1983, and 1984) answers that question. Isthmus secretary A. Gerald Spalding wrote a note on the bottom of the form letter that went to Outler asking for each member's evaluation: "If you check the arrows carefully on the 'summary of response,' you will notice that you had the highest average score of all the talent used in 1982, 1983, and 1984. That is no surprise, but it is nice to see."

10

As a Methodist

Outler's being reared in a Methodist parsonage, serving as a Methodist local church pastor, graduating from a Methodist seminary, teaching in a Methodist seminary, and serving as a United Methodist delegate to six General and Jurisdictional Conferences qualify the man uniquely as a *Methodist*. His influence on the law of the Methodist church (long before it was changed to United Methodist) is written in the minutes of the General Conferences he attended as a delegate. However much he may have affected the law of the Methodist church, *that* was not the power he finally trusted. He always looked to something (Someone) higher.

A Vote Against Merger!

Outler was looking to Someone higher when he voted *against* the original Methodist/EUB merger plan. How could Outler, Mr. *World* Methodist, vote *against* the merger at the November 1966 General Conference held in Chicago? In a February 19, 1968, letter to Mrs. David A. Nelson, Outler gave the answer when he said: "It is true that I voted against the EUB-Methodist merger proposals, but not because I was opposed to the *fact* of the merger.

What had happened was that, both before and during the Conference, the ad hoc Committee had railroaded *their* plan, with open contempt for the consultative and parliamentary processes by which true consensus and union might have been achieved. Amendments were offered and the one amendment (on the 'ecumenical paragraph' in the constitution) that the General Conference rose up and passed (over Mr. Parlin's contemptuous opposition) was then scuttled in joint committee. In short, this particular plan of merger was rammed down our throats on the plea that the idea of the merger was so good that nobody in favor of Christian unity would object. But, passionate ecumenist that I am, I *did* object both to undemocratic means to ecumenical ends and to the spirit and form of *this particular plan.* The essence of this plan is merger with minimum change: *union without reform.* The only ecumenism I believe in or want to support is one that encourages reform and renewal in order to more effective mission. Under the circumstances, I *had* to register my convictions by voting 'No.' It was a spiritual agony that still saddens and disturbs me.

"All of this is to say that union is not an end in itself nor is it an end that justifies any means used by a small group in their manipulations of the large generality of church members. The means in achieving a union are crucially important to the validity and quality of the union, and any act of union is itself a means to reform, renewal and a higher level of dedication and Christian service. Thus, I am not unhappy with the fact and prospect of the United Methodist Church, but I do not approve of the way this business has been, and is still being, handled. And I believe that we still have a great deal of soul-searching and reform to undertake before the UMC can fulfill even a part of its potential and promise.

"This is, I think, wholly consistent with my lifelong ecumenical devotion, and I would hope that you and your class will recognize the distinction I have suggested between a worthy end and unworthy means to that end. If so, you will understand why I can exhort you to keep the ecumenical faith and yet also keep your fingers crossed about the practical details of this particular example of ecumenical mismanagement."

One aspect of Outler's reluctance to vote for the merger, which was left out of this letter, was written by Spurgeon Dunnam in the December 1, 1966, *Texas Methodist:* "But, as previously indicated, other important factors were involved in his [Outler's] negative vote. Dr. Outler strongly objected to the name of the new church: The United Methodist Church. He stated that Methodists have been arrogant enough in the past calling themselves THE Methodist Church when there were other churches also in the Wesleyan tradition. He thus considered it a compounded felony to be THE UNITED Methodist Church, a name which, by its very nature, is a false description. In typical Outlerian humor, he observed that since according to the new constitution, the name will have to be changed on all public documents, 'I guess we'll have to change the name of Southern Methodist University to SUMU. I wonder what that will do to our school song "Varsity"?'"

When the EUB-Methodist union did come in the April 1968 General Conference, Outler not only voted for the merger, he was asked to give the Uniting Conference sermon. In the sermon, he emphasized what he saw lacking in the first efforts of General Conference merger: "a church truly catholic, truly evangelical, truly *reformed*."[139]

General Conferences as an Itch for Disputing

Outler knew that it took more than a conference for organic union in order for the church to be alive in the Spirit. In a May 19, 1987, letter to M. Elton Hendricks, Outler wrote in reference to the loss of church membership that the United Methodist Church has suffered through the years: "We could, therefore, do with a miracle—even as a *historian, I believe* in miracles. But you can't schedule them in our quadrennial emphasis." While Outler appreciated the honor and responsibility of being a General Conference delegate, he was never inspired by the power plays of the various self-interest groups. Rather than being exhilarated, more often he left the conferences feeling depressed. A handwritten note in his files states: "The itch for disputing is a sore on the church's body."

Without a Doctrine of the Church

At one time in the history of the Methodist church this sore did not exist. "We became a church without a doctrine of the church that we became. We became a church in a kind of negative way. We became a church because the society had become inhabitable. It had been taken over by the sectarians, by the holiness people and *that* came to define Methodist sectarianism. Still does. And so we became a church and got away from being a society. [Wesley never regarded the movement as a church.] Moreover we became a church without any self-need of a doctrine of the church and its ministry because we had already developed our admirably effective polity—profoundly coherent, mobile, adaptable, sensitive—beginning to be less mobile, less sensitive toward the end of the nineteenth century. Done so well with polity that there was not any special need for thinking up a doctrine of the sacraments or of the ministry."[140]

Outler talked about "being in the institution, but not obsessed by it. [He felt we] could do the housekeeping and the homemaking chores; but we could sit loose with denominationalism, to parochialism without being rootless. [He called for us to] really learn to live toward a future that contains the providential choice when we can best serve the kingdom by losing our life in a more authentically catholic (in terms of continuity and inclusiveness), more evangelical (with its eschatological, *sola fide*, and good works emphases) and reformed community (watch this catholic business *and* this evangelical drive lest either emphasis produces a humbleness as proud as Lucifer). [This calls for] poise; self-criticism; aspiration; assurance; general rules of the concept of Christian discipline and perfection. These are the things that have been distinctive in our tradition. And these are the things that could be distinctive in our future. And these are the things we could offer as our contribution to the coming great church."[141]

Chair of Doctrine and Doctrinal Standards

Outler felt that the best that the United Methodist Church could do in this age (or any age) was to strive toward stabilizing church doctrine. That is what he tried to do as chair of the commission that brought an unprecedented statement on *Doctrines and Doctrinal Standards* of the United Methodist Church to the 1972 General Conference. Why the establishment of this commission? "By the end of the nineteenth century, and thereafter increasingly in the twentieth, Methodist theology had become decidedly eclectic, with less and less specific attention paid to its Wesleyan sources as such. Despite continued and quite variegated theological development, there has been no significant project in formal doctrinal re-formation in Methodism since 1808."[142] That is, until under Outler's tutelage in 1972.

Outler sought the help of one in particular to bring it about. He saw to it that he had the crucial support of a "friendly" secretary in the election of Robert Thornburg, who served superbly, in the opinion of Outler. This was not an easy secretarial assignment for Thornburg. Sometimes Outler tended to go into orbit over the heads of the commission members. Those "high" moments were hard to record. Bishop Emerson Colaw recounts how difficult it was at times for some on the commission to understand what Outler was saying. One layman, who was a member of the Texas Supreme Court and a friend of Outler, on occasion as Outler soared in pursuit of a particular theological concept, would interrupt and say: "Albert, will you please tell us what you are talking about?" Outler would quietly rephrase his idea in a more common language.

Too Much on His Plate?

Dow Kirkpatrick offers the following observation leading up to the 1972 General Conference: "The 1968 General Conference (Dallas) was the occasion of the uniting of The Methodist Church and the Evangelical United Brethren. The process was quite complicated, resulting in an overload on the agenda. The General Conference decided to defer action in three areas. Commissions were appointed to study the issues in each and propose action to the 1972 General Conference [that was] to meet in Atlanta. The three were: *Social Principles* (Bishop James Thomas was elected to chair the separate social creeds of the uniting churches and recommend a single statement for the United Methodist Church); *Theological Statement* (Albert Outler was chosen to chair a study of the theological statements of the two churches, and bring them together); and *The Structure Study Commission* (I [Kirkpatrick] was elected to chair this commission to bring together the variety of general agencies of both churches).

"During the four years of the working of these commissions, Jim Thomas and I sought to have joint meetings of the three. It seemed it would be useful for us to share our separate processes while in progress. Albert refused.

"However, the night before the convening of the General Conference in Atlanta, Albert spearheaded a mass meeting at The First United Methodist Church, nearby the Civic Center, the site of the Conference. The intent was to defeat the Structure Commission Report. His efforts failed, and the Conference adopted the Commission's recommendations almost in entirety. This created a widespread judgment (true or not) that Albert really wanted to take over all three study commissions."[143]

There is some legitimacy to this claimed attempted "takeover" by Outler on this occasion. But one has to look at what "takeover" meant in his thinking. In his thinking, what the Structure Study Commission had brought to the General Conference was overloaded with bureaucracy. This is apparent from his subsequent actions to correct what in his mind was a top-heavy structure with too many chiefs. Those curiae running the general agencies of the newly structured United Methodist Church soon began to feel that it was they who had the power to run the new church. This led to what Outler referred to as "The Constitutional Crisis" of the new church. Was it the curiae who were to oversee the church or was it the bishops, as the constitution of the United Methodist Church prescribes? Because of the power that the new structure gave the curiae, Outler often in his writings referred to the lawbook of the church as "the cross-eyed *Discipline*," with the curiae eye looking at the situation one way and the constitutional eye looking at it another way.

But why didn't Outler meet with the other two commission chairs and work out their differences earlier? A good question with only speculative answers. But one answer that he surely must have given had to do with his already overscheduled calendar. During the 1968–72 quadrennium, along with his full class load of teaching, he gave seventeen major lectures, while taking on some weekend and one-night stands giving information and answering questions, writing articles and one book, *A Methodist Observer At Vatican II* (Westminster: Newman Press, 1967). By any standard, he had a full plate. This much is known: whether in a one-night stand or in a prolonged four-year study, Outler was going to try to move the program in a direction he felt it should go. He very well might have influenced the Structure Study Commission had he worked with them during the quadrennium, with Dow Kirkpatrick being his friend and a friend of his family. But as it turned out, he spent the rest of his days lobbying for structural changes that would topple a top-heavy bureaucracy in the United Methodist Church.

Doctrinal Standards

Outler witnessed the fire storm that surrounded the doctrinal standards as defined by the 1988 General Conference. His last lecture (he died September 1, 1989), given at Lake Junaluska, July 3, 1989, at the convocation of the UMC Historical Society, dealt with this subject. He contended with confidence and conviction with his last public breath that Wesley's sermons and notes *were* doctrinal standards (and not mere subsidiary models of exposition that clarified the Articles of Religion and the two Confessions of Faith). They point to the very root of Wesleyan evangelism. The Wesley sermons and his *Explanatory Notes Upon the New Testament* are a live dynamic that witness the Christ-centered faith by grace (of all sorts) that saves. This live, Spirit-filled witness is a different standard in kind from the written doctrinal beliefs, creeds, and confessions. Wesley worked "out a working distinction between 'the heart of Christian faith' and the doctrines and 'opinions' that grew up in reflection and debate about this inner core of heart religion. Almost ruefully, he concluded that true religion does not consist in orthodoxy or right opinions: [In] *The Way to the Kingdom,* 1.6., [Wesley says that] 'neither does religion consist in *orthodoxy* or *right opinions;* which . . . are not in the heart, but the understanding. A man may be orthodox in every point; he may not only espouse right opinions, but zealously defend them against all opposers; he may think justly concerning the incarnation of our Lord, concerning the ever blessed Trinity, and every other doctrine contained in [Scripture]. He may assent to all the three creeds — . . . Apostles, the Nicene, and the Athanasian—and yet 'tis possible he may have no [heart] religion at all. . . . He may also be as orthodox as the devil [who understands orthodoxy perfectly] . . . and may all the while be . . . a stranger to the religion of the heart. This alone is religion, truly so called. . . . The Apostle sums it all up in three particulars—"righteousness, and peace, and joy in the Holy Ghost.""[144]

Wesley acknowledged that the devil believes orthodox doctrines, and the devil knows the strength and weaknesses of them. But there is no faith experience for the devil. Even the essential orthodox doctrines laid out in their most reasonable order remain a dead orthodoxy until they are lived out in the faith experience. Rational assent to the most finely tuned orthodox doctrines does not save. It is the Holy Spirit who stirs our consciences, assures us of sins forgiven, and makes efficacious the means of grace that save us through faith.

Outler reminds us that not even Wesley's heartwarming Aldersgate experience vaulted him into world evangelism: "It was in early October 1738 that John Wesley [in a walk from London to Oxford] first encountered Jonathan Edwards' *Faithful Narrative of a Surprising Work of God in New England* and was so deeply stirred that he promptly undertook an agonizing reappraisal of his own doctrinal foundations.

"After a full month of troubled soul, Wesley finally turned back to the origins of his own Anglican tradition and found there the resolution that would thereafter serve as his doctrinal charter."[145]

After Wesley had his initial stab at doctrine written down, a problem remained. He had not yet fully experienced with his heart what his head had affirmed in the stated doctrine. The "saving ('lively') faith" had eluded him.

It finally did come to him in the spring of 1739, as he reluctantly preached faith to the miners in the fields of Bristol. Wesley was so overtaken by the faith response to the message of God's grace of these tough-minded miners (all that they were accustomed to had been the oppressive power of authoritarianism) that *his* faith became alive to the point that now he knew in his mind and heart the "witness of the Spirit" in the assurance of his salvation. His faith experience prompted him to tell his followers to "preach faith until you have faith," a faith that comes out of the faith of those to whom you preach. Outler made strong the case that without that unique conversion experience (Wesley's fourth), there would never have been the Great Revival.

With that faith experience Wesley brought to his original "bare bones of basic doctrine" (extracted from the Homilies of the Church of England) a fifth doctrine: "What is missing from this earliest summation of his Anglican heritage is any explicit emphasis on Christian perfection. *That* was Wesley's own distinctive contribution—at least in his own unique fusion of it with the main themes of central Anglicanism. He had come upon this notion of the goal of the Christian life in the course of his Oxford studies in patristics. It is this *interaction* between the divine and the human that counted crucially for Wesley. Thus, Wesley took the idea of 'the fullness of faith' as the capstone of his doctrinal mix; it gave an upward and forward thrust to the whole: faith *and* good works, justification *and* sanctification, God's sovereignty *and* man's freedom, spontaneity in the spirit *and* ascetic *self*-discipline in the Christian life. Out of his lifetime concern for a Christian message that would be both vital and balanced, John Wesley amassed a splendid legacy—orthodox and stable at the core, but always open at its growing edge."[146] Those stable doctrines of sin, atonement, Trinity, etc., as well as "growing-edge opinions," are found in the *Sermons* of John Wesley, which in their total witness are our doctrinal standards.

According to Outler this doctrinal pilgrimage of Wesley is the templet to be applied to the UMC's present-day doctrinal quandary. The standard of doctrinal preaching is the faith dynamic that gives life to what otherwise would be a cold and dead creed. A mental assent now given to the essential doctrines is grounded in a God-given faith.

Wesley's Functional Doctrine

Outler labeled that faith dynamic as Wesley's *functional* doctrine that gave expression to the *essential* doctrines grounded in Scripture. This functional-faith doctrine has a power that a mere assent to orthodox doctrines fails to provide.

Fourfold Set of Theological Guidelines

That faith dynamic deals with essential doctrines (such as those laid out in the creeds and confessions of faith) from four perspectives: the Scripture as the font of revelation, tradition as the memory of the Christian community, reason as the ordering principle of truth (even if ineffable truth), and experience as the individuation of *living truth* in self and society. These guidelines made their way into the 1972 United Methodist *Book of Discipline* as Outler chaired the commission that wrote the "Theological Task." He called these Wesleyan guidelines a "quadrilateral," a word he coined and later regretted having done so because too many took it to mean that the four guidelines were *equal* in importance. In Outler's mind the four guidelines were not *equal*, but complementary, with scripture holding forth as primary. He kept insisting that one does not compare a font with a memory or a principle or an experience ("quadrilateral" in considerations, not properties). Without the font of revelation there would be nothing to talk about, remember, or experience. These four influences mix, not like oil and water, but like four fruits of the vine. God as Truth through the presence of the Holy Spirit is the Vine and the Mixer. Thus, for Outler, the *quadrilateral* was not a doctrinal standard; it was Wesley's way of dealing with doctrinal standards.

Pluralism

The overwhelming majority vote by the 1972 General Conference favoring the Doctrinal Standards report surprised and pleased Outler. But he was far from elated over the acting and actions of the Conference itself. In a June 2, 1972, letter to J. Robert Nelson he said: "I've been deeply depressed since General Conference. Even though our Doctrinal Standards thing went off all right, the Conference as a whole was a disaster. As of now, at least, I'm resolved, irrevocably, to call it quits with my 'institutional church' involvements and devote my remaining years (?) to what has been my vocation all along: study-teaching-writing."

Had Outler seen in 1972 what was to happen with his Doctrinal Standards in the 1988 General Conference, the words "depressed" and "disaster" in the previous letter would have been magnified many times over. The reason being that the new doctrinal statement dropped any mention of theological or doctrinal *pluralism.* "Pluralism" was muted out of existence. This was not a total shock to Outler. He had seen something of this sort coming since the 1984 General Conference mandated the formation of an episcopal committee to prepare a new statement on the theological task of United Methodists. The Council of Bishops appointed the Committee on Our Theological Task (COTT), which worked throughout the quadrennium preparing the statement called for by the 1984 General Conference. The 1988 General Conference, in following the draft of the COTT, killed and buried "pluralism."

A Shift Toward a "Confessional Principle"

What was this "pluralism" animal that had been laid to rest? Here are some of the crucial statements that, when left out of the 1988 *Discipline,* created a shift toward a "confessional principle" rather than a "conciliar principle" (the vehicle for "pluralism"): "But, even as they [UMC pioneers] were fully committed to the principles of religious toleration and doctrinal pluralism, they were equally confident that there is a 'marrow' of Christian truth that can be identified and that must be preserved. This living core, as they believed, stands revealed in Scripture, illumined by tradition, vivified in personal experience, and confirmed by reason. They were very much aware, of course, that God's eternal Word never has been, nor can be, exhaustively expressed in any single form of words. They were also prepared, as a matter of course, to reaffirm the ancient creeds and confessions as valid summaries of Christian truth [truth remains above and beyond *summaries* of truth]. But they were careful not to invest them with final authority or to set them apart as absolute standards for doctrinal truth and error.

"In this same spirit, they also declined to adopt any of the classical forms of the 'confessional principle'—the claim that the essence of Christian truth can, and ought to be, stated in precisely defined propositions, legally enforceable by ecclesiastical authority. Instead, they turned to a unique version of the ancient 'conciliar principle,' in which the collective wisdom of living Christian pastors, teachers, and people was relied upon to guard and guide their ongoing communal life. Wesley's agency for this collegial process he called the *Conference.*"[147]

". . . the Articles survived in the *Discipline,* where their prominence has seemed to suggest that they were more of a doctrinal 'confession' than had ever been intended."[148]

"This act of deletion [of a confessional principle] was a notable instance of a conciliar spirit in a time of bitter controversy."[149]

"We do not possess infallible rules to follow, or reflex habits that suffice, or precedents for simple imitation.

"In this task of reappraising and applying the gospel according to the conciliar principle, we recognize under the guidance of our doctrinal standards and guidelines the presence of theological pluralism. It is true that some would wish traditional doctrinal statements and standards be recovered and enforced; others would demand that they be repealed; and some would urge that they be perfected; others would insist they be superseded. When doctrinal standards are understood as legal or juridical instruments, it is easy to suppose that a doctrinal statement of some sort could be drawn up that would be normative and enforceable for an entire Christian body. Many persons with quite different views on doctrine insist our inherited statements ought either to be reaffirmed and enforced or superseded by new propositions. The effort to substitute new creeds for old has a long history of partisanship and schism.

"Our older traditions and our newer experiments in ecumenical theology provide a constructive alternative to this confessional tradition [as seen in the Augsburg Confession, the Catechism of Trent, the Westminster Confession, and Otterbein's Heidelburg Catechism]. This is fortunate because the theological spectrum in The United Methodist Church ranges over all the current mainstream options and a variety of special-interest theologies as well. This is no new thing. Our founders supported what Wesley called 'catholic spirit,' which also prevails in much contemporary ecumenical theology. But theological pluralism must not be confused with 'theological indifferentism'—the notion that there are no essential doctrines and that differences in theology, when sincerely held, need no further discussion.

". . . Rightly understood, our history of doctrinal diversity in the United Methodist Church has been a source of strength, producing fruitful tension when accompanied with a genuine concern for the vital unity of Christian truth and life. United Methodists can heartily endorse the classical ecumenical watchword: 'In essentials, unity; in nonessentials, liberty; and, in all things, *charity*'" (love that cares and understands).[150]

"In charting a course between doctrinal dogmatism on the one hand and doctrinal indifferentism on the other, The United Methodist Church expects all its members to accept the challenge of responsible theological reflection. The absence of a single official theological system does not imply approval of theological perspectives currently dominant in the church, nor disapproval of any serious exploration across new theological frontiers or the confronting of new issues, of which there are many. Indeed, it welcomes all serious theological opinions developed within the framework of our doctrinal heritage and guidelines, so long as they are not intolerant or exclusive toward other equally loyal opinions. . . .

"United Methodism in doctrinal lockstep is unthinkable. . . .

"All claims to Christian truth deserve an open and fair hearing for their sifting and assessment. The viability of all doctrinal opinion demands that the processes of theological development must be kept open-ended, both on principle and in fact.

"No single creed or doctrinal summary can adequately serve the needs and intentions of United Methodists in confessing their faith or in celebrating their Christian experience."[151]

While the 1988 General Conference muted "pluralism," they inadvertently kept its ghost alive through a liberal usage of the word "diversity." There will always be words to describe "more than one" doctrine.

The History of Sermons and *Notes* as Standards of Doctrine

How did Wesley's *Sermons* and *Notes* become standards of doctrine for Methodists? Given the situation of Wesley's many assistants, uneducated in things theological, who were preaching in his preaching houses, Wesley came up with a plan that historian Outler put together for us: "[Wesley] put negative limits to the business of preaching in the Wesley preaching houses. He produced a set of sermons. They are written sermons and are not at all like his oral sermons. They are sermon essays which, [among] the forty-four of them, cover the ground that Mr. Wesley regarded as essential to the Methodist perspective and the Methodist message. It is within this broad perimeter of doctrinal reference that you are expected to find yourself at home. And the rule is that you will not preach doctrines that are contrary to the doctrines in *Sermons on Several Occasions*. This does not mean that you will simply take the forty-four

Standard Sermons and reproduce them in your own inimitable
way. What you will do is to make it an affair of conscience that
you will not preach any doctrine that contradicts straightaway
and straight out the fundamental notions in the forty-four sermons. This was and still is the Methodist standards of doctrine:
the *Sermons,* the *Notes* and finally the Twenty-Five Articles."[152]

Sermons and Notes as Pluralistic Doctrines

Outler could never seem to win when it came to changing the
leadership style of bishops. While he cried for them to stand up
and be counted, when one actually did, Outler very nearly fainted.
He was aghast at the banishment of the word "plural" from the
glossary of United Methodism by Bishop Tuell in his 1988 Episcopal Address at the General Conference (especially since Bishop
Tuell had sought Outler's counsel in writing the address). Once
Outler gained his composure about the matter and could write
about it, he said: "Methodism has been the most fissiparous
[producing new units by fission] of all the mainline American
traditions; and the least disturbed about the diversity of the doctrinal premises of its teachers.

"[With all these obvious diversities] we are now forbidden,
by episcopal mandate, to use the p-word ('pluralism') with reference to *diversities* among United Methodists. (When asked by a
United Methodist if Free Methodists were really free, Bishop
Paul Ellis of the Free Methodists quipped, "Free Methodists are
at least as free as United Methodists are united!") The announced
reasons for this episcopal interdiction were embarrassingly unso-
phisticated: the chief one being a perceived equivalence of 'pluralism' and 'indifferentism.' (This is, of course, a lexical mistake,
and a logical eccentricity.)"[153]

How anyone could make those two words synonymous blew
Outler's mind. The preposterous idea that you can believe anything and be a United Methodist amounts to *indifferentism*, and
that does not represent Methodism's understanding of doctrine.
What Outler, and Wesley before him, and the church fathers
before Wesley, and the New Testament church before them, called
for were essential doctrines (the marrow) grounded in Scripture.
Those doctrines are listed in our Confessions of Faith, the Twenty-
Five Articles, and the historic creeds of the church. Beyond those

essentials it is a matter of "think and let think." In time this thinking about the essentials resulted in theological interpretations that became accepted as doctrines. Wesley took the essential doctrine of grace and enlarged it to include prevenience (God's loving presence working in our lives before saving grace and oftentimes in spite of us).

Wesley also interpreted the scriptural doctrine of perfection (Matthew 5:48), not as perfected perfection, but as perfecting perfection. These two Wesleyan opinions have become unique *Methodist* doctrines that presently contribute to the ecumenical dialogue. Who knows but that some day those opinions-turned-doctrines for the Methodists will become accepted as essential doctrines of the whole church. Meanwhile, Wesleyan Methodists extend the hand of fellowship to all those who share the faith experience of knowing God through Jesus Christ. *That* is doctrinal *pluralism,* and in no way is it identified as *indifferentism.*

In fact doctrinal *pluralism* offers the best offense against the *indifferentisms* of antinomians, immoralists, Pelagians, et al. This happens when the essentials (the marrow) of our faith (as expressed in our confessions of faith, historic creeds, *Sermons* and the *Notes*) come alive in a faith witness of God's rule of grace in our lives. "Come alive" is the key. One can accept conceptually and give assent to the best laid-out doctrines (including assenting to the *functional* doctrine of faith witnessing) and be far from the kingdom of God. The devil is *that* orthodox! Until one comes alive through the influence and presence of the Holy Spirit, *that* is dead orthodoxy.

The *Sermons* and *Notes,* by referring us back to the biblical essentials, guide us in our faith witnessing, whether written or oral. We are not plagiarizing when we use the themes of these resources in our witnessing. These are expressions of scriptural truths that are given to the whole church. *Indifferentisms* offer excuses for our questionable actions; *doctrinal pluralism* offers life-changing options.

Faith and Good Works

The dynamic *functional* doctrine of faith is never truly functioning without good works. Outler put it this way: "You can't tell an awful lot about faith, but you can tell an awful lot about good works. It is better not to go delving an awful lot into a man's innards spiritually—unless this is indicated by what does in fact appear in behavior. Christian faith has some sort of evidence in Christian behavior. [This is] the heart gist of Mr. Wesley's notion of salvation, that righteousness is imputed in faith. And faith that remains in any vitality for any length of time acquires the character of faithfulness. And faithfulness is evident in some respect in behavior. [You] can go by the fruits of faith. [It is] not good works that *prove* you have faith; but [it is] good works that prove that faith that you *do have*."[154] The ironic nuance is subtle, and it is there to ponder.

This wedding that Outler gave faith and good works, grounded in the life-giving love of God, involves a commitment: the best laid-out plan of *doing theology* carries with it the grace-filled obligation of *doing* something about it. Outler called this the mission of the church. *That* is the evidence of Wesley's functional doctrine at work changing lives and circumstances of needy people (that includes both the rich and the poor).

The Restrictive Rules of 1808

The Restrictive Rules of 1808 state: "*Article I.*— The General Conference shall not revoke, alter, or change our Articles of Religion [*Article II*—and our Confession of Faith] or establish any new standards or rules of doctrine contrary to our present existing and established standards of doctrine." "Or" to Outler introduced something of equal value to that which went before. What went on before was the use of the *Sermons* and *Notes* by Wesley's preachers as far back as the beginning of the Wesley movement. For historian Outler the *Sermons* and *Notes are* constitutionally grounded doctrinal standards, and not mere appendages of "doctrinal exposition."

"But as they say in Australia, 'Not to worry.' The United Methodist Church *is* a traditionary church [kept alive with the great themes preached in the *Sermons* and *Notes*], whatever any current *Discipline* may say, and the *Sermons* and *Notes* will continue to exercise as much or as little influence on United Methodist doctrinal self-understanding as if we knew, precisely, what the First Restrictive Rule really means. The earthly remains of the last United Methodist theologian decisively influenced by official stipulations in the *Discipline*, against his/her convictions otherwise, lie somewhere in an unmarked grave."[155] An implication of that statement would be: If such a theologian, who permitted a *Discipline* to dictate his/her beliefs, were discovered, that person's remains *would* (and *should*) be placed in an unmarked grave. That "theologian" would be a disgrace to the church. In this regard Albert Outler's grave is *marked.*

Are Doctrines Ever *Finalized?*

Some in the church insist that doctrines become finalized, never to be touched again by anybody. Outler asks: "Can *any* form of words *conclude* the task of doctrinal interpretation and development?"[156] Outler recognized that words cannot nail down all the ramifications of the things that have to do with the relationship between the wondrous mysteries of God and the mysteries of God's handiwork in humankind. Yet he was one of the first to cry "Heresy!" and begin redefining the doctrine in question, only to realize in the end how far from perfect was his defense of the doctrine he sought to rescue from the heresy. Church doctrine is simply another field of play where Good and Evil (God and Satan) have at each other until finally for that particular moment in time a resolve comes in the form of an "orthodoxy" that survives for a while until once again a new search for a proper "orthodoxy" begins as it encounters another heresy. History has declared pluralism here to stay. Each newly defined doctrine creates a "new" doctrine.

Do Methodists Have a Doctrine of the Church?

A reading of Outler's address *Do Methodists Have a Doctrine of the Church?*, given at the 1962 Oxford Institute on Methodist Theological Studies at Lincoln College, Oxford (of which John Wesley was a Fellow), answered in some measure that question. While Outler in his latter days may have spoken with emotion on the subject of doctrine (when did he *not* speak on *any* subject *without* emotion?), this paper delivered to Methodist theologians from diverse Methodist bodies (under the sponsorship of the World Methodist Council) revealed a well-balanced, historically grounded statement on Methodist doctrine, very much the same that guided him in the drafting of the 1972 doctrinal statement for the United Methodist Church. In it he said: "The drift of these comments is that Methodism has never lost the *essence* of a *functional* doctrine of the church but that, by the same token, it has never developed—on its own and for itself—the full panoply of bell, book, and candle that goes with being a 'proper' church properly self-understood."

While a far cry from the state of "A 'proper' church properly self-understood," the *functional* doctrine of a vital living faith witness (as revealed in the Wesley *Sermons* and *Notes*) is the dynamic that wins and keeps souls in the kingdom of God. "And what is faith? Neither orthodox doctrine nor submission to external authority of any sort. Rather, it is the twin awareness of God's reality as the Encompassing Mystery in which we live and move and love, and of a willing, radical trust in God's upholding power and unfaltering care. It is the willingness to be upheld in God's love and to be uplifted by it to our potential. Faith is our awareness that our existence is from, in, and to God and our being glad to have it so. Faith is the human acceptance of *theonomy*, and anything less or other is faithless."[157]

Some Evangelicals and Pluralism

In sniffing out the antinomian winds of the seventies and eighties, some evangelicals rightfully pegged such heresies as the worship of Sophia, but wrongly condemned pluralism as the root cause of the problem. Toward the end of his life Outler penned on a small note pad paper these words:

> The evil that men do lives after them,
> The good is oft interred with their bones.
> (*Julius Caesar,* Act III, Sc. 2, Line 81f)

"So let it be with the commission that produced Part II of the 1972 *Discipline* and the delegates of the General Conference that approved it with a mindless majority of 960 to 17. The earnest evangelicals hath told us that doctrinal pluralism is a heresy— and if it were so, it was a grievous fault, and grievously has the old Part II [of the 1972 *Discipline*] answered it."

This is one of the tragic ironies of Outler's life. He lived and died a Wesleyan evangelical and fought to get the evangelicals places in positions of authority in the United Methodist Church. Yet some of those who carried the evangelical flag either never heard what Outler was saying or heard it and simply rejected it. It is difficult to know the truth of the matter.

Outler's historic practice of questioning friends if he got the message across was never asked regarding his presentation of the Wesleyan message of doctrinal pluralism. Feedback came without his asking, conveying that he never got his message across. Some never caught the absurdity of making *pluralism* and *indifferentism* synonymous: *Pluralism* means "more than one." *Indifferentism* means "a matter of no importance." "More than one" and "a matter of no importance" do not mean the same thing. There is more than one doctrine in the church. That is the way it is whether one accepts it or not. But this does not mean that all doctrines are of equal importance. Wesley calls for tolerance where doctrines do not strike at the essentials of Christianity. And when they do, it is time to cry, "Heresy!" Until then it is "think and let think." Truth, through the witness of a saving faith (as *functional* doctrine), never makes peace with the Prince of Darkness who knows doctrines as well as any. And uses them to deceive. When the dust of history settles, truth will shine through the essential doctrines and show others up for what they *are not*. Outler said: "Faith God in Christ in the Scripture and then mind your language! And if you do not 'mind' your language properly, somebody will *re*mind you that your doctrine might well be heresy."[158] Of all people Outler cannot be accused of being indifferent toward doctrines. His life was spent trying to keep them coherently in line—the Wesleyan way.

Good News

This gross misunderstanding over such a crucial issue forced a sad Outler (as his letters openly admit) to begin distancing himself from those in the Good News movement who equated "pluralism" with "indifferentism" (not all evangelicals did). This was to Outler "a lexical mistake and logical eccentricity." Outler was always uncomfortable being identified with a cause that ignored history. Especially was it a problem when that history had to do with Methodist doctrine.

It is interesting to note that some of those same United Methodist evangelicals are now joining evangelicals from other denominations in combating common secularisms and heresies. While in this common cooperative mood, these ecumenical evangelicals have accepted their comradeship without making any significant reference to the various doctrines that their denominations represent.

Unwittingly the participating United Methodist evangelicals have confirmed what Outler was saying all along. And that is: some of those doctrines that the churches have given *essential* status are indeed essential and some are not *that* essential after all. They are theological beliefs (opinions) that have been given the status of doctrine in the different churches, a theological pluralism (diversity) that has been turned into a doctrinal pluralism. And now in a time when a common moral crisis threatens all denominations (e.g., the acceptance of the *practice* of homosexuality as a viable Christian lifestyle; the killing of unborn babies, etc.) evangelicals in those denominations unite in the *functional* doctrine of a live, vital, dynamic life-changing faith witness that God through Jesus Christ, the Lord of our lives, in the presence of the Holy Spirit is the agent of change.

That is the essential doctrine of our faith—"our" meaning persons in any church, anywhere, anytime, who have accepted God's way through Jesus Christ in the presence of the Holy Spirit as their way. At this melding of *forgiven* human spirits with the *forgiving* divine Spirit a sacredness of and for life comes into being. *That* is what counts. *That* is the heart of Christianity. *That* is essential. Beyond *that* it is a matter of "think and let think." To this spontaneous led-of-the-Spirit present-day ecumenical evangelical effort, Outler with a smile on his face would say, "Go for it!"

One can see this "distancing" had to do, not with the basic moral and ethical emphases of Good News, but with the direction some were taking with their doctrinal *thinking*. On practically every other point the two seemed to be on the same wave length. Good News did agree with Outler's contribution regarding the Wesleyan Quadrilateral, and in turn was recognized by Outler as the only official caucus of United Methodists who ventured to *do* theology the Wesleyan way. In Outler's eyes they were *doing theology* well in making Scripture their primary authority, in studying tradition and allowing the Christian faith experience its due influence, but in his estimation some (not all) were not *doing* the process adequately with their best reasoning.

Since Outler's death many rank-and-file Good News persons, with increased understanding (reasoning), have accepted doctrinal pluralism ("think and let think") without allowing that level of tolerance to interfere with the essential doctrines of the faith experience. *Those* evangelicals and Outler walk the same road without any distance between them.

And then there are evangelicals who are distancing themselves from Outler's Wesleyan Quadrilateral. William J. Abraham caused a minor ripple with his oracle appealing for an awakening from "doctrinal amnesia" as he questioned the wisdom of the church's acceptance of Outler's understanding of Wesley's practice of doing theology (Wesley's Quadrilateral). And then John Wesley scholars W. Stephen Gunter, Scott Jones, Ted Campbell, Rebekah L. Miles, and Randy Maddox calmed the waters and established for the twenty-first century other words dealing with the same Quadrilateral laid out by Outler. This is their common pronouncement:

> We believe that the Quadrilateral, when defined as "the rule of Scripture within the trilateral hermeneutic of tradition, reason, and experience," is a viable way of theologizing for United Methodism. We believe that this dialogical way of theologizing is in harmony with the teachings of John Wesley. And we believe that the theological application of this new Neo-Wesleyan interpretation of the Quadrilateral is the most faithful way for The United Methodist Church to end the twentieth and begin the twenty-first century.[159]

And so it is—some evangelicals like a part of what Outler had to say, and not another. Some disagreed with others concerning Outler's view of Wesley's doctrinal teaching. And in so doing vindicated Outler's claim that there *is* theological and doctrinal pluralism (even within the ranks of evangelicals).

An Evangelical Scholar

Outler could not totally break with those in Good News who disagreed with him because, after all, he was a Wesleyan scholar.

This meant that he was evangelical. When Ed Robb told Outler that he (Robb) was a Wesleyan evangelical, Outler is said to have answered, "If you are Wesleyan, you *are* evangelical."

Outler could not break with Good News because he could not deny his own history with that evangelical organization. A history filled with paradoxes. Strange as it may sound today, earlier Good News evangelicals were crying for pluralism to be practiced by the architect of theological/doctrinal pluralism, Outler himself! The following September 15, 1972, letter from *Good News* magazine editor Charles Keysor stated that position: "Dear Friend, we appreciate your taking time from your busy schedule to comment on our editorial, 'In the Aftermath of Atlanta.'

"Frankly, your letter disappoints us. From one of the world's leading ecumenists we had expected disagreement—but not diatribe. From a man who has often championed dialogue, we had not expected to be written off just because we see things differently. From one with so deep a knowledge of the complexity and diversity of Christian tradition, we had expected some sensitivity to our tradition.

"My brother, can't you see the radical contradiction between your letter of August 29 and your stance as Ecumenist and Statesman of the new pluralism?

"Good News had hoped to take part in the deliberations of your commission. This had seemed a reasonable expectation, since many United Methodists share our perspective, and to our knowledge we are the only organized evangelical movement within the denomination.

"On September 18, 1969, I wrote to your commission secretary, Dr. Thornburg, offering you 'input' from Good News. A copy of this letter is attached. I received no reply. Several times I wrote to you, hoping to continue building a constructive relationship begun at our luncheon in Dallas in 1968. You never replied.

"This silence mystified us—until we learned, on reliable authority, that you consider the Good News viewpoint invalid because you know of no spokesman with academic credentials acceptable to you.

"Be that as it may, the significant thing is that a new doctrinal formulation was developed without involvement—to my knowledge—of United Methodism's only organized evangelical voice and movement. How strange that a document stressing the importance of 'pluralism' should, in its inception, violate this very principle.

"But all of this now lies behind us. We are not bitter; we are sad for the unrealism of those who would build a house of pluralism upon non-pluralistic foundations. Had you taken the trouble to hear us earlier, you would not have been so surprised at our point of view. Had we been allowed to participate in forming your document it might have been modified so we could have written a different editorial.

"We find it ironic to hear you saying that our editorial shuts the door to dialogue. As I have already noted, there was no dialogue from you until after the editorial, so it seems that publishing more editorials is the way to increase dialogue.

"As we speak, we expect that God will pronounce the final judgment upon us for truth and conformity to his Word. We hope that you will be content to leave our condemnation to the Lord and that you will exemplify true pluralism by extending the hand of friendship in spite of our disagreement."

The ironies of the Good News/Outler relationship were compounded even further as Good News, who once pleaded for a pluralism that included their opinions, struck off in the direction of equating pluralism with indifferentism. They initially cried foul that the new doctrinal statement of the United Methodist Church in its inception had not practiced the pluralism it had professed. The letter from Keysor was plainly *for* pluralism, which included pluralistic theologies and doctrines. What else? There was no hint in Keysor's letter of equating *pluralism* with *indifferentism*.

Good News' *new* position of equating *pluralism* with *indifferentism* in turn sent Outler proclaiming loudly in writing and speeches that the 1972 doctrinal statement *was* in fact including the evangelicals, even though Good News was not at the table when the deed was done. He held this position while having differences of opinions with them. He fervently disagreed with Ed Robb's statement at Lake Junaluska that the historic Wesleyan biblical perspective was not being presented in United Methodist seminaries (Robb says this was taken out of context by the news media). But this did not keep him from reconciling those differences with Robb. They came together on the common ground

that pluralism was needed on United Methodist seminary faculties. Outler's concern for pluralism was the same as that expressed in Robb's August 8, 1975, letter to Spurgeon Dunnam:
"My great concern is that we practice pluralism in our educational institution on the theological level. I do not believe that
any fair-minded objective person can contend that this is done to
any great extent in our schools." In the end they came out supporting a common program in the formation of AFTE (A Foundation for Theological Education). In the years to come this
foundation would make available evangelical scholars in the
Wesleyan tradition for Methodist seminary faculties.

Outler was satisfied that established liberal schools of theology could now practice their "liberalism" by allowing bona
fide Wesleyan scholars grounded in that evangelical tradition
to teach in their seminaries. Robb was satisfied that seminaries
could now hire evangelical scholars with academic credentials.
Both acknowledged that, while there is the inevitable plurality
of theologies and doctrines, the unique Wesleyan flavor deserves to be heard. Outler also knew that these Wesley scholars, with their own obligation to think and serve in the Wesleyan
tradition, would be properly credentialed to deal with the subtle-
ties of present (and future) doctrinal confusions concerning pluralism or any other "ism" that might rise to divide the house of
the evangelicals.

Evangelical scholar Outler was for the evangelicals, but not
for a stance (e.g., anti-pluralism) that some evangelicals would
take. In his mind, this would be another case of "shooting oneself in the foot," a counterproductive move. He was not for anything that would hurt the evangelical cause. He maintained to the
end that evangelicalism must be wedded to a church reformed
and catholic.

A Mixed Bag

The 1988 General Conference left the United Methodist Church
with a mixed bag: On the one hand, all references to pluralism
were put to rest; on the other hand, ghosts of pluralism were
raised in references made to the acceptance of diversity.

Church historians are still arguing over whether the *Sermons*
and *Notes* were included in the 1808 First Restrictive Rule as

"our present existing and established standards of doctrine." This mixed bag of doctrinal confusion has provided theological fodder for years to come. It started when Outler charted the course in 1972. He watched it veer off course in 1988, and he took the brunt of the criticism that brought about this change. He was the victim of his own doctrinal insight expressed in the 1972 *Discipline's* (p. 82) *Conclusion of Our Theological Task*: "Doctrine and doctrinal standards are never an end in themselves, nor even a resting place along the way. They must be a springboard from which we are propelled into creative living and our tasks as agents of reconciliation in the name of the loving God." He did not mean for United Methodists to go shopping for a new springboard every four years, but to use the one he had given them.

Was It Vanity?

Some say that Outler was personally offended by this new 1988 statement, and that vanity and pride expressed through hurt feelings accounted for his not accepting the new statement. Regardless of how Outler may have felt, the debate still rages at this writing. And Outler's feelings have nothing to do with that debate. This fact would lend some credence to Outler's charge that the "new" Doctrinal Statement is *not* an acceptable statement of the United Methodist Church's Doctrinal Standards. Some of those who wrote it would agree with this assessment.

A Foundation for Theological Education

One of Outler's proudest involvements was with A Foundation for Theological Education. In 1994 Bishop Hunt said: "He [Outler] called me. It must have been fourteen or fifteen years ago and asked me to become a member of the Board of AFTE. I almost declined, and he turned on his charm. He told me that it would be no more unusual or incongruous for me than it was for him. He said we both have a duty to the Church. He said the orthodox element of Christian thinking is not having adequate representation in the seminaries. We have got to supply that from the kind of resource that is intellectually respectable. And I became a founding member of the Board of Trustees at his insistence. And the most remarkable phenomena in our religious world in recent years is the friendship that developed between Albert Outler and Ed Robb—which is a tribute to both of them. It was Albert Outler who broadened and mellowed Ed Robb."[160]

Inglorious Beginnings

No human gets any glory in the founding of AFTE because of its so obviously inglorious beginnings. Here is how Outler tells the story: "The rise of 'the evangelical movement' is well known by now—in numbers, strength, and self-confidence—is one of the major developments in American Protestantism, and has been for at least the past two decades. It is also common knowledge (usually explained away) that this development has not yet been registered, in any significant proportion, within the liberal theological establishment. During these decades, of course, the evangelicals have done very well for themselves with their own seminaries, from which it has also been argued that this division makes for a comfortable and mutually acceptable arrangement (the old 'separate but equal' slogan in a different context).

"On the other side, it has long seemed to many of us in the 'establishment' that the standard 'evangelical' denunciations of our seminaries, *toto genere*, have been both unfair and unhelpful. In the United Methodist Church, for example, one of the evangelicals' favorite target since 1972 has been our denominational statement on 'Doctrine and Doctrinal Standards'—largely because of its open avowal of pluralism as a theological principle. The irony here is that one of the conscious aims of that statement had been to make welcome room for the evangelicals within the inclusive Methodist theological enterprise—even while it was also trying to wall off the extreme dogmatists from the 'right' and the barn-burners from the 'left.'

"Thus, in 1975 when Dr. Robb (then president of the 'Good News' movement) leveled a blast at all the United Methodist seminaries, claiming that in none of them could an evangelical student hope for a decent exposure to the Wesleyan heritage, there were not many of us in an other-cheek-turning mood. My own indignation was especially 'righteous' since I was deeply involved, with others, in a protracted, earnest crusade to recover and re-present John Wesley (not only to Methodists but to other Christians as well) as a significant theologian and as a fruitful resource for contemporary ecumenical theology. My response was less than conciliatory; after all, what was there to expect but another salvo in reply?"[161]

And "salvo" it was. Outler's August 1, 1975, letter addressed Robb, not with a warm "Dear Sir" but a cool "Sir." He began the first paragraph with: "If, as reported in the *Texas Methodist,* you said: 'I know of no United Methodist seminary where the historic Wesleyan biblical perspective is presented seriously, even as an option,' then I solemnly charge you with having, willfully and premeditatively, violated the Ninth Commandment (Ex. 20:16)." And then a deeply wounded Outler turned the heat up and admonished Robb to repent for the sin he had committed.

"It was, therefore, downright disconcerting to have Dr. Robb and some of his friends show up in my study one day with an openhearted challenge to help them do something more constructive than cry havoc. Needless to say, I've always believed in the surprises of the Spirit; it's just that they continue to surprise me whenever they occur!"[162]

A more detailed description of the events leading up to that momentous meeting of mind and heart between the two men resembles more a surprise in the making than a sudden flabbergast. Following Robb's sweeping denunciation of United Methodist seminaries and professors (as reported in the news media), John Wesley scholar Outler fired a scathing rebuke to be printed in *The United Methodist Reporter.* Publisher Spurgeon Dunnam called Ed Robb and read Outler's article to him and asked if Robb wanted to write an article that could be placed side by side with Outler's in *The United Methodist Reporter.* Ed responded, "I am going to give that some thought," and he did "think about that" in prayer to God.

It was easy for Robb to pray, "Lord, what am I going to do?" because he respected Outler more than any theologian in Methodism. Robb called Outler and talked about the comments and concerns expressed in his (Robb's) controversial 1975 speech at Lake Junaluska. Robb asked Outler if it would be all right to come to see him. Outler responded in the affirmative but not enthusiastically. Robb laid bare his heart and told Outler how much love and respect he had for the Wesleyan scholar. In that visit and those that followed, Outler and Robb found themselves on the same page of evangelical concern.

Where Robb in his speech had suggested that two seminaries be turned over to evangelical trustees so that evangelical students and scholars would have a place in United Methodism, Outler suggested a different approach: to seek and develop a cadre of evangelical and Wesleyan scholars (John Wesley Fellows) trained and committed to serving the church, and whose quality of excellence would be such that United Methodist seminaries would want to hire them. AFTE was formed according to the Outler formula. At the time of Outler's death, seventy John Wesley scholars had received fellowships and were making a positive impact as they were accepting posts in seminaries, universities, and local churches.

Such was the appreciation for Outler that at the first AFTE Board of Trustees meeting in 1977, Robb proposed that Bishop Finis Crutchfield chair a committee to raise one million dollars for the Albert Outler Chair of Wesley Studies at Perkins School of Theology. Bishop Crutchfield thought for a few minutes and said, "I'll do it." Bishop Crutchfield put it before the Texas Annual Conference, and it was voted that the million dollars be raised through an apportionment over a period of four years. Bishop Crutchfield reported that this was some of the easiest money the Conference ever raised, which supported the claim of Ed Robb: "Albert Outler has influence beyond any name in Methodism!"

While at the time of his death Outler was disillusioned about much that was happening in the United Methodist Church, AFTE was the one shining light of which Outler was most proud. He said, "Here, obviously, was a heaven-sent opportunity not only for a reconciliation but also for a productive alliance in place of what had been an unproductive joust. Moreover, as we explored our problem, some unexpected items of agreement began to emerge. For example, there was the recognition, first off, that too many evangelicals (especially in the Methodist tradition) had made it all too easy for the liberal establishment to freeze them out on the grounds that they had not paid the going price for full academic respectability. All too often, John Wesley's warmed heart is celebrated by those who ignore the . . . scholarly tools that he kept burnished throughout his long career. [Some in the liberal establishment could not (or would not) see any good coming from such an organization as AFTE. In 1997 AFTE Ph.D. Scott Jones was hired by Dean Robin Lovin to fill the McCreless

Chair of Evangelism at Perkins School of Theology. That makes the following comment of Dean Quillian, now deceased, all the more prophetic: "An AFTE scholar will teach in Perkins over my dead body!"[163]]

"We also discovered a second agreement, variously expressed: that theology in the Wesleyan spirit must be truly ecumenical, or it is not truly Wesleyan. The evidence for this assertion is scattered throughout the Wesley corpus but is best summed up in his sermon on 'Catholic Spirit' and in his open 'Letter to a Roman Catholic.' On a third crucial point we also found ourselves in genuine consensus: 'evangelism,' in the Wesleyan spirit, must speak of justice as earnestly as of justification, of Christian nurture and discipline as emphatically as of conversion, of Christian social action as boldly as of personal salvation.

"It was these agreements that became the working charter for AFTE. For here were men and women willing to put their money and time where their convictions lay—and so they have. Since 1976 [speaking in 1996], fifteen Wesley Fellowships have been awarded for doctoral programs in England and America. This means that soon there will be a larger 'talent pool' of fully credentialed scholars than we have ever had before—with more in the pipeline behind them.

"Given so much, we may be justified in believing that such a venture may honestly be reckoned as a grace-full sign of hope, even in these rattled times."[164]

In 1998, eighty Wesley Fellowships had been awarded for doctoral programs in England and America. Sixty-two of these have been granted the Ph.D. degree. Eighteen Wesley fellows are pursuing that degree.

In a May 15, 1989, letter to Edmund W. Robb III (Eddie, who had been a student of Outler's at Perkins) Outler in describing his Bradenton situation, whether intentionally or not, laid out a warning to evangelicals in these words: "Church life in these parts is un-lively and motley; amicable sectarianism is simply a fact of life (sixty-one 'denominations' listed on the 'Religion' page, plus nine independent congregations); the prevailing theological perspective is what I've come to think of as an 'evangelical Pelagianism' (i.e., Jesus Christ is Lord, sent to help us to save ourselves, by moral efforts and a sentimental mysticism)." Toward the end of this letter were his last written words concerning AFTE: "You've still got your priorities right in the AFTE formula: evangelical, above all; Wesleyan in the best sense (i.e., with Wesley more as mentor than patriarch!), and academic 'star quality.' But it may be that you can't ratchet up the academic standards by a little without downscaling 'the first things.'

"And it is more than just an old man's bias that our theological schools, generally speaking, are less impressive places than they used to be (what with quotas, coteries, academic dilutions, and all *that*).

"'Take then the torch; be yours to hold it high'—not to 'break faith' with AFTE's founding vision."

Outler was pleased with the accomplishments of AFTE and saw even a brighter future. That vision put a smile on his face.

Outler and *Some* Bishops

Outler ridiculed those who felt high and mighty, and that included some United Methodist bishops. At times that ridicule turned into an unabashedly pronounced judgment on monarchical bishops. A careful reading of his sermons/lectures in the first three volumes of *The Albert Outler Library* will reveal his basic distrust of sinful persons politicking with a *humble* demeanor for positions of power, viz., the episcopacy; and, once elected, inevitably corrupting the office with their abuse of power. Outler recognized that the most fertile soil that existed for growing a good opinion of one's self was the exercise of power over people's lives. But he also knew that this craving for power corrupted their power once they got it. And left them unfulfilled as humans. "No other animals are anywhere near to man in their incontinence and instability, in precisely those dynamics that set the *human* off from its animal matrix: (1) intellectual curiosity, (2) the hunger for freedom, (3) the need for *conferred* dignity (as distinguished from status fought for and won at some other animal's expense!), (4) the love of loving and the need to be loved."[165] This understanding accounted for Outler's basic disagreement with the highly politicized system in which United Methodist bishops are presently elected—a "clawing" system that robs the elected of "conferred" dignity.

Outler recognized that humans "grounded" in *un*fulfillment make poor spiritual leaders. It was not the bishops per se who bothered Outler; it was the abuse of power on the part of some that he recognized as demonic. And he told them so, sometimes in bone-dry sarcasm: "Where the pious lust for power; for God's glory, of course, what else?"[166]

"Telling them so" could be done only by Outler. That was the opinion of Bishop William C. Martin given in a May 8, 1979, letter to Outler: "Our neighbor, Paul Galloway, told us of the enthusiastic standing ovation with which the Council greeted you when you had finished the address [given at a recent meeting of the Council of Bishops]. And why not! You had insightfully and courageously dealt with some areas of episcopal responsibility that are urgently calling for immediate attention. Even the relatively small number who tended to disagree with some of the convictions which you expressed could not be other than grateful to you for directing attention to issues which must be fearlessly dealt with if the UMC is to fulfill the mission which we believe God has in mind for it.

"And you were considerate enough to propose some handles which can be used in taking hold of some of these problems. For this we should all be grateful to you.

"I am confident that I am not alone in the firm belief that there is not another person in all of Methodism who could have rendered the much-needed service to our Fellowship which you have done in this statement of episcopal responsibility."

Much of what was said in this 1979 address to the Council of Bishops was put into print in a 1982 *Circuit Rider* article titled "Politics and 'Scriptural *Episkopoi.*'" In it Outler clarified what Wesley meant by "*episkopoi.*" And it was not what Asbury had come to grips with as he insisted upon the title, not of "general superintendent," but of "bishop." To him Wesley wrote: "How dare you suffer yourself to be called Bishop? I shudder, I start at the very thought! Men may call *me* a knave or a fool, a rascal, a scoundrel, and I am content; but they shall never by my consent call me Bishop! For my sake, for God's sake, for Christ's sake, put a full end to this!"[167]

Yet this same Wesley later said, "I firmly believe that I am a *scriptural episkopoi*, as much as any man in England."[168] In Wesley's thinking this statement was no contradiction with his earlier outburst at Asbury. "The key here is Wesley's radical distinction between spiritual *authority* and secular *power*. He knew that, in the New Testament, the term *episkopoi* reflects no aura of arbitrary power. More importantly, he had found (in Matthew 20:25–28 and elsewhere) a positive model for the notion of the 'scriptural *episkopoi*':

> "But Jesus called his disciples to him and said, 'Ye know that the princes of the Gentiles exercise dominion over them and they that are great exercise authority upon them. But it shall not be so among you; but whosoever will be great among you, let him be your minister; and whosoever will be chief among you, let him be your servant. Even as the Son of Man came, not to be ministered unto but to minister and to give his life as a ransom [a *lutron*] for many.[169]

What has happened to Francis Asbury, this competent defender of the faith, the compassionate pastor, the effective spiritual director? Outler's answer: "The nineteenth century brought both fabulous expansions for American Christianity and a series of class and culture shifts among the Methodists. With these changes came altered images of the episcopacy. The old-fashioned field commanders gave way to new *commanding officers of troops in garrison*—and then to still another image: arbitrary dispersers of clerical patronage. This is the negative stereotype that all too many United Methodists carry about in their collective unconscious to this day: leaders who hold themselves above contradiction, jealous of their episcopal prerogatives and yet not really great theologians or statespersons and not always suffering servants. In this confused development Wesley's image of scriptural *episkopoi* got blurred and overlaid."[170]

Outler went on to say that so blurred and overlaid is our voting for bishops in Jurisdictional Conferences that the elections are "strikingly similar to those fancy cattle auctions we have in the Southwest or to those tumults on the floors of stock exchanges. Those who liked that old temple with its money changers would have loved some of the conferences I have been in, with wheeler-dealers and kingmakers in full cry!"[171]

How did the bishops take this criticism? The majority accepted what Outler said with receptive hearts and minds. Some did not. And he was the object of their ridicule. Outler's friend Bishop Monk Bryan ended a September 30, 1977, letter with this paragraph: "You know you are joked about because you have been so prominent before so many people. Nearly all of this joking about you is with respect and affection. In that vein somebody one time said that you would some day realize that you were not infallible. To which I replied, 'Maybe Professor Albert Outler will come to the point that he thinks he is not infallible, but I doubt if I will ever reach that place.'"

While some bishops joked with each other in private about Outler, Outler made some bishops the butt of his jokes before hundreds. Here is such a story told by Thomas Stransky about the incomparable Bishop Fred Pierce Corson, then president of the World Methodist Council and observer of Vatican II: "At each of the four autumn sessions Fred would shop at the clothing hangout for clergy, bishops and cardinals, on the Piazza Minerva. Gradually he acquired a bizarre ecclesiastical wardrobe. Much to the Methodist annoyance of Al [Outler], who told me at the Council's closing when he saw Bishop Fred in the Observer's Box: 'Thank God, no fifth session; by then Fred would be showing up in all white!'"[172]

Outler enjoyed telling these stories about Bishop Corson: "[Corson] came to the Council in an outfit that outrivaled the pope. The Romans were greatly impressed as they are by all costumery. Wearing the same outfit he came back and went to the meeting of the Methodist Council of Bishops. Whereupon a colleague said to him: 'Fred, you look like the wine steward on the *Queen Mary!*'

"There is another Methodist bishop who insists on being addressed as 'His Thrice Eminence' and who wears a Triple Tiara!"[173] Outler revealed through his humor that he never took seriously those who took themselves seriously.

Bishop Earl Hunt said about Outler: "[When it came to bishops] he was always like a feisty dog snapping at the bishops' heels and interfering with their morning walks. No doubt about it. He enjoyed this. He was constantly aggravating them, but with a constructive purpose."[174] Bishop Hunt illustrated this Outlerian tendency with this story: "Well, I've been a bishop forever—since 1964. We invited Albert to come and give a major address to the bishops. He came, gave the address, and it was masterful. But he inserted in the address at strategic points little jibes at the bishops. He had a constant concern—a real concern—that the bishops were not exercising their constitutional mandate and were not giving adequate oversight to the spiritual and temporal affairs of the church. He never let us forget that. Incidentally, I think he was right. But I remember the reaction of some of the senior bishops—Bishop Arthur Moore, Bishop Fred Corson, Bishop Don Tippet—Don Tippet especially was sorry we invited him. But he was good-natured about it."[175] Outler's letters confirm Bishop Hunt's observations. The bishops sought Outler's critical comments, got uptight and undone and sometimes downright angry when he spoke them, yet sought him again—and again!

An Advocate for Episcopal Term Limits

The abuse of power by *some* bishops motivated Albert's father John Outler to take up the cause of episcopal term limits long before Albert was born. Sister Fan in a May 6, 1976, letter to Carla and Albert wrote: "We have been following the AP reports of the Portland, Oregon, General Conference and realize from this morning's headlines that Albert's efforts to limit life tenure for bishops did not win; but I hope that it will not represent too deep a disappointment as his father was [disappointed] before him. Papa fought life-time tenure all his fifty years and at all the quadrennial conferences he attended from 1922 in Hot Springs until his retirement, so that if it is all added up, both of them were at least fifty years ahead of their constituency, or colleagues, or 'peers' (ha!) or superiors (hearty ha! ha!). Certainly no political group could be expected to preside over its [own] dissolution, be it ecclesiastic or lay, so once again we hear the guttural growls of a Churchillian monolithic mind (no pun intended). I am truly sorry, because time for Albert is running out, in that he will not physically be able many more quadrennia to keep this battle going. Nor can he expect the younger and upwardly-mobile place-seekers to go against their manifest self-interest in currying favor with their appointive masters."

A Balanced Attitude

Bishop Hunt further stated: "But Albert balanced this chronically critical attitude toward the episcopacy with a deep innate respect for the office. And with a widespread personal friendship with the individuals. Many of us looked upon Albert Outler as a dear and trustworthy friend. On many occasions we telephoned him and asked for his counsel. I remember I had to give a key-note address at the World Methodist Council at Dublin in 1976. I wanted to check the accuracy of my viewpoint on one or two issues, and check some sticky facts. I called him and he treated it as though it were his address. He called me back to give me additional information."[176]

Letters from bishops seeking Outler's counsel confirm this to be true. In one letter the bishop questioned Outler on the meaning of *sin*, especially as it related to the bishop's own life. The man had wanted to become a bishop; his friends got him elected; and now this *thing* called sin fiercely bothered him. At the time he felt that he ought to be happy over having won the election. But he was not. Instead, he was miserable. In a six-page single-spaced letter Outler spoke directly to the man's situation and of the grace of God through forgiveness as the answer to his problem. Outler let the man know that one is closer to the king-dom of God in one's convicted state of sin than those are who are so proud of themselves and their power that they could never humble themselves to ask forgiveness from anyone against whom they had sinned.

An appreciation for Bishop Hunt by Outler was expressed in the last paragraph of an April 22, 1988, letter. The move from Dallas to Bradenton was soon to be made. "As for future involvements in more than the fellowship of a local church, this will take some counseling (especially with you), along with much prayer and some 'fasting.' We do hope to stretch out this 'last chapter' of our lives in optimum ways, avoiding deadlines on the one side, and boredom on the other (even though, for a while at least, a bit of 'constructive boredom' would be preferable to living 'by the day timer,' as I had to do for much too long). Mostly, it will be a blessing just to live quietly and peaceably among cherished friends (like you and Mary Ann), and to make some new ones (a prospect that looks promising already). In any case, we are looking forward to having you all for 'neighbors'—for counsel and guidance, and most of all, for our fellowship in Christ."

Another friend of Outler's was Finis Crutchfield. When Bishop Crutchfield died of AIDs, Outler strongly maintained, in the midst of all the alleged contrariwise evidence, that his friend had lived an exemplary life and the lifestyle charges were unbelievable. In those dark hours Outler made pastoral visits to the Crutchfields in person, by phone, and by letter. In a November 4, 1988, letter to Charles Crutchfield he wrote: "—In all those memories, your father's role has been (and always will be) tremendously significant over the years even if more episodic than constant. We were instant friends from our very first meeting at Duke: he the bright young graduate student, I the eager young instructor. Then when we came to SMU from Yale, he was the first influential churchman in the region to get me involved in practical church affairs. Now that *that* is all behind us, I have come to realize more and more how un-typical my career was during those nearly four decades in the South Central Jurisdiction, and that your father's role in this was decisive.

"At Duke and Yale, I had been busy (and as they say 'upwardly mobile') in the academic world; but otherwise I was a marginal figure in the working life of the church. This would almost certainly have continued to be the case at SMU, just as it is the case of most Methodist scholars in other schools and other times. Except, that is, for your father and Bishop William C. Martin. Between those two, though not in collusion, I was given opportunities and assignments in the churches, conferences, and councils of the church that would never have come in the ordinary course of things. As you know, Methodists have always had a problem as to what to do with the few eggheads that keep turning up in our midst. In my case, it was your dad and Bishop Martin who, more than any others, saw to it that I was enabled to do what I could to combine the otherwise disparate roles of an *academic*-cum-*churchman* at one and the same time.

"Your Dad was himself a remarkable combination of a distinguished church statesman (never fully appreciated for his vision) and a practical, can-do church executive. He had a shrewd head and a caring heart and hand. I have, therefore, had good reason to admire him and to enjoy his unfailing and affectionate friendship, over so many years, in so many ways. Moreover, nothing has happened (or will) to sunder the bonds of our abiding friendship and mutual affection.

"The circumstances of his homegoing were sorrowful, but less for him (I was deeply moved, in my visits with him, by an inner peace and serenity I saw there) than for your mother and for you and your family. The 'journalists' who live by gossip and slander were worse than usual in their vicious *Schadenfrende.* But Mrs. Outler and I continued to admire, and be grateful for, your mother's quiet dignity and strength through it all, as well as for your loyalty, courage, and candor. More than once, the vision of Hebrews 12:27 has come into view; what still remains unshaken in the tragedy is the undeniable eminence and distinction of your father's ministry (to which so many of us, and so different a range of us, bear proud and grateful witness) and the upholding power of a loving and loyal Christian family, such as yours."

With these previous readings, suffice it to say that Outler knew *some* bishops as friends; and that he was less than friendly with *some* who lorded their power over others as church bosses rather than leading by the persuasive powers of truth and love.

Episcopal Elections a Sub-topic

In answer to a query from Walter Underwood about "a theology for episcopal elections," Outler in an October 10, 1980, letter said: "It's a special sub-topic within 'a theology for church politics,' which is generally a theological perspective for the distribution and sharing of 'power' in the church. Is it really the same as the parceling out and sharing 'power' in the *saeculum*—as so many people say in defense of '*church politics.*' Luke 22:21–30 says something rather different. Sometimes it seems to me that we have slid into an almost unconscious justification of the patronage systems of the world around us—without the honesty of that world in acknowledging that *the* rule of any patronage system is mutual self-interest!"

"Some have asked if I [Outler] would accept an election to the episcopacy or a college presidency or a deanship. I always answer no to such questions. My basic vocation is to be a scholar-teacher for the church. I could not become a bishop because I would have to answer questions one and eight 'no.' I do not consider myself called to that job (#1), nor can I say that I would work at it with enthusiasm (#8). I must stay with my current work: demonstrating the continuity of historic Christianity in the contemporary world."[177] He added later: "I would not have made a very good bishop."[178] And he would not have, if by "bishop" one means "caretaker of the cathedral."

Roles of Bishops and the Curia

"Instead of episcopal potentates (good riddance to them!) we now have episcopal populists—some with billowing spinnakers to catch the shifting winds of opinions; others with gonfalons to wave in single-issue causes. Meanwhile, our curia continues to assume many of the tasks of general superintendency in the church at large."[179]

While he knew he was fighting an uphill battle, Outler tried to convert bishops from *playing* church to *being* the leaders that the office called them to *be*. He felt that the United Methodist Church was languishing as much from lack of spiritual leadership as much as anything else. He made it clear that, if they would take seriously the constitutional *responsibility* for "planning the temporal and spiritual interests of the entire church," the church would at least be free of one of its problems; the boards and agencies would no longer be running the show in the promotion of their own self-interests.

"Never mind our cross-eyed *Discipline*, in which responsibility for *planning* [the temporal and spiritual interests] is mandated to the Council of Bishops and the *doing* of these plans left to the curia. 'Everybody' [sarcasm intended] understood that the real center of gravity in *The Discipline* is not in Part I [the Constitution], but in Part IV and specifically chapter 5. I have known the first three presidents of the Council of Secretaries; I count them friends and can vouch for their dedication, probity, and personal modesty. And yet I have heard each of them speak openly of their settled conviction that the presidency of their curial Council was (and was designed to be) co-equal with the presidency of the Council of Bishops [which in effect makes them equal to the bishops in their wielding of power]. The wonder, then, is not that a polity with such radical anomalies wired into it has not worked well, but that it is still working as well as it is."[180]

On another occasion Outler spoke of the matter in these words: "The Council of Bishops is thwarted from its constitutionally mandated responsibility to oversee the spiritual and temporal interests of 'the whole church' by the huge fact that they exist alongside three other councils and six boards and agencies, all of whom see 'the whole church' as their fiefdom and who regard themselves as co-responsible with the bishops for the 'spiritual and temporal interests of the whole church.' It is as if in 1968 we designed a church that would look like it would run well from the top—and yet could not, even with better people in all those curial posts."[181]

So convicted was Outler regarding this constitutional crisis of the church that he in 1977 wrote a paper by that title. He and Bishop Crutchfield came up with a slate of subjects that needed to be addressed by the 1980 General Conference. Outler asked Crutchfield to search me out and see whether I would chair an ad hoc committee of preachers and laity in the church to propose legislation and petitions for presentation to the next General Conference. I agreed to do this, and I met with Outler at his home on September 6, 1977, to go over his constitutional-crisis paper and an agenda for the meeting that was to come on the next day at the Dallas/Fort Worth Airport.

With my wife, Doris, acting as secretary, I called to order the thirty-seven (out of sixty invitations mailed out) who attended the meeting. Bishop Crutchfield was at the DFW Airport Hotel planning to attend the meeting. When I told Bishop Crutchfield that Outler on the previous day had strongly urged that he (Crutchfield) should not attend the meeting, the bishop did not question Outler's advice. He stayed in his hotel room while the committee met from 10:00 A.M. until 5:00 P.M., with a break for lunch. The group elected Highland Park United Methodist Church pastor Leighton Ferrell to chair what was labeled by detractors as the High Steeple Churches Committee.

In an October 24, 1978, letter to me Outler wrote: "As we agreed, I've sent off that annotated sheaf of proposed legislation to Leighton, with a covering letter with suggestions as to strategy and tactics. Meanwhile, I've an interesting letter from Dr. [Ned] Dewire, of the General Council on Ministries, proposing a visit here in late January, 'to discuss a number of concerns' (and that's literally all he says about *his* agenda). It's easy to guess, though, that he's come by a copy of your legislative proposals, he's heard that I've had a hand in them, and they've fluttered his dovecote somewhat at least. It's also easy to guess that you and your colleagues will find this as interesting a development as I do (and as unexpected?).

"He's welcome to come, of course; I'm as willing to discuss these issues with him as with anybody else. Besides, it would never do to be inhospitable or negative in a circumstance like this. Why not assume that he wants constitutional reform, too, in some sense or other—and so find out how far he is willing either to help us or interested in our helping him! There could, quite conceivably, be a real advantage in my getting a firsthand 'reading' on such a point, before the General Conference skirmishings begin in earnest.

"But that will mean that I'll need to be briefed, as fully as possible, on the progress of your project as of the middle of January so that I'll know as much as possible about your game plan and the then current score. Don't spread the word about this visit of Dewire to Dallas—just know about it as you plan, and appraise your planning. And keep me in touch."

In the days prior to the General Conference of 1980, Outler and I stayed in touch with face-to-face, telephone, and written contacts. Outler sent me a copy of his address (more of a lecture-to-direct than a speech-to-entertain) to the Council of Bishops before he gave it in the spring of 1979, asking for red-penciled additions, corrections, or deletions to be placed in the margins. I responded as Outler directed, and, along with the edited copy of Outler's speech I sent the following March 8, 1979, letter: "Thank you for 'waking me up' to the need of more legislative materials that speak to the 'amenability' problem [the curia are amenable to the Council of Bishops]. I will work (and when necessary, 'wire work') to get this into the hands of those ad hoc committee members in an acceptable form.

"As for your speech to the bishops, you might express the 'vote problem' in a manner that would wake up the bishops in this way: 'An eye-witness [by which I mean myself] told me that there was, amidst a 44 for/29 against vote, utter confusion on the floor of a Chicago ad hoc committee meeting concerning a paper with which I am *familiar* [Outler wrote it!] titled 'Accountability and Amenability to the General Council on Ministries—A Constitutional Crisis.' This means somebody (bishops are some of those 'bodies') had better get on the ball in Annual Conferences and do some educating soon. This check-and-balance legislation must come off this General Conference. Every Annual Conference should be alerted to the constitutional crisis that does exist.

"You hit 'em from 'the top' and I'll hit 'em from out here in the bottom land."

The point to be made here is not high-steeple preachers, but the world-renowned historical theologian Albert C. Outler was the one behind the scenes calling some of the crucial plays that moved the 1980 General Conference to become more open and accountable to the grassroots church it represented. The man was as busy writing history as he was interpreting it.

The Outlers as Reformers

Could Albert Outler's lover's quarrel with the United Methodist Church be reflections of his father's similar experiences? Certainly there are similarities. Outler said, "In a way my father was an old-fashioned conservative Methodist preacher as far as his tastes and theology were concerned. But I can see now, in retrospect, that he was also a genuine reformer—both in the church and in the communities he served. And I have come to appreciate this interesting mixture of theological conservatism and social vision and activism.

"For example, he was a pioneer in the Christian education movement long before it was a universal cause. And in the missionary movement. And in the very early stages of Methodist labor and race relations, at a time when these were pretty far out.

"It was my father who taught me how to be a free and loyal Methodist. Free in a tight connectional system; loyal to the system and yet independent of its power to repress.

"We lived under a series of very authoritarian bishops in Georgia—Bishop Candler and Bishop Ainsworth and the lot—with whom Mom and Dad were acquainted, for he was sometimes presiding elder and at other times preacher in large city churches. And his relations with these bishops and the conference organization were almost always tense—in some sort of loyal opposition. He was, himself, never intimidated nor subdued. And we lived in congregations that we loved—as I remember it—and who loved us—as I remember it—but whom

Mother kept out of our hair by insisting that the parsonage was *our home.*

"Now this was important because it helped me to relate to people as a preacher's kid and yet, also, to keep my own stance and agenda—without too much pressure to conform, on the one hand, or to rebel on the other."[182]

Conformity was never considered as a way of life for Outler; neither was rebellion for the sake of rebellion. But for the sake of *being* the church he had some other thoughts in his later days: "'Do not be weary in well-doing,' saith St. Paul—although I confess too much weariness in much of what was intended as well-doing, in light of what has come of all my efforts, over a long lifetime of watching American Methodism reap the slow but inexorable penalties of a century's renunciation of its heritage and of turning to Pelagianism without even knowing the term for what it was doing.

"Maybe the time has come for some of us to do what Wesley and his folks did: stop bothering to look *up* to the hierarchy and bureaucracy, and to look up to something higher (the Scripture and Christian tradition), to look *around* (at the churches who actually are alive with the gospel message and with networks of nurture and concern), and to look *within* (to the Holy Spirit's prevenient callings to repentance, faith, and forgiveness and assurance and reconciliation and holiness defined as love of God and neighbor, in that order)."[183] The effect of such experiences would be the true church—catholic, reformed, evangelical.

In Outler's sermons at church conferences and in local churches one can see over and over, on the one hand his independence from church authorities, and on the other hand his loyalty to the heart and mind of the church as it *ought to be*: "A church in the mode of maintenance is less attractive to the unchurched than a church on the march with a sense of excitement, intensity, monomania in mission!"[184]

Outler could barely tolerate General Conferences; he was never at home in those situations. There was too much rancor. And at times he found himself in the middle of the muddle. It was the mission of the church that captivated him. He once said: "A Methodist General Conference is one of the most debilitating experiences I ever had [he attended six of them as a delegate]. And yet even in this spiritual desert there springs an oasis—

urban churches that are not only alive, but life-giving; suburban parishes that are not falling victim to the suburban malaise or turned into sensitivity-training groups, etc."[185]

The maintenance mode of the United Methodist Church, with its incessant tinkering with structure, its preoccupation with strategy, its threatening hierarchy maintaining its control over the church led to this classic Outler reply to those who questioned the future of the United Methodist Church: "I am firmly convinced that the United Methodist Church will be marching strongly down through history, long after Christianity is dead and gone!"[186]

World Methodist Conferences

Outler's involvements in World Methodist Conferences are legion: plenary address (London), 1966; plenary address, Conference on Evangelism (Jerusalem), 1974; lectures, World Methodist Conference (Honolulu), 1981; World Methodist Executive Committee, 1976–82; and then there were the plenary lectures, Oxford Institute on Methodist Theology 1962, 1981, 1987; Oxford Institute for Theological Studies, 1982, and others. At the eleventh World Methodist Conference on August 22, 1966, in London's Central Hall, Outler, in speaking to the advertised lecture title, "What Is God Saying to Us in Contemporary Theology?," changed it to a more manageable title, "The Current Theological Scene: A View From the Beach at Ebb Tide." This avoided apocalyptic answers that too many theologians dogmatically (or cavalierly) give. "It was more than mere annoyance that prompted the mutter: 'Quit faking and talk plainly!' Last month, when the new prophets at Geneva had finished their tirades against practically everybody, it was more than my prejudices that wondered where they got their credentials to omniscience.

"'Contemporary' theology is still a lively business, but there are now few fixed positions and no broad consensus as to method and rhetoric. A favorite indoor sport among theologians today is the game, 'disclaimer'—and any number can play. You start by stating an extreme or novel notion in which the key terms are neologisms or old words in new usages. Then the rest pounce on you, and your move is blandly to deny that they understood your real meaning. The one who enlists the largest number of friends *and* foes in the effort to explain what he *really* meant is the winner—until the *next* brouhaha begins! You can't quote a man against himself today if the quote is older than yesterday. There is the early Barth and the later Barth, the early Heidegger and the later Heidegger, the early Robinson and the later Robinson—and each *prosopon* has its partisans."

Of the death-of-God morticians he said: "They have done us a service—one of God's backhand volleys!—of raising the question as to what, if anything, we mean when we sing out: 'I believe in one God, Father Almighty, maker of heaven *and* earth, and of all things, visible *and* invisible!' But they gave no answer."

Toward the end of the address he said: ". . . the theologians we do have scatter over the entire theological spectrum—with advocates of every known position, and some that aren't. You name it and we've got it somewhere—good, bad, and indifferent, something old, something new, something borrowed, something *piu*! When we mislaid our Wesleyan heritage (which was itself eclectic enough), we began to be a sort of theological cafeteria. Knowing that a man is a Methodist will tell you very little about his beliefs—until you know his seminary, his vintage, his major; or, if he's a layman, the succession of ministers he's had.

"This, certainly, is better than its opposite: lockstep confessional consensus. But why do we go on ignoring the better way: of reclaiming the substance of our Wesleyan heritage as our common treasure and working together at the several ways in which *that* tradition can be updated and oriented toward the Christian future?"

Not all audiences gave Outler standing ovations, and this bothered him. That bother was expressed in an extraneous paragraph in a September 1, 1987, letter addressed to James S. Udy. It was not intrinsic to the information Udy was asking for, but it was on Outler's mind. And it agreed with some of Outler's friends who attended and heard Outler speak at the 1987 Oxford Institute of Methodist Theological Studies. Here is Outler's assessment of that occurrence: "This summer [1987] I summoned my dwindling reserves (of energy and effort) to go to the Oxford Institute, and to do the 'keynote address.' The better part of two months went into the address, and (as Wesley used to say of some of his failures) 'I delivered my soul.' The response was cordial, but the impact was minimal. A fortnight of 'conferencing' made it plain that 'World Methodists' are more interested in their contemporary 'causes' (which are so disparate as to be discordant) than they are in 'heritage' and in the classical consensus of the churches in the early centuries. We had a few competent pathologists there, but the Institute as a whole was more interested in their 'babel' of 'experience,' and in Scripture in support of this or that, than in 'Scripture and Christian Antiquity' (to borrow again from Wesley)."

"A Belly Full of It"

As was attested to many times, people flocked to hear Outler talk. And he would talk as long as they would listen. But, as indicated above, not all shared this fascination with Outler's penchant for talk. What Outler had to say on one occasion was a bit more than at least one person could handle. He was Bishop Bill Cannon, possibly the closest long-time friend Outler ever had. Cannon's concern and care for Outler can be seen in this October 8, 1973, letter: "You have a brilliant mind, and your devotion to God is so sincere and deep that you have worked yourself to a frazzle in service. Please pace yourself more. That is essential. We need to keep you here for many more years to come. You have the brightest and most influential scholarly mind in Protestantism today. We in Methodism are proud to claim you. How grateful to God I am that I have you as a deep and intimate and wonderful friend!"

More sincere words were never spoken. But friendships are similar to marriages; there are moments when one is tested. In a Roman Catholic/World Methodist dialogue held in Bad Soden, Germany (October 3–6, 1977), Bishop Cannon was tested. After a couple of days of marvelous interventions on the part of Outler, Bishop Cannon took Joe Hale aside and said: "He's scintillating, brilliant, and all of that, but after awhile you get a belly full of it!"

Outler was invited to address the World Methodist Council Executive Committee in High Leigh, England, which met October 30–November 3, 1978. He gave the history of the Roman Catholic/World Methodist dialogue that continued following the close of Vatican II (to which he had been appointed as observer by the World Methodist Council). As was the case in 1977 when he spoke on the same subject but to a different audience, there was dialogue with those who chose to linger and talk. And Bill Cannon was there. If he got "a bellyfull of it," he kept it to himself.

At the World Methodist Conference in Hawaii, 1981, Outler gave a response to an address by Dr. Nikos A. Nissiotis, the moderator at that time of the Faith and Order Commission of the World Council of Churches. At that 1981 Conference Outler also served on a panel that discussed Wesleyan humor. His comments, laced as always with wit and humor, revealed a Wesley capable only of unintended humor.

The Oxford Institute of Methodist Studies

In August 1982 at Keble College, Oxford, Outler was a co-convener, along with John Turner, of the Wesley Studies Group at the Oxford Institute of Methodist (Theological) Studies. Outler prepared the agenda, and at the conclusion he and Turner, assisted by Timothy Smith, produced a paper based on its discussions. That paper, edited by Douglas Meeks, was published by Abingdon Press in 1985 under the title *The Future of the Methodist Theological Traditions.*

The mix of Outler and Oxford's noted historian John Walsh furnished some interesting dialogue for the group. When Outler said, "*The Arminian Magazine* has a marvelous montage of jewels and junk," Walsh responded, "It is the junk that interests the historian," and they were off and running.

The two scholars literally did run together. As Outler worked on the Wesley *Sermons* project in Oxford University's libraries he was often a guest in the home of Walsh. Car rides in and about Oxford permitted the two men to come to know the landscape of their minds as well as the face of the earth. Walsh said of himself, "I am a historian, not a theologian." And of Outler, "He was a great scholar—a bit of a prima donna, but that's all right."[187] That was vintage Outler—he transcended himself as he *became* a primary actor in whatever public forum he joined.

A World Methodist Theological Statement

Toward the end of 1984 an ailing Outler explained to World Methodist Council General Secretary Joe Hale that his angina problem would not permit him to attend a World Methodist Council workshop in Jerusalem that was to meet early in 1985, at which time they were to develop a theological statement. But he did send to Hale a very long letter saying how this might develop and gave his own input. Hale "cut" a part of the Outler text that he felt would not be well received by the British. The final text was perfected and voted on by the World Methodist Council meeting in Nairobi in July 1986. While some of what Outler said cannot be found in the document, it is difficult to find any part of it contrary to his thinking—*except* there is far more to Methodist doctrine than cognitive propositional truths. About the adopted Nairobi statement Outler said in an address titled *Methodists in Search of Consensus* at the Oxford Institute of Methodist Theological Studies (July 1987, Oxford): "What was finally agreed to at Nairobi is edifying (and I am grateful for it); but it is not authoritative, nor does it pretend to be. In my judgment, we should learn to speak of our conciliation with the classical Christian tradition (God's *actus tradendi* in Christ), the traditions of the church (*constitutivae* and *interpretivai*), *and* the various traditions of the divers church (*consuetudines*). We should learn to theologize more self-consciously *coram Deo,* from the premise that it is the Spirit who alone can turn cognitive-propositional 'truth' into 'faith energized by love.' We should avail ourselves of all critical resources in our intent in rightly dividing the Word of Truth in Holy Writ. We need to correlate Scripture and tradition in the right order, to redound the disciplines of reason to the glory of God, to help liturgy to surpass its aesthetic components, to rescue 'experience' from subjectivity, and thus to surpass both sentimentality and ideology. We should cultivate the intellectual love of God in Spirit-filled minds and hearts."

Outler had a "word from the Lord" for Wesleyan Methodists. And still does. Outler's name is still honored when World Methodists meet. Wherever World Methodists are gathered, on the floor and in major addresses Outler is quoted and is recognized in that respected prophetic role by church leaders of the world. Preeminent theologian Reinhold Niebuhr puts Outler in his place with these words: "I am indebted to Albert Outler, the century's foremost Methodist theologian."[188]

11

As an Ecumenist

Senior Statesperson

Outler exemplified Wesley's "catholic spirit" through his many ecumenical involvements. And that is the way the church universal saw Outler. To them he was primarily an ecumenist. "There is no doubt he was the senior Statesperson of Christianity in America," said church historian Martin Marty of the University of Chicago. In the October 1989 issue of *The Christian Century,* Marty said following Outler's death: "In all the obituaries, memorials and remembrances of Outler, one word surfaces more than 'Methodist' —'ecumenist.' He was conscious of the ways that John Wesley's theology drew on biblical and historical sources shared by other Christians. He taught us how the *traditum,* the 'handing over' of God's gift in Christ and the church, differed in many ways from the *traditiones,* the behavior patterns, practices and teachings that the faithful and the faithless alike pass on in their sometimes more trivial pursuits. He was engrossed by the former and amused or put off by much of the latter, but never failed to show courteous interest in those who represented both. Most of these were not his fellow Methodists."

Outler's interest in the ecumenical church began in the earliest stages of ecumenism when he was a Yale graduate student as he helped redraft Calhoun's paper to be given at Oxford. In his later years Outler called himself "a grizzled ecumaniac with a wealth of golden memories." A glance at his ecumenical involvements shows how he got *that* grizzled:

Delegate to the Third World Council on Faith and Order at Lund, Sweden, 1952

Co-chairman of the Study Commission on Tradition and Traditions, 1952–1963

Member of the Faith and Order Commission working committee, 1953–1974

Co-chairman, Faith and Order Study Commission on Tradition and Traditions, 1954–1963

Delegate (gave plenary address), North American Conference on Faith and Order in Oberlin, 1957

Delegate, COCU, 1960–1976

Delegate, Third and Fourth assemblies of the World Council of Churches at New Delhi, India, 1961; and at Uppsala, 1968

World Methodist Council delegate-observer to the Second Vatican Council, 1962–1965

Delegate and vice chairman, Fourth World Conference on Faith and Order in Montreal, 1963 (gave plenary address). (It is interesting to note that in 1963 Outler turned down an "inquiry" about any interest in the post of theological secretary of Faith and Order.)

Vice president, Commission on Ecumenical Affairs and chairman of Ecumenical Study and Liaison Committee, 1964

Methodist Church Commission on Ecumenical Affairs, 1964–1968

American Catholic Historical Association; first Protestant president, American Catholic Historical Association, 1972–1973

Member, Academic Council of the Ecumenical Institute for Advanced Theological Studies, Jerusalem, 1965–1978

Member, "Bilateral Conversations" between the Vatican's Secretariat for Promoting Christian Unity and the World Methodist Council, 1966–1982

Uniting ceremony sermon in Dallas before the combined General Conferences of The Methodist Church and the Evangelical United Brethren Church, April 23, 1968

Chairman, Evening Session at the Sixth International Congress
of Patristics, Oxford University, September 6–10, 1971

Member, Board of Directors of *The National Catholic Reporter,*
1971–1981

Lecturer, Public session of the World Methodist Historical Society, Bristol, July 1973

Member, World Methodist Council Executive Committee,
1976–1982

Founding Fellow, Dallas Center for World Thanksgiving, 1977

Associate editor, *Journal of Ecumenical Studies*

In a September 9, 1977, letter to Fred Maser, Outler judged
these ecumenical involvements in this manner: "My most significant projects have been the work (co-chairman) of the Theological Study Commission on Tradition and Traditions (1952–63)
of the World Council of Churches and as a member of Faith and
Order's 'Working Committee' (1953–74); plus my assignments
as a 'Delegate-Observer' from the World Methodist Council to
the Second Vatican Council and my subsequent involvement in
the Roman Catholic–United Methodist 'bilaterals' (the first from
1965–72 and now the new one being launched, October 3–7, in
Germany; it is scheduled for a five-year run)." To all of these
ecumenical audiences Outler had this word: "Our work is not to
finish the job, but to get on with it."[189]

A Profile of Outler As an Ecumenist

Oxford's Henry Chadwick observed how Outler "worked the
crowd" during Anglican/Roman Catholic discussions. And gave
a profiled description of Outler at work in any ecumenical setting: "He was a fine person who was the embodiment of goodness, intelligence, and shrewdness. He had an insider's
understanding of ecumenism as an art, of reexpressing Christian
convictions without using language or terms which carried polemical overtones and sharp edges for one or other of the conversing parties. He astonished people by illustrating with
apparently no sleight of hand about it. He saw clearly that in
drafting ecumenical statements it was perfectly possible with
total integrity to avoid all language that was going to annoy
some group that was a party to the discussion. So he largely
anticipated the method employed in Anglican/Roman Catholic

discussions with a degree of success that astonished the participants in the commission, though it bewildered some who had not
been exposed to the white heat of really serious self-scrutiny
before the searching investigation of other Christians who love
God and his Church and apparently draw different conclusions."[190]

The World Council of Churches

The previous description of Outler performing in the ecumenical
environment reveals that he was "at home" *working* in those
settings. Sometimes there was more "white heat" than light. This
was certainly so with some of his involvements in the World
Council of Churches. Outler made lasting friends with many of
those participants. But not all. One with whom he felt least "at
home" was William A. Visser 't Hooft. In a blistering October
26, 1966, letter Outler reprimanded Visser 't Hooft for making a
false judgment (about Outler) based upon a news release and
spreading the "news" in such a gossipy manner: "Besides the
disquieting thought of being 'discussed' in such company, I found
the whole thing astonishing on at least two separate counts. The
first is that this is the first and only time in my twenty years of
service in the ecumenical cause (in one capacity or another) that
I have been aware of any particular notice by you of *any* notion
of mine, real *or* alleged. That such a notice should come in such
a context is at least mildly outrageous. The second ground for
my astonishment is that you have raised a question about my
'loyalty' (and presumably the loyalties of the others in the *Una
Sancta* symposium) *before* you had read the relevant texts. You
were a scholar once and your academic conscience is surely not
yet shrunk to the point where you would raise basic questions
about a man's basic ecclesiological stance with his ecclesiastical
superiors on no more evidence than an NLC news release!" This
stern rebuke continued for three pages, single-spaced.

   Visser 't Hooft counter-reprimanded Outler with his defense
in a November 11, 1966, letter, which in essence was a put-down
concerning Outler's becoming "explosively indignant."

   Then came Outler's one-page reply in a November 15, 1966,
letter with this concluding paragraph: "Here we may as well let
the matter rest. But *if* there should ever be any 'next time,'
please either read the *texts* involved or come at me directly.

Meanwhile, if my name disappears from (or fails to appear in) various Methodist ecumenical commissions, you'll understand that there are those who have *their* reasons to be able to murmur, 'Have you heard that Visser 't Hooft has raised some questions about Outler, etc.?' I've run into it already, at our General Conference in Chicago last week. It begins to look as if this—and much else, of course—will drive me back to the academic work I should have been concentrating on all along—and that may be the best outcome, anyway." A lack of further correspondence suggests that this matter between Visser 't Hooft and Outler was laid to rest.

Tradition, Traditions, and Traditioning

"The way into the community is not, in the first instance, by way of doctrinal understanding—but rather through encounter with Jesus Christ, as he is remembered, proclaimed, and interpreted by the community and its tradition. The heart of Christian faith and the living center of the Christian community are one and the same, the Lord Jesus Christ."[191]

"There is—an authority for *all* Christians. It is the origin and center of our faith and our community. It is God's self-manifestation in Jesus Christ who possesses all men who receive him (John 1:12). It is God's prime act of *tradition* or 'handing over' Jesus Christ to share our existence and to effect our salvation. 'For he who did not spare his own Son but 'handed him over' for us all, will he not also give us all things else with him?'" (Romans 8:32; cf. also Romans 4:24–25).

"There is simply no prospect whatever that we shall reduce the different church traditions to a universal uniformity. What is more, the Christian community would be the poorer if it should lose a large diversity in its traditions—of doctrine, liturgy, and polity. What matters is that it be diversity-in-unity, and that the unity shall center in our common loyalty to God's 'tradition' of Jesus Christ and to the Spirit's 'traditioning' of Jesus Christ in the church. This is the unity which we have received, which even now we know in foretaste. The further fullness of this unity turns upon our willingness to move toward the Center of our community—the Head of our one Body—in order that we may move closer to one another!"[192]

"There is still a long uncharted road before us in our pilgrim journey toward the unity we seek. And the rules of the road must include at least the following: *force no issue; avoid none; eyes center!*"[193]

Consultation on Church Union

With "eyes center" Outler forced no issue and avoided none as he became involved with COCU [Consultation on Church Union] in the early sixties. "Remember in the beginning that Methodist representatives in all these things were people who were closest to the policy-making, decision-making processes in the church. But after the 1964 debacle at Princeton—when Mr. Parlin, in effect, put COCU on notice that the price of Methodist cooperation was their agreeing to the Methodist model as a kind of paradigm, which the rest promptly disavowed with some vehemence and disgust—after that debacle we started out to find a new style of participation and dialogue, and that was the time when I got appointed to COCU and continued until 1970—from 1964 to 1970.

"In this period I had a hand in drafting the new plans—the chapters on "Our Common Faith" and on "The Ministry," and was also on the drafting committee for the Ordinal. As early as 1968 we knew we were in trouble. The liberals weren't interested in the real 'faith and order' questions of sacrament, ministry, or the terms of a mingled membership in a united church. For they saw the church as either an arm of social revolution or not as terribly relevant to the crises of the 1960s. And you have to keep remembering that the 1960s were a different decade from the one we live in now.

"The conservatives never had been committed to ecumenism at the cost of any real change in their cherished denominational traditions and patterns. So that in 1968 we began to realize that the Achilles heel of the whole enterprise was not the old cluster of thorny issues that *had* divided the churches—doctrine, liturgy, ministry, apostolic succession, all of that sort of thing or even the primacy of scripture—but instead were structure, polity, the organization of the institution. And there the practical people simply failed us. They were obsessed with the model of merger and a corporate structure that was pyramidal in form with juridical processes divided—church courts at every level. To Methodists all this looked very Presbyterian and Episcopalian. To Presbyterians and Episcopalians it looked like nothing they had ever really believed in, in terms of polity. To the Disciples and the Congregationalists, it looked awfully Methodist. And this was the rock on which COCU foundered.

"Now if merger is not the answer then the question is whether organic unity is something other than spiritual ecumenism, practical cooperation, or uniform institutionalization. And the answer, I think, is quite clearly some formula of mingled memberships, mingled sacraments, mingled ministries. This will create the only kind of Christian unity we need, the only kind that will actually translate itself into effectual mission. All that can be achieved without a uniform institutionalization."

To an interviewer who asked what Outler meant by COCU being "dead in the water," Outler responded, "I meant that the institutions were sitting down and dragging their feet—if you don't mind a mixed metaphor!"

Outler's Mix with Vatican II

The approach, *force no issue; avoid none; eyes center*, also guided Outler as he went reluctantly to observe officially from a World Methodist/Protestant/ecumenist viewpoint what was going on at Vatican II. For the Christian world (Roman Catholics and Protestants alike) it came as a bolt out of the blue when on January 25, 1959, Pope John XXIII announced he was planning on convening a Second Vatican Council (the First Vatican Council was held 1869–1870) with the express aims of a means of building up the people of Christ, but also as a call to the separated communities for a search for unity. Within months Pope John instituted the Secretariat (same as Commission but with more freedom) for Christian Unity, naming his newly appointed Cardinal Bea as the president, who in turn submitted the name of Cardinal Willibrands to the pope to be confirmed as the Secretary of the Secretariat. Outler came to know very closely these two cardinals (as well as the charismatic Cardinal Seunens from Belgium) as colleagues in the search for unity.

Unlike Vatican I where non-Catholics were invited but did not attend, at the opening session of Vatican II fifty-plus observer-delegates from churches over the world were present at the plenary session where 2,495 Catholic cardinals and bishops assembled. Of the three full observer-delegates representing the World Methodist Council, Outler was the only one who attended all sessions of Vatican II from its first session (October 11, 1962–December 8, 1962) through the second session (September 29, 1963–December 2, 1963) and through the third session (September 14, 1964–November 21, 1964), ending with the fourth session (September 14, 1965–December 7, 1965).

At the conclusion of the first day of the Council in 1962, Outler and Roman Catholic Thomas Stransky, during the long walk from St. Peter's Cathedral to the hotel, talked excitedly about John XXIII's startling speech/homily. Could this bridge to the 'separated brethren' be for real? That was the question. When the progressives got a strong head start and moved fast with their push for change, the world came to know the bridge was in the process of becoming a reality. In recognition of the extraordinary changes in liturgy, where participation between clergy and congregation would no longer be clergy *dominated* and people *subordinated* but where all would be on the same level before God, Outler said following the second 1963 Session, "Never has there been such an obvious intervention of the Holy Spirit as in this Council. Changes that in ordinary times would take decades have come in two years!"[194]

An astutely observant Outler also saw the ridiculous mixed with the sublime. In one of the final meetings of the Second Session of Vatican II (1963) the Protestant observers, dressed in their academic robes with colorful stoles and hoods, mingled with the more elaborately decorated Roman bishops and cardinals as they exited St. Peter's Cathedral and processed across St. Peter's Square. Benedictine monk Godfrey Diekmann, professor of patristics at St. John's University in Collegeville, Minnesota, walked beside Outler and began a conversation. Observing this colorful plumage fluttering about on the bishops and observers, Outler said to Diekmann, "Protestants have always taken great glee in pointing to the Romans in their colorful garb. Look at us in all these fancy academic gowns and colors of all kinds. Reminds me of a bunch of game cocks in a mating season!"[195]

No one recognized and appreciated the excelling abilities of dilettante Outler more than his friend and colleague Howard

Grimes, who in his book *A History of the Perkins School of Theology* wrote about Outler: "His [Outler's] participation in Vatican Council II took him beyond Protestant ecumenism and was important for the Council, since he not only understood the Catholic tradition better than many bishops but also helped them with their Latin, in which he was a specialist. A story—I'm sure apocryphal—is that at the opening meeting of one of the sessions of Vatican II, the Pope scanned the assemblage carefully and finally, with gusto, asked, 'Where's Albert?'"[196]

An audio tape sent to me following Outler's death reveals this moment. First, a look at the setting for the occasion: The Council delegates had met for nearly two months in the first session; had gone home for approximately ten months; then returned for the second session with the new Pope Paul VI (the beloved Pope John XXIII had died earlier that year on June 3). With the new pope unproved regarding things ecumenical, tension filled the air when the memory of a keen-minded, good-humored and quick-witted Outler came to the rescue. The convener came to the podium, rapped his gavel, and in a strong, well-trained resonant voice declared: "The second session of Vatican Council II is now called to order." He then paused and said, "But where's Albert?!" The congregation of delegates erupted in laughter. Which eased the tension and helped get the second session off to a good start.

This tape sounded so perfect. It fit Outler to a "t." It sounded just like something one would expect. But it did not happen. Letting Bishop Duprey and Monsignor Salzmann in Rome and Thomas Stransky in Tantur, Jerusalem, hear the tape proved Grimes was right. It is apocryphal. What started out as a spoof had the ring of possibility and was repeated as if it really happened. A signal of its inaccuracy: The session was called to order in Latin, not English.

Most Quoted

According to *The Catholic Messenger,* Outler was "quite likely the most quoted man on the Second Vatican Council with the exception of Pope Paul VI." One can see why such a statement might be said when his interviews are added up. During Vatican II there were two ABC Radio interviews by a man named

Whitehouse; a broadcast over Vatican Radio for the Canadian Broadcasting Company on "Methodist tradition, the Methodist views and history of bishops, the way bishops are chosen and the kind of bishops we have, Methodist polity and discipline"; three ABC-TV broadcasts; an interview by Claud Nelsus for his News Service; a TV broadcast for the NBC station at Pittsburgh; Italian Radio interview; and a CBS-TV interview. Add to these Outler's many writings and speeches, quotes in religious and secular newspapers and one comes to the conclusion that Outler was "quite likely the most quoted man on the Second Vatican Council with the exception of Pope Paul VI."

Not only was Outler quite likely the most quoted, he was also the most quoted *to*. During Vatican II he seemed to have spies everywhere reporting to him. Presbyterian observer-delegate Robert McAfee Brown said this about Albert Outler: "I doubt if there is a single person, whether cardinal, bishop, Pope, or mere observer, who had a more comprehensive understanding of what was going on throughout than did Al. This is partly because he had those special linguistic gifts that made it possible not only for him to listen to Latin, but to be able to write in Latin as well. His keen historical mind always made it possible for him to be drawing precedents from past events of conciliar history or to see parallels in previous theological positions held by the Catholic Church. This meant that he was usually two jumps ahead of the bishops, who were at least one jump behind their favorite *periti* [searchers and dispensers of the latest news].

"My favorite illustration of the way Al operated came sometime toward the end of the second session. I cannot remember the precise detail of the document under discussion, but the sequence went something like this: Late one evening while I was visiting with a group of priests, I got by the grapevine the word that a special document was circulating among influential bishops trying to get their support for a change in the conciliar procedures. By talking to these priests, I began to get a little idea that something rather important might be happening, so the next morning, when we got to the *aula,* instead of staying for the opening speeches by the cardinals, I left the observers tribune immediately after the Mass had been finished and began my circulation of the coffee bars. By virtue of a number of friends made in these places over the preceding weeks, I pieced together considerably more information about the document under discussion which, although it had not been released, was clearly in existence and was by some invisible Vatican telegraph being gotten to the important people.

"In the course of conversation with a number of *periti* and a few bishops and in general circulation in the aisles of St. Peter's, I had pieced together a fairly reliable secondhand account of the nature of the document and some of the probable signatories. About two hours later I went back into the observers' tribune flushed with a sense of being on the edge of a terrific ecumenical scoop. Al was sitting in the tribune, listening to the speeches quite distanced from any one of the translators into English, since he had no need of these mediation devices, and I went up to Al and started to tell him a bit about what I had found out. He listened for a moment or two and then reached into his coat pocket and pulled out the full text of the document in question along with the names of the signatories. Somewhere during the night or early morning Al's own troops and/or spies had not only heard of the document, but had been able to secure a copy of it for him. He was already miles ahead of the rest of us before the day even began."[197]

Outler's influence at Vatican II continued on the American scene following the Council. Roman Catholic theologian David L. Balas puts it plainly: "After Vatican II, Dr. Outler did, in my judgment, more than anybody else (including most Catholic participants of Vatican II) to help Americans, especially American Catholics, to understand, appreciate and assimilate Vatican II."[198]

Another "Apocryphal" Story

Another "apocryphal" story describes Outler speaking in St. Peter's Basilica before the pope and the nearly twenty-five hundred assembled delegates. His first words were: "I wish mama could see me now." That sounds precisely like something Outler would say and very likely did say in a similar setting.

At the close of the Council in 1965, Outler was a worship leader in a liturgy of the Word (Common Bible Service) that was held in the Church of St. Paul Outside-the-Walls. This statement would fall into the apocryphal category if it were not for a Vatican photograph that shows Outler speaking behind a podium with Pope Paul VI in his chair to the right and the observers to the left and the bishops before him. His text was 1 Chronicles 29:10–18 (RSV): "David said: 'Blessed art thou, O Lord . . . We are strangers before thee, and sojourners . . . a house for thy holy name comes from thy hand and is all thy own.'"

It is not hard to believe that he spoke in Latin because he did that often. This could very easily have been the setting where he made his wish for the presence of his mother.

Separated Brotherhood of St. Longinus

Outler also addressed the Roman Catholics on two other occasions. The first was during the Second Session on November 8, 1963, when he spoke at the ecumenical reception in Rome's Grand Hotel given by the Paulist Fathers and their congregation of Santa Susanna, "the American Catholic Church" in Rome. His speech entitled, "The Separated Brethren Of St. Longinus," began with the typical Outlerian wit and humor they had come to appreciate: "Your excellencies, Venerable Fathers, Beloved Brethren in Christ: I speak to you this afternoon as a member of a new and not yet authorized order which has sprung up in the course of this council. It is the Separated Brotherhood of St. Longinus— for, as you know, the tribune of the observers is placed under Bernini's great statue. And, as you can guess, the centurion's spear was quivering this morning!" The tone of the speech is captured in this comment: "You must realize (and not be offended by it) that the burden of our reservations toward you, from both Orthodox and Protestant sides, has not been that Rome is *too* catholic, but rather not *catholic* enough."[199]

The tone of Outler's second address was even more challenging to his Roman Catholic audience than the first. When the Paulist Fathers were faced with the picking of an observer to speak during the final 1965 reception given in the Grand Hotel, they focused once again on Outler. In his speech titled "Reformation Roman-Style" he stated where he saw them in *aggiornamento* (Pope John XXIII's slogan, "bringing the Church up to date"): "Thus, one of the important consequences of your Reformation Roman-Style is that in it you have continued to maintain a stable community in terms of unstable theories about that stability and these theories now require re-examination. This, too, is an item in your budget of unfinished business."[200]

Outler's Writings Continue to Enlighten Catholics

Outler's writings continue to enlighten Catholics on their history. In writing Cardinal Augustin Bea's biography Stjepan Schmidt made, as he calls it, "particular use"[201] of Outler's book, *Methodist Observer at Vatican II* (Newman Press: 1967; 189 pp.).

What Set Outler Apart

A unique turn of events happened with Outler at Vatican II. He went there to observe and, as it turned out, many there began to observe him. Paolo Ricca, professor of Church History and Ecumenics at the Waldensian Seminary in Rome, whose school had hosted the non-Catholic observers, spoke what many thought: "Professor Outler was different; the other observers were what I would call 'churchmen'; he was a scholar"[202] A scholar who was as entertaining as he was knowledgeable in his relationship with others at Vatican II.

A Man of Conviction

A comment from Rome concerning the Council, made in an October 8, 1964, letter by Outler to Jesse Hobson, then vice president of Southern Methodist University, revealed a conviction that affected every social situation in which he found himself. A conviction that allowed himself over and over to be caught in the middle—sometimes to be attacked by the conservatives, sometimes by the liberals. His words speak that strong persuasion: "Over here, I'm having a wonderful, though strenuous time, struggling to keep on top of a swirling burst of activity in a Council suddenly galvanized into divisive action. The last dozen days have changed the history of the Roman Catholic Church past all recognition (or reversal)—and the 'victory' of the 'progressives' is so nearly overwhelming as to be alarming to one who believes, as I do, in the necessary *polarity* of conservatism and liberalism in any dynamic society. Anyhow, it's all very exciting to observe, and this time I've access to some of the inner workings of the operation and can understand it better, as it unfolds."

In this instance Outler's ambivalence was evident and accounts for some of the complexities involved in understanding him. In other writings as an observer Outler aligned himself with the progressives; yet he says here that the progressive movement is "alarming." Closer scrutiny shows that he wanted the progressives to win but not at the expense of steamrolling the conservatives. He saw as a historian of the world and the church the need of polarity as a means of not permitting the principles and practices of one part of the dynamic to squelch the other, which inevitably would lead to oppression of the opposition.

One can see how it happened that this belief of necessary polarities opened the door for accusations made from both the liberals and conservatives that "Outler left himself *open* for such criticism."

One Church

But when it came to the one church, apostolic and universal (catholic!), Outler left himself open to no misinterpretation. Roman Catholic Bishop Pierre Duprey, Secretary of the Secretariat for Christian Unity (1997) summed up that undebatable truth about Outler in these words: "What struck me about Albert Outler was that he was totally convinced, totally convinced that there was one church. He really believed that."[203]

A Theologian's Theologian

Vatican II revealed that Albert Outler was more than an equal to European theologians (earlier letters disclosed that their snobbery was a tad more than he could bear), that he was in fact a theologian's theologian. Their acceptance of him revealed that he indeed was *their* teacher. That had to be for Outler one of his most satisfying experiences.

The late United Methodist Bishop Paul Galloway, who observed Observer Outler at the Second Vatican Council, said: "In the corridors and on the walkways in or near St. Peter's Cathedral in Rome an entourage of Roman bishops followed Outler wherever he went—asking questions, seeking counsel, admiring. That was one of the most unusual and exciting events of the entire Council."[204]

What was it about this bushy-browed, bespectacled 5'10", 160-lb. man, unassumingly dressed in drab greys and high-topped shoes, that attracted a crowd wherever he went? It was what came forth from the man that attracted them—an infectious smile that made others want to try the same, eyes that pierced when piercing was called for or light up with a sparkle when moved with enlightenment or excitement, a uniquely pleasant baritone voice that was bathed in a Georgian accent that did not reach the more advanced drawl that some Georgians trade on (in Rome they loved to hear Outler order his meal from the restaurant's menu in Italian!), a quick wit that sometimes erupted through a quick temper and as quickly into a lecture on why it is the way it is, whatever "it" is. The man was a walking encyclopedia, and they *read* him with the same joy, excitement, and commitment that he projected.

The 1987 Pax Christi Award

In presenting *The Pax Christi Award* to Albert Outler in 1987, St. John's University acknowledged him as heir of Saint Benedict in spirit. The following excerpts from the certificate reveal how providential was the life of Albert Outler for the Roman Catholic Church at Vatican II: "Who would have thought that a Methodist minister brought up in Georgia and teaching in Texas would become for many of the bishops at the Second Vatican Council their most valued and trusted interpreter of what they themselves were doing? . . . [Official observers and Council Fathers saw him] as the historian who knew the context, the theologian who knew the language (and the languages), and the gregarious human being whose wit and humor spiced ecclesiastical life in Rome during those long weeks."

The program also contained a statement that moved Outler deeply: "Professor at Duke University and Yale University, and then for a quarter-century at Perkins School of Theology at Southern Methodist University, you have been—and still are—

the embodiment of the responsible and imaginative quest for Christian unity. By a happy providence we are gathered here to honor you on the holiest day in the Methodist calendar. It was on May 24, 1738, two hundred and forty-nine years ago today, that John Wesley went, reluctantly, to an Anglican society meeting in Aldersgate Street, London. Of his experience there, while hearing a reading from the preface to Martin Luther's *Commentary on Romans*, he reports: 'I felt my heart strangely warmed. I felt I did trust in Christ, Christ alone, for salvation.'"[205] No one planned for this award for Outler to be an anniversary occasion. The Benedictines declared, "Wrong! By 'a happy providence' *Someone* did."

Organizer and Lecturer
of Notre Dame Colloquys

Sixty theologians from eleven denominations met on the campus of Notre Dame in the fall of 1980 to read papers, study and discuss *The Loss and Recovery of the Sacred.* The idea was born in the heart and mind of Albert Outler; the sponsoring agency was AFTE [A Foundation for Theological Education], headed by evangelist Ed Robb.

Outler's penchant to attack vigorously an unacceptable theological position sometimes, to his regret (but not always!), came off as a personal censure. This happened during the final report-writing of the colloquy as Professor Gabriel Fackre candidly criticized the direction the process was taking. Outler did not realize that his crisp counter remarks had left Fackre feeling unwanted for Colloquy #2 that was to come in 1982. When Fackre (who felt the 1980 Colloquy was a landmark event and felt inclined to attend the 1982 Colloquy) sought Outler's counsel whether to attend or not, Outler wrote this letter: "I was *dismayed* by your note—and the thought that our momentary impasse over that drafting job at Notre Dame last fall should have left you with the impression that it was, or could have been, more than a passing 'crisis' that did, in fact, contribute to a better outcome of our Colloquy than we could have expected otherwise. No one realizes more clearly than I, nor more *gratefully,* the quality and spirit of your contribution to the Colloquy (your *very* useful response to my paper, your helpful work in the 'working groups,' *and* your notable service on the drafting committee!). But now I realize that I failed to *express* my gratitude—and to assure you of my warmhearted *affection* for you, as well as my high regard for your theological colleagueship!

"It was, therefore, especially gracious of you 'to leave your gift there before the altar,' to be 'reconciled,' and this moves me both to gratitude—and to 'repentance' that I had left you with an unresolved worry about having offended me. We *are* reconciled—and bound all the more firmly by ties of love and mutual self-respect.

"Please, therefore, say 'yes' to Art Landwehr's invitation: it was mine, too. For we *need* you at this 'sequel' to that first Colloquy, for all sorts of reasons. I would be disappointed if you weren't there—and devastated if I had been the cause or occasion of your not accepting our hearty and eager invitation. I believe that this next Colloquy can top the first one—and that you can help to make it so, as few others can. In my view, you occupy a very strategic 'spot' on the spectrum of representation. We need you in such a 'coalition'—and, in my heart, I am eager to welcome you there again as a cherished friend and co-laborer in an important project! Grace, peace, and love, Albert"

Professor Fackre attended, contributed, and fulfilled all of Outler's expectations. Further differences between the two never affected their friendship, now grounded in Matthew 5:23-24. The *sacred* that they discussed in the 1980 Colloquy was now validated in this mutual experience, and set the tone for the proposed November 1–5, 1982, Colloquy where the same participants, plus a few other *Who's Who in Theology* gathered on the Notre Dame campus and shared thoughts and experiences concerning *The Hallowing of Life*. Outler's files of letters written and received on these two colloquys reveal that, in his heart and mind, the Sacred Word of Life in our secularized societies was spoken, heard, and, he hoped, taken back home, *lived* out, and received by others.

Outler's Ecumenical History

Told in his own words here is Outler's ecumenical history: "The Methodist Episcopal Church, South—into which I was born in

1908—was a warmhearted, evangelical matrix in which to grow up. It was also (and naturally enough, in those times) fervently denominationalist and tribalist. There were all those other denominations 'out there'—though we never knew quite *why*. There weren't many Lutherans in our midst (as far as I knew), but it was explained to us that *they* were strong on the doctrine of justification and weak on the doctrine of sanctification. Our differences with the Presbyterians came closer home (predestination, mainly!), *and* with the Baptists (infant baptism!) *and* with the Episcopalians (formalism and worldliness!). We had no dealings whatever with the Roman Catholics—except to guard against their aims of taking over the United States (as, indeed, most of us thought they were threatening to do in 1928)! We also mistrusted 'those *Northern* Methodists' and we were widely separated from the three black Methodist denominations.

"My recollection, however, is that we were less preoccupied with polemics or conscious rivalry than we were with our own affairs: deeply engrossed with each other in evangelism, Christian nurture, missions—in Wesley's phrase, the 'works of love and mercy.' And there was also this tacit understanding—and we shared it among ourselves and saw it shared among our separated brothers and sisters—that denominationalism was actually a positive good—providentially arranged for different strokes for different folks, a sort of ecclesiological Darwinism, the survival of the fittest, which would of course be *us*. Our Methodist triumphalism was relatively unaggressive and almost unconscious—as it was in the other denominations. We did our bragging among ourselves and we supposed that they did the same. We even had a so-called 'ecumenical movement' of our very own (with 'Ecumenical Conferences' of Methodists from around the world, every ten years).

"I was educated in a Methodist college and seminary and joined my father's Annual Conference, as a matter of course. But my decision to go to Yale for further graduate study was with the expectation that this would be a more adequate preparation for the pastorate. This created a crisis: My bishop felt strongly that I was already well-enough prepared academically ('overeducated' if anything) and that a Yale Ph.D. would do me—and the church— no good. He warned me that if I persisted there would be no way back into the pastorate in the conference—*my* conference and my *father's* conference! I scarcely believed he could be that unreasonable and so I went on to New Haven hoping for the best. But he wasn't kidding and with my Ph.D. in hand, I had to find a teaching post, which is how Methodism got themselves another professor instead of the pastor I would rather have been.

"The younger ones of you here will scarcely understand how brave and unexpected 'a new-world' graduate school was in those ancient days—for me, for others too. There was that brown-bag lunch when I asked the man next to me what church he belonged to. 'I'm a Schwenckfelder,' said he. And I had this odd feeling of an encyclopedia article coming to life before my very eyes! Then there was the exciting experience of doing legwork for Professor Robert L. Calhoun, in his preparations for the Oxford Conference. And, beyond this, there were all those discoveries of wider and deeper theological grounds for Christian social concerns than I had before. There was Richard Niebuhr explaining 'the social sources of denominationalism.' And there was my classmate, Liston Pope, already preparing to revise Troeltsch as far as the American context was concerned. And there was Roland Bainton, lecturing on Luther!

"In the process denominational lines got blurred for me and the suspicion began to grow that triumphalism was actually a defense mechanism. My ecumenical perspective was widened as I read various ecumenical statements (that stand now as 'classics'): the Jerusalem statement 'on the meaning of the Gospel' (1929), 'On the Grace of our Lord Jesus Christ' (1937), etc. As my ecumenical interests grew, so also did my ecumenical involvements. This has been a singular blessing, that I have had more ecumenical opportunities come my way than there ever was a rational accounting for them. There was our Methodist Union of 1939. Then there was my first large-scale ecumenical celebration involving seven denominations in Charlotte (1940). I was appointed to Amsterdam but could not go (to my everlasting regret). But then when my appointment to Lund came, I did go—to be ushered into yet another wider and richer world (fabulous and confusing). Thenceforth there followed three decades of exciting times in that fabulous and confusing world.

"At Lund, we were trying to find the way beyond 'comparative ecclesiology.' As I listened to the discussions, the notion began to form in my mind that one of the reasons why our differences could not divide us forever was that we also shared 'a common history as Christians' that was longer, deeper, and richer than our histories as 'separated brethren.' After Lund there came the five study commissions that were instructed to report to the next Faith and Order world conference ten years later. Mine was the one on 'Tradition and Traditions'; it was mandated to examine the interrelationships of Scripture, History and Tradition. That ensuing decade ushered in yet another graduate program—with Jary Pelikan, Georges Florovsky, Wilhelm Pauck, Eugene Fairweather, K. E. Skydsgaard, S. L. Greenslade, Gerhard Ebeling, and Erick Dinkler as my teachers. The upshot of it all was a reconceptualizing of the role of tradition in Christian life and thought—not only in our minds but more generally. Actually most of us have come to think positively of 'tradition'—but none more impressively than Professor Pelikan, as you can see in his monumental work, *The Christian Tradition.*

"Meanwhile all of this (including the work of the other four Faith and Order commissions) was going on without the Roman Catholics (save for a few informal contacts, like those with Fr. Tavard). On our side [Protestants] we kept our defenses manned and ammunition ready—with my copy of von Hase's two-volume manual for controverting all Roman charges and claims in its seventh edition!

"This is why John XXIII took everybody by surprise with his call for a Second Vatican Council. We knew, and wondered why he didn't know, that Vatican I had already made a successor council redundant. Then, also out of the blue, came my appointment as one of three delegated observers from the World Methodist Council—the only one not *ex-officio* (which meant that I was supposed to be there all the time and not just for the great occasions). [Outler attended every session.] Here was an utterly new venture, for which I was as well-prepared as I am now for space travel. Classical Rome I knew and the Rome of the early Christians. But papal Rome? How would I have known—or cared?

"The four years turned in still another postgraduate study program; it seems as if I have stretched beyond my expectations and capacity, for my whole lifetime—since seminary. Talk about continuing education, I have had it all my life, in the most rewarding fashion, largely fortuitous. There in Rome I saw a great church in the throes of a critical self-examination that almost died aborning. The story of the progressives in that Council is the most dramatic one I know in the whole compass of church history, and watching it at close range was an incomparable opportunity (history being made before one's eyes). The observer corps at the Council was an influential factor (and this, too, was unprecedented), but many of them never shed their suspicions that the whole show was another Roman trick, more spectacular than most but none the less devious.

"When Faith and Order met in Montreal in the summer of '63, one of the WCC [World Council of Churches] officials warned the Conference (and the world) not to trust the Romans. When Douglas Horton and I offered a friendly resolution to be sent from the Montreal Conference to the new pope, the Executive Committee turned it down—flat. When we then proposed that, at the very least, we might express our thanks to the Secretariat for Promoting Christian Unity for their hospitality toward the observers, that too was rejected. In Rome, when the Council celebrated the 400th anniversary of the adjournment of Trent— making of it a special bid for burying the hatchet—*all* the Europeans and some of the Americans boycotted the whole occasion, leaving the scene to the Orthodox, to Douglas Steere, Douglas Horton and me, sitting forlorn in the Tribune of St. Longinus. I mention these unpleasant things so as to remind you once again of how far we've come from where we were.

"Meanwhile, and as yet another dimension of the ecumenical experience, the impulse to church union in America was getting a fresh impetus from the so-called Blake-Pike proposal that went on to evolve into the Consultation On Church Union. From fairly early on, I was on the working committee of COCU, and found it a less exciting experience than Vatican II had been, but still instructive. We began with the notion of resurrecting the old Seabury Plan (of union between the Episcopalians and the Presbyterians), and then discovered that a larger conspectus was needed. The administrative types in our churches set up our agenda for us: first, clear up the doctrinal difficulties, then liturgy, sacraments and ministry—after which they would dispose of all matters of polity as, of course, they honestly believed that they could do. I always thought (was it cynicism or realism?) that they had counted on the theologians getting hopelessly bogged, leaving the curia exempt from the charge of stonewalling.

"Our work was not easy, but we did make astonishing progress in doctrinal consensus, *toward* shared views of sacraments and ministry. Then we discovered what we should have known all along: that *polity* was to be the actual shoal on which our project would get bogged down. The Episcopalians were stuck with the problem of episcopal orders (despite Rome's view of theirs—and Constantinople's, too), and the Presbyterians were stuck with their traditional conviction that there is a single church polity revealed and decreed in Scripture.

"With no immediate prospect of organic union before us, COCU then turned into a very useful continuing forum for ecumenical dialogue, with a covenant of mingled memberships that is still in process of being ratified in practice. In the course of all this, we learned that both Christian unity and Christian union are deeply influenced by what C. H. Dodd taught us to call 'nontheological factors.' Ecumenism is both helped and hindered by the way we carry about the weights of our several traditions.

"I must say that COCU has helped me realize the deeply intransigent character of ecclesiastical power and its tendencies toward denominational self-maintenance.

"Now, what has all this varied experience added up to? I scarcely understand it even yet, and this is not for want of trying. Part of my difficulty turns round the fact that the fixed factor in it all has been the constant of the unexpected. None of the ventures in my career has turned out in any of the ways I had planned or foreseen them. Each had entailed a major redirection of my plans and my personal preferences. But each has opened up new frontiers, new encounters, new challenges and opportunities. And now, at the end of it, the patient part of me can look back over it and say, in honest wonder and praise: 'what hath God wrought?' But the impatient part sees all the missed opportunities, all the high-minded foot-dragging—not to mention that far-off promised land that I will not live to enter, and another cry wells up 'How long, O Lord, how long?'

"Even so, it seems to me that my ecumenical experience can be summed up under six fairly brief heads:

"(1) The older patterns of unity as uniformity have been replaced by a general concept of unity-in-diversity, wherein our unity is in Christ and our diversities reflect legitimate differences in 'the showing forth *of* Christ.'

"(2) [The discovery in other traditions] of authentic Christian faith, piety, grace and good humor, moral discipline and social passion (equal to anything I could point to in my tradition and often more) has given me a sense of the length and breadth and height and depth of Christian tradition in the Christian community.

"(3) Concurrently, the discovery of other traditions had the effect of sending me back to rediscoveries in my own tradition. This had surprising results, for it has meant finding a set of norms whereby to judge the strengths and weaknesses of contemporary Methodism on some other basis than my own biases. Hence twenty-five years of searching out Wesley's *sources* and of seeing an inductive thesis emerge and crystallize—viz., that Wesley was more of an interesting and fruitful theologian than he has ever been reckoned (by Methodists and the others) and that he now is more significant for ecumenical theologizing than we had thought. No longer in the old ways, of course: Wesley is off his pedestal as the Methodist's cult-hero and patriarch (revered but not studied). My studies have calmed my Methodist triumphalism to an extent that some of my Methodist brethren find alarming!

"(4) With this firmer anchorage in tradition—my own and others—my ecumenical experience has given me a wider swing on a longer theological tether, which has meant a liberation from the invisible barriers of a single tradition into the larger treasure-store of the Christian Tradition entire. God forbid that this should be construed as doctrinal indifferentism or any loosening of my tether to its anchor: *solus Christus.* To live in Scripture is also to live in tradition; to live in tradition is to face the problem of its rootage in and consonance with Holy Scripture.

"(5) It was in the course of my ecumenical experiences that I came to see, more and more clearly, that Christian union (or even unity) is not an end in itself but only a means to the urgent ends of the Christian mission in the world: to offer Christ, to nurture, to proclaim the Rule of Grace.

"(6) The ecumenical experience generates its own crop of visions and dreams of the Christian future which God is still holding open for us. When and if we are ready to offer up our 'distinctive traditions' as gifts to the whole family of God, willing for them to be refined and transmuted even so as by fire (1 Corinthians 3:15), then we may also be ready for God's gracious gifts of truly effectual renewal in our mission, and of joy in *God's* service."[206]

"Saint" Florovsky

Outler said, "I am a Protestant—devout and on principle—and yet, Eastern Orthodoxy and Medieval Catholicism have always been a living option for me."[207] A major reason for this Eastern Orthodox attraction came to him through the unique spiritual qualities of one of that church's saints. Talking about the Eastern Orthodox, Outler said: "The care of the soul in its spiritual journey (the overriding concern of Eastern Christianity, then and now) is the function of those already on that journey, (priests or not). This is why the greatest Orthodox theologian (and saint) that *I've* ever known—Georges Florovsky [Russian Orthodox]— has always been more interested in the Quakers and the Pentecostals than in any of the other Protestant groups."[208]

And Florovsky also expressed a keen interest in Outler, which elicited from Outler this comment: "Florovsky was a decisive force in my life."[209] Outler once said, "The people I have known who knew themselves as saints haven't been. And I've known a few who have been and didn't know it." Outler asked, "You know, Father Florovsky, you are a saint, don't you?" To which Father Florovsky answered, "Albert, don't be stupid!"[210]

In this instance Outler was testing his saint. Outler knew that, if one felt one was a saint, it was a sure sign that person was *not* a saint. And Florovsky's answer indicated that he knew that Outler knew better than to have asked it. Outler realized that he was caught and felt the way Florovsky had admonished him not to be—stupid!

Outler talked about their relationship in these words: "For ten years, I served on a Faith and Order Commission with Father Georges Florovsky, the greatest Russian Orthodox historian/theologian of our century—and a saint. There was nothing maudlin about Fr. Florovsky and nothing too easily familiar. He chewed me out more than once and, what was worse, he was, almost invariably, right! But what a wonderful man. He was, almost literally, 'full of grace and truth.' In his presence, strange and wonderful things happened, to quite unlikely people (which is to say, to some highly temperamental and pig-headed ecumenical negotiators). His was a *grace* manifested in integrity, in dignity, in patience—and we were utterly confident that his unfailing trust in Christ was unfailingly trustworthy. He was more than a distinguished acquaintance. His graciousness was, and still is, a decisive force in my life. There is, as he would insist (but deny it in his own case) an analogy on earth between created grace in human hearts and the uncreated grace of God in Christ—whose Rule of Grace he served so gracefully."[211]

Intervening on Florovsky's Behalf

Outler knew that the created grace of God in the heart of Florovsky would providentially care for his saint. But Outler also felt that it was God's providential call for him (Outler) to intervene on Florovsky's behalf whenever proper respect was not being offered his saint. Outler wrote Carla on March 5, 1957, from Princeton concerning an experience he had while chairing a meeting of the Commission of Faith and Order: "I'm back in my 'tower,' and for once, glad of it. The weekend was extremely wearing, and not very productive, at least of *immediate* results. Actually, it was all I could do for a while to keep the commission from blowing up or falling apart. The differences in viewpoint that exist in the group have created a good deal of intellectual tension, and Friday it got very close to being personal between Pauck and Florovsky. Young Clebsch was there and he proved a staunch ally for Pauck—so I had to cut them both down. Friday night I didn't get much sleep and would have readily tossed the whole thing up. But we made a new beginning Saturday and that strange transformation that so wonderfully characterizes ecumenical groups began to happen. We worked for the rest of the time— but so little material has been produced that I'm almost embarrassed to report to the World Council of Churches. But everybody promised to do better and have a full paper by next time—even Pauck! He said at the close that he had finally come to see what it was we were working at and from now on he would work with us much more earnestly! If something concrete comes of this, it will have been a significant session." In this instance Outler came to the aid of his "saint" Florovsky, who Outler indicated just sat by, confident in his own faith statement, and let it happen.

A 'Byzantine Methodist'!

If Florovsky was a saint to Outler, what was Outler to Florovsky? The answer comes in this comment from Outler: "Every now and then we are in the presence of created grace in an unmistakable manifestation [in Florovsky]. And we realize almost as if it were a fresh discovery that grace in a human being is an actual force in the literal sense. Professor Florovsky once said that he didn't know how it happened, but that I [Outler] had somehow turned into a 'Byzantine Methodist'!"[212]

Christ Was His Center

In whatever company he found himself Outler exhibited an unquenchable and inexhaustible ardor-of-soul that burned with a desire that the truth be expressed (by somebody). He radiated a warmth that persuaded his hearers to believe in *him* even though his ideas might not be accepted. In Outler was the power of grace that made it possible for him to love sinners, but not sin— in himself or others. Over and over he would (and could) go onto the turf of the various denominations and point out their part in the sin that divides the body of Christ.

Outler let it be known in those settings that "denominational theology, if it ever had a past, has no future. [And that] theology aimed at any denominational concern makes no sense."[213] "The United Methodist Church has a theological problem with its Article VIII [from the Evangelical United Brethren]: 'God was in Christ reconciling the world *to himself,*' which is exactly opposite to the classic substitutionary theory of atonement rendered in Article II [from the Methodist Church]: '[Christ came] to reconcile his Father *to us.*'"[214] This Christological problem is not unique to the United Methodist Church. It is the church's problem that affects all denominations.

The church had one of its finest voices in Outler as he found himself on various denominational turfs. He recognized the sins of the church in its history as well as present times. Warnings to the church pervade his writings and lectures as a means to alert the church to its pitfalls. He strove to save the church from those who would destroy it. He warned, "The church has buried more than those who have buried the church. Seen in retrospect, you can see God at work, a mystery, but real in experience nonetheless."[215]

Audiences warmed to his warmth and wit and humor that helped to get his point across without alienating. Readers of the *National Catholic Reporter* preferred to call Outler "huggable."[216] His hosts felt that he was a part of that unity that they wanted to be a part of, a unity whose common Center was Christ. Outler was a Methodist variety of the church; catholic, reformed, and evangelical.

12

As a Community Person

Outler feared public apathy. On the other hand he held little hope for the modification of society by outward revolution. The change must come from within, and can be aided with the help of positive experiences. Through manners, art, music, and poetry—through the finer experiences of life—Outler could see graciousness spread through the whole human community. Real change came, not merely through exposure to these events but through an appreciation for them. Further still, through a sense of gratitude to God for them. Outler said: "Gratitude is my gift, which is the grace I may bring to the bounty of the givens. Gratitude to God, in action, is the most powerful, constructive, ethical force in the world! This is, I believe, literally true."[217]

Thanksgiving Square

In the early sixties Outler carried this conviction into a group of educators who conceived Thanksgiving Square religious park in downtown Dallas. At One Main Place the present three and one-half acre downtown facility was built in 1976. In the 1969 booklet *The Spirit of Thanksgiving,* Outler wrote the initial article

"The Idea of Thanksgiving" and ended with a three-page statement "A Summing Up Thanksgiving—Root, Flower and Fruit." The universal dimension of gratitude has been an essential part of Thanksgiving Square with its array of international guests. Outler played a major role within that all-inclusive company. To the question, "How did you fare as host for the Dalai Lama?" Outler said, "No one has to be other than who he is."[218]

Cardinal Koenig in the early 1980s suggested that a Declaration of World Thanksgiving be composed and honed each year. Outler was the guiding light in seeing that this was done. And consented to be the first rector (1976–1988) of Thanksgiving Square.

On October 8, 1996, Elizabeth Espersen, Roy Harrell, William T. Stephenson, and Louise Cowan in a special Thanksgiving Square presentation brought a program remembering *The Life and Work of Albert Outler*. Richard Heitzenrater was the featured speaker with Roman Catholic theologian David Balas, ecumenical executive Patrick Henry, and Rabbi Gerald Klein serving as responders. Thanksgiving had played a large role *in* the personal life of Albert Outler; on that day of celebration thanksgiving played *the* key role in the lives of the participants for the life and work of Albert Outler.

Serving His Community

Experienced gratitude to God was the spirit in which Outler served his community. Some of those involvements were "Goals for Dallas" political reorganization effort of the 1960s, The Outfit (ad hoc meetings of ecumenical ministers), The Discussion Club, The Spring Valley Athletic Club, The Elizabethan Club, and the Dallas Council of Churches. Some persons from all of these organizations attended the Dallas Great Bicentennial Celebration of Religious Freedom on Sunday evening, November 9, 1975, at the Dallas Convention Center. This event sponsored by the Dallas Council of Churches provided thousands the opportunity to hear Outler speak on the descriptive title "Two Down— One More To Go."

In recognition of his stewardship of the gift of time, in 1985 Outler was given an award for excellence in the area of religion. The *Dallas Morning News* reported: "Fourteen outstanding men and women will be presented the fourth annual Awards for Excellence in Community Service for their significant contributions to the quality of life in Dallas... We salute the recipients for their energy and dedication to making this city a great place to live!" While the world was his parish, his community was a large part of that world.

In these community involvements one finds no barrier in Outler's thinking between his so-called "professional" and "social" affiliations. Both affected people near and far and at all levels and qualities of human experience. When he served as member and president of the American Society of Church History, the American Theological Society, or the American Catholic Historical Association, he kept what was being done in the context of church tradition, and tried to effect in his comments and actions a hopeful picture of the future of not only the local community but the world community. One recalls the words of his sister Fan: "As Albert spoke in the present, he was fifty years ahead of his time!"

PART 3

The Person *Behind* the Dilettante

13

He Was Human

fter a perusing of the interests and involvements of Outler, which establish him the dilettante that he saw himself to be, it is time now to go behind *what* he did and discover *who* he *was* in all that he did.

Beyond all his abilities, insights, accomplishments, and involvements that exceeded those of ordinary people, Albert Outler was *human*. His abilities as a historian, theologian, writer, and speaker were so pronounced that he was seldom thought of as a person who had to wrestle like the rest of humanity in being a husband and raising a family. He loved his wife. His love for Carla was expressed as strongly in his last days as it was in his first days with her. Martin Marty states in his interview of Outler in the February 29, 1984, issue of *The Christian Century*: "Historians need contexts, and Outler has found his in conversations, colleagues and, most of all, the family. Some sages may be hermits, but this one shows that he is not. What about Carla, the children, the other grandchildren?—'That's the most interesting thing of all that's happened to me,' the professor sparkles back. 'The gift of the family. I have always had an invincible notion that we were all special to each other.'

347

Carlotta Grace Outler

"Why, the question comes to mind, is this family context so rich with you, but suppressed by many with whom we speak? Outler lets this pass with a confident mumble about 'grace.' 'Of course, he says, 'no marriage is pure romance. We think of ours as a negotiable partnership at times. But if I have pursued my own ambitions, as she has hers, we have mutual respect, though we do not share all the details of each other's life.'"

There were disagreements. He admitted that at times he was *disagreeable*. In this regard he fitted the pattern of humanity. But he would not hesitate to ask forgiveness, and Carla Grace Outler forgave. And understood. She knew him and his needs better than he knew for himself. He admitted this. Others came to realize that aspect of their relationship too. When Bob Schuler of the Pacific and Southwest Conference of the United Methodist Church called to talk with Outler about speaking in that Conference in 1984, he ended his call with a brief conversation with Carla. She left these words with Schuler: "I am sending Dr. Outler to you well. Please try to see him returned to me in this same condition."[219] Schuler wondered how well Outler was when the time came for the first lecture and there was no Outler. A worried Schuler left sixty or so clergy singing and hurried to the hotel and an empty room. Returning to Pasadena's First Church, Schuler found a well Outler, who apologized for his tardiness. He had overslept. Later when he began his second lecture, Outler smiled and said, "It's good *not* to be the late, Dr. Outler."[220]

Sister Fan summed up the Albert/Carla relationship in this January 7, 1974, letter: "I give up on Albert: he is driven by the same sort of compulsions that have driven me all my life: We cannot have them excised or exorcised. They just devastate us, and everybody else gets to pick up the pieces! Thank God he's got you to love him and be patient with him. You are an eighth wonder of the world to be so tranquil."

Children and Grandchildren

Marty continued in his article in *The Christian Century:* "Dare I press one step further and ask a learned savant to unbutton his vest and risk sounding simplistic by translating all this for children? I, for one, make this a central test for sages. Are they spiritually available—do they have Gabriel Marcel's *disponibilité* —to children? How would Outler talk about any of this version of the Christian tradition to, say, his six-year-old grandchild during a walk in the woods? 'How would I? I have!' It goes something like this, without apologies for the corniness of family namings. 'So many things happen to us,' he tells the child, 'but look twice. Someone who is loving has been fooling around here, bringing excitements and joys even in the midst of the bad things that happen in life. That someone is not just 'Nanna and Gaffa' or 'Mom and Dad'! What the child would really like to know is: 'Am I cared for? Do I matter?' The gospel, says Outler, murmurs its 'Yes, yes'—to carry the child through the harder questions and times. 'And so,' Outler tells the six-year-old, 'it's a joy for us to be around.' Then comes an afterthought: '. . . and a joy to be around *you*.'" Granddaughter Melissa, as a child, lived in the Outler home. She called him Gaffa and counted him her best friend in all the world.

It bothered Outler that his studying, lecturing, attending conferences, and his many involvements kept him from being the father and grandfather that he truly wanted to be for his family. He expressed this sentiment many times in his letters. To compensate for this lack of presence, he sometimes went somewhat overboard in accommodating his children's desires. For instance, there was the time when his junior high school son, David, "declared his interest in things agricultural over things urban and we had accordingly arranged for him to commute to the nearest small-town high school where they had a Future Farmers of America program. As it turned out, it included an animal husbandry project conducted at home; and it was sheep! Two bred-ewes in the fall and winter, three lambs in the spring, and all of this in the sizable backyard of an upper-middle class neighborhood in Dallas. 'Neighborhood' is right, too, thank goodness. The neighbors were wonderfully understanding through it all and our sheep became something of a neighborhood project, especially with the kids. You will doubtless be willing to be spared the details of how everybody in the family (including the dog) became amateur shepherds and how Dad had to turn into an unlicensed veterinarian (since city vets take a dim view of sheep and country vets charge outrageously for city calls). The upshot of the whole business was that it brought home the pastoral imagery of the Bible more vividly than anything else quite could."[221] It also showed something of the character of Outler that word descriptions fail to reveal.

A 1966 "Happy Father's Day" card from son David describes well their relationship at that time. On the front of the card are the words: "I don't care if you are a mentally superior, culturally aware, socially well-adjusted college graduate . . ." Inside the thought continues,: "I like you anyway!"

Outler's favorable notoriety as a scholar, speaker and writer was so pronounced that he was seldom thought of as a father and husband who had to wrestle like the rest of humanity in being a husband, in raising a family. In that domestic setting Outler was treated as the ordinary human that he was in his own mind. And he enjoyed their acceptance of him based on that understanding.

Time for Others

Time was a most gracious gift of God for Outler, and through him, for others. His retreats into solitude blessed him with healing, and others as well. He was gregarious with groups, and obviously helpful or they would not have followed to hang onto his every word. Every letter written to him was answered. He received many letters asking for copies of his speeches, and he was very willing to send them. People questioned him on everything from gardening to jurisprudence. And more times than not, he gave lengthy answers. In every instance he was giving himself.

He wrote Carla from Princeton on May 31, 1957: "Last night I had dinner with a professor in philosophy and a doctor and his wife, who all were very much concerned about the problem of evil and suffering. So we had quite a session that turned out actually very well. Then, one of the professors in religion here is involved (with an ulcer) in a very difficult decision and I've had to take time out to help him. And this morning, in the midst of everything a chemistry student came in to ask if there is any respectable way to believe in God. Another two hours—but this, too, came out well. So I can't begrudge the time." His open-door policy allowed people into his life and he into theirs as long as he was able to relate.

Almost all of his letters to those seeking counsel or seeking him for speaking engagements received the kindest letters one can imagine. He started begging forgiveness for his tardiness for not answering sooner. By the time he got through describing how full was his cup, the inquirer was entirely sympathetic. His statement that, if there were one person he wanted to accommodate, it would be the one to whom he was writing. And that, too, was totally believable. Here was the way Ira Gallaway, who was at that time associate general secretary of the Division of Evangelism, Worship, and Stewardship of the Board of Discipleship of the United Methodist Church, described the believability of an Outler sympathetic rejection: "This is in reply to your letter of March 21 concerning my invitation for you to address the forthcoming World Consultation on Evangelism to be held at Lake Junaluska in October. As a friend of mine said to me recently, "You say 'no' in such a beautiful manner that I am almost glad you didn't say 'yes.' Seriously, you know how very much I regret that you cannot make this address, but I do understand, especially when you say you are 'at the end of your tether.'"

Outler had an interest in things, events, all the "ologies," but his greatest interest was in people. The pastor-part of his early calling never left him. He made persons feel that whatever was important to them was important to him. He felt their hurt, their pain, and when he could he related to that hurt by his *being* there. A thousand words could not describe better the pastoral presence of Outler than these made by Patrick Henry as he recounted the grace of caring that came from Outler during the days following his father's death by suicide in May 1983: "He [Outler] was just *there*."[222]

Friends

Outler was a friend to people. Yet, strange as it may sound, he felt deeply that he had few close friends. Some permitted their awe of him to distance them from him. But then on the other hand, the complexity of his makeup confused some of those potential friendships. In many ways Outler's study of John Wesley was a study of his own life. In a lecture on Wesley he said: "It is a sobering and yet strangely consoling thought—John Wesley was a compulsive, obsessive neurotic and although he was saved and much mellowed by grace, he remained one all his life. He was a driven man and a driving man. His emotions were held in tight rein. He would not, his father complained, go to the toilet without a pause for decision. He had a multitude of acquaintances who cherished their acquaintanceship. He had a sizeable number of friends and colleagues who were devoted to him and yet not really close bosom friends—not even his brother Charles who came the closest."[223] This was indeed a "sobering and strangely consoling thought" *for Outler.* This knowledge of Wesley surely helped him live with the problem that plagued all his days: He had a host of admirers but few very close friends. This keen awareness of his human condition served to accentuate the revelation experience of God's saving grace, the subject that monopolized his life.

One of the reasons Outler did not have bosom friends was his commitment to the truth as he saw it. "On an occasion at St. Simons Island Ira Gallaway [who was a participant with Outler in a prayer group when he lived in Dallas] was to give an address. He chose as his subject 'off-color' Catholics (not the ones recognized by the pope). The tone of the paper embarrassed the old professor. So Outler managed to have something else to do during the presentation. This programmed absence offended Gallaway."[224] There is no telling how many times similar occurrences caused schisms between Outler and his friends. Regardless the consequences, *that* was Albert Outler. He lived out the truth as he saw it regardless of whom it offended.

That truthfulness was also known to alienate. When people asked him for an honest evaluation, they got one. In a letter to a man who asked for Outler's "honest evaluation," he got it. Outler's underlined parts of the paper with accompanying remarks such as "Not correct," "Bad faith!?," "Self-pity," "Is this evidence one-sided?," "Where are alternatives?," "Is this a fair and full statement?," "Presumption here?," "Inconsistent," "Peevish," "Nonsense," "Immature," "Everyone equally?," "Who's kidding whom?" And then Outler left him this head-scratching comment: "*Creative* scholarship!" It is difficult to believe that this final cryptic comment secured a "friend" for Outler.

At times the man inevitably contributed to his own feeling of alienation. In one sense he could not help but contribute. His seemingly unlimited knowledge on practically any subject sometimes intimidated people. "Having a conversation with ACO is like playing chess with someone who always checkmates you on the second move."[225] That sense of being intimidated kept them safely within the category of "admirers," rather than "friends." There were times he glimpsed this happening. But he was trapped. No way out. This self-entrapment was something he had to live with.

Testing Time

And then there were times Outler unwittingly contributed to having many admirers, few friends. Those closest to him never knew when he might pull a test on them (again, the professor coming out). Never knowing when one was going to be given a test was in itself a test, a test to see whether one dare show up for a possible-test occasion. The natural tendency is not to put oneself into such a position to be tested. The following episodes (tests) told on myself could be told by others in similar settings: On one occasion when Outler still had his office in the Bridwell Library vault, I arrived at his office a little early for a luncheon appointment. As I walked in, I saw that Outler had his back to the door. I quietly waited, not wanting to disturb him, but he sensed that I was there. After a few moments, Outler vigorously spun around in his chair and asked, "What did John Wesley mean by 'convincing' grace?" Stung by such a greeting, I sat on the corner of the desk (more the result of a faint coming on than the urge to find a comfortable seat). I replied in words that seemed to come out of nowhere, something to the effect that grace conveys its own convincing powers in the experience of salvation. Outler responded, "That's what John Wesley said it was. Let's go have lunch." That was for me a glorious day. I passed the test without having read the book! One never knew, with Outler, when that test would come. Knowing *that* tended to create "admirers," not "friends."

Not only was Outler known to test one's knowledge of subjects, but he would also test one's value systems and how one might react to his value system. This experience of mine was totally out of character for Outler—until one realizes that Outler was "in character" with *his* testing game. Sometime during the early seventies in the Outler's Lakehurst, Dallas living room Outler lit up a cigarette and "smoked" in a manner incongruent with smokers. I, being an ex-smoker, recognized the incongruities.

In the first place he never inhaled. In the second place he did not know how to hold a cigarette (he held it between the thumb and forefinger as if holding a pencil that was on fire). In the third place, after about three or four puffs and no reaction from me, he sought to put it out and couldn't find an ashtray!

One will never know what was on his mind (exactly what the test was about) that day. But it is known that smoking was not his *habit.* And that it was his habit to test a person, the *whole* person. I do not know whether I passed the test that day. But I could tell from Outler's demeanor that a test was on. This behavior accounted for an irony in the man: For a professor who disliked *grading* his students, he certainly enjoyed *testing* his friends.

Loneliness

Even when some people expressed love and appreciation for Outler, for whatever reason *those* were not the emotions he was feeling. Then again, sometimes his feelings seemed justified. In an April 13, 1970, letter to Perkins colleague Howard Grimes, he said: "I was appalled by the sight of the abyss of misunderstanding and tension opened up in our [faculty] committee meeting this morning, and I am truly sorry for my part in provoking your climactic statement. In a way, though, it *was* constructive.

"For if *you* are 'tired' of our relationships here in this 'academic community,' you might be willing to consider how 'tired' I am also—and why. You know, as no one else here knows, of my reception here, and how and why I have never felt at home. For all its rewards, my career here has been almost tragically miscast and I've often rued the decision that brought me here in the first place. Until lately, though, there was always the hope that the situation and my place in it would be more satisfactory to all concerned. Now, however, it's easier to think of serving out my time rather than attempting a fresh start elsewhere. But don't count on that.

"My main point is that, in my case, the sort of understanding, compassion and support that has been generously offered to some here has not been accorded *me*—or has not been so perceived by me—and this crossed my mind this morning when you spoke of 'consistency,' 'fairness,' and 'inhumanity.'

"I've made my peace with my alienation (sort of) and have developed ample compensation for my frustration (as we all have in one degree or another). But I *am* 'tired'—*desperately* tired!—and I remain hopeful that if we aren't able to develop adequate *modi cooperandi* with our 'community' here, we can at least manage some sort of *modus vivendi* that will save us from the worst consequences of our mutual alienations. Maybe your candor this morning was a contribution to that end."

Outler's "inherited" Wesleyan sense of loneliness within a crowd intensified in his later years. On one occasion when he was expressing his loneliness in not having many friends, I reminded him that Jesus had only twelve close friends, and that one betrayed him while none of the others understood him (until after the Resurrection and then in a *faith* mode). The statement did not seem to phase him, which, in effect, verified his own psychotherapeutic understanding: *Hearing* the truth as it applies to oneself is not the same as *receiving* it. In this regard Outler was as human as all humans.

"Book Friends"

The ones whom Outler always enjoyed and felt totally accepted in their company were his "book friends." Outler carried on his continuing education with books mainly in his study, first at the seminaries where he taught and then in retirement at his home. His mind was method; his constitution was order—for society and his study time. But the place where he did his work looked a mess. At first glance one would think that a tornado had hit his study. Closer observation would reveal that the "storm" had left papers in neat piles here and there on his desk and all around the room. His desk and wall-shelving were a triumph of chaos.

Cosmopolitan Outler was also a down-home sort of person. He felt at home, whether researching in a London library, conversing with an Australian aborigine, having lunch in Rome, or digging around the countryside in Israel. And in his last days he was more at home with his books, referring to them as his "friends." As Albert would leave his Bradenton apartment to go down a floor to his study, he would say to Carla, "I'm going down to visit my friends." While preachers he listened to may have failed to preach the Word of God, his "friends" never failed to give him meat to chew on.

"Friends" describe well Outler's loving attitude toward books—not only for what was in them, but for what they were made of, how they were bound, how they were handled. At the time he attended the Texas Annual Conference to speak and autograph his Wesley Works books, a browser thumbing through one of the books accidentally dropped it. The book survived the fall, but Outler did not. He was genuinely pained and showed it as he rubbed and petted the book back to a semblance of the newness it once had.

At one time Outler's Dallas library held over eight thousand volumes; at Bradenton he had fewer than five-hundred.

Ambivalence

Outler's tendency toward perfection coincided with his some-time efforts to hang on and not let go, all the while knowing he must. This can be seen in some of his efforts at publishing in his later years. Time was up but he could not let go of imperfect papers though he knew he had to. And he did, with the help of those who worked with him *gracefully*. That was the power that he recognized, respected, and to which he responded as he made his way through ambivalences of all shades and colors.

Vanity

Some called Outler a vain man. If by that one means "empty," no. He was not empty. Lonely at times, yes; but empty, no.

If by "vain" one means "unreal," no. Sarcastic at times with his humor, yes, but a real man getting a real point across in the use of his humor.

If by "vain" one means "a deceptive self-confidence," no. It was he who said, "To say that your self-confidence is adequate is a form of self-deception."[226]

If by "vain" one means "a deceitful person," no. He was too open with his comments on any subject or person to be considered deceitful.

If by "vain" one means "producing no good results," no. His life was filled with good results, the like of which few in this age have matched.

If by "vain" one means "ostentatious," no, because he was never fond of showing off *himself*. And he did not appreciate that attitude in others. In a September 22, 1971, letter written from London to Carla he wrote: "The walk down City Road to Epworth House is depressing: the roar, the stench, Wesley's Chapel hunkered down midst the glowering skyscrapers all around (with a congregation under a hundred) and Colin Morris (whom you may remember as our Conference Preacher last June), the pastor, who is chock full of brave, radical ideas with nobody much responding (except in some of his broadcast talks), who has just fled the old manse for a home in the suburbs. I don't blame him, but it ought to qualify his radicalism by a bit—and yet he is still as cocky as ever."

Worship of others or himself by others was never a temptation for Outler. And he disdained any encouragement or practice of cult heroism. In the same letter mentioned above, he wrote about the icons in his London workplace: "Epworth House has been sold for offices (except for the basement), but they haven't any tenants on the first floor. So I go into this deserted-looking building and grope down the darkened stairs to the Archives. They are relatively bright, clean, and cheerful. I've a little room, crammed with Wesley busts and other icons and two little statues made out of horses vertebrae—so Bowmer (the archivist) swears!—and painted and dressed to look (a little) like John Wesley with wings! Hideous little reminders of how much of a cult hero John Wesley was (with or without his encouragement, I'm not quite sure)." True, Outler's brilliance, wit, humor, and grace came across loud and clear. Never as a means to glorify himself. But to glorify God.

If by "vain" one means "conceit," no. The charm of his public personality would not permit that interpretation.

If by "vain" one means "greed," no. Outler once described greed in these words: "What I have is mine and what is mine is me."[227] *That* was not Outler.

Vanity Equals Pride?

If by "vain" one means "pride," yes. As he admitted in these words: "I accepted this invitation [Yale Taylor Lectures] with the usual mix of gratitude and vanity," and "There is a hint of perfectionism in all professions."[228] In Outler's case the "hint" resembled more of a reasonable delight than a covert suggestion. And then there was a dark side of that reasonable delight. His letters indicate that he wrestled with this thing called pride all his days. In the heat of debate Outler sometimes reacted as if one's dislike of his statement was a dislike of him. And he did not like that! But even on those occasions his graced charm would take over, and he would leave the scene a champion. But like others in the human family, he was known to carry on the debate behind the scenes.

He would never outwardly promote himself. He prided himself as one who would never ask anything for himself. And he wouldn't. To those inquiring what he "charged" to speak on an occasion, his stock answer was that he would like to have his expenses paid, but, other than that, he preferred not to know. He did not care for the knowledge of the honorarium to spoil his stay, one way or the other.

He would not promote himself. But he could plant the need in another's mind in such a way that one could not help asking *for* him! On occasion he would "permit" Carla to be his advertising agent. Those closest to Outler knew what he was doing. Thus, it never revealed itself as a problem. It was simply that his need, never to ask, was in his mind paramount to the specific need that plagued him at the time. And his friends felt duty-bound to honor that unique trait as they dealt with the exigencies of the moment.

A Downside of Pride

Outler's pride was known on occasion to put pressure on himself. While in London in the fall of 1971 digging into the Wesley Archives, he wrote Carla on September 19: "There was the business of settling in and finding where things were—not a finished exploration by any means. The collation at the Archives is tedious, exacting and rather more extensive than I had expected. What is more, there's more of the holograph material in shorthand and cipher than I'd supposed—and I haven't dared ask Bowmer (the archivist) if *he* could read John Wesley's shorthand and cipher or even to wonder if he'd give me a hand, for of course I can't make it out and have no time to learn it. The alternative, though, is to turn to the tender mercies of Frank Baker and Richard Heitzenrater, and that would be galling even if they agreed to help (from microfilm or xerox copies, that is). Thus it is hard now to forecast how long this will take." However long it took, it was longer than it would have been had he called in some help. But *that* was Albert Outler. *He* was the scholar chosen to do the Wesley *Sermons*. And *he* was going to do it. It was this prideful determination that would not allow Baker nor Heitzenrater nor anybody else to dominate totally his editing decisions. When he did accept editorial changes, it was *his decision* to accept. And as the result of *his* labors, the church has the unparalleled scholarship exhibited in *The Works Of John Wesley*.

Pride in What He Did

One did not have to be a close acquaintance of Outler's to see that he took pride in what he did. Just hearing him speak made one aware of a reasonable delight regarding what he had to say. It bothered him to think that maybe he did not get his message across. Outler's redeemed pride in his accomplishments resulted in some exceptionally fine writings, scholarly and otherwise, in many areas of interest (the bibliography at the end of this book attests to the truthfulness of this statement). While pride in his work brought about great good, he did not allow himself to dwell upon the good that he did. He was well aware that such narcissistic displays pronounced huge debits to one's credit.

A searching curiosity about what was happening in the moment and how this might affect the future never allowed him to dwell on accomplishments of the past. He once wrote, "Academically, my proudest 'moment' was my appointment as Timothy Dwight Professor of Theology at Yale (that was the post I resigned to come here [Perkins] in 1951—once my professional vanity was slaked)."[229] Perkins offered no prestigious chair to appeal to Outler's professional vanity. The school did not have one! The challenge to resurrect a seminary and the new horizons that the challenge offered (and it was happening in the South) combined to squelch the professional vanity that the Yale appointment once satisfied.

A Pride Without Condescension

Outler left no doubt that *he* believed in what he had to say. In no way was his pride tainted with contempt, disdain, scorn, arrogance, ostentation, or *hubris*. And he abhorred the actions of anyone in any corner of life who displayed such airs of patronage. In a November 17, 1975, letter to the Woolf Brothers, Outler wrote: "Thank you for your letter and its expression of concern. Mrs. Outler and I don't buy as many clothes nowadays as we used to and, as you know, Dallas has many fine clothing stores, including yours. We don't expect perfect service anywhere, of course, but it is our impression that *some* of your people in your Dallas-Northpark store are just a mite *lofty* when their routine is upset. For example, last winter, I went in looking for charcoal flannel slacks (admittedly not the fashionable thing, but I've worn them over the years and intend to continue doing so). It was, of course, all right that they didn't have what I was looking for; but they couldn't conceal what I took to be a faint disdain." For Outler, condescending attitudes were never acceptable in anybody, including himself.

He was never intrigued with positions of power that allowed a strutting pride to walk over others in order to get desired results. He felt deeply that the power of the Holy Spirit had opened the doors for him. "In the Methodist Church normally you have to have some sort of office in order to have very much influence. I don't know how much influence I have had, but it looks as though I've had more than the average preacher, yet with no corresponding office. You take professors of theology, even when they are involved with annual conferences, do not amount to much . . . This last fall Bishop Earl Hunt wrote and said they were having a meeting of the Doctrinal Commission in Dallas and they would like for me to speak at it. It was a friendly letter. So I wrote back a friendly letter and said, 'No, thank you.' Then came the letter that said, 'You've got to do it.' And so I did.

"I did not ask to go to the Vatican Council. I hadn't asked to do any of the other things that have happened in this church or in the ecumenical movement; I have never had an office of any sort in the church or the academy."[230] Outler summed it up for others as well as for himself: "Where arrogance is, faith has lost its touch."[231] He also said: "If you've got a real solid case of bigotry, it is hard to see yourself bigotting."[232] Outler might well be called any number of things, but neither friend nor enemy would call him a bigot. And would never describe him as arrogant, a condition that his faith would not allow.

A Sense of Providence

Instead of forging his own way in his life's vocation, Outler was possessed by a sense of Providence. To the question, "When did you have the inclination to be a theologian?" he said, "A conscious decision was never made on my part. I have always thought of myself as a pastor/teacher in the church. Circumstances in every single case have charted, or opened, or strung out the way I've gone." To the comment, "Isn't this providential?" he said, "I think so . . . I've never had a script to go by since Ainsworth scrapped the script I had." Outler pondered a moment and said, "I cannot now remember a door I knocked on. I remember I wanted to go to Emory, but under the circumstances it was inappropriate to knock on that door and ask for a job. I never asked for an assignment, a lectureship, or whatever. Something happens and somebody says, 'Can you do this?' I never foresaw a closing of the door because if one door had not opened, another one would have. I never had one, that was opened, closed on me. Some things have gone well; some things have not gone well; but the things that have not gone well became part of the rubble that the things that went well were built on."[233] Outler's sense of Providence kept in check the vanity that could have overwhelmed him.

How to Deal with Pride

Outler defined this haunting human condition called pride as: "exaggerated or disproportionate self-concern that seeks all available pleasures and avoids all avoidable pain."[234] He went on to say how this "mother of sins" reveals itself on what would seem the most innocent of occasions: "I myself was made aware of how marvelous and subtle these temptations were because when I was given a passport, I became a VIP inside San Pietro [Basilica of St. Peter]. You would go up to a Swiss Guard and you would take out your passport and you would show it to him. He would take his halberd off and bang it on the pavement and your vanity would flutter—even when you knew that this was corny and ridiculous."[235] Outler laughed at his fluttering vanity, referring to "the jailbirds and general scum of England and Europe that are our ancestors in some of the First Families of Virginia.

"Terribly impressive," he remarked. "As a Georgian I take very great pride in the fact that most of our ancestors were deadbeats!"[236] That sense of humor helped Outler live with his own incongruities regarding the temptation to pride. He drew from his own experience when he said: "Pride is the imperative to unlimited freedom, to unqualified dignity, to the trappings of power—an absence of trust, of acceptance of one's being at and from the hands of God and being glad to have it so. And so people reach for the pinnacle of freedom, of self-determination, of self-assertion. Everyone of us does it. There is no way to decline to do it. That is, all except me! [Said with a clearing of the throat, "humph," signaling a hyperbolic humor-at-self.] And content with the frustrations of my reach for freedom—like Margaret Fuller and Thomas Carlyle: With Margaret (following deep meditative thought finally) accepting the universe and Carlyle growling out, 'Gad, you'd better!'"[237]

The following paragraph is from a January 15, 1943, letter to a former student who was finding it tough in the pastorate. Outler drew upon his own experiences with pride to advise the man how to deal with his problem: "You can rationalize this [his pride problem], of course, but it does not repair the mischief. I know the limitations, the unexamined prejudices, the inertia and the perverse stupidity of people in a community like Bartow or Tennille (or Gordon, or Macon or the Duke Divinity School). I know what it is like to be stymied, thwarted, frustrated; to feel like failure. Who doesn't? But the fact remains that bleak unhappiness and despair, even in such a context, is fundamentally a symptom of one's own maladjustment, one's own lack of faith and hope and love. 'The fault, dear Brutus, is not in our stars but in ourselves.' That we are neurotic means there is some inner abscess of unredeemed pride, of self-will, of unrealistic and naive determination to impose my own ideals (my will) on other people in spite of their resistance (their wills). In short, there is always sin on both sides and I can't do much about theirs until I have done more about my own." But Outler recognized that *he* compounded his problem when he tried by himself to get to the bottom of it. "When we try to probe [into ourselves] more deeply, we run into an infinite regress: Where, what, and who is the self that is appraising the self, and who appraises *that* self, and so on and on? All these selves are *one* self (if we are at all healthy and whole) and the inmost secret of that one self is never really intelligible until we recognize the whole as a specific creation and project of God."[238]

All that Outler *was*, including his pride, was God's project. Only through God's grace was his pride redeemed. Outler "did more about his own sin" by letting grace do for him what he could not do for himself. He once wrote, "The best antidote to pride is gratitude."[239] And gratitude to God was Outler's ready response. This was dramatically illustrated in his involvements with Thanksgiving Square from its inception.

Outler described himself when he wrote: "Paul was a humble man, in his own proud sort of way, and he was utterly confident of the chief business of his life—the proclamation of the Gospel of God in Christ and the outreach of the evangel to the furthest limits of his world."[240]

Self-doubt

A large part of Outler's pride dilemma was derived from this perfectionistic tendency in an imperfect world. No doubt his mother and sister Fan's perfectionistic tendencies influenced his ability to spend thousands of hours poring over the footnotes of Wesley's sermons without climbing the walls or throwing up his hands in disgust when he could not find the source of a comment Wesley made in his sermons. These feisty lady saints of the church lived on in Albert as he preached with the flair of a perfectionist who seemed to pull it off. But in his own mind he knew that he had never done his best.

This concern was often expressed to preachers in the audience whose judgment he trusted. After he had rung the bell, reached the portals of heaven, saw a new heaven and a new earth, and helped his hearers see it too, he would in a most serious manner ask his trusted critic, "Did the message get through?" It always did but even when one told him that it did, he never was quite sure. His audiences thought he did *his* best because it was the best they ever heard. He always wondered whether he had.

He expressed those doubts in the early years of his academic career. In an April 19, 1943, letter to Edward Harris he said: "You made me feel very proud and happy with your letter of invitation to preach in your church on the Sunday of Pastors' School. I have delayed in answering because I had a rather vague and tentative engagement elsewhere for that Sunday but, on checking, I find that I will be free, and I shall be glad, though a little awed, to preach to your people and to the visiting brethren. I trust that you realize that if I could really preach I wouldn't be teaching; hence, you must not get your hopes up for 'great utterances' or models of homiletic art."

Harris responded with a May 10, 1943, pride pricker: "It was good to have your letter of acceptance for the preaching engagement for Pastors' School. In spite of the apologetic utterances about your preaching ability, I still plan to subject my people to your merciful ministrations. By the way, was that humble attitude toward your homiletical ability acquired at Yale or Duke? I can't remember much evidence of it at Emory!!!" And then proceeded to mend any possible fence breakdown with, "Seriously, I have no fear about the effect of your ministry on the spirits of my people—and that is a genuine compliment, for they are wonderful people."

Outler had a way of failing in these moments of self-appraisal. This proved giant of the church really felt that he was second-rate amongst his peers. He never seemed to see himself as successful as he was in the eyes of others, which bodes well within the context of Christian truth. He never doubted grace. This mix safeguarded him against the human's most self-destructive state of hubris—of soaring with the gods—which, viewed from God's vantage point, resembles more the fleeting shades of Hades. Had Outler recognized his incomparable excellence, he would indeed have been most difficult to live with.

The following quote from a 1956 Princeton letter suggests that some of the doubting of his unique capabilities waned somewhere around the end of the fifties: "Curiously enough, I'm not very much interested in doing the Cole Lectures now—although five or ten years ago, I would have broken my neck to get 'em into the schedule no matter what. I truly believe that this need to be 'in demand' is waning inside me—and maybe it's high time." Indications are that he was reaching a level of importance in the world of scholars that should have relieved him of the anxiety brought on by the question: Would he or would he not measure up to his self-inflicted demands for scholarly perfection? The list of lectureships at the back of the book reminds us of the popularity of the man. The invitations he declined in 1989 alone were more than many scholars receive in a lifetime.

Undue Self-deprecation

Outler's tendency toward perfection caused him to be hypercritical of himself all the days of his life. He always expected more of himself than he could ever fulfill, and self-deprecation was a way of dealing with those self-imposed targets of excellence. This came out in many of his papers and letters, and was a strong part of his nature from early on. He wrote while a graduate student at Yale: "Now about my religious beliefs: they are an awful hodgepodge. I have been in turn a fundamentalist, then a radical, then a 'social gospeler,' an exponent of religion by nurture and education and each of these has left its trace in the complex of my beliefs. In addition, the approach of psychology has led me to an interpretation of motivation and personality which gives color to all the rest. However confused, and a little proud to be without label or party, I am still convinced of the authenticity of my earlier vision: to follow Jesus, as I can see him, so long as my faith holds. I do intend that the main lines of its future development shall stay as close as possible to the core of what has been the Great Tradition in Christianity. When I can no longer do that, I shall feel dutybound to renounce religion as an illusion and make friends with the mammon of unrighteousness."[241]

And then Leroy Howe wrote an editor's note concerning the paper from which the previous quote was taken: "The only comment Professor Hartshorne seems to have made on this rather remarkable effort of his young graduate student is on the essay's very last sentence. Hartshorne suggested that it was neither a logical inference nor an emotional consequence of what went before, and that, as such, it seemed merely 'superimposed on an otherwise intelligible and attractive structure.' On the returned paper Outler wrote, 'One is inclined to agree with Hartshorne's comment.' In retrospect, this little interchange portends much. It hints that even from his earliest writings, Outler exhibited a curious predilection for undue self-deprecation that became wellknown to his colleagues and friends, and that almost invariably appeared incongruous with the quality of achievement of the very writing in which it appeared."[242] Readers can judge for themselves how strong a portent that last comment might be, but Outler's "predilection for undue self-deprecation" midst the highest quality of performance and scholarship was, without question, the haunt of his life.

Down in the Dumps

A 1957 letter written to Carla puts Outler squarely in the middle of the human condition of self-doubt/self-deprecation: "I'm in a real king-sized slump. Out of yesterday and today, with nothing else to do, I've managed to get the bibliography done and Chapter IV almost finished—but not a word on V and not too many good ideas. Tomorrow, Sockman is preaching in the Chapel and I must go—and have lunch with him thereafter. Then Merry comes—or at least I *suppose* he'll be coming, for I haven't heard from him in reply to my note suggesting train schedules and asking him to let me know which was his choice. Worse yet, in my present state, I shan't be very good company. For I'm in another spell of 'agonizing self-appraisal' and you know what that does. Here I am, with half my career over and gone, with a thousand different things accomplished, but no shape or really distinctive pattern emerging from the lot—a gifted dilettante!

"The immediate occasion for this Black Saturday was the dinner, last night, of the Conference Committee of the Faculty and the Curriculum Committee of the Board of Trustees. Mike Oates asked Peter Hempel and me to speak to the joint committee about our work in the Council of the Humanities. We did but it was a *very* ordinary performance. As bad luck would have it, Pit Van Dusen was presiding (as chairman of the Trustee's Committee) and Pit damps me down. Beside, whenever I'm among the high and mighty, all my insecurities roil up—and I don't have what the old preachers used to call 'liberty.' This, I suspect, is what others sense in me and why *they* know my place is in the study and classroom. But for that I ought to have a specialty or a cumulative program of scholarship—and I have three or four, not one, and I'll never master them all. And so I shall master none of them, and leave few 'footprints on the sands of time.' What follows? That I should work harder? But how can I? Or, relax and take it easier here on out? Who would be content with that?"

Perfection

While Outler wrestled with the ambiguities of his own humanity (a fierce pride on the one hand and self-doubt/self-deprecation on the other), he kept the faith that by grace gave him courage to fight the good fight and finish what Providence had given as his particular missions in life. For this God-given faith he was most thankful. It was in *that* spirit of gratitude that Outler experienced the perfection he preached. His was never the Latin version of perfection: a pluperfect perfected perfection (a condition attained and maintained) but a perfecting perfection (a condition in process).

A perfectionist preaching perfecting perfection. What an irony! And yet the grace that he preached as the power of "perfecting perfection" worked in his life. It accounted for his repeated apophatic utterances of glory, praise, joy, and peace in the presence of the Holy Spirit. His faith in the unlimited grace of God helped him to live with the limits of his humanity.

Curiosity

One unlimited human characteristic Outler made use of was his curiosity, the drive that he exhibited from his earliest years in the Appalachian hills of North Georgia as a boy. It continued to drive him in his scholarly quests for Wesley's sermon sources. He took off on every tangent of information that Wesley offered. In 1972 Outler wrote to Texas historian Frank Tolbert: "I need some material on that frog." The inquiry resulted from an article Tolbert wrote on a frog that had lived entombed in a cornerstone. A similar thing happened in John Wesley's day. Wesley mentioned in his sermon "On Living Without God," this story: "A late incident . . . [that] cannot reasonably be doubted, there having been so large a number of eye-witnesses. An ancient tree being cut down, and split through the midst, out of the very heart of the tree crept a large toad, and walked away with all the speed he could. Now how long, may we imagine, had this creature continued there? It is not unlikely it might have remained in its nest above a hundred years. It is not improbable it was nearly, if not altogether, coeval with the oak; having been some way or other enclosed therein at the time it was planted. . . . it had lived that strange kind of life at least a century."[243]

In his researches at Oxford and London Outler traced the source of Wesley's story about the toad in the oak tree to a little-known eight-volume work of Oliver Goldsmith called *An History of the Earth and Animated Nature,* published in 1774. Outler waded through six volumes and then found in the seventh volume these words: "What shall we say to [a toad] living for centuries lodged in the bottom of a rock or cased within the body of an oak tree without the smallest access for nourishment or air, and yet taken out alive and perfect . . . we have highest authorities bearing witnesses their truth, and yet the whole analogy of nature seems to arraign them of falsehood. Bacon asserts that toads are found in this manner; Dr. Plot asserts the same."

Outler's curiosity pushed him further than simply finding the source, as difficult as that venture actually was. For his own satisfaction Outler wanted to find out from Tolbert if "that frog" story were really true. "That frog" Outler was referring to was Old Rip, the pet frog a child named Will Wood placed inside the cornerstone of the Eastland County Courthouse July 29, 1897. The event was witnessed by county dignitaries as the toad was sealed in the cornerstone.

Tolbert writes: "Will Wood was still living in Eastland when the cornerstone was opened on February 18, 1928, at a time when the old courthouse was being torn down. Several days before the cornerstone was opened stories had appeared in newspapers all over the country about Mr. Wood putting the toad in there 31 years before. So there were about 1500 witnesses gathered for the opening of the cornerstone. With two Eastland preachers and County Judge Ed S. Pritchard charged with the duties of watching every move from the time the wall was pulled off until the workmen's picks broke through the cornerstone. The Rev. F. E. Singleton pointed a finger into the cavity when the cornerstone was broken open and said: 'There's the horned frog!' Eugene Day, an Eastland oilman, reached in and brought out the living lizard by the tail.

"After that Old Rip became one of the most famous creatures on earth. First Will Wood took his pet to the White House for [President] Coolidge to see. In St. Louis 40,000 people turned out to see the ancient toad. Old Rip died on January 19, 1929, probably from the rigors of a theatrical tour. His body was embalmed and is now on display in the Eastland County Courthouse.

"The witnesses get angry if you suggest there was some slight of hand when the cornerstone was opened. I've spoken with many of those 1500 witnesses. They're all convinced the toad taken from the stone in 1928, was the same one placed there in 1887."[244]

While Outler did not refer to Old Rip in his footnotes to the sermon "On Living Without God," he did lend further credence to Wesley's frog story by listing the sources of Goldsmith, viz. , "Francis Bacon, 'Doctor Plot,' and the Memoirs of the Academy of Sciences as credible witnesses, and added a third accredited instance ('near Nantes,' 1731) of a toad that had survived 'in the heart of an old oak,' 'not less than eighty or a hundred years without sustenance and without air. Three interesting accounts to the same effect had appeared in *Gent's* Magazine (1756, pp. 74–75 and 240–241)."[245]

The frog story revealed a curiosity in Outler that went far beyond the footnote need at hand. Outler pushed for an answer that satisfied his own mind. Did (could) the frog live through such a tombed environment? Old Rip corroborated Wesley's frog story. While Outler kept quiet concerning his own conclusion, he made every effort to reveal that Wesley without a doubt believed.

It was such probing studies as this that led people to get the idea that Outler had opinions on everything. After he studied you-name-it, he had an opinion on it. In this instance it was frogs.

The World of Psychic Gurus

Outler's curiosity regarding parapsychology was established early in his career. Yet, his interest went beyond that into the world of the psychic gurus. His approach to the whole psychic scene is described in this excerpt from a 1974 Peyton lecture at SMU:

"I've sophisticated friends who speak of PSY-phenomenon as casually as all groups do of sports and politics. Dr. Gilbert Holloway of Deming, New Mexico, of all places for this particular purpose [audience laughter], is cited in a recent *National Observer* piece as 'the hottest psychic just now in the crowded field of psychic surgeons and medicine men who are emerging to red-hot respectability among the rootless seekers of peace of mind.' The lead article in the *Current Horizon* is all about 'ESP, psychokinesis, minions, psytrons and ghosts.' Plus twelve pages of annotated pictures of America's more famous gurus. *Time*'s cover story last month was on 'Witches Cradles and *Their* Revelation.' To ignore all of this is to play ostrich. To swallow it uncritically takes you straight inside the Cave of the Witch of Endor. Their common credo is human autonomy. Their conviction is that humankind must, and can, manage their own destiny. Which is, of course, idolatry."

No-o-o-o-o! You Don't Mean It

Based on Outler's long-time interest in parapsychology his visit to psychic Dan Fry would not only be justified but expected. But now comes the real shocker. Fry was also a practicing astrologer and gave Outler a reading. When Outler let that be known to family and friends, there was one long whisper of disbelief, "No-o-o-o-o! You don't mean it." After all, what business does a Christian teacher, whose life is grounded in grace through faith, have with the antithesis of that faith? An answer for the average Christian to the question would be, "No business."

But anybody who knew Outler realized that the man was not "average." He was a theologian/philosopher whose overactive curiosity lured him into investigations of how other persons thought. He could study astrono*my* out of books, but Outler had in Fry a personal study of astrolo*gy* through a card-carrying astrologer. After all, being the historian that he was, Outler knew that kings prior to the Enlightenment had astrologers parked in the wings of the castles. In this instance he would go into the inner sanctum of the astrologer and find out how the real practitioner performed. In the scripture Outler could read the revealed Word of God; with Fry he got a man-initiated reading of the twelve signs of the zodiac as they related to his life.

When astrologer Fry completed his reading, he asked Outler if he had any questions. To which Outler replied, "I scarcely know how to frame any. You've covered an enormous range. I'd want to ruminate on most of it."[246] After listening to the taped reading, here are some of the things he would have chewed on:

(1) Differences between his grace-grounded counseling techniques and those of an *adviser*. Fry to Outler: "You are not going to like this. But if you were my little boy, I would have held you at gun-point until I got you to go into law with the idea of getting you into political life."

(2) The *adviser's* control tactics. "I don't want you to become involved in anything that is going to be limiting." "I don't want you to become so fixed on the idea that you have to go into quiet obscurity."

(3) The matter of reincarnation. Outler had studied the Eastern religions that embraced the teaching. In this instance the subject became personalized in Fry's comments: "I always feel like a fool when I talk to someone like you about reincarnation; there is a broad path of learning from past life times." Outler gave no indication that he even *tasted* that bit of information, much less *chewed* on it.

(4) The effect of astrology upon his belief system. No indication exists in letters, tapes, papers, or diaries to suggest that his experiment altered in the slightest his beliefs or his sense of a providential divine destiny.

History reveals that Outler never entertained the idea of becoming involved with secular politics (his observation and sometimes involvement in denominational politics had already rankled his spirit). It was never his thing to pursue any particular destiny. He often stated how astonishing were the events of his *God*-given destiny.

While at first it might seem out of character for Outler to accept this offer of a psychic reading, a second studied thought reveals that he was in character for that situation. There Fry was the adviser; Outler, the client. In this setting Outler allowed Fry room to do his thing, and Outler responded with conversation that showed respect for the seer and in what he believed. There was no serious exchange of ideas. No debate. Outler honored the parameters that he assigned to *that* situation. And from the tone on the tape I conclude that Outler enjoyed himself, even as he did later when he and Carla were dinner guests in the home of Dan Fry.[247]

Outler could never play the ostrich on any subject. And on this one he did not find himself in the Cave of the Witch of Endor but in *his* own classroom of testing *his* subject.

One can imagine how things might have gone had Fry seen Outler for Christian counseling. Given Outler's penchant for argument, a probing debate on "Be it resolved that the heavens declare . . ." would have sent Outler soaring.

An Unlimited Knowledge?

As one looks back over Outler's lifetime involvements, one sees a curiosity that enticed him to go in all directions to discover what was going on in this world, and especially what God had to do with it. He was, in Rabbi Gerald Klein's words, "a true Renaissance man who knew something about everything from cooking to baseball to whatever."[248] His storehouse of knowledge had strong retainer walls; he seemed able to keep and dispense, as need be, the valuable information he came onto. This accounted for apocryphal comments such as, "This man knows something about everything," or "What is there he does not know?" or "He is the most knowledgeable person I've ever met." The last comment could be said with a straight face because, for many, it would be true. There would be nothing apocryphal about it. That part of the lore was written in reality. But the previous two would be apocryphal simply because only God knows everything about everything. And Outler knew that.

At times he might have talked over the heads of his audience. But not of God! He told about a student he had at Duke who had a habit of overshooting his audience: "He was sent down to a little seacoast town in North Carolina. He wife agreed to give him a wiggle of the finger when she thought he had overshot the audience. At which point he would say, 'Now I have been trying to say . . .' and he would go over into simple form. This seemed to work very well until in the midst of a prayer she . . ."[249] Outler knew that nobody talks "over the head" of God. Only God knows what God knows.

But Some Criticized

And then there were those who, because of Outler's extraordinarily gifted intelligence, criticized him for not being as perfect in his intelligence as they had assumed he felt he was. They thrilled at revealing an error in his recall as one would spike a ball in the end zone. Catching him using a wrong name or date was like discovering a rock midst a bag of diamonds. It was the rock that should not have been there that got all the attention. This remained a cross that his genius had to bear.

Knowledgeable Yet Not Dogmatic

As his curiosity grew through the years, new worlds of knowledge showed up. Relentlessly he set out to conquer them, all the while admitting that he missed more knowledge than he had gained. In everything he learned, he discovered there was more that he did not know. This did not deter his curiosity; it made him all the more curious. But that curiosity was never applied to his assurance that God loved him. He said: "I'm sure I must have heard something like this from childhood and I must have believed it, at one level of understanding or another, with my mind and also in my heart. But I can remember even now when it was that I first came to be so utterly sure of it that nothing since has ever shaken my basic faith. This is *not*, let me hasten to add, a claim that my life has been without its share of intellectual toil, uncertainty, agony. After a half-century of wondering and pondering about God and the mysteries of life, there's very little now that I know for sure, very little that I hold so dogmatically as to denounce those who think differently. I've still more problems than answers, but I've learned to live with the problems in the certainty that their answers are somehow focused in that one certainty that remains after all the rest are shaken [i.e., that God loved him]."[250]

It was obvious that Outler knew more than the average person, but he never claimed to know everything. In a February 14, 1955, letter to Mrs. Erminie Lantero, Outler declined to write a review for the Christian quarterly *Religion in Life* of a new book coming out by Hindu philosopher Radhakrishnan: "I don't know enough about Indian thought to do a competent job on

Radhakrishnan." It did not take Outler long to hone up on his understanding of Indian thought and add that to his repertoire of philosophical thought. When he found out that he did not know something that he should know something about, he set out to find the answer. If somebody else knew something, he wanted to know it, too. And did not hesitate to ask questions. Ignorance of a subject goaded him into learning about it. He always knew that he ought to know more than he did. By applying himself he simply got more out of his humanity.

A Startled Awakening

Outler knew he had a vast storehouse of knowledge. He had worked hard enough for it. But God had a way of keeping him humble concerning his knowledge in any given moment. Such a moment came to him at Vatican II. It was time for the Eastern Orthodox to do their thing in St. Peter's Cathedral. "With Coptic liturgy in hand and incense in the air the people came in beating drums, with the most wonderful kind of five-tone minor key music I have ever heard. You get used to a little Greek and to Byzantine music and you think you've got your western ears attuned. And then 'ghee' [an attempt to create a musical sound] comes along and you realize you are still a boy from Georgia struggling to be cosmopolitan and failing practically every crucial new test."[251]

Curiosity, Work, and Sickness

This curiosity, that pushed Outler into various areas of inquiry and labeled him a dilettante, at times overburdened him with too many irons in the fire and literally made him sick. To begin with he was born a sickly baby whose situation demanded close supervision by family and friends. The hectic pace he placed on himself time and again exacerbated his inherent physical problems. He turned down thousands of invitations to write and to speak and still was overworked. The point is well taken—he "stretched" (a word that he often used to describe his situation) himself into a sickness that a more relaxed pace could well have avoided. On occasion, when he was stretched too far, he retreated to the hospital, home, or hotel room to recuperate and regain the vigor needed to carry on his work.

One suspects that what he continually referred to in his letters as "the flu" (always in quotes) was in reality total fatigue. Periodically he needed a time out because in his words he was "bone tired."

However, this was not always the case. He genuinely suffered many ailments. His letters indicate some of the illnesses he experienced—diverticulitis, hemorrhoids, hernia, peptic ulcers, flu, ileitis, virus infections of one sort or another, lower back pain that turned out to be gout, intestinal problems of undisclosed nature, angina pectoris, migraine headache, etc. In his Vatican II diaries he writes, "A ghastly night. The strongest sleeping pill I had lasted until one o'clock and then two pain pills. Got through the night. This is another actual ulcer—the worst one yet. I dozed all morning, too sick to read or even care what went on."[252]

In June 1975 he wrote that in a six-month period he had "one cold and sore throat, two 'rotten eggs' diarrhea and nausea bouts, two back spasms, insomnia and fatigue, constipation and hemorrhoids." He had causes for his interest in medicines. And knew better than any the psychosomatic nature of *some* of his illnesses as well as those that attack the human being in ways still unknown. Outler was well aware that his life's hyperactivity at times literally made him sick.

But he also knew in his own heart and mind a power that could take his workaholic weaknesses and bring about great good. In his words: "We all know the story of the farmer who explained to his more sophisticated son that he wasn't farming, even then, as well as he knew how. We all know how aptly that applies to our own living. *My* unsolved problem is where to find the energy, motivation, courage (or humility) to do what I know needs doing; and to do what a part of me, at least, would *like* to be doing, or at least to see done. But where am I to get that necessary energy and motivation—if not from the Holy Spirit within; from my willingness to let *him* rule and guide my priorities with his promptings? The great good news, which flows from faith in Christ, is just this: that the Spirit who raised up Jesus from the dead is the same Spirit who will not only quicken our mortal bodies but who, meantime, will help us defy the tyranny of sin."[253]

Outler knew by experience what he was talking about when he said: "When you've got your health, you *think* you've got your health. And then the next time you go the doctor you discover you've got high blood pressure or low blood pressure or you've got something and he does not know why. He says, 'Have you had it before?' And you say, 'Yeah.' And he says, 'Well you, you've got it again!' As my doctor used to say to me, 'Now remember, I am giving you a clean bill of health. And it is guaranteed to hold until you get to the bottom of the elevator and walk out onto the street. And that's about as long as I can verify it. Because you could have a coronary before you get home.' The point is: all this illness is undignified. There is not any way that you can be ill and not be aware that your work has been diminished. Illness is a temptation to resentment or to self-indulgence. We know people who try to deny the plain fact of illness or who complain of it and want it whisked away by some magical wonder worker [the doctor/priest]. On the other end of the spectrum are the people who enjoy poor health. Who wallow in sympathy and attention. In either case the ego is working overtime. And one's interest is being turned inward instead of being drawn and pointed outward. And that, of course, is one form of meaninglessness and one retreat from the hallowing of life. And of the recognition of the hallowed life. But illness can be hallowed. And always by the same description. This too is of grace. Therefore it may be managed with some measure of *style.* Which is to say 'grace under pressure.'"[254]

With the many life-long illnesses Outler experienced, he surely must have experienced the temptations of the ego working overtime. This much is known: those illnesses were hallowed by grace. They ultimately did not defeat him or what he was about. His death was managed by grace in the same way. He dealt with his illnesses and faced death in *style,* "grace under pressure."

Outler reflected on his experiences of sickness with a sense of humor, which he knew to be a gift of the Spirit. He likened his exhaustion and "tired blood" to that of one of his favorite colleagues, Hal Luccock. "After a long preaching circuit at some colleges and universities, Hal came home one afternoon and wanted to rest. Mary [his wife] said, 'There is a good lecture down at Woolsey Hall.' Hal answered, 'Mary, I am just worn out. I'm too tired. May be a good lecture. I just don't want to go.' Mary told him, 'Hal Luccock, your tongue is going to wear out before your ears do.'"[255]

A Catch-22 Situation

While Outler, in faith and good humor, learned to live through his fatigue, this picture of the man working himself "to death" caused concern for friends and admirers and put them in a catch-22 situation. If he did less and got more rest, he could have been a healthier man; on the other hand, had he done less, the church and his brothers and sisters in that church would not have today his multifarious gifts he shared with them and that gave meaning to their lives. Outler would say that this is precisely the kind of situation out of which God can bring great good. And this is what God did. God used Outler's faith that he had accepted by grace, the faith that gave him his grace and good humor, and took him through eighty years of pain, physical and mental. And now Outler is "home" and all is well—peace at last. His friends and admirers are better off for having him just as he was.

Rising Early

Outler is so identified with John Wesley that often they are made to act and think alike in all instances. Not so. Outler did not share all of John Wesley's thoughts and ways. Far from it, especially when it came to rising early. In discussing Wesley's methods for study Outler said, "Here is number one—what method of continuing education would you advise preachers to follow? Answer: We would advise them first always to rise at 4:00." And then Outler added: "This is where I am normally lost because I can lecture when I am asleep, but I can't do anything else."[256]

Outler did not rise early, and he did not retire early at the end of the day. He had a system for rest that was all his own. He punctuated his days with short naps. Many who entered his office probably thought his couch, which resembled a psychotherapist's, was for his "patients." In fact, however, it was for, in his words, a "short rest stop that gets me on the road again."

Time in the Study Prepared for Time in the World

Outler's work in the study had a purpose in the world. For every ten hours in the study he spent one hour airing his thoughts out on the sidewalk, in the hallway, classroom, symposium—wherever he had an audience. His best "airing" came when he sidled up to a truck driver and talked about the latest truck-driver music. Or to a farrier about blacksmithing in general. Or to a farmer about his tomatoes. Or to a rancher about his cattle. He discovered Plato's secret: to express abstract truth he drew illustrations from sources disdained by the polite academia: from sheep, pigs, cows, dogs, butchers, cooks. His salty, sharp, laconic words were so alive that they would bleed if you cut them. He used words that walked, ran, skipped, tiptoed, swam, flew, swirled.

Giving

Even Wesley's dictum to "earn all you can; save all you can; give all you can" was not followed to a "T" by Outler. Never ostentatious, he saved all he could, which was not much. He drove in the Texas summer heat a non-air-conditioned Plymouth Duster "George." He gave all he could. Immediately after Albert died, Carla put $160,000, which had accrued through the years from the $70,000 gift of the Crisman family for his library books, into an archives fund for the Bridwell Library. They decided on this before his death. But he never attempted to earn all he could. What kind of fortune could a mind like his have amassed had he set that mind to it?

Personal Comfort

Personal comfort was not high enough on his list of values. As Outler drove "George" (they named all their cars) through the hot Texas summers, he never complained. Not so with many of his friends. They looked forward to the day that he would enjoy the comforts of a larger, better-equipped automobile. When told he *deserved* it, he cringed at the thought that his friends never heard that grace cannot be deserved. But it was a graceful cringe!

The Albert C. Outler Prize in Ecumenical Church History

Following her parents' death, Carla received her inheritance. She wanted to do something *with* Albert concerning $50,000 of the money. That had been her relationship *with* Albert through the years. It seemed only right for her, with Albert's help, to write to Winton Solberg, president of the American Society of Church History, and make the gift. Typical Albert, in doing this, again played down himself in it and made sure that it did not appear that he was *asking* for anything. Great joy was expressed as he contemplated the good that would come from the earnings of the investment for ecumenical Christianity. The award, established in 1986, is given to encourage the critical study of ecumenical history, broadly conceived, and to facilitate the publication of such studies. The prize consists of an award of $1000 to the author and $3000 toward expenses in getting the work published. This award emphasized Albert's concern for the church catholic, his lifelong "workplace" and "home."

Passing on His Desk

The oak desk that Outler used at Perkins came from a close friend and colleague, Clarence Tucker Craig, who was first a heroic scholar-missionary in China and thereafter a distinguished professor of New Testament at Oberlin and Yale. Much of the work that Craig did as a member of the Revised Standard Version team of Bible translators was done on this desk. As were his major contributions to the ecumenical movement, especially during the early days of Faith and Order. Craig left Yale to become dean of the Divinity School at Drew University. At that time he gave his desk to Albert, who brought it along to Dallas when he moved there in 1951. Outler had special feelings for this desk, both because of its association with "Tuck" Craig and because it had for forty years been the solid base of numerous scholarly endeavors such as collations, scribblings, and wrestling with perplexities. With these fond memories Outler left it to the Bridwell Library, hoping for its continued usefulness through the years.

His Gifted Life Was a Giving Life

Outler was multifaceted, complex to the point that he could not write a "Who am I?" essay and give answers that would satisfy his own professorial critique. Yet he made it easier for those who knew the *pastor* in the man to love others—because they knew Outler's love and acceptance.

Outler said, "It [life] comes down finally to a radical choice: life under the Rule of Grace *or* life under the rule of self-interest. Under the Rule of Grace our lives are acknowledged as gifted, and lived out in basic trust in God's upholding love." All of life's secondary values were accepted by him as useful, even necessary but never paramount.

Humor

These pages have been filled with the wit and humor of Outler. In introducing Outler, colleague Douglas Jackson once said, "He not only has a deep sense of humor, but the timing of a Jack Benny; the ability to wait for his laughs; and then let you have the second laugh. We are proud of Albert Outler. We are proud that the world has discovered him—he is *our man* for this time."[257]

For Outler to be recognized as a great person on the one hand, and for him not to know it on the other; to be evaluated first-rate by colleagues and friends on the one hand, and to feel in his soul that it's not so; to be appreciated and needed by so many on the one hand, yet feeling left out on the other—all this placed Albert Outler squarely in the tragic fabric of human existence. His humor often revealed a connectedness to the tragic side of life: "When I first heard Anna Russell do her wonderful spoof of Freudian morality (back in 1960 as I recall), it seemed hilarious (an obvious cosmic fantasy):

> At three I had a feeling of
> Ambivalence toward my brothers,
> And so it followed naturally
> That I poisoned my lovers.

> But now I am happy; I have learned
> The lesson this has taught:
> That everything I do that's wrong
> Is someone else's fault.

"*Now,* as I take my daily dosage of heavy pieces explaining mass murders, prison riots, promiscuity, hijacking, terrorism, and ripping off as a lifestyle (this litany is random and also endless), I feel like the post-operative appendectomy case: it hurts only when I laugh."[258]

It is no wonder that Outler preached and practiced grace. Shooting through all the negatives of his existence was that power of God called grace. Midst all the personal deficiencies, that *he* felt were his *was* the great *I AM,* whose Rule of Grace gave meaning even to meaninglessness, faith amidst self-doubts, and unquestioned love that finally challenged and satisfied all the questions that plagued his existence.

Outler's recognition of these incongruities within himself and others accounted for his unusual sense of humor. He couched his observed incongruities in ironies, sarcasms, hyperboles, litotes, rhetorical questions, oxymorons, and paradoxes. There was his use of syllepsis in the quote: "Mind over matter—no mind; never matter."[259] Sardonics in: "Do you remember the flamboyant pastor of _____? I do as a matter of history, but not as a matter of interest."[260] Sometimes he was laughing as he described what he saw, sometimes not. But at all times his audiences saw and heard intellectual wit/humor at its best.

Outler's wit and humor endeared him to the historians of the Churches of Christ. The following story told by Church of Christ historian Everett Ferguson reveals that Outler elicited that same humor in them. During the time that Outler lectured at Abilene Christian University (July 1985) on the restoration theme in various church bodies "there was an anecdote that he [Outler] liked to tell with reference to Churches of Christ and that he brought up with some at lunch during the conference. The cornerstone of the University Church of Christ reads:

> Church of Christ
> Established in Jerusalem
> A.D. 33
> This Building Erected
> A.D. 1951

"Outler took delight in that as capturing the essence of a 'restorationist' vision, yet lack of consciousness of history."[261]

That anecdote had its beginning with Outler's first discovery of such a cornerstone in the First Christian Church in Sweetwater, Texas, and continued as he saw other similarly inscribed cornerstones on other older Church of Christ buildings across the region. In an article titled "Church History by the Cube," Outler wrote, "This was as short a survey of church history as I had ever run across. Later I would learn that it was a long-accustomed format in many Churches of Christ in the area and elsewhere: a 'restoration' statement in stone."[262]

Overlapping this highly intellectualized genre of humor was another that was uniquely of the Outlerian flavor. The intellectual humor was always up and running. But now and then another unusual type of humor came into play. It was a matchless mix of his superior intelligence and playful childhood hillbilly experiences (recall the story told by Carlyle Marney about the squirrel hunter with the St. Vidas dance). On the speaker's platform the audience saw and heard a southern gentleman endowed with gifts and graces far beyond the average. His poise, infectious smile with an intermittent chuckle, "uh-uhs" signaling words trying to catch up with a fast-moving intellect, and his unquestioned sincerity combined to charm his audiences.

When that image was struck by such unexpected words and phrases as "He fit a good fight," "plowing too shallow in fallow ground," "bust the middle of the furrows that we have already plowed," "one ditch of the road over to the other," "mule-headed" (remember, he once owned some), "whipsawed," listening to people "gaggle," "lapping at the Pierean spring," "flogging a tired horse uphill," "heard tell," "barn-burner radicals," "wings free to flutter," "cat amongst the pigeons and you've got a lot of flurrying about," "cows staring at horses and dogs with what may be an equivalent of bovine (meditative) wonder," the audiences laughed as the unexpected came from a man who did not fit those backwoodsy comments. Such comments were incongruent with who the audience felt he was. But what most did not realize was that his folksy, backwoodsy comments were congruent with who *he* felt he was. His experiences as "an Appalachian hillbilly" never left him. This genre of humor delighted his audiences and caught his detractors off guard. Before they knew it, they were laughing too. He, in turn, was delighted to see that they *could* laugh.

His use of the ludicrous was picturesque. Observing some people becoming acquainted, he said, "They are like dogs getting acquainted on stiff legs!"[264]

Outler did not offer a series of groaners or one-liners of a stand-up comic. Whenever an incongruity jumped at him, the humor was there. Al Smith relates the time the Perkins newspaper, *The Log,* came out with this definition: "Theological professor: A man who takes young theologs, leads them down a dark alley, and blows out their torch!" Someone circled it and put it on the lecture stand from which Outler was to lecture. When Outler came in, he picked it up and read it, smiled and said, "Uh, Uh, no, no, I would rather say, 'A theological professor is one who keeps young incendiaries from burning the church down!'"

Outler enjoyed a laugh *with* others as much as any person. He appreciated any good humor others displayed toward him. One of his female students from earlier seminary days wrote him a letter with this salutation: "Dear Most Adored Professor (except by contrary women!)." Their correspondence indicated a mutual friendship grounded in good humor. Outler once wrote, "A pastor without a sense of humor ought to be blocked early on."[264] This particular student was not "blocked in her ministry early on."

Humor at Self

Outler once wrote: "In these bleak times humor has come to be 'in' (high fashion and low). We almost have too much of it: irony, satire, sarcasm, 'one-liners,' buffo! Our communicators have been encouraged to become our entertainers—to ease the pressures of our anxieties, to conceal their own perplexities. And yet it is simply the fact that humor at its best lets good ideas sparkle as they can only in the play of wit and irony. The comic gift is precious, especially when it punctures pomp without contempt, when it pokes fun at human foibles without holding the human up to scorn."[265]

Outler laughed more than most because he saw more than most the myriad of inconsistencies that people project, including himself. Once when I flew my plane into Love Field, Dallas, the Outlers picked my wife and me up at a Fixed Base Operator's lounge for a visit and lunch. Following lunch the Outlers drove us back to the airport. I directed Albert to drive onto the tiedown area and take us directly to our plane at the far end of the ramp. He did and before he knew it, he was winding in and out and around numerous large and small planes. He seemed genuinely uneasy being in such threatening surroundings. He said to me, "What would you say if an airport policeman stopped me and asked what I was doing out here?" I answered, "I would say, 'He just picked us up. I do not know this man.'" At that point Outler flushed red with loud laughter at himself in *that* situation. This was one of the few times that he was caught speechless.

The depth of this humor-at-self can be seen in the following letter where he elicited a laugh at his name in hopes of getting his name spelled right. To Perry Prentice at *Life* magazine he wrote on January 8, 1938: "I am continually amazed at the inefficiency of the circulation of a publication with the reputation of *Life*. And I am really becoming annoyed at the number of communications I am receiving from you.

"About a month ago I wrote you, calling your attention to the fact that our name is misspelled on the mailing list stencil, and saying that we would send a check for our subscription the first of the year.

"The check was sent on the sixth of this month, with a note on the bill calling attention to the fact that the spelling of our name still had not been corrected. We renewed our subscription for two years, as the check for seven dollars indicates.

"I really don't mean to be fussy about our name, but when one has an odd name like Outler, it makes it much worse to have it spelled Ostler. Even though our name has come from 'Outlaw,' we have become sufficiently civilized to want to conform to law and order—So, please, make the necessary correction.

"The check for seven dollars has been properly credited to the Outlers, and not the Ostlers, who do not exist as far as I know.

"Thank you very much. I'm sure you have been unusually busy during the Christmas season, but I think it is far enough past now to get this straightened out finally." In this instance Outler used humor-at-self to get across his point.

Outler's humor-at-self revealed a confidence (in spite of his insecurities) midst his critics. He recounted Merrimon Cuninggim's comments made at a Kent Fellowship meeting, where they had gathered to read papers. "Merry's part was to do an impressionist imitation of me. He started out with a perfectly clear clause and went on. It was all, I thought very interesting. He went on and on and finally he said, 'If anybody here knows where this sentence is going to end, he is a better man than I am!'"[266] The fact that Outler told this story on himself indicated that he could take the ribbing while he continued to write page-long sentences and read them with a flair during a lecture.

While Outler was not a standup comic, he easily recognized the comic in life. As a member of the audience of this human comedy, he laughed more than most because he saw more incongruities. He in turn helped others laugh at the comic human situation through his humor and ready descriptions of the ludicrous. His ability to laugh through tears revealed an Outler in touch with Truth—the light that illumines incongruities and triggers the humor. The Outlerian smile, punctuated by hints of laughter, oftentimes prepared one for the humor to come. Those signs alerted one that the revealing of an incongruity was on the way. This ability to recognize and expose human inconsistencies enabled him to see more of what it means to be human than most humans will ever understand, which is to say that, in this regard, he was *more* human than most humans.

When Outler was called upon to address the Council of Bishops concerning his experiences at Vatican II, he remarked that Pope Paul XXIII "was so human that he could have written the script for *Bonanza*."[267] That, to a point, described Albert Outler. Any writing of *Bonanza* by Outler would reveal a humanness that allowed a full view of God's saving grace.

14

He Was a Bridge Builder

artin Marty, in his interview of Outler in the February 29, 1984, issue of *The Christian Century,* said to him: "The most complex lives are those who can be reduced to an informing phrase. Such a phrase or word summarizes a vocation, a profile, an impact. 'I/Thou,' 'The Courage To Be,' 'Aggiornamento,' 'The Responsible Self,' 'Creative Fidelity,' 'Freedom!' What is Outler's? After a split second during which his [Outler's] brow furls to spell sheepishness, he recovers: 'Is it too corny just to say of me, "Bridge Builder"?'" No, it is not corny at all. He can be assured that his self-image matches the impression others have gained.

I continue with excerpts from *The Christian Century* article.

Christianity and Psychotherapy

"'Well, my life has been all bridge building.' To build bridges assumes that one has firm footings on both sides. Sides of what? 'Christianity and psychotherapy, for instance.' Who else was bringing the therapists and theologians together back in 1954, when Outler published *Psychotherapy and the Christian Message*? 'I am still thrilled to see traffic on that very bridge,' he says.

Christianity and Philosophy

"A second bridge was between Christianity and philosophy, at least in respect to their histories. Graduate student Outler learned from ancient Origen. Has he conversation among current philosophers, or do they dismiss theology and force him to talk solely to those who speak only through books?—'There's less company than there was in the heyday of process theology,' he answers . . .

Denominational Bridge building

"As for denominational bridge building, he does not have to spell matters out. Mergers as such interest him less than shared Eucharists across boundaries, mutually acceptant ministries among the formerly competitive and participation in each other's gifts. No wonder the Methodists chose him to go to Vatican II, And Vaticanologists chose him to represent so much of Protestantism.

Mainliners and Evangelicals

"Outler has put energies recently on a tense and promising front: that between mainliners and evangelicals. One might speak of this front as being at 'the right of the left and the left of the right,' for his mainliners care for tradition and his evangelicals are open to other voices. 'No one of these gatherings is called to compromise, but we do come up with astonishingly fresh formulations.' Some hardlining evangelicals may suspect that Outler is here subverting groups that might otherwise engage in some political takeovers, but have instead stayed around to speak *and* to listen to the moderate-to-liberal camps. Some hardlining mainliners may surmise that Outler is suspect as one more 'neocon' who has gone over the hill and, like other apostates, spends his career taking revenge on his own spiritual past and the colleagues he thinks he has left behind. Neither stereotype works for this subtle and supple mind, and one of his main contributions may lie in helping to destroy such stereotypes . . .

Logos Incarnate Bridges the Gap

"Entrepreneurs and impresarios come and go; theological bridge builders need a sustaining philosophy. Outler leans forward when asked about his principle: 'Does this sound too formal? I honestly believe that the Logos incarnate does in fact 'compromise,' and is, in fact, a sort of bridge . . . I work with the conviction that all truth is an emergent co-incident with this movement of the Logos between God and man.' What this means needs spelling out, and his life and conversation are exercises in such spelling . . .

Life Goes On

"Outler makes no pretense that life is all one 'have-a-good-day' smile, and his pleasant expression bears the marks of being worn by someone who cares and has cares. As for his own transits, for instance, 'I've had a terrible time with retirement, as I watch my school get on with the next chapters to which I know it must turn without me.'

John Wesley

"I mentioned the four theological sages whose names come up when you inquire about those who influenced Outler most. Who helps in the bridge building between the biblical worlds and our own? John Wesley . . .

"Outler has not only dug, he has used what he came up with. Wesley, he says, 'got the order of salvation right,' and that order Outler spells out in eight stages. Why, one cannot resist asking, does today's Methodism so seldom get this order and its consequences right? 'There may be more of us who do than you realize. We've done what we could, and it wasn't enough.' More sadness than defensiveness in his voice.

Origen

"Origen [another bridge builder]. 'Does that surprise you?' Outler asks. The son of the Georgia Methodist parsonage encountered Origen when philosophy pressed hard on his young mind. Origen connected the Bible with contemporary culture 'and it is desperately important that we learn to do so, too.'

Karl Rahner

"Among the moderns Karl Rahner stands out [as bridge builder]. 'His Christian wisdom is certainly for the ages. What does he [Rahner] mean by 'God's self-communication'? We'd be well advised to reflect on that . . . And Rahner's *Spirit in the World* (Crossroad, 1968) opens us to a psychology that goes far beyond what Christians usually work with.'

Church Morale

"If this historian of theology is well aware of the surrounding world and the church today, he has to be concerned about the malaise many currently identify with mainline Protestant life. He knows that many of its local churches and movements are vital. But has he a diagnosis for low morale on the national and international levels? Instantly two come to his mind.

"'First, the churches have overbought the managerial revolution.' Outler cannot think of a church body that has not put too much hope in expensive and energetic restructuring during the past 25 years.

No Romantic Simplest

"Bridge builder Outler will not, however, let the simple antibureaucrat come charging in with a lance against 'the organized church,' even at this vulnerable point. No romantic simplest, he is on good terms with the elected and managerial leadership of the churches. He simply insists that to look for evangelical reform from structural reshuffling is a diversion. Look elsewhere. Such as?

Networking Is Way to Go

"'Such as networking.' He almost apologizes for a term that sounds faddish, but recovers. 'I know that sounds like a slogan, but it is really very apt. Look around you and you will see.' He describes spontaneous combustions, voluntary associations, movements which come into being without a charismatic leader or celebrity to whom members swear fealty and from whom they pick up jargon. The good ones of these outlive their founders. They are not 'parachurch' rivals to the churches. Their members do not turn their backs on everyone else's congregation; they live off the church and feed into it. Outler is reluctant to cite examples, since exposure often makes the networks vulnerable to public-relations hype and consequent disappointment or decline.

Still Living in Enlightenment Rationalism

"Outler's second case against the mainline is that it has not, in code language, recognized the expiration of Enlightenment and Enlightenment rationalism. (An irony: the evangelicals have not noticed it either, and misfight it in some of their charges against 'secular humanism' and adopt it in some of their rationalist defenses of biblical authority . . .)

"Instead, Outler feels, 'mainline congregations would be well served if they were told not, 'You *must* love' (which is true and which they've heard often enough), but rather 'You can love' because 'You *are* loved.' This message centers on the personal encounter with Jesus Christ. 'You are loved. Therefore , you are free to be thankful. You are free to be useful.' Is this a long way from Origen and Wesley and Rahner? Not in Outler's mind. 'We can tell the congregations this, or we can try one more time to say, "Pull up your socks, set your goals, you can do it!" Wise people , however, realize how default that is.'. . .

A Benediction

"We need a benediction from this Wesleyan: can he find something in the question, 'What is the Holy Spirit for us today?' Outler chooses the words with care: 'The Holy Spirit is the personal presence, the power of God, building and making the church, building and making human community.' And, we might add, building and making bridge builders like Albert Outler."

In these quotes from *The Christian Century,* Marty allowed the reader to hear Outler describe himself as a bridge builder and then to *watch* Outler go to work in different areas describing the process.

What Makes the Bridge Builder?

How was it that Outler was a bridge builder when so many others were not? One obvious answer is that he had a mind as deep as it was expansive. This thinking capacity allowed him to see perspectives, angles, and insights that the various sides could not see in themselves. Some of the Romans of Vatican II declared that Outler knew more of what was going on there than their own theologians. With these insights he saw bridges where others saw chasms.

Another part of that answer is that he had a piety that matched his knowledge; he knew the Source of his knowledge. He knew his God. That search for and with Truth provided him with bridge images. He did not set out to build bridges. He set out for the truth and the bridges came into focus. A major contributing factor in getting his bridge images across to different viewpoints was the man's ethos. Others could say the same words that he said in building that bridge, and their audiences would never hear it. When Outler spoke, they listened.

They listened because they sensed he was listening—to God. And was willing to listen to what they were also hearing from God. Outler told a story that illustrates this openness: "When we moved from New Haven to Dallas, I soon made friends with one of American Judaism's true giants, Rabbi Levi Olan, and for twenty-five years, we were close friends and he my chief mentor in things Jewish. Last summer, when he died, I was honored by the invitation to pronounce a heartfelt eulogy at his funeral in Temple Emmanu-El. [In this instance Outler was a Christian pastor to a Jewish rabbi's family. He proved in that situation the truth of Rabbi Gerald Klein's observation: "Albert understood the Jew and Judaism."[268]]

"This is not a mere anecdote; it is one man's witness to the fact that one can be involved in the Christian ecumenical enterprise and in the Jewish-Christian dialogue and interreligious dialogue of all sorts at one and the same time. The struggles of Christians seeking their way back to some sort of authentic unity (without betraying their own traditions, *at their best,* and yet discarding the remnants of past hatreds in their ongoing heritage) opens up to the wider horizons of God's self-disclosures to others in his human family besides ourselves. It was the ecumenical experience that led the way, not only to dialogue between Christians and Christians, Christians and Jews, Christians with Moslems and Hindus and Buddhists, but that also opened the way to cooperative social action in the great human causes of war and peace, the holy crusades against racism, poverty and injustice."[269]

This openness experienced in Outler's relationships with others (excluding the obstreperous or *hubris*-haunted) reached beyond them into the past, and then came back to influence those personal relationships in a unique Outlerian manner. Outler went back in history and studied Wesley; went back behind Wesley to Wesley's sources, the church fathers and the Bible; and brought all this history forward to affect the whole church with all its denominations in today's world. In effect, Outler permitted history to influence history as it was being written in his day and is being written today and the days to come. He used his bridge across history to build bridges across chasms that divide in any given situation.

What was the source of the power that allowed Outler to stand in the tension between opposing views? He gave an answer to that question in an address to students of Virginia Polytechnic Institute in the early 1940s: "Somehow, so far I have managed to live in tension, to bridge those sagging days between one period of stability or creativity and the next, by holding fast, no matter what, to the faith that the basic values in human life are never repealed, never outmoded. The value of a good home and work to do, of life in a community with steadily broadening horizons, the reality of friendship and the willingness to trust the power of unselfish love in and beyond the human level, the expanding spiral of values in life—all derived from and consummated in God, the revelation of God in Jesus Christ, and the continuing life of God's spirit in the Christian Church through the ages— these things for me are basic values which I cannot deny nor disparage, although God knows I neither understand nor exhibit them very well."

He addressed YMCA leaders in the National Cathedral at Washington D.C., in 1966: "Peacemaking is the enterprise, carried through suffering to a cross if necessary, to overcome evil in the world and estrangement between people, by love. Peacemakers are those who place themselves by choice in the midst of human conflict—to do and to speak the truth in love at the cost of the cross, with their vindication expected, not from their worldly success, but from God's blessing and unconquerable providence."

While Outler bridged opposing views with an encyclopedic mind that saw more facts on all sides than those sides knew existed, the *thing* in the man that made others stand up and take notice was his faith. Indeed, therein did lie the power that fed the energy loosed in his mind. His faith saved him from snobbery and won for him and his cause many converts.

15

He Was a Prophet

ometimes Outler's stands in the midst of the fury of debate were moments of great pain. Often he pleased nobody and gravely offended some. Early in his pastoral ministry he felt the call of the prophet—the call to speak a word from God to the people—no matter who the people might be. This did not necessarily mean that he could read the future; it meant that he had a strong reading (conviction) on the present state of affairs; and if things did not change, the future was obvious for anyone to read. In a November 14, 1975, letter to Charles Milford, who had asked him his "views of the future for the next twenty-five years," Outler wrote: "I'm very hard pressed just now to cope with the next twenty-five days." But within that twenty-five days he would have told anyone in the blink of an eye, in his words, "how the [proverbial] cow ate the cabbage." And if things did not change, doomsayer Outler would picture a bleak future.

Outler sometimes used humorous asides in dealing with pronouncements upon unethical or immoral human behavior. "Chivalry first meant you had a horse and second meant that you knew how to behave—which does not follow from having a horse."[270] For Outler this genre of antinomian logic was unacceptable.

Offending Bishops and Bureaucrats

More than once Outler pronounced judgment upon bishops and bureaucrats; and more than once he felt the scorn of the high and mighty. He described such a situation in these words: "Once I wrote a little piece that upset the bishops and bureaucrats in my church. [His usual challenge to bishops was "to bish or cut bait."] I did not mean to cause a row, but I had to speak my mind and it did cause a row. [Outler believed, when the situation called for it, in going "past amiability to genuine confrontation"[271]] A short while later I had to be at one of those meetings of our movers and shakers in one of those hotel conferences where you have a whole battery of committees meeting in different rooms. Where they all get together and gaggle in the lobby. I got into the hotel and registered and started across the lobby, where many VIP friends were conversing. I was allowed to go through them like the children of Israel through the Red Sea—midst blind eyes and frosty glances. At least for the nonce I had a sense of ungrace as *dynamis*. And I confess to a certain amount of loneliness in a crowd of old acquaintances."[272]

Outler never meant to cause a row, but a row seemed to occur every time he spoke prophetically. To the speech "What Price Methodist Reform?" given at a Methodist Conference on Christian Education in Dallas on October 10, 1967, a District Superintendent from Minnesota wrote: "I disagree strongly with what you said about the appointive system and even more strongly with the way you said it. This kind of radical talk cannot come out of a broadly based knowledge of the facts. I think that in your attacking the appointive system that you have tackled something you know very little about."

That last clause lit Outler's fuse. He responded with a stinging defense of his position set forth in his address. After the man got through reading Outler's reply, he realized that Outler knew more about the appointive system that he ever dreamed existed. He wrote in answer to Outler's instructive argument: "I think if you still have a copy of my letter and would expunge the entire last paragraph of it, you would have removed from it some of what I did not really mean to say as I gave it a more careful reading in response to your statements that I was saying you didn't know what you were talking about. Sadly enough, your reference to the modification of our appointive system is all too true." In this instance Outler's prophetic voice triggered a response that in turn allowed him to win a convert.

Dulaney Barrett wrote Outler for a copy of the address. Here is the gist of Outler's reply: "Here's a copy of my address to the Conference on Christian Education, "What Price Methodist Reform?", last November. Would you believe it was meant to be *constructive?* My main notion was that the best practices of our best bishops in many cases should be codified into a basic policy for all bishops in all (or nearly all) cases of pastoral appointment or ministerial placement—and it oughtn't to be too difficult to do this.

"The reactions [over forty responses] to the thing have been diverse to the point of bafflement. The 'establishment types' have *unanimously* regarded it as a dangerous assault upon the central nervous system of Methodist polity—to be rejected out of hand, and with the explanation that their matching numbers [officials] in other churches envy *their* power and responsibilities! [It was precisely this gloating over *their* power that Outler saw as the bishops' Achilles heel.] There have been some who have agreed with the bishops that I'm trying to wreck the Methodist citadel—and are cheering me on to the demolition! The rest fall in between—agreeing that reform is needed but doubting that it has much hope or prospect. I'd be interested in your reactions—and especially so if you can think of any constructive revisions or modifications."[273]

An Ecumenical Hostile Encounter

Outler's tendency to speak his mind sometimes got him into trouble with his ecumenical colleagues: "When I first proposed at Lund in 1952 that Western Christians might quietly drop the *filioque* ["the Holy Spirit 'proceeds' from the Father *and the Son*] from the neo-Constantinopolitan Creed, I was made quickly aware of having committed an egregious *faux pas* and felt properly squelched. Now, as you know, there will be a proposal to do this very same effect at Faith and Order in Vancouver next summer. Thirty years is about as swift a fruition as any unwelcome idea ever gets. [What was a hot *new* proposal in the eighties was a hot potato for Outler in the early fifties.] Which is to say that I have had a few hostile encounters as you have. And none of them brings out the best in any of us."[274] Outler accepted confrontations; he never enjoyed them. Outler knew that these confrontations did not "bring out the best in any of us," but he also knew that the best could not be served if he kept silent. He said what he felt he had to say and did what he felt he had to do. But in the expressed opinion of Patrick Henry, one who knew him long and under many trying circumstances, "He was not mean-spirited. Nothing about him was mean."[275]

Abortion

When the subject was abortion, Outler was a prophet with the personal experience of knowing what he was talking about. Speaking to a conference on abortion Outler said: "It has, occasionally, been explained to me somewhat impatiently, that an aging, WASP, male, theologian cannot possibly understand human realities and the human damage of unacceptable pregnancies—and, therefore, that all my notions about abortion are 'academic.' My response to this is also *ad hominem,* and it comes in two parts: the one is frankly sentimental; the other, grimly prophetic. My personal sentiments in this matter root in the fact that our two children and our son-in-law were all adopted—and none of them would have seen the light of day in these new times. To tell me *now* that the social values that might have accrued to their three anguished mothers (had they aborted) would have outweighed the human and personal worth of these three persons is, I'm afraid, literal nonsense.

"And as for my prophetic forebodings, it seems certain that in America alone, over the next few years, millions of fetal lives will be snuffed out—*with little moral outcry!* There are ways of arguing that this is not comparable to the Nazi holocaust, or to the tragedy in Indo-China, or the widening stains of child abuse here at home. But it will be comparable statistically—and morally it will be even more ominous, for it will be sponsored by many whose professional ordinations are to healing and compassion. Moreover, it will have for its rationalization theories of fetal life defining it as a chattel to a mother's private value-judgments. Who then will be surprised if our human sensitivities are still further calloused, if sex becomes yet more promiscuous—with our scruples against euthanasia crumbling and the moral cements of our society dissolving?"[276]

Homosexuality

Outler rattled the rafters with a speech concerning homosexuality on the floor of a plenary session of the 1976 General Conference: "Mr. Chairman—Just before leaving home for Portland, some of us finished Charlotte Saikowski's eight-part series in *The Christian Science Monitor* entitled 'After Permissiveness, What?'—one of the most thoughtful essays I have seen on the moral crises in our society as a whole. Her conclusion—a renewal of moral standards or a further drift into militant antinomianism—comes to mind now, since we are here being asked to answer Saikowski's question, 'After Permissiveness, What?' with 'More Permissiveness, That's What!'

"The essence of the issue before us is not Christian nor pastoral compassion for homosexuals or their civil and human rights. That's provided for in the text of the 1972 *Discipline* [which Outler helped draft]. Nor is it some imagined difference between welcoming homosexuals into *membership* and refusing them ordination. Membership in the UMC is itself an ordination on the basis of sexual orientation if the UMC has said that any sexual orientation is as fully allowable as any other, on Christian principles!

"No, sir, we are being asked, here and now, to condone homosexuality and to *welcome* avowed, militant, missionary homosexuals into our membership. We are being asked to vote for or against antinomianism, in an acid test case. We are being asked to vote for or against moral decadence, in one of its most characteristic forms. We are being asked to endorse sexual promiscuity in the case of homosexuals (since we do not stipulate their marriage), which logically entails endorsement of sexual promiscuity for other United Methodists.

"Besides being contrary to biblical interpretations of sexuality and the whole tradition of Christian ethics, homosexuality is at least *doubtful* as a positively equal sexual option in the view of many (if not most) modern biologists and moralists. Moreover, the evidence is very far from solid that pederasty or homosexual liaisons are positively good and humanly fulfilling.

Nevertheless, we are now being asked to ignore all of this and to pass directly from homosexuality's decriminalization (1972) to its positive institutionalization (in 1976) and mark you well, to ordination in 1980.

"This is *wrong,* this is *unwise,* this is a foolproof recipe for irreversible disaster in the United Methodist Church and in the Christian world. I wish there were time and that this were a sufficiently rational forum in which to debate this matter more calmly and completely. As it is, I can only say, with all possible emphasis, that the import of this issue goes way beyond a practical judgment of a pragmatic sort. It is an issue of conscience; and for me, I aim to vote against antinomianism (as any heir of Wesley would), to vote against moral decadence—and I appeal to this Conference to do the same, decisively!" Outler was often heard to say, "There are still antinomians walking around loose—very loose!"

The General Conference supported Outler with a chorus of applause and votes.

Outler did not touch on the problem of AIDS in that speech because *that* was not the issue at hand and also because that particular problem had not reached the epidemic proportions that were to come later. A part of a paragraph written in an April 2, 1987, letter from him to R. W. Younts issues a succinct warning statement on the subject: "Our ignorance about AIDS is embarrassing and scary, but this much still seems clear: AIDS may or not be a *homosexual disease,* but it is one (may be the worst) of the fruits of sexual *promiscuity* and of reckless drug use. Any church, therefore, that condones homosexuality and other forms of promiscuity is aiding and abetting (even if without deliberate intent) the worst plague that humankind has seen since the Black Death in the 14th century. What is more: we have hardly seen the 'first act' of a looming tragedy that is all the more demoralizing in a society that trusts medical technology and the virologists more than any ancient code of sexual morality. The Black Death was spread, as we know now, by *fleas.* AIDS, as we already know, is spread by *human* body fluids, and by aberrant acts. We have not begun to understand what this may do to the further demoralization of a decadent society. But all this is lost in a process where zeal has driven out reason, and I've grown tired of arguing with the zealots on both sides."

Further comments concerning homosexuality came in an April 12, 1982, letter written by Outler in rebuttal to United Methodist Bishop Wheatley's well-publicized statements on the subject: "The first point for United Methodists, of course, is the statement in *The Discipline* (par. 71). I know what it meant, because Harold Bosley and I wrote it, in Atlanta, in 1972. It says nothing about homosexual *orientation*; it speaks explicitly (twice!) about homosexual *practice*. What we had in mind was the analogy between homosexuality and adultery, fornication, incest; there are strong 'orientations' (inclinations) in those *cases* too (biogenetic?); they cannot be controlled by law or resolution. But their practice can, to some extent, and ought to be controlled as far as possible. This passage in *The Discipline* was passed by a large majority in 1972 (after a weird debate), retained in 1976 (after the most depressing display of confusion I have ever experienced in any General Conference), and then reaffirmed, without change, in 1980. If I were vowed to uphold and implement the decisions of the United Methodist General Conference, (including some I have disagreed with), I would think that this particular passage is as clear a mandate as any. If bishops are to ignore *The Discipline,* we are in for more and more disorder in the church by other people who regard their 'own sweet wills as heaven's will, too' And there goes the ball game— 'connexionalism,' the Social 'Principles' and so on.

"Bishop Wheatley's argument seems to amount to this: (1) Homosexuals are persons (right!); (2) deserving of respect, compassion and their civil rights (right!). But then: (3) Compassion toward homosexuals includes understanding them (right!); (4) understanding them opens the way to condonation (wrong!); (5) condonation involves acceptance of homosexuality as an alternative lifestyle (wrong!); (6) Advocacy of homosexuality as an optional Christian lifestyle (wrong!). Finally, (7) homosexuals are 'gay by birth, not choice'—and this, too, is wrong. By the same general argumentation, he could legitimate ministers living in adultery (provided, of course, it was 'a meaningful relationship,' since heterosexuals are as prone to adultery as homosexuals to promiscuity). It would also legitimate *any* practice allegedly rooted in genetic predetermination—including incest and promiscuity.

"As for Bishop Wheatley's appeal to 'authority,' it is shockingly amateurish and one-sided. He speaks of his 'authorities' as 'biblical scholars' (none is, except in the sense that you and I are); all are militant advocates of militant homosexuality.

"The upshot of it all was summed up by an excellent psychiatrist here [Dallas] with whom I work as 'theological consultant' and whom I asked about the *current* state of the question: 'Homosexuality is not a *single* psychiatric entity; it is a syndrome or spectrum of psychological aberrations. It rarely sustains long-term relationships (five years is the statistical maximum) and is, therefore, a modality of sexual promiscuity. A minority of biologists—and fewer psychiatrists—regard it as biogenetic or congenital. It is now harder to treat than ever, since it has become a politicized issue. The churches are not helping us much!'

"You realize that I have begun with the psychotherapeutic aspects of this problem—and its place in the larger tangle of problems generated by the phenomena and mysteries of human sexuality. *That's* where it roots—and our present hopeless confusion (as incarnate in Bishop Wheatley) stems so largely from leaving scientific questions in the hands of well-meaning amateurs.

"But the doctors cannot *settle* moral and spiritual questions. They can warn us, though, against being trapped in the 'gay by birth and not by choice' slogan—since all the biologists I know who advocate biogenetic predetermination of sexual orientation include it under their larger principle of biogenetic predeterminism as it applies to the *rest* of the range of human options. Thus, they flatly deny 'free will' in any meaningful moral sense (e.g., the socio-biologists and the behaviorists). The majority view is that we are 'hardwired' for heterosexuality, soft-wired' for sexual aberrations. It is, therefore, 'culture that makes the difference' (to them).

"There is also the entry into the [Reformed] *Encyclopedia Judaica* ('Homosexuality'): 'Whereas the more liberal attitude found in modern Christian circles is possibly due to the exaggerated importance they accord the term 'love,' Jewish law holds that no *hedonistic* ethic, even if called 'love,' can justify homosexuality, any more than it can legitimize adultery, incest, or polygamy, however genuinely such acts may be performed out of love and by mutual consent. And it would be rash (anti-Semitic) to contend that the Jews do not understand their Bible and the law and that we can correct them both!

"Now, given all this, I would like to see the question pondered in terms of our United Methodist Church's 'fourfold standard' of doctrinal judgment (Scripture, Tradition, Reason, and Experience). I have probed the efforts of certain biblical scholars and amateurs (many of them homosexual!) to line Holy Writ up for the gays—and have been over the commentaries (including Käsemann on *Romans*—the lexicons and the social history of the biblical world). Result: those who argue that the Bible regards homosexuality as an allowable option deserve more credit for ingenuity than probity (the evidence for this would take a long paper) and those who ignore the correlation in all the ancient civilizations between homosexuality and decadence are one-eyed or blind. Then, there is the plain fact, that in the Christian tradition, from St. Paul to Karl Barth there is no condonation of homosexuality by anybody, even where 'compassion' is the pastoral rule. Wheatley is in the exciting position of having discovered what no Christian generation before his ever dreamed of—and of being right where *all* those old fogeys were wrong. If that were not tragic it would be amusing; but it hurts me when I laugh!

"As for 'Reason', two crucial points may be made. Point one: The bulk of the evidence points away from genes and hormones to 'culture'; what harm is 'caused' by 'culture' must be 'cured' by culture. Point two: Homosexuality is a form of *promiscuity* and any church that condones *homosexual practice* is well on the way to condoning sexual promiscuity in general, including incest. And let's face it: incest is the next taboo to be discarded in the name of freedom and consent. And in every age where the church has made alliance with moral decadence of any kind, it has been infected by it. There is no more bold a *graffito* on history's walls than this one!

"The question of 'Experience' is difficult to formulate, but its import is clear. The testimony of United Methodists to the overall superiority of conjugal love, fidelity and mutual support in old age over homosexual liaisons is overwhelming. Some of the older homosexuals whom *I* have known (including at least one in Bishop Wheatley's bibliography) are having a bad time of it in their old age—or have died graceless deaths. This is not just a chess game with words and concepts: it is an arena of agony and tragedy. Homosexuality is a profound problem; nobody is helped by its sentimental approval, even by church folks! Homosexuals deserve the best the church has to offer— but that does not include approval of overt or militant practice. For United Methodism to become inclusive by embracing *sexual promiscuity* of any kind is to insure its doom (a just one, too)."

Outler referred to these let-it-all-hang-out "antinomians running around loose—some very loose! as . . . *avant garde,* who are *avant,* maybe. But *garde,* no!"

Writing It Down and Discarding It

Prophetic statements by letter or orally given by Outler were carefully handwritten (mostly on yellow legal-sized pads), corrected with rephrases and words more to the point, and then typed for delivery. Some were painstakingly written and not delivered. The wastebasket caught many such speeches. He wrote them down, vented his thoughts and feelings on paper, and discarded them. Oftentimes it turned out to be not the time nor the place for his interpretive utterances.

Something happened in the North Texas Conference that triggered this strong voice of conviction: "Mr. Chairman, I beg the privilege of the floor of this house on a point of urgent and high personal privilege." [Chair: "State your point."] "If it is at all in order, I desire to state, quite briefly, why I propose to withdraw from this Conference and from the United Methodist Church. If it is not permitted that I do so here and now, I can do it later and elsewhere. Mr. Chairman, I find that *what* this Conference has just done (and the way it has been done), is literally intolerable: both to my best judgment and to my Christian conscience. My judgment tells me that this action is disastrous and that it opens the way to further disaster. I do not, however, insist upon my judgment; many of you know very well *that* has been overruled before and I have only grumbled. But in this case my conscience is involved and it tells me that what you have done is morally *wrong* (wrong before God and his moral law). And it is never safe for a Christian to ignore or evade a deeply offended conscience—his own or any others. I do not wish to argue the point: I merely state my reluctant, but deeply pondered conviction.

"I was born into the Methodist Church; I've never had any other church nor ever expected to seek another unless it were an enlargement of this one. It is, therefore, a shattering experience to find myself convinced that I can no longer live and work in what this church has now become in good conscience, or to defend this action of yours, even in ambivalent terms. I feel shattered by the prospect of severed ties with so many men and women whom I have loved and labored with—and I do not now see my own way ahead. I leave you, however, without rancor—only with an overwhelming, tragic sadness that a church, that has been known to invoke John Wesley, could have done what he would have been unable even to comprehend, much less approve.

"Parting words are all too often either banal or bitter. Mine are meant to be loving, even if also heartbroken: 'Father, forgive them—for surely they cannot have known, really, what they have really done.'"

It is not known what was done (or about to be done) that caused this speech to be written. But for the good health of the church (whose pains were bad enough already) it was never given. The United Methodist Church needed Outler, and still needs to heed his warnings and counsels. Whether written and delivered or written and discarded, Outler's speeches oftentimes fell within the genre of the Old Testament prophet Amos: "I hate, I despise your feast days, and I will take no delight in your solemn assemblies. [This was not a nice thing for Amos to say in their solemn assembly.] But let judgment roll down as waters, and righteousness as a mighty stream."[277]

Frequently Outler would write people asking their opinions of papers before he gave them. But in these extreme cases of getting it off his chest nobody was invited to critique his statements. In some instances he wrote letters or speeches, put them in envelopes, and stamped them for mailing. But never mailed them. He discovered the good habit of "sleeping on *it*" and then sometimes putting *it* to sleep. Sometimes he mailed the letters and made the speeches.

In his strongest judgments, written (sealed or sent) or spoken, Outler's statements were sharp but not peevish. Where he could, Outler avoided petty controversies and acrimonious disputes; but when these arguments were raised to a level where they threatened some good cause, with a sense of abandonment Outler bore in with the truth as he saw it. Some words were understood; some were not. But they always came together in such a manner that his audience felt he knew what he was talking about. And their answer, if they had an answer, could not match the wit and sarcasm bathed in a sea of intelligence that had nailed them to the wall.

Doctrines and Prophecy

Tied closely to Outler's judgments upon issues and ethics was his Wesleyan understanding of doctrine. The doctrinal essentials (as dogma), i.e., original sin, prevenient grace, repentance, justification by grace through faith, regeneration, and sanctification (spelled out in the Nicene Creed) translate into a faith experience (the Wesleyan *functional* doctrine) that in turn makes biblically grounded judgments on what is right and what is wrong. This salvation process is more than a compelling of people to be just. It is more than assenting to a given set of orthodox doctrines. (When one merely assents to its validity, orthodoxy remains dead.) The Devil knows the great beliefs of orthodoxy. The Devil knows *about* grace, *about* faith. But the Devil knows no grace, no faith. Outler spoke his convictions concerning issues out of his expansive knowledge/experience.

He often cried "Pelagianism!" whenever he saw people attempting to save themselves. "Liberals, turning to Wesley's stress on moral character, lapsed into Pelagianism without knowing what it was they were lapsing into by title, but rather liking it by substance."[278] Once *they* decided what was morally right (what *they* wanted), they devised all kinds of arguments and ways to achieve those goals. Pelagians choose their own lifestyles and find arguments *they* choose to justify their actions. *They* choose the scripture they want and twist it to fit their choice; *they* choose (fantasize) a tradition that leaves them comfortable; reasoning amounts to self-justification; and skewing experience by choosing and acting according to convenience. They, too, claim the faith experience; but it is faith in a freedom of their own making.

One can see how natural a thing it was for Outler, and Wesley before him, to condemn doctrinally the immoralities of Pelagians on the one hand and the let-it-all-hang-out antinomians on the other. Outler acknowledged his precarious position in these words:

"When the historian and analyst turns prophet, he is skating on thin ice. But we ought, because we must live on it."[279] His skirmishes within the larger Christian community (the Second Vatican Council, ecumenical councils, United Methodist Council of Bishops, etc.) gave him moments on the thinnest of ice. Every now and then it looked as if he might go under. But after awhile he would come huffin' and puffin' and saying something like: "Never has any power on earth or hell been able to extinguish the divine fire of faith which the church has always cherished."[280] Thus were the sayings of Outler, the historian/analyst, and the ice-skating prophet.

Patron Saint: St. Sebastian

Now one can see how it was that Outler's patron saint was St. Sebastian—the saint whose picture is depicted as having arrows lodged in him from all sides! Outler said: "Arrows on the right and left. That seems to me to be where theologians ought to be. If most of his arrows are from the front, then he has been charging too hard; if most of them are in the back, he's been slow on the uptake; if he has any from the right, it ought to be mildly offensive to the left—he gets punctured all around. This is not, I think, a masochistic longing for scars. It's just that I avoid trouble when I can; when I can't, I don't."[282]

There are those who continue to shoot arrows at Outler (in spite of the fact that the proved scholar is not here to fend for himself). Strange as it may seem to the reader, *that* would be totally acceptable to the "grand old man of Methodism." What would bother him, however, are those aiming their arrows at him and totally missing him because they are aiming at something that is not there. What they "hear" Outler saying was never said by him at all. They work from a basis of complete misunderstanding. And yet they by God's providential grace serve a good: They bring attention to the doctrinal dilemma that faces the United Methodist Church. And to the perspective that Outler offers as the premier John Wesley historian/theologian of this century.

This commitment to the truth as he saw it, regardless of what people thought about it, stayed with Outler all his days. No matter the stance that Outler took, he could not fend off the arrows of criticism coming from all sides. He was always willing to let people know *where* he stood. It was up to them first to find the target and then to hit it.

Outler's Last Prophetic Stand

Outler was never one to back down from the challenge of addressing bishops of any ilk, but he did not always get the response he was hoping for. He addressed the Council of Bishops in the late 1970s in Boston. He told them that the United Methodist Church was in the midst of an identity crisis and it was their task to help the church find its heritage through their teaching role. He came back very disheartened: "They didn't hear me—they were playing to the reporters who lined the room, saying there was no crisis and that their primary role was the appointive role."

Richard Heitzenrater had it right when he said: "Such occasions did not diminish his subsequent attempts to be heard in and by the church; but because of who he was and how he could cast a spell on a crowd, not everybody always heard exactly what he was really saying. [In his] last speech at Lake Junaluska [he was] chastising the present generation of United Methodists for not taking the Wesleyan doctrine of the Holy Spirit seriously; projecting dark consequences for the denomination, not only with conviction but also with the typical Outler smile, humor, hesitance, and grace so that nobody really heard the bite of the message or noticed the blood dripping from the denominational banner in the corner. He received a standing ovation, everyone smiling at hearing the 'great man' speak, while he himself was trying to wipe away the tears of grief over the tragic vision he had just projected of his beloved church."[282]

Outler was a theologian who as a prophet represented a combination of which there were few, if any, superiors in his day.

A Bridge Builder and a Prophet?

The question has to be asked: "How can a person be a bridge builder and a prophet at the same time?" These two callings represent precisely who Albert Outler *was*. It was the moment, the situation, that called forth the appropriate response from him.

If the moment called for a persuasive argument to bring sides, ideas, opinions, or persons together, the man's thought processes, wit, and charm worked wonders. But when the moment called for a proclaimed commitment to the truth as he understood it, a torrent of judgment would fall upon his hearers. He never confused unconditional love with unconditional approval. Grace allowed him to love the sinner but not the sin. Thus he never attempted to build bridges for sin but for sinners who were open to God's justifying and convincing grace. The roles of a bridge builder and a prophet were compatible in his being, according to what he was called *to be* at the time.

16

He Was a Churchman

This biography has borne out the fact that Albert Outler's home and workplace was, as he suggested, the *church.* What did he mean by "church"? The story has been told in these pages. Always his church was evangelical, reformed, and catholic. He insisted that these emphases function as one experience. While he recognized the expressed evangelical faith to be the essential ingredient of Christian experience, he would not allow any one of the three to reign exclusive to the other two. This resulted in a Christian witness with fewer distortions.

Outler brought this Christian witness to the academy as well as to the organized church. His life affected those institutions in ways that he had never planned. He felt at home in those workplaces because he was where God wanted him to be.

Abhorred Triumphalism

Outler never lifted up denominationalism. He abhorred triumphalism in any shade or shape. What he meant was that he carried into any situation *his own* tradition, understanding, and experience of the body of Christ. This put him at home with the church fathers as well as the church bureaucrats of his day. There were agreements and disagreements with all of them. He co-mingled with them in his workplace. While John Wesley was his mentor, he felt free to take on Wesley when his own understanding pushed him to that point. But he did it as a "think and let think" Methodist. On the essentials of the faith Outler with Wesley held steady. This thoroughgoing ecumaniac always tried to make it plain that, beyond the dialogue, all Christians shared a common essential faith tradition.

The Academy and the Local Church

While a February 3, 1960, article in *The Christian Century* was written in his mid-career, it sums up his church involvement for a lifetime: "In 1949 I was on the faculty at Yale and pastor of the Methodist church at Wallingford, Connecticut. It was an arduous and vastly stimulating situation. It signified that I wanted to be in close touch with the life of the church, to fill out my understanding of the Christian tradition and the contemporary world, and to work out a theology on historical foundations. Presumably I could have done this as well at Yale as anywhere else. But like many another Southerner who 'left home,' I was feeling a strong pull to go back—to help with the development of theological education in a region where Protestantism was still vigorous and to work directly with the churches through a university set down in their midst. The call to Southern Methodist University in 1951 seemed to provide such an opportunity. So we moved, though not without a few backward glances in the course of the early years. On the whole it has turned out rather as we had hoped.

"In this new setting I have become a more loyal churchman than I was before without ceasing to love *academia* one whit the less. I think I am as critical as ever of the churches' failures—of nerve, of wisdom, of vision. Certainly I am still distressed at the stale, flat and unprofitable business that often goes by the name of Christianity in all too many places. But I have also found an opportunity to work for something different and better within the churches themselves and to help with the training of ministers furnished for the future with the resources of the past. Moreover I have discovered more authentic life and power in the churches themselves than even the pious critics ever see. The residence of the Holy Spirit among the people of God is still a reality—and this has given both promise and hope, even in the midst of discontent.

"This closer involvement in denominational affairs has had the effect of strengthening my commitment to the cause of ecumenical Christianity. I know now that the way to unity does not lie in the aggressive reassertion of our respective virtues or the recombination of the separated members of Christ's body. If it comes at all, it will be through the mutual discovery and affirmation within the separated churches of the common Christian history which we share as Christians."[283]

Through this first person witness Outler reveals how he brought Christian traditioning to the community of scholars and students, and how those experiences in turn went out to the churches through preachers in ministry. He was at home in the academy because it offered him a workplace that permitted him to hold together human culture and high religion. In that sense the church *was* in the academy.

The Kingdom of God: His Home

Outler could never be accused of being enamored of an authoritarian bureaucracy or hierarchy of any church, including the United Methodist Church. While he was elected as a delegate to six General and Jurisdictional Conferences, and contributed greatly to the dynamics of those bodies, he did not hold some of their highly charged politicized agenda with high regard. (That sometimes evoked the man's righteous indignation akin to wrath.) For Outler the church catholic was not a pyramid but a network, a network of souls living under the power of grace. They made up his *home* wherever he was in the world.

Outler bared his soul in those church situations that oftentimes resembled more the kingdoms of the world (power over people) in their actions than the kingdom of God (the power of grace). He worked in those places because he wanted to improve his home; he could not stand by and permit some evil force destroy his home; he worked to make the church exemplify the kingdom of God. *That* was his lifelong quest. *That* was his home. He was always at home with the faithful of the church. He *belonged* there. And he worked to maintain the integrity of the institutions that claimed to be the witness of God's kingdom. This all amounts to a very complex look at the church that was his home and his workplace. But it fits the makeup of the man.

PART 4

A
Retrospective

A Retrospective

While moving from community to community with his itinerating Methodist preacher father, Albert's home was their Young Harris cabin nestled in the mountains of north Georgia. His summers there as a boy provided him with visions of a world far beyond what he could see at the time. Curiosity pushed him to know more about what was "out there." Early on, from as far back as he could remember, his Christian faith was his taproot within the kaleidoscope of human culture. The energies for such probings came from an insatiable curiosity and a restless drive to more faith toward understanding without losing the sense of the sacred, encompassing Mystery in which he lived and moved and had his being.

Albert, a Special Project

That insatiable curiosity and restless drive was awakened to a large extent by the efforts of his sister Fan, who herself had it and passed it on to Albert. All of the Outler children were challenged to be their best by "The Little General." In a September 20, 1982, letter to her niece Helen Lankford (daughter of Jason Outler) Fan wrote: "Mama had a phenomenal memory, but in order to tell anything, she had to go into every detail, so that she

417

could never reduce anything to a passing reference. I guess I have a good memory like hers; but Albert has the curse of total recall from her. I always said we should never ask him what time it is if we didn't have time for him to explain how a watch is made! The works! Mama's infinite and boundless resentment of the various parsonage committees that oversaw our lives down to the last detail makes for very harsh, very vehement voicing of her loathing of being patronized by well-meaning, meddling biddies, and the result is a great deal of rancor. She did not share Papa's sunny disposition; they really made an odd couple. The capacity to show affection was zero in mama; and yet, she would speak kindly of me to someone else. I suppose she was afraid I might be spoiled, more than I was. It took me a long, long time to realize that I never would succeed in getting a 'well done' from her; but it broke my heart back in the years when a kind word would have made a difference—We are fearfully and wonderfully made, *n'est-ce pas*?"

All her life and past her life in this world, Fan was Albert's foremost teacher. In a September 10, 1985, letter to Donn Gaebelein, president of the Westminster Schools in Atlanta, Albert apologized for his not being able to attend the September 16th dedication of the Frances Outler Memorial Room. He enclosed a musing for the school officials to use as they wished. The middle paragraph of that writing says as much about Albert as it does about Frances: "It was often said of Frances Outler that she was 'a born teacher'; that very well may be. What I can vouch for, at least, is that when she was eleven and I was four, she singled me out as a special project—later, I would learn that all her students were special projects!—and continued as my domestic tutor till she went off to college. Thereafter, of course, I had many other teachers (a few of genius class) but none better than she at what I came finally to learn for myself is the quintessence of good teaching: the kindling of the love of learning, the shaping of consciences forever discontented with mediocrity, the arousing of delight in every sort of excellence."

Albert *and* Carla

Against the advice and consent of their local bishop, Albert and Carla set out to explore the further reaches of scholarly study at

Yale, not in psychology of religion (as he had first intended), but in patristics (made possible by the bonus of his Wofford education in classics). The words, "Albert *and* Carla," are used intentionally. She was the stabilizing influence in his life. The following quote from a May 10, 1957, letter from Princeton is typical of dozens of comments he made in letters to her: "In this [the problem at hand] I'll need your help—your help in understanding, in absorbing my irritation and hurt feelings when things go wrong, your help in doing some of the tasks of scholarship and your help in turning what free time we have into real re-creation." Carla described her role in these words: "We are a very middle-class family. It is for me to keep the wheels of the machinery of our lives oiled."[284] And she did—even when he did not ask for it! The practical wisdom of Carla had a sobering effect on Albert.

Diverse Influences

The decisive influences on Outler at Yale were as diverse as Robert Calhoun (an unpublished genius and incomparable mentor) and two other great scholars more widely known: Roland Bainton and Erwin R. Goodenough. Outler's dissertation, "Faith and Reason in Origen," was a particular angle of vision on a perennial problem that he continued to probe through all the years, in various contexts and different perspectives.

Outler took seriously the teachings of those about him who had something worthwhile to say. This included family, friends, theologians, whoever. It is an ontic fact of life that, to some extent, one takes on the characteristics of those with whom one associates. Just as surely as Albert took on his parents' and Fan's orientation toward life (strong-willed, intellectually bent, their manners and personal charm), his "friends," the books, talked to him out of the past and influenced who he *was*. One can read his comments about Origen, or Augustine, or John Wesley and see that, in fact, in some instances he was giving descriptions of himself. A reading of these men's lives reveals that his comments about them were valid expressions of the truth. Colleagues and friends of Outler verify that indeed some descriptions by Outler of these giants who traditioned the church can easily be seen in the demeanor, ways, beliefs, and habits of Outler himself. He did not pattern these great men after his life, but *they* influenced who he was *to become* in this world. An unveiling of a fairly accurate portrait of *their* thoughts and actions comes in the viewing of the life of this grand old man of the church, Albert Outler.

New Directions

Yale Ph.D. in hand, Albert headed back home, to South Georgia, expecting a pastoral appointment. This was refused by that same bishop whose earlier advice had been ignored. Thus, forced into teaching as a substitute for the pastoral ministry long-intended, Outler found himself teaching at Duke. As he tells it, "vanity" won the battle of the mind as he later accepted the invitation to return to Yale as associate professor in theology and then promoted to Dwight Professor of Theology. However, after six years, still concerned with the challenges of ecumenical scholarship in a denominational seminary (somewhere in the Sun Belt) and attracted by the academic vision of Umphrey Lee and Merrimon Cuninggim, he and his family headed for Texas and the brand-new quadrangle of the Perkins School of Theology at SMU.

Local and Regional—the Cocoon

Outler sensed keenly his movement out of the cocoon (his word) of Methodist triumphalism into the wider world of the church catholic, out of biblical and racial bigotry into a world more tolerant of those unlike himself. But the geography cocoon of the South offered him a comfort zone that stayed with him all his days. He traveled the world and was cosmopolitan in many ways, but his perch remained in the South.

In the beginning, the horizons were local and regional; then they were focused on humane arts and letters. At Wofford, he was trained in classics and English literature; and at Baxley he was aide to Caroline Miller in the writing of her Pulitzer Prize-winning novel of 1930, *Lamb in His Bosom*. Another horizon came into view while he was engaged in pastoral ministry and writing his B.D. thesis at Emory on pastoral counseling, a new and fertile field at that time. He was bred to an interest in "Western civilization" before that became a staple in college curricula. Then came a chance encounter with H. Shelton Smith (Duke), who opened up a new and still wider horizon: the adventure of a

Yale *graduate* education. He distinguished himself as a renowned historical theologian at Duke and Yale.

Outler's Final *Pied-à-terre*

At SMU, over and beyond the adventures that came with the development of a "new" School of Theology in the midst of rapid social change in the region and in the face of a vigorous entrenched denominationalism, there were always the excitements of global horizons of the ecumenical movement in its golden years. Outler was caught up in them.

Texas turned out to be Outler's *pied-à-terre* for wider explorations than before. In 1952 he went to Lund, Sweden, as a Methodist delegate to the Faith and Order Conference, and thereby began a thirty-year stint of service with Faith and Order, the World Methodist Council, and COCU. It was Perkins that made possible his attendance as a Methodist observer at Vatican II at the invitation of the World Methodist Council; Perkins helped support his work on the Wesley *Sermons* right up to the time of his retirement in 1979.

Wanda Smith

Any mistakes found in Volume 4 of the Wesley Sermons can honestly be hung on Outler. Before the book went to press, the last galley passed under the scrutiny of perfectionist Albert Outler and the well-trained eyes of his efficient secretary, Wanda Smith, who worked with him on the project. The adjective "efficient" is used to describe Wanda because *that* was the only kind of secretary Outler could put up with or who could put up with him. Outler was a perfectionist and nothing less than a secretary of that same bent could satisfy him. Other secretaries had come and gone in tears. From the beginning they were afraid they could not make the grade. And most did not. "We could not please him," was their complaint. And they really could not. They simply could not do the job that his tedious work demanded.

Wanda sympathized with their dilemma. At times she wondered if she could handle the pressures. Especially was this so in the beginning years with him. As time went by in her research for Wesley notes, she developed her own expertise in Wesley studies—to the point that Outler looked upon her as a partner and colleague. When one listens to those dozens of audio tapes with notes to be typed, one realizes that an unsung hero in the Wesley Works project is Wanda Smith. Outler realized this and made a gesture of appreciation toward Wanda when in 1984 he contributed $250 in her name to the Restoration of Lovely Lane Church in Baltimore, making her a member of the Francis Asbury John Goucher Society.

He wrote in a February 10, 1988, letter to her: "One of the few regrets I have from that remarkable collaboration of ours (and a lasting embarrassment, because I could do nothing about it) was the pittance that you received from SMU for a demanding job that you did so faithfully and well, over and beyond the call of duty.

"You may recall that one of the 'arrangements' made by the Editorial Board was that recompense for the unit editors was to be fixed at a uniform rate of a thousand dollars per volume. Now that the *Sermons* unit is finally published, my part of the project is over and done with—with fond memories of the excitements and rewards we had in the doing of it and with fading memories of the hindrances and aggravations that turned it into a nightmare before it was over. As of now, I don't know which I dread most: reviews that will zero in on its shortcomings, or the 'friendly' silences of perfunctory reviews that will 'damn the whole project with faint praise.'

"At any rate, the honorarium for Volume 4 came a couple of weeks ago, and it occurred to me that it might help a little if you and I shared it. There is, of course, no question of recompense, nor even a 'gift.' It just occurred to me that, on your next adventure or so, this sharing might make 'something extra' possible. That would please me very much.

"Just as Carla will remember all those chalupas, so I will remember all those chores that we managed between us and the friendship that sustained it all and that has survived. Thanks, therefore, and all the best!"

A Summary of Outler's Affair with Wesley

In a January 10, 1989, letter to Randy Maddox, Outler sums up his affair with Wesley in these words: "As you may know, I had never set out to study Wesley (I am a patrologist by training and trade, and a historical theologian by experience) and I began to take Wesley seriously *as a theologian* only after having taught the history of Christian thought for twenty years at Duke, Yale and SMU. He had always been easily and naturally 'located' as a minor figure between such folk as Baxter, the Turrettini, Jonathan Edwards—and, on the other side, the Enlightenment Protestants, like Schleiermacher. Finally, on a challenge (by the Editorial Board of *A Library of Protestant Thought*) I began to read Wesley seriously (in the atmosphere of a Faith and Order Study Commission that included Jary Pelikan and Georges Florovsky). And I began 'hearing things' that sounded like and unlike the early Eastern 'fathers'.

"The question of Wesley's readings of patriotic *texts* is, as I came to see, 'undecidable,' in any rigorist sense; his 'Letter to Conyers Middleton' would get a failing grade in any patristics seminar. For example, how can it be 'proved' that Wesley had absorbed the participation anthropology of Gregory of Nyssa? But *if* Wesley *was* one of the 'ante-Nicene Father redivius' (Kenneth Rowe's jibe at me), many of the anomalies in his theological comments make sense—and they illuminate many of his controversies (from both sides). And it would also illuminate Wesley's Christocentric notions of grace and his *trinitarian* pneumatology. If, therefore, Wesley's 'scriptural Christianity' has an Irenaean (or 'Eastern') anthropology, a Cyrillian Christology and a Cappadocian (or Alexandrine) soteriology (*metousia theou*), he *is* an interesting theologian who has something to offer our theological future now looking *beyond* the past three centuries. If not, he really was a minor character in the epoch that is already on its way into eclipse.

"At any rate, and as a historian, I have found *Methodist* theology, in general, boring and mediocre. As a historian (and in my personal *agon* for faith, hope, and love), I have found *Wesley* a real refreshment, and still do."

The Baker/Outler Battle

The Baker/Outler battle that waged midst the Wesley Works Project, as uncomfortable as it was for both men, illustrates once again that scholars need the redeeming grace of God as much as (and in some instances more than) ordinary folk. The nature of scholarship is to be picky, picky, picky. Those inclined in that direction tend to make better scholars. The more picky they are in perfecting their work, the better the work. Scholars of the stature of Outler and Baker are *blessed* with an extra portion of pickiness. In their cases neither would allow himself to be out-done by the other in this *blessedness.* An italicized *blessedness* signifies another catch-22 situation—the scholars needed to hone in on the fine points of their evaluations, but how far could they go with their *digs* without maligning the other's character? In both instances a move to either pole would have weakened the emphasis they represented.

In order to get the best possible results of their labors a chairman, Bishop Cannon, was assigned to mediate the two men's positions. Neither got all he wanted; neither was totally pleased with the outcome, but both were grateful that the monumental Wesley *Sermons* task was finally accomplished.

But Was It Worth It?

But was it worth twenty years of his life? Would scholars take seriously his work with the Wesley *Sermons?* That was Outler's nagging concern until the end of his days. The answer to that question varies according with whom one talks. Some say "no"; some say "yes." But there are signs that indicate the winds are blowing favorably. The sales of the four volumes of Wesley *Sermons* have exceeded the publisher's expectations. In fact theologians of other denominations are taking a hard look at Outler's catholic John Wesley.

Church of Christ historian Everett Ferguson acknowledges that "one of his [Outler's] *most enduring* scholarly contributions will be the critical edition of the *Sermons* of John Wesley for the Bicentennial Edition of *The Works of John Wesley.*"[285] And then there is presently at least one prominent Roman Catholic theologian, Francis Frost at the Ecumenical School at Bossey, Switzerland, whose specialty is John Wesley. A Roman Catholic John Wesley scholar who liberally quotes Outler in his lectures! It is highly probable that there are and will be other non-Methodist theologians who will make it their life's primary work to study the "folk theology" of John Wesley. To no small degree that will be due to Outler.

The jury will never come in with a verdict that will please every scholar on this question posed by Outler: Would scholars take seriously his work with the Wesley *Sermons?* But has any jury on any question ever offered a verdict that pleased everybody?

How Is Outler Remembered?

Strange as it may sound, if John Wesley's sermons are read and studied and utilized as sermon material, the context will be ecumenical. *That* was the way Outler "read" John Wesley. Wesley belonged to the church universal (catholic). There is no doubt that Outler wanted to be remembered by the church catholic for his editing of the Wesley Sermons.

The question remains: What was the contribution that Outler wanted the United Methodists to remember? That answer came in a September 9, 1977, letter to Fred Maser who was creating an Outler entry for a revised edition of the *Dictionary of Western Churches.* Outler wrote: "Within our own denomination, I'd hope to be remembered for my work as chairman of the Theological Study Commission on Doctrine and Doctrinal Standards (1968–82)—and its contribution of Part II to the 1972 and 1976 *Disciplines.* Time will have to tell how useful that document is, but it could have an influence on the theological climate in the UMC over the next generation, if taken seriously."

That Commission statement included doctrinal *pluralism,* meaning "more than one." This did not mean for Outler that all doctrines were equal. They are not. Some are *essential* such as scripturally grounded grace. Then along came John Wesley who preached *prevenient* grace. Initially *prevenient* grace was his *opinion.* After awhile he and his followers believed it so profoundly that it became a hallmark doctrine of the Methodist movement. It became an *essential* doctrine. But then there were many other *opinions* that he gave the church to *think* about, e.g., convincing grace, accompanying grace, etc. Those *opinions* fall into the category of *theological pluralism,* having not yet reached the importance of meaning that would warrant *essential doctrine.* It is out of diverse (*pluralistic)* theological *opinions* that the status of doctrines is reached. What one church body may deem *essential,* another may not. Other groups have their own *essential* doctrines.

This doctrinal *pluralism* is tolerated until a heresy arises. And then, as Outler said, "The fat is in the fire!"

Outler, as Wesley before him, implored people in their thoughts about salvation not to depend upon their mental assent to the best-phrased orthodox doctrines available. But to depend upon grace that gifts God's people with faith.

Outler was emphatic in saying that this understanding of doctrinal *pluralism* has nothing to do with an intolerable doctrinal *indifferentism.*

And how is Outler remembered concerning his doctrinal statement? We are well into the "next generation" and can see that what Outler did as chairman of the Study Commission has been taken seriously—seriously enough to cause the denomination to study it, and consequently to come out with a statement that will provoke debate for years to come. Outler's work has given reason for rank and file United Methodists to think about doctrine. What he has done influences not only "the theological climate in the United Methodist Church over the next generation" but will continue over the next and the next and the next.

Outler's Place for Sermons in Worship

It was interesting to note in the editing of Outler's sermons on various occasions (in the first three volumes of *The Albert Outler Library)* that he oftentimes lapsed into the same mode of sermon writing as John Wesley; he also neglected listing his sources.[286] Yet there was a motivational difference between the two men; Wesley published his sermons for his preachers' use; Outler never intended publication in the writing of his sermon "notes" (the term he used to describe them).

Preaching, for Outler, was an effort in aid of vital worship and of an inward understanding of the Gospel's meaning and power in a given group at a given time and circumstance. Those who knew him best agree that, while he rarely took himself seriously in his sermons and lectures (that anxiety usually came before and after his presentations), he always took God's self-communication in Christ with utter seriousness. To a great extent this accounted for his preaching on the New Commandment text (John 13:34) more than any other. It is a text that fit well within his favorite theme—the grace of Christ in one or another of its aspects. His understanding of grace began and ended with the Holy Spirit as the immanent giver of grace in the human heart, the church, and the world. That was the heartfelt power of the reasoned judgment found in his sermons.

The Holy Spirit

With this picture in mind one can understand why it was that the old hymn "In the Garden" was not one of Outler's favorites. He would paraphrase it irreverently: "And he walks with me and he talks with me, and he chuckles me under the chin!"[287] Views of God like this would prompt a thirty-minute lecture on how people are misled into a false sentimental relationship with the divine.

While Outler admitted he did not understand the mystery of the Holy Spirit, he knew who the Holy Spirit is, and he was sure the Holy Spirit does not stagger beside us like a tired servant or act like a pal in a buddy system. Any hint of mushy sentimentalism regarding the Holy Spirit sent Outler up the wall. Gratitude to God for bringing alive the spirit of Jesus Christ through his Holy Spirit—that attitude gave him a sense that the gospel light was dawning. For him the Holy Spirit is the Giver of life! Lord of life! Guide and Consummator of life—the agent of God's goodness in creation.

Aversion to *His* Systematics

Outler's aversion to writing his own systematics (while he expertly taught the systematics of others) came early in his career as he studied patristics. "He was never interested in writing a systematic *summa theologica,* and would have been incapable of producing a balanced digest of his multifaceted teaching. Thus, if he is to be read wisely, he must be read widely—and always in context, with due attention to the specific aim in view in each particular treatise." This quote sounds like a comment *about* Albert Outler. Rather, it is Albert Outler referring to St. Augustine.[288] In continuing that theme Outler *did* say this in an August 18, 1975, letter to William Cantwell Smith: "For Wesley, all authentic religious knowledge is intuitive; he speaks of our 'spiritual sensorium' and of 'sight' and 'assurance'—since divine reality is radically mysterious—and all honest religious language is apophatic. There is a paradox here, for Wesley was also a Lockean empiricist with respect to the finite creation and he was an Aristotelian logician by trade. This is why you can get the term 'doctrine' used to mean 'teaching' (its Latin root) and 'opinions' to mean 'speculative interpretations,' both 'propositional.' But when you ask him what are the essential Christian truths and their necessary linguistic forms, he comes back at you with a bewildering series of 'doctrinal summaries'—all nearly alike but all different, too. There is method here; he refused to write a systematic theology (conceptualizations have a tendency to say 'absolutely' when one means 'on the whole'; 'totally' when one means 'generally' and 'precisely' when one means 'nearly') and chose instead to publish a series of sermons as his 'little system of divinity'—knowing full well that the sermon, as a literary genre and a logical form, is not chiefly 'propositional' but 'persuasive.'

"For the same reason, he strikes off *aphorisms* in place of closely reasoned arguments—and they are meant to generate insight rather than to supply proof (which is the main point, in the Aristotelian view, to propositions set in order). That oft-quoted (but seldom analyzed) aphorism of his about 'thinking and let think' was always linked with 'opinions' and by opinions, Wesley always meant theories, 'doctrines,' interpretations which are not absurd and yet which have never been settled in the Christian mind in the course of Christian thought. His favorite example of this was 'predestination,' but in his mellower moments included transubstantiation.

"And although Wesley has the typical 18th-century views of 'Mohametans,' he refused to exclude them (or anybody else) from the 'extraordinary grace of salvation' if they did what was 'in them' according to their highest lights: *fac quod in se est* and all that."

Readers of Outler will note that there were no *systematically* planned presentations from him, but rather that his thoughts were *coherently* expressed in numerous essays. In no way did his *coherent* theology advocate disorganized theology. Outler expressed it this way: "Saying the first thing that came into your head may be all right. But having said the second thing that came into your head without thinking about the first thing that came into your head is not all right at all. This axial theology organizes and makes coherent rather than systematizes and makes things neat and slotted. It opens up a lively conversation with other theologians in terms of dialogical accommodations rather than rivalry or a factious church search for that one true theology—that one elusive theological holy grail."[289]

Outler defers to St. Augustine in finding words that describe the wonder and mystery of the apophatic approach (as over against the nitpicking eyeglass approach of *systematizing*) of talking about those axial scriptural themes that have to do with God. One begins to understand Christian mission in the world as one is "speaking out of the vision of God and out of the inspiration of the Spirit and out of his grappling with the problems and the frontiers of and horizons of Christian life."[290]

"This [apophatic] is the theology that tries to take the mystery of God with utter seriousness and stops short of platonic ontologizing. . . . the kind of theology that works with language as if it were inherently inadequate for conceptualizing any fundamental and completed truth about the Godhead. And this is the theology that refuses to take the mystical plunge and stays within the brackets of the rational analysis of problems and the liturgical response of the rhetoric of worship."[291]

When Outler said, "All religious language is apophatic," and then proceeded to make use of that language in his essays and sermons, he was in the mode of the early church fathers. Rather than systematizing their thoughts *about* God, they dealt with the mystery of God through silence, meditation, parables, prayer, liturgy, and expressions of longing, despair, hope, and ecstasy. Outler read the Bible and the early church fathers with an ear to the hearing of faith. And spoke to the issues at hand with the faith language of his sources. And it made sense to his hearers.

In this catalytic approach to theology (where his reaction was accelerated by a response to a revealed truth), Outler arrived at his presentation by praxis (the practice of *doing* theology rather than speculating *about* it). Yet what he had to say was reasonable. "The Bible is obviously not very good at systematic theology. But we get pretty good at making a systematic theology out of an unsystematic theology of the Bible without noticing that this may not have been what the Bible had in mind."[292]

Coherence was a reasonable process for Outler. But what made his particular *coherence* palatable was the manner in which he spoke his reasoning. As a speaker he was sometimes aggressive and energetic in making his argument, sometimes emotional in his apophatic utterances, always inspiring and persuasive. It was not merely his fast-moving southern accent that captured his audience; it was the particular Southerner who spoke in a manner that his audiences appeared to understand because *he* was the medium of the message. Even his Latin, or Greek, or Hebrew, or German, or French (that few could interpret) was accepted and appreciated by the ordinary audience because Outler was saying it. His speeches, carrying a matchless felicity, an intuition and insight, and a power to use these gifts to the required heights of passion and inspiration held audiences spellbound.

Another Bridge-Building Episode?

Theologians for the last four hundred years (since the Reformation), including those surrounding and continuing past the life of Outler, have produced "systematic theologies." Will Outler build a bridge between those and the coherent theologies of the church fathers and the Bible itself? Only time will tell. If indeed that does happen, he will be recognized in that role as one of the great ones in the history of theology.[293]

Was He Liberal or Conservative?

A question often asked about Outler is, "Was he liberal or conservative?" In the context of a note he wrote and passed on to a friend in Bradenton is found an answer, not to the either-or question, but to who he *was* in his Christian witness. (The statements at the end of each paragraph, revealing my evaluation of who Outler *was,* will be bracketed): "There is an *attitude* that can be called 'the *liberal spirit*' : i.e., of open-mindedness, and tolerance, of confidence in free and critical inquiry. Wesley called it 'catholic spirit,' and has a sermon with that title. 'Liberal,' in this sense, is a priceless value. Its main instrument is *persuasion,* rather than the force of law. [In this sense Outler was liberal.]

"There is also an *ideology* that wears the same label, 'liberal,' the claim that human beings hold their destinies in their own hands (with or without 'God's help'). Liberals in this sense profess that human well-being is their chief concern and that the chief instrument for achieving this is the force of law (civil or ecclesiastical). The theological presupposition (where it is not wholly secular) is called 'Pelagianism.' [In this sense Outler *was not* liberal.]

"Evangelical has an equivalent double meaning. In classical Christianity it has pointed to 'the evangel' as the heart of 'the Christian gospel,' i.e., 'salvation by grace through faith' in Christ alone. Its chief interest is Christocentric and often (though not always) with the doctrine of substitutionary atonement. [In this sense Outler, without substitutionary atonement, was evangelical.]

"There is also an 'ideological evangelical' who insists on one or another rigid and doctrinaire 'scheme of salvation,' 'the primacy of Scripture' (ranging from proof-texting to a doctrine of inerrancy), the memorialist view of sacraments, and a political view that 'saved souls will save society.' [Outler *was not* evangelical in this sense.]

"Finally, 'fundamentalism,' in American church history, has had a connotation of bigotry, intolerance, along with a fondness of legalism. Many 'fundamentalists' sincerely believe that if they and their political allies controlled government (national, state, and local) they could 'make America a Christian nation.' [Outler in this sense *was not* a fundamentalist.]

"Historically, 'the fundamentals' have been that core of indispensable beliefs 'by which the church either stands or falls.' The classic summary of these fundamentals, accepted by most churches in one way or another is the so-called Nicene Creed. The exact formulation of 'the fundamentals' may vary; their essence is necessary for a community of believers to warrant the title 'Christian.' This is what Wesley meant by his repeated dictum: 'As to all opinions *that do not strike at the heart of Christianity,* we Methodists think and let think'. [Outler in this sense was a fundamentalist.]

Was Outler liberal or conservative? The answer is neither "yes" nor "no"; it is both. And more than either. He was evangelical, reformed, and ecumenical; always *fundamentally* Christian in his *coherent* scholarly reasoning. This can be seen in this non-crowd-pleasing statement: "But in this either/or process—'saving souls' or 'liberation'—what has gotten short shrift is the original impulse to, and authority for, missions: the heralding of God's kingdom and the effort to understand and live by the parabolic mysteries of the Rule of Grace . . . if 'evangelicals' understood the real meaning of grace and the Rule of Grace, their soteriology would not be so narrow and otherworldly. If 'liberals' understood the meaning of grace and of the Rule of Grace, they would not put so much of their hopes on secular aims and strategies."[294] This judgment pronounced upon "evangelicals" (conservatives) and "liberals" leaves him clearly outside the narrowly defined label of either. He had seen how those who sported labels in too many instances perverted the gospel they so earnestly wanted to present.

Think and Let Think

Outler was willing to think and let think, but he would not let others think they were thinking right when in his heart he knew they were thinking wrong. In conversation and in writing he frequently targeted persons playing well outside the bounds of orthodoxy as *Pelagians:* "Pelagianism is now more loosely and pejoratively used by some to designate any view which champions *freedom of the will*, or rejects the doctrine of original sin, or argues that guilt can only be properly attached to a free and conscious act."[295] In Outler's way of thinking, "God is love" (1 John 4:8), "God was in Christ, reconciling the world unto himself" (2 Cor. 5:19), "For by grace are you saved through faith; and that not of yourselves: it is the gift of God" (Eph. 2:8), etc., were essential doctrines that gave meaning to *his* faith experience wherein his practical application of witnessing became the most "essential" doctrine of all—a *functional* doctrine illuminated by the presence of the Holy Spirit. Outler espoused doctrine not *about* God (as important as those doctrines may be; and they are important!) but *of* God's active presence in the Person of the Holy Spirit (the witness without which the crafted essential doctrines lie lifeless on a piece of paper).

God Help Us!

This mix of properly well-defined, carefully crafted doctrines and the witness of the Spirit (*functional* doctrine) can be seen in this humorous aside Outler used in a sermon/lecture: "One tall Texan, whom I think was genetically determined to have been a Pelagian, came by one day to complain that I sounded as if human sinning were something deeper and more mysterious than a lapse of will or a moral failure. He was interested in such a strange idea and asked about suggestions for further reading. At the time John Whale's *Christian Doctrine* had just been published. So I mentioned that. To his very great credit he tackled Whale. But then was back again, still more baffled. For Whale was much more of a Calvinist than I have been. After some further talk about this business he delivered himself of a real outcry from the heart that I shall always remember: 'Well,' said he, 'if we don't have the power to decide to sin or decide not to sin, then all I've got to say is, "God help us!"' This of course was a sort of obvious cue to point out that he had just betrayed himself into involuntary orthodoxy."[296] The man realized that if one as knowledgeable as Outler was a sinner, it was truly a matter of "God help us!"

Knowledge and Experience Important

In the majority of these encounters with Pelagians or whatever antinomian stripes they might represent, Outler relied upon his understanding and experience of Wesley's "doctrine" of prevenient grace with all of the attending functions of grace, i.e., justifying grace, convincing grace, sanctifying grace, accompanying grace, etc. as the *theological* reasoning that more adequately explains the *essential* doctrine of grace represented in scripture. "Think and let think" implied that doctrinal collision need not be lethal. It was meant to be helpful midst doctrinal differences. It definitely was not synonymous with "it doesn't matter at all what one thinks." Rather it was a matter of doing the best thinking one can manage in order to counteract less-than-adequate thoughts from those whom one has "let think." It meant for the Pelagians "think but don't think you can get by with what you are thinking!"

The Matured Scholar

One can sense the Spirit *growing* Outler into a mature scholar. His earlier letters (Yale days) indicate an insecurity when he was in the presence of some of the great theological giants of the church. He constantly saw himself less than what he was in the minds of others, including scholars. While his works were of highest quality in those pre-Vatican II years, in his own mind he doubted. In a May 10, 1957, letter to Carla from Princeton he wrote: "SMU is not going to become a great university in my time; and I am not going to become a great theologian in spite of SMU's mediocrity. So I must find a satisfying and rewarding role that does not rest on either of these two as preconditions. It'll take a bit of doing—and a lot of help and understanding from you and my friends." He said this at the time that his scholarly career was about to blossom and bloom into one of the most popular scholars of this age. In the post-Vatican II years Outler's concerns about his place in relation to the giants faded. He ceased to talk about the matter. (For a while he was too busy dealing with Baker!) When he did comment, he spoke as a responsible critic.

In his later years while Albert Outler was no longer intimidated by the *greats*, he would never in his lifetime put himself up to the level of the Florovskys, the Tillichs and the Niebuhrs (though Reinhold Niebuhr named Outler *the* Methodist theologian of this century).

But whether he was a *great* theologian or not is not in his (or anybody else's) province. But it is in the hands of "history," which is to say "God" because the true history (whatever that is) is written by Truth, which *is* God's nature. Who impacted the ecumenical scene more than Albert Outler? He blazed a trail for all denominations, which, in his words, are already "together" in the common experience of salvation by grace through faith. *That* is our common tradition. In this trail-blazing role he may be more widely known than any other.

Never Tutored a Graduate Student in Wesley Studies

Through his Wesley Sermons Project Outler gained the reputation of being the foremost scholar on John Wesley. While some Wesleyan scholars would challenge that statement, not many would challenge that Outler was among the most proficient of that elite few. Outler counseled many graduate students as he read and critiqued their doctoral theses. With all his other irons in the fire, Outler, while choosing not to take on a single graduate student in Wesley studies, accepted the role of unofficially becoming a tutor for many graduate students studying Wesley. AFTE scholars can attest to the invaluable deliberations they had with Outler regarding their doctoral research.

Outler's Pilgrimage

Seen from the outside, the course of Outler's pilgrimage seems to have been a meandering one—from one-room rural churches to ecumenical lectures in New Zealand and Australia to reading a Scripture lesson to the Pope and assembled bishops of the Roman Catholic Church (during the closing ecumenical service of Vatican II, in the basilica of St. Paul's-Outside-the-Walls in Rome), to a seminar with four Nobel Prize-winning scientists at The Isthmus Institute in Dallas (on "Science and Religion"), to "A Thanksgiving for the Children of Abraham," in the chapel of Thanksgiving Square (Jewish, Christian, Moslem), to shared services with the Dalai Lama on the occasion of his visit to Dallas.

On these myriad occasions this "walking encyclopedia" (a term given him by his associates) seemed to be able to throw at the listener more than one could ever digest on nearly any subject chosen. Dean Joe Quillian once approached Outler and inquired about an incident that occurred in the fourth century and then added, "But please, Al, don't tell me any more than I can bear while standing on only one foot."[297]

Zan Holmes did not have to stand on both feet as he sat by Outler as both were delegates at the 1972 General Conference in Atlanta. Holmes said, "I sat next to Dr. Outler for two weeks during the General Conference, and I got an education in world history, ancient history, anthropology, and parliamentary procedure. He is unreal."[298]

Outler's audiences will always remember how these utterances were laced with wit and penetrating humor. One Roman Catholic executive in Dallas once remarked about Outler, "I'd walk across town to hear him read the phone book."[299]

Outler would never let one forget that all these far-flung horizons were all linked to a single center: his Christian faith, and its interactions with whatever human context in which he had found himself. He *believed* it all happened by that Providence "whose grace is over *all* God's works." His explorations into history always had a religious focus, as also did his interest in arts and letters, in contemporary science, and in its chief secular interface, psychology.

This incessant and unfolding dialectic between Christian Gospel and human experience gave a certain integration to Outler's mind and heart in the somewhat "disorderly order" (to use a phrase of Wesley's) of his career.

Faith and Christology

Crucial for Outler was the *essential confession* of the Christian faith experience, brought dynamically alive in the presence of the Holy Spirit. "This is a confession of Mystery and *designata,* not a doctrinal statement in the strict sense. It acknowledges the Mystery of God in Christ, but it does not provide a theoretical explanation of any problematic correlate of that Mystery. It is more apophatic than analytic. It is better suited to remind believers of their common Lord than to aid them in a dogmatic construction of a Christological doctrine."[300]

"Faith, at bottom, is a divine gift; Christology, at its best, is still a human enterprise,"[301] an enterprise that began in the first century. "It is no accident that the notion of heresy arose *before* any firm notion of a mature 'orthodoxy' was nuanced. What happened was that the mainstream of Christians went about their business until somebody came up with a divergent view that stretched beyond their elastic limits of diversity; and not until *then* was there a ruckus. As a matter of fact, the church got on fairly well for a full century without a canonical New Testament, without a creed or confession, without official norms of teaching until heresy arose and had to be walled off. The canonical New Testament is the church's defense against a heretical canon; the Apostles' Creed a defense against outlandish formulations by the Gnostics. Official norms of teaching had to be identified over against the false ones or those *so-called.* And in each case, the crucial function of the creed or the teacher's self-binding rule of faith was to affirm and also to safeguard the New Testament paradox [the full deity and the full humanity of Jesus Christ]."[302]

The full deity and full humanity of Jesus Christ was settled for Outler and the church in the Council of Chalcedon (451 A.D.). Few were as expert as he when it came to knowing the ins-and-outs and ups-and-downs of the happenings of that council. And he knew it. This was evident in the following statement from an April 18, 1957, letter to Carla from Princeton where he was the Visiting Senior Fellow, Council of Humanities: "Everything here is pretty much as I left it. The Council meeting this afternoon featured a report from Carl Hempel—and it provoked some very lively discussion. My turn comes up on May 15th and since I'm speaking on Chalcedon, it's unlikely there'll be very much of a hassle. Most people don't know Chalcedon from a hole in the ground—and could hardly care less. But the ones who brave it may find in it a good deal more than a theological brawl."

Outler's Christ? "My commitment is a simple and personal one. For me Jesus Christ is the wholly adequate and indispensable revelation of God to man. . . . His patient and penitent disciple can look at life's illusions and realities and mark the shadow and the substance."[303]

Striving Toward Orthodoxy

The striving toward "orthodoxy" began with a first-century Christological dispute and continues in every age of history as divergent views (theologies) stretch the elastic limits of diversity. When those divergent views are perceived as doctrines, the heretical viewpoints are confronted with an "orthodox" confession of faith, where the Holy Spirit does the justifying, causing the half-truths of heresy to fade away, only to come back again in another form on another day. There is no room in doctrinal pluralism for a heretical doctrine. (When I asked Outler about the "Sophia" phenomenon that was beginning to make its way in the late 1980s, he said: "That is goddess worship." Those who lucidly reasoned that Sophia was God, and prayed to "her," failed the crucial Christology test.) While the dynamics of this Spirit-filled confession (witness) face the heresy at hand, diverse ways of expressing "orthodox" beliefs (doctrinal pluralism) continue full steam ahead—until once more the elastic limits of diversity become just too much for "orthodoxy" to put up with.[304]

Both terms, "doctrinal pluralism" and "diverse doctrines" (including the words in these paragraphs) are being used to describe the one *essential* experience of the Christian faith—God in Jesus Christ was and now is, in the presence of the Holy

Spirit, reconciling the world unto himself. That mysterious *essential* faith experience is laid out as an *essential* doctrine of the church that the church never ceases to deal with as a theological problem. When it comes to *how* by grace God justifies, *how* God sanctifies, *how* God does all that God does—for Outler, and Wesley before him, it was "think and let think" (doctrinal pluralism). But just let somebody go too far, and the "orthodoxy" quest will lunge forward with spirited debate and rout the heresy.

Throughout his life Outler continually strove for more adequate expressions of his Christian faith, but he was not tied to a lifetime of trying to defend a *systematic* statement made years ago during other situations that did not necessarily speak to his present world. This accounted for his sometimes challenging those claiming orthodoxy. He never questioned their sincerity; he questioned their tunnel-vision view of their claims. It was not so much a matter that they *couldn't* think of more adequate ways of expressing their beliefs in the unfathomable mystery of God in Jesus Christ, but a matter that they *wouldn't*. Their way of talking about God was *the* way and there was no other. They were stuck on trying to get others to think their way; Outler was stuck on trying to get them to think.

His Need of an Agenda

Outler seemed to have an agenda for every occasion. Richard Heitzenrater recognized this at the 1982 Oxford Institute: "He [Outler] and John Munsey Turner (British scholar) co-chaired the working group on Wesley Studies (ten-day conference with daily working-group meetings, plenaries, a concluding session with reports). He mentioned to Turner after the first meeting that they should go to his room to talk about the final report. ([Isn't it] a little early for that?) ACO had a draft prepared already [with the explanation]: 'When you start into things like this, it's always good to have some idea of where you are going.'"[305]

As one reads the life of Outler, one sees a mind full of agendas always at work. He saw where the situation was; where it needed to go; and set about using his influence to get there. He would talk with participants privately but never deceitfully. On occasion he was known to release his agenda well in advance of a meeting. *Ecumenical Review* (April 1952) published his essay,

"Agenda *for* Lund." In his mind he would not be doing his job properly if he did not use all his wits and energies to persuade his colleagues to go the direction he felt they ought to go. This approach was at work in his bridge-building efforts, was a part of his prophetic utterances, of all the conferences of every bent and color.

Yale's Jaroslav Pelikan

Yale's Jaroslav Pelikan pointed to this agenda-setting aspect of encyclopedic-minded Outler's *modus operandi* with these words: "My own association and friendship with Albert Outler came out of two projects that also were not 'necessarily harmonious' [this quote within a quote came from the previous paragraph of Pelikan's letter referring to Outler's 'solid grasp of the several facets of . . . life, including patristics, psychotherapy, ecumenics, Wesley studies, the theoretical foundations of higher education']: (1), the 'Commission of Tradition and Traditions' of the Commission on Faith and Order of the World Council of Churches; and (2), the Editorial Board for *A Library of Protestant Thought,* published by Oxford University Press.

"To the first of these Outler brought his conviction—'intuition' may be a better word—that behind and beneath the varieties of Christian teaching and experience there does lie a shared tradition/Tradition that is longer and deeper, and that in the discovery of its resources lay a path or *the* path to 'the unity we seek.' By a mixture of the 'non-directive counseling' techniques he had learned from the psychotherapists, wide reading, and sometimes non-stop monologues from the chair, he cajoled and led the Commission to some rather far-reaching conclusions. I shall always be grateful to this project because it brought me closer to Father Georges Florovsky, who became my πατηρ πνευματικος."

Pelikan's "spiritual father" was also Outler's. This common respect for their mentor in the faith made for a unique friendship between these two scholars.

"The *Library of Protestant Thought* involved some of the same people, including Sydney Ahlstrom and me, but also several scholars who did not have even nearly so close a tie to the organized churches. Here it was Outler the encyclopedist that prevailed, with some of the same techniques, especially the non-stop monologues and free association. He seemed as a generalist to have read everything that each of the others had read as a specialist, and he tied things together in ways that were sometimes baffling but never dull. The volumes of that set were the work of many hands, but his fingerprints are all over them."[306]

Outler came to meetings prepared. Sometimes fireworks broke out in the process of give-and-take as they worked toward a stopping place or a consensus, if possible. Whether from the chair or the floor, to the consternation of some and the delight of others, Outler had an agenda with which to work.

The Rule of Grace

The common faith experience has been the bond for the church, inside and outside organized churches, through the centuries. And, thanks to the efforts of Outler, his colleagues in the faith, and the pioneers of the faith before him, it is finding its way midst the fabric of human existence through the healing ministries of pastors, psychotherapists, and other committed people of God. Faith proves to make *the difference* wherever it appears. "By grace through faith" was the "little red wagon" that Outler pulled and pushed whenever and wherever he could. His unfinished manuscript, *The Rule of Grace,* unveils those highest and most important thoughts on his mind at the time of his death. Its thesis: the kingdoms of the world exhibit the pecking order of power-over-people through threats, intimidation, and coercion. The kingdom of God brings a different kind of power midst the powers of the world—the power of grace, the power of persuasion through faith *working* by love (Galatians 5). This persuasion in one's heart allows one, when the need arises, to rebuke or refute; and is used by the Holy Spirit to convert. The Rule of Grace is over against any rule of self-interest. Outler's heart was made heavy by this observation: Too often the church repels its Spirit-led power by mimicking the powers of the world. As a church historian he knew all too well those times where corrupt leaders have initiated violence in the name of God. He warned his hearers to watch for anyone who drags theology into a scheme of coercion.

And he warned those who enjoy exercising their power over people of the nemesis of the power they express. Those who have been dehumanized by such abuse of power (by lying, betraying, humiliating, etc.—all efforts to subdue and kill the spirit of those dominated) will have the last word for those who have lorded it over them. With calmness they will reflect just how much of a nonentity the former power broker in the end has turned out to be. Their faithful resolve in the face of spirit-killing power plays by those in authority will prove to have sustained them. ". . . the body they may kill;/God's truth abideth still;/his kingdom is forever."[307] Grace carried for Outler a strength that an intimidating power could not penetrate; and *that* frustrated and diminished the threats of the power brokers.

A "Last" Setting for Proclaiming the Word

As Outler's physical life on earth was reaching its lowest ebb in his last days, his spirit in the faith (by grace) stayed busy probing the mysteries of that faith and enjoying the contentment that faith brought to him and Carla. At the invitation of the World Methodist Council, Outler preached at Lake Junaluska two sermons on "World Methodist Sunday—A 250th Anniversary." The title for the morning was "World Methodism's World Parish—Then and Now" and for the evening "The Measure of Greatness" (both in *Albert Outler the Churchman* in the *Albert Outler Library*).

A November 22, 1988, letter to me illustrated this mental/spiritual posture: "Here is a copy of that second sermon for Lake Junaluska on 'World Methodist Sunday,' last July 10th. Unlike the commemorative sermon, this one tackles one of the profoundest wonders that I have been pondering for more years than I can remember: how God is truly sovereign, as he must be—else our faith is in vain—and how his sovereign grace allows for human defiance (as both biblical and secular histories attest to) . . .

"As you would understand, this effort to probe the paradox had an obvious 'occasion': i.e., the eve of a Jurisdictional Conference. In the congregation that night there were *seven* men who were about to be elected United Methodist bishops and dozens more who were hungering and thirsting so to be! But the most touching comment of the evening came from my old friend, Bishop Bill Cannon. 'Albert, I found myself admiring this morning's sermon; I found myself convicted tonight!'

"In any case, it was about as much as I had in me to bear witness to and maybe it belongs somewhere in the files, and so I am sending it along." Outler had seen too many times in his life where "good" persons had been elected bishops and had lost *their* grace in the process and ultimately became failures in their highest moments of "success." And then there were those plodders out there in the boondocks who never got "up there" and yet were grace-full in serving God and humankind. This sermon (one of his last) took out of Outler "about as much as I had in me to bear witness to"; which indicates how important he felt the subject was for the good of the United Methodist Church.[308]

Apocryphal Stories

Apocryphal stories are told about persons who are not the ordinary run-of-the-mill variety, about those with unusual talents and traits. *That* was Outler. And that is why apocryphal stories will continue to be told about him and why they will be believed. Outler was *that* unusual. Tall tales are told about him. But I have found that, by going back to the sources of the stories told, one will find that, more often than not, they can be verified as essentially true. Apocryphal stories began to create an Outler legend long before the story of his life was completely told.

Dying Happy

Some have said that Outler was a better John Wesley scholar than John Wesley *was* a scholar. The study of Wesley, and the tracing of his sources, proved to be one of Outler's most fruitful and rewarding (and at times the most disappointing) of all his explorations. He said: "If at all possible before I die, I hope to convince a fair number of able people about this conviction of mine—about Wesley being an interesting theologian as over against being an eponymous hero.

"What is interesting in him is not merely the fact of his popular impact. There were people in his time who were as popular as he, and there were people who were better preachers than he. And I don't think it was the organization that made the thing tick as much as it was the message.

"That message is quite unique. It is rational and coherent, but not a systematic way of understanding and expressing the Christian faith and the vision of the Christian life. If that is so, then he deserves better than he has had from Methodists on the one hand and non-Methodists on the other. If that's not so, then I have wasted thirty years.

"Can I convince enough competent witnesses, a large enough jury, to see Wesley as a competent theologian?"[309]

A Fund for Theological Education

One can see now why it was that Outler was so genuinely pleased during his last days about the creation and growth of AFTE (A Foundation for Theological Education). He was seeing dozens of Wesley scholars spreading their versions of John Wesley as a theologian. He saw with his own eyes how John Wesley was being understood as a theologian. He saw his desire fulfilled. In an August 24, 1987, letter Outler said to Ed Robb, Jr., "to see AFTE take root and grow into an entity in its own right and with its unique identity is one of the relatively few parts of my career that I can look back on with a lively sense of 'love's labors' *not* lost." Outler died a happy man knowing that his investment of thirty years of his life with John Wesley was not wasted.

The Outler Legacy

Outler preached a bold message while he held a modest view of himself. With full knowledge that he never *attained* the perfection he preached, Outler continued *to be* himself under the grace he preached. He knew that grace through faith redeemed the good he would do even when it did not sound so good to those to whom he was doing it, and that it was up to history to place him where he belonged midst the giants of his day. He recognized how fleeting was fame and popularity in one's present existence. In his last days he said: "Tillich could excite a sizable audience in any university in this country. Tillich was already beginning to be turned off in the last years of his life at the University of Chicago. And was greatly puzzled by it. I recall a conversation that he and I had with Langdon Gilkey. He said that he was sort of being tuned out by the young and wondered why. All the comfort Langdon could give him was that he [Langdon] was, too. This is a miserable thought of solidarity. I am prepared to swim against the stream, though my arms are getting tired and my breath short."[310]

Outler knew that he would never be another Florovsky. It would bother him if the thought ever occurred to him that he could! Such was his respect for his mentor. This deep awareness humbled him. In that awareness he was possessed by a humility that was not of himself alone; it was the gift of God. Outler, warts and all, lived under the rule of grace. He talked, taught, and preached that the role one plays in the experience of salvation is the hallowing of life. In that graced context he practiced what he preached.

Albert said: "The time for the theological titans may come again, and we can trust the Lord to raise them up for us in the fullness of his time. Meanwhile, the whole lot of us, great and near-great, right, left, and dead center (like myself), have the task before us of refocusing our theological spectacles or regrinding their lenses so that the Word of God may be seen and proclaimed, truly heard and believed, understood and explained, confessed and lived. . . . [Yesteryears' old haunt of "standing in the shadows" of theological giants had no place in Outler's later years. By this time he knew that God had done his thing in this little Appalachian boy's life, and he was content with *that,* whatever *that* happened to be.]

"I have no serious ambition to be a theological pacemaker and no serious expectation of affecting the theological climate of the future. But because I am deeply convinced that Christology is one of the 'new' questions in our time—yet one of the perennial issues in the history of Christian thought—I have been trying to gain a historical prospective on the Christological tradition in the hope of being able to speak a word about it to the theological parade that is passing before our eyes. . . .

"The next crop of geniuses will be thrown up out of a new situation fashioned from a different template, in which the modes of theological work will seem bound to be a sort of interregnum. We stand, then, at or near a threshold of a new age where the theological future is even more open than usual, though less predictable than at any time since this terrible and wonderful new century began."[311]

This modest view of himself in no way indicates what God ultimately has in store for Outler's theological contributions. In fact that modest view of himself means that he has passed the first test of being recognized as another great one in the theological life of the church. Those who think they are the greatest will never be—except in their own minds. This much we know: Outler has left a rich legacy for the church in its ministry to the world.

Who Are Outler's Apologists?

One wonders if Outler's doctrinal and theological contributions with their different functions will withstand the onslaught of critics. Who will be his apologists? We do know that some who never knew him personally are greatly influenced by the life and teachings of the man. Randy L. Maddox, professor of Religion and Philosophy at the University of Sioux Falls in South Dakota, says this about Outler: "While I never had the privilege of studying under Albert Outler in the direct sense of that term, my own work as a 'Wesleyan theologian' [not an AFTE fellow] has been profoundly influenced by his writings and his impact on the academy. Central to this impact is Outler's rehabilitation of Wesley *as a theologian*. Outler helped broaden the renewal of Wesley Studies beyond its initial historical focus. He taught us to place Wesley in his theological context in a way that Wesley could be recognized as engaged in serious theological activity throughout his ministry. More importantly, Outler himself came to an increasing recognition that Wesley's *model* of theological activity had positive value that could serve to call into question the current reigning separation between academic theology and the life of the church.

"Outler also was central to moving the initial renewal of Wesley Studies beyond the agenda of showing how 'Protestant' Wesley was, helping us to see in Wesley a potential mentor in helping bridge the longstanding split between the Christian East and West. In short, Outler framed out the basic agenda upon which I (and many others) have been seeking to build: to return to Wesley's model of theology pursued in integral relation with the life and practice of the Christian community, and to press forward exploring the potential of Wesley's distinctive 'balance' of the central themes of Christian teaching."

Randy Maddox represents a group of young scholars who have latched onto Outler's John Wesley and are expanding on those directions pointed out by Outler. Maddox and others of his bent assure that the Outler flavor in Wesley studies will not be lost.

Disciple Bible Study

The lifelong experience of being sought for life's new ventures dramatically took place in regard to Outler's involvement in the *Disciple Bible Study.* It started with shaky beginnings. Bishop Richard Wilke, who along with his wife, Julia, have coordinated and designed the *Disciple Bible Study,* tells this story: "Dr. Outler was one of the key advisers . . . After Julia and I had prepared twenty-five principles for *Disciple*, a consultation was called at Flower Mound (an Episcopal retreat center near Dallas). It was made up of about twenty-five consultants. Dr. Outler was one of the speakers. And as you can imagine, he spoke quite a bit."

When time came for the Wilkes' program to come together, Bishop Wilke said to the project's editor, Nellie Moser, "Be sure and get Dr. Outler to do a video."

Nellie Moser called one day and said, "Dr. Outler refuses to do a video."

Bishop Wilke replied, "He has to do a video. He is *the man,* of course." At that point, the following telephone conversation ensued:

Wilke: "Dr. Outler, we need you to do a video. This is a key part of the biggest thing in the twentieth century."

Outler: "Well, Dick, I just can't do it."

Wilke: "Why can't you do it?"

Outler: "For two reasons. One is they want me to do the authority of the scripture in nine minutes. I take the Perkins students, spend six weeks, three hours a week, talking about the authority of the scriptures. And they want to give me nine minutes. It's impossible. Can't be done."

Wilke: "What is the other reason?"

Outler: "Well, the other reason is: I am scared to death of that camera."

Wilke: "Dr. Outler, you speak to tens of thousands people for an hour and hold them in the palm of your hand!"

Outler: "Well, I am afraid of it. That is a medium I never worked in."

Wilke: "Well, I will help." [At this point Bishop Wilke laughed at himself and said to himself, "Me! Help Dr. Outler!" He was shocked at the thought of what he had just said. But it was the push Outler needed.]

Outler: "Well, Dick, if you will help me, I will do it."

Then came the day for the video filming. Bishop Wilke described the occasion: "It's Nashville, Tennessee—the television lights and cameras all around. And here is Dr. Outler coming in with his notes, page after page, written over, scratched on the side. Oh no, we are in trouble, big trouble. Outler said, 'I've got it down to twenty minutes.' Which meant he had about sixty minutes plus anything he added.

"The technician said, 'We are going to put that camera on your [point to me] shoulder and we are going to let you ask him questions.' That was the first time I had heard about this. Frankly, I did not know what I was going to do. I got over in the corner and wrote some really brainy questions like: 'Dr. Outler, why do people read the Bible? How do people know what is truth in the Bible?' etc. Those were my brilliant questions. Here were the cameras about to roll, powder being put on the face, and Dr. Outler with his notes. Zan Holmes introduces the occasion and I said, 'Dr. Outler, we are so glad you are here. This will be fun for us to talk. Why do people read the Bible?' Outler laid down his notes and began to talk, and looked at me eyeball to eyeball. Because of the camera position on my shoulder, it looked as if he were looking into the camera. When Outler finished talking about the greatness of the Bible, the mystery, he came alive with these words, 'And that is just Amazing Grace.' And now he is in heaven and 450,000 people have seen that video, and at this time [1998] the audio on the video has been translated into German, Cantonese, and Mandarin with more languages to come."[312]

Julia Wilke spelled out what Outler accomplished in *Disciple* with these words: "The Bible shows us where we are without Jesus Christ. It is this human condition. Wherever you are in your life today, you ask, 'How can I handle this condition? What does the scripture say to the human condition, whatever it is? What does the Christian do?' Dr. Outler's answer was not one of determinism (where God does it to you), but where God transforms you by grace through faith."[313]

These examples of God's providence in Outler's life through the *Disciple Bible Study* have become the examples of God's providence in the lives of hundreds of thousands. And more people are finding it so every day.

How Will It Play Out?

Will this Outlerian influence continue to grow in the years ahead into a general acceptance of Outler as one of its main players on this particular stage of ferment and change? And how much of what he has done and has to say will remain and for how long? Since he based his life intrinsically upon an ecumenical understanding of the faith, will he become a primary spokesman to and for the whole church? Will Presbyterian theologian John Leith's following observation become a viewpoint generally accepted? "There is no one I know in American theology who is today the equal of Albert Outler in knowledge, theological sensitivity and wisdom, and in faithfulness to the great heritage of the Christian theological tradition. In one sense, Professor Outler's intentions were modest. He did not set out to write the great new theology [a new *systematic* theology]. He did set out to be a faithful and responsible interpreter of the Christian tradition in the context of contemporary culture [*doing his theology* and making it *coherent*]. In fulfilling this intention he has no equal."[314]

Will Outler's emphasis on *coherent* theology with its *apophatic* utterances become a bridge builder between the titans of *systematic* theology (Tillich, Barth, the Niebuhrs, et al.) of his earlier days and the titans of some future tomorrow? If his Wesleyan approach of *doing theology* in a manner that makes it *coherent* catches on, *that* very well may vault Outler into his own unique position as a titan in his day.

The list of questions goes on: Will his "psychotherapy and the Christian faith" message be accepted as the grounded foundation that has eluded the various psychological theories? Will his self-diagnosed Sisyphus syndrome, which allowed all the great stones of good causes he managed to nudge so near the top of so many rueful hills finally be broken? For these questions there are presently no answers. Only time will tell.

Signs of the Times

But the signs of the times indicate that his interpretation of the doctrinal standards of the United Methodist Church are getting an ample airing out. The attacks made on them by unsuspecting critics are unwittingly helping his perspectives become better known. And his Theological Task section of the United Methodist *Book of Discipline,* the first official statement of the denomination formed in 1968 by the union of the Methodist and Evangelical United Brethren churches, has piqued the thin skins of theologians who feel as if they have been slighted by the audacity of a church accepting one theologian's word without their input. From all accounts at the present time, the rancor they are causing serves only to promote the four guidelines that Outler coined *Quadrilateral.* He admitted that the misunderstood coined word may very well be dropped, but the four guidelines are undroppable; they are simply there. They may be rejected, but they will always be there to reject. The paradox is obvious: The arguments against them serve to spotlight the truths of them.

The Difference One Man Makes

Outler often said, "If John Wesley had retired at seventy, we would not have the Methodist Church today." If Albert Outler had actually retired at seventy, the healing ministries, the United Methodist church—indeed, John Wesley's theological vision of the world church would not have the quality of renewal being experienced today. Look again at the faith direction Outler gave psychotherapy, the effect he had upon Vatican II in the sixties, the "traditioning" effect he had upon the world church through decades of involvement in the Faith and Order Commission of the World Council of Churches, the bringing to light the folk theologian John Wesley through Wesley's *Sermons,* and the sobering effect his paper on the "Constitutional Crisis Of the United Methodist Church" had on the 1984 General Conference at Baltimore. The truth cannot be denied: the Holy Spirit has used Albert Outler in giving the United Methodist Church, as well as the church catholic, direction for his day and for years to come.

The Glorious Mystery of the Man

These pages have hopped, skipped, and jumped through the life of Albert Outler, told the story of a dilettante, and gone behind the scenes to look seriously at the person. Yet they have not come close to capturing the mystery of this complex man. But more is now known *about* the man by the general public than was once available. I hope that the picture of Outler in these pages reveals both the mysterious and the commonplace in the man. For one who was so down-to-earth in his relations with others, his mind and spirit reached far beyond what ordinary (and even extraordinary) people could comprehend. The essence of the man can best be known and appreciated by those who know the Spirit who moves *graciously* in all of life and who in a particular way moved in the life of Albert Outler.

Prayer Too Deep for Words

The Holy Spirit, moving in Outler's prayer life, oftentimes left him speechless. He shared with humankind the inability to know precisely how to pray. He knew, through his own inarticulate groans and stumbling speech, the Spirit pleading on his behalf. God, who knew the secrets of his innermost heart, heard his prayer because the Spirit was pleading for him. Outler *knew* the nature of God through Jesus Christ, through the works of God in history, through the works of the Holy Spirit. But there were those prayer moments when his mind reached the point of nonthinking and simply *was*, with the Holy Spirit carrying the prayer load. He knew he had not even made a beginning in expressing the mystery of prayer. At times he ended his sermons/lectures with a prayer, and fell silent when he sat down. His prayers were too deep for words.

"Craft of Dying Well"

Albert Outler never preached that he believed or practiced "the art of holy dying." He was caught up in faith by grace in this life. He said it well in this one sentence: "The Christian style of life is not so preoccupied with 'the life of the world to come' as it is with the reflex significance of the Christian hope for life in and for this world."[315] But his living in faith by grace allowed him to experience the Christian "craft of dying well" (that had come to him most directly from Jeremy Taylor via John Wesley). He said much about faith, a dimension that kept him vitally alive in the face of death every day. He accepted growing old gracefully and in good humor diminished the power that death claims. When he returned to Duke University in 1983 to give the Gray Lectures, he recognized that Harvey Branscomb was in the audience and expressed how wonderful it was to have present *his* dean at Duke when he was a professor there forty-five years before. He told about their private visit the previous evening and said, "To have him back at the same time I am here is one of the best antidotes to hypochrondia and self-pity (laughter) that I have had in many a moon because he's enough older than I am to make me ashamed of feeling as old as I do!"

Hope was an uplifting aspect of all his sermons—whether spoken or unspoken. Death in all its phantom forms shrank before that spirit in his preaching and teaching. Many of his sermons ended with a doxology. Some started with it! His cup, filled with the unmerited favor of God, overflowed through his life and ministry. One only had to hold out a cup to receive. Grace became so much the subject of all subjects of his life that, for many, *he* became the subject of grace.

Though he realized that death was soon to be the big event of his life, Albert Outler by grace was given the will to live *through* it. Even as death approached, he was preoccupied with *living*, a *living* that came from more than this world could offer. That *living* came, not from tubes and needles and medications geared to keeping his worn-out body parts functioning, but from his faith. As far as he was concerned, when his quality of life *in this world* was gone, *he* was gone from this world.

He carried on his work as long as health would permit. During the last months of his life he would settle into his big, comfortable lounge chair in front of his desk (behind his desk a long shelf across the wall held his papers), and worked off a lap board. Lamplight bathed his papers and his right arm as he wrote. To shield his right arm he had an old white cotton sock, with the toe cut out, pulled up past his elbow and protecting his forearm. He called it his gauntlet. In describing similarities between his old-sock gauntlet and those worn by warriors, he said, "It protects me from the enemy—not a costly armament; doesn't look too spiffy; but it works!"

On that day when I saw Outler wearing his gauntlet, he was writing an article on the subject of a new hermeneutic. "New"— that pictured the posture of Outler in those twilight days of his life. An old man with new ideas, an old man who still lived as he did in his younger days.

One can appreciate the confusion that the comment, "the grand old man of Methodism," brought to many. Which "grand old man of Methodism" did it refer to? Wesley or Outler?

Laughed the Laugh of God

Of all the blessed traits of Albert Outler (and there were many), his experience of salvation by laughter uniquely stands out. He was equipped to handle tragedies of human existence with a sense of humor—at self as well as others. "He who sits in the heavens laughs" (Psalm 2:4). Outler laughed the laugh of God at human incongruities on earth, including his own. Now he knows the joy of the Lord in Paradise without the baggage of human tragedy.

He Remains with Us

Yet he remains with us. We will know it as we research his thoughts in his letters, papers, sermons, lectures, and prayers through this, his life story. His message is God's message for the people of the world who, for the receiving, can know salvation through grace—sovereign and persuasive, the work of the Holy Spirit, forming in us the mind that was in Christ—grace prevenient, awakening, justifying, convincing, regenerating, accompanying, sanctifying.

This *was* Albert Outler's prayer. Now it belongs to God's people in the world. We do not *end* with it. We *go on* with it:

> Unto God the Father, who first loved us and
> accepted us in his Beloved Son; unto God
> the Son, who loved us and washed us from our
> sins in his own blood; unto God the Holy Spirit,
> who loves us and sheds the Father's love abroad
> in our hearts, be all love and glory for all
> time and eternity! Amen.

PART 5

Biographical Data

Biograhical Data

Education

Wofford College, B.A., 1928
Emory University, B.D., 1933
Yale University, Ph.D., 1938

Appointments and Offices

1. Pastor, Methodist churches in the South Georgia Conference, 1928-1935
2. Professor, Duke University, 1938-45
3. Professor, Yale University, 1945-51
4. Professor, Southern Methodist University, 1951-79
5. Professor Emeritus, Southern Methodist University, 1979-89
6. Professor, Texas Wesleyan, 1983-84
7. Professor, Union Theological Seminary (summer terms, 1943, 1953, 1957)
8. Visiting Senior Fellow, Council of Humanities, Princeton (1956-57)
10. Mellon Visiting Professor of Religion, Davidson College, Spring, 1980
11. Chairman, The Graduate Council of the Humanities, Southern Methodist University, 1960-63
12. Member, North Texas Annual Conference, UMC, 1952-78
13. Retired member, North Texas Annual Conference, UMC, 1978-89
14. Delegate, The General Conference of the Methodist Church, 1960, 1964, 1966, 1968, 1972, 1976
15. Preacher, Uniting Conference, 1968
16. Commission on Ecumenical Affairs, 1964-68
17. Member, World Methodist Council Executive Committee, 1976-82

18. Chairman of the Theological Study Commission on Doctrines And Doctrinal Standards, 1968-72
19. Member, Task Force, Kennedy Foundation, 1977
20. Honorary Chairman, Southwestern Association for the Study of Religion, 1976

Membership in Professional Societies

1. President of the American Catholic Historical Association, 1972-73
2. President of the American Theological Society, 1960-62
3. Member, The American Society of Church History (vice president, 1962-63; president, 1963-64)

   (Outler was the only person in his lifetime to have served as president of the previous three professional societies)

4. Elected to alumnus membership in the Wofford Chapter of Phi Beta Kappa, 1948 (past president of Gamma)
5. Member, The Erasmus Club at Duke
6. Member, Editorial Committee, *A Library of Christian Thought*
7. Member, Editorial Board, *Wesley Works Project*
8. Founding Member in 1965 (served three terms), Academic Council, Jerusalem Institute for Advanced Studies, Jerusalem, Israel
9. Member, the Wofford College Council of Associates, 1966; commencement address at his graduating class's fortieth reunion, 1968
10. *World Outlook* "Methodist of the Year," 1966
11. Fellow, American Academy of Arts and Sciences, 1966
12. Society for the Arts, Religion, and Contemporary Culture
13. Member, American Academy of Religion
14. Fellow, The Academy of Texas, 1969
15. Member, Executive Council of the Society for the Scientific Study of Religion
16. The National Society of Religion in Higher Education and the American Academy of Religion
17. Member, Board of Directors of the *National Catholic Reporter*
18. Member, Texas Institute of Letters
19. Member, Duodecim Theological Discussion Group
20. Fellow, American Academy of Arts and Sciences
21. Member, Task Force, Kennedy Foundation
22. Honorary Chairman, Southwestern Association for the Study of Religion, 1977-
23. Member, Board of Directors, A Foundation for Theological Education, 1977-

24. Chairman, Planning Committee, Colloquy on "The Loss and the Recovery of the Sacred," Notre Dame University, 1979, 1982
25. Dallas Historical Society
26. Honorary Fellow, Wesley College, University of Sydney, Australia
27. Academy of Senior Professionals, Eckerd College, 1986-

Honors

Honors came to Outler in many forms. Following are the more outstanding ones:

1. Honorary degrees
    a. Wofford College—D.D., 1952
    b. Kalamazoo College—D.D., 1962
    c. Lycoming College—L.H.D., 1964
    d. Notre Dame University—L.L.D., 1966
    e. Ohio Wesleyan University—L.H.D., 1967
    f. General Theological Seminary—S.T.D., 1967
    g. Emory University—Litt. D., 1968
    h. Duke University—L.H.D., 1974
    i. Southwestern University—Litt. D., 1975
    j. Loyola University—D.H.L., 1978
    k. Catholic University of America—D.H.L., 1979
    l. Texas Wesleyan University—Sc.D., 1984
    m. Southern Methodist University—Dr. of Humane Letters, 1986
2. Listed in *Who's Who in America, Outstanding Educators of America, Who's Who in the World,* and *The Blue Book*
3. A special Spring 1974 issue of *Perkins Journal* dedicated to Outler (with a virtually complete bibliography of Outler's published writings to that date)
4. A Festschrift: *Our Common History As Christians: Essays in Honor of Albert C. Outler,* edited by John Deschner, Leroy T. Howe, and Klaus Pengel (Oxford, 1975)
5. A "profile" of Outler appeared in *The Christian Century* (February 19, 1984)
6. Dallas' 1985 Award for Excellence in Community Service
7. Wofford College Alumni Distinguished Service Award, 1987
8. Southern Methodist University's Authors' Series
9. Honorary Fellow, Wesley College, University of Sydney, Australia
10. The Albert C. Outler Prize in Ecumenical Church History
11. Endowed Albert Outler professorship established at Wofford College, 1968

12. The Albert C. Outler Award in Theology at Perkins School of Theology established in 1976 by Barbara West and her husband
13. Albert Outler Scholarship established by Mr. George Pirtle at Perkins School of Theology
14. An endowed million dollar Outler Professorship in Wesley Studies established by The Texas Annual Conference, 1983, at Perkins School of Theology
15. The 1987 Pax Christi Award, given by the Benedictine Order of the Roman Catholic Church
16. Posthumous honors:
    a. Albert C. Outler Scholarship Memorial Fund, Perkins School of Theology (Given by Carla Outler for international students in recognition of her husband's contribution to the Commission on Faith and Order and the ecumenical movement)
    b. Institute of Religion, Houston, Texas [I was chosen by Carla to receive the humanitarian award on her behalf, and I told those present at the black tie affair: "This occasion was to be a special time in his [Outler's] life. Just days before he died he said to me: 'I have canceled all my engagements except the shindig that Bob Nelson's pulling off in March of '90. That will wrap it up for me. Grace also tells you when to hang 'em up.' He canceled all appearances except this one. And somehow I get the feeling after listening to comments made tonight that indeed you have helped him keep this appointment. In the spirit of the occasion he is here."]
    c. Honored by the 1993 periodical *Journal of Early Christian Studies* with essays by Denis Farkasfalvy, David L. Balas, James A. Brooks and Leroy T. Howe
    d. A principal inspirator of the *International Catholic Bible Commentary*, an international and ecumenical enterprise with a denominational mix of 118 scholars from six continents (including third-world countries) scheduled to be published in the fall of 1998 simultaneously in three languages: English (Liturgical Press), Spanish (Verbo Divinod) and Italian. French and Polish editions will follow.
    e. At the Eighth Oxford Institute, Outler read a paper titled "Methodists in Search of Consensus." The papers of the Institute were published after his death. The volume is dedicated "To the Memory of Albert Cook Outler."

Lectures

Albert Outler lectured on many special occasions. Major lecture-ships are as follows:

Hazen Conference, Hazen Foundation, Swannanoa, North Carolina, August 1945

Pacific Northwest Hazen Conference, Hazen Foundation, Moore, Washington, 1953

Objectivity and Commitment in the Study and Teaching of Religion, Indiana University, April 1953

Peyton Lectures, SMU, 1953

Merrick Lectures, Ohio Wesleyan University, 1953

Mead-Swing Lectures, Oberlin University, 1953

Lectures, National Council of YMCA, Pittsburgh, Pennsylvania, May 1954

First Quadrennial Convocation of Christian Colleges, Denison University, Granville, Ohio, June 1954

Episcopal Theological Seminary of the Southwest, Austin, Texas, February 1955

Richards Lectures, University of Virginia, Charlottesville, Virginia, Autumn 1955

Ecumenical Institute, Bossey near Caligny, Switzerland, August 1956

World Council of Churches, Consultation of Church Historians, Ecumenical Institute, Bossey, Switzerland, September 1956

Dudleian Lecture, Harvard University, Cambridge, Massachusetts, 1956

Scott Lectures, Texas Christian University, Fort Worth, Texas, 1957

The Princeton Lectures on Aquinas, Princeton Theological Seminary Princeton, New Jersey, January 1957

Ayer Lectures, Colgate-Rochester, New York, April 1957

Greene Lectures, Andover-Newton Divinity School, October 1957

Methodist Conference on Christian Vocation, Cincinnati, Ohio, November 1957

Colloquium: The Future of Theology, Princeton University, Princeton New Jersey, April 1958

Cole Lectures, Vanderbilt University, Nashville, Tennessee, April 1958

American Baptist Convention, Des Moines, Iowa, 1959

Minnesota State Pastors' School, January 1959

Lectures, St. Stephens Golden Jubilee, Edmonton, Alberta, February 1959

Smith-Willson Lectures, Southwestern College, Winfield, Kansas, October 1959

Southern California Convocation of Ministers, Claremont, California, January 1960

Gallahue Conference, Menninger Foundation, Topeka, Kansas, March 29, 1960

Zimmerman Lectures, Gettysburg Theological Seminary, May 3, 1960

University of Virginia Lectures, University of Virginia, Charlottesville, Virginia, November 1960

Ott Lectures, Davidson College, North Carolina, November 1960

Institute of Religion, Texas Medical Center, Houston, Texas, January 1961

Caleb Davies Lectures, University, Enid, Oklahoma, May 1961

Grey Lectures, Duke University, Durham, North Carolina, October 1961

Chancellor's Lectures, Queen's University, 1962

Curry Lectures, January 1962

Christology and Christian Faith, Luther Theological Seminary, January 1962

Noble Lectures, Harvard University, Cambridge, Massachusetts, March 1962

Oxford Institute, Lake Junaluska, North Carolina, July 1962

Bridwell-DeBellis Festival, Bridwell Library, Perkins School of Theology, Southern Methodist University, Dallas, Texas, September 1962

Quillian Lectures, Emory University, Atlanta, Georgia, January 1963

Faith and Order World Conference, Montreal, Quebec, June 1963

Barton Lectures, Barton, Oklahoma, 1964

Scott Lectures, Texas Christian University, Ft. Worth, January 1964

Fondren Lectures, Perkins School of Theology, Southern Methodist University, Dallas, Texas, February 1964

Rockwell Lectures, Rice University, Houston, Texas, March 1964

The Jerusalem Institute for Ecumenical Research, Catholic Press Association (South Central Region), Austin, Texas, September 1966

Norton Lectures, Southern Baptist Theological Seminary, Louisville, Kentucky, March 1965

Peyton Lectures, Ministers' Week, Perkins School of Theology, Southern Methodist University, Dallas, Texas, February 1966

Rall Lectures, Garrett Theological Seminary, 1966

Willson Lectures, Southwestern University, Georgetown, Texas, 1966

Ohio Pastors' Convocation, January 1967

James Sprunt Lectures, Union Theological Seminary, Richmond, Virginia, March 1967

Lyman Lectures, Sweet Briar College, April 1967

Colliver Lectures, University of the Pacific, Stockton, California, 1968

Perkins Lectures, Wichita Falls, Texas, 1968

Religion and the Healing Arts: New Frontiers, The Institute of Religion, Houston, Texas, October 1968

Schultz Lectures, Evangelical Theological Seminary, Naperville, Illinois, January 1969

Earl Lectures, Pacific School of Religion, Berkeley, California, February 1969

John Wesley As a Preacher, United Theological Seminary, Dayton, Ohio, April 1969

Texas Pastors' School, Southwestern University, Georgetown, Texas, July 1969

Willson Lectures, Texas Tech, Lubbock, Texas, 1969

Francis Memorial Sermons, Highland Park Methodist Church, Dallas, Texas, 1969

Showers Lectures, Lebanon Valley College, Annville, Pennsylvania, October 1969

Institute of Theology, Princeton University, Princeton, New Jersey, June 1970

McFadin Lectures, Texas Christian University, Fort Worth, Texas, June 1970

Short Lectures, Louisville Annual Conference, Louisville, Kentucky, May 1971

Denman Lectures, New Orleans, Louisiana, January 1971

The Ecumenical Institute for Advanced Theological Studies, Tantur, Jerusalem, September 1972

Mendenhall Lectures, DePauw University, Greencastle, Indiana, January 17, 1973

Ecumenical Lecture Series, Little Rock, Arkansas, April 1973

Tager Lectures, Perkins School of Theology, Southern Methodist University, September 1973

Willson Lectures, Wesley Theological Seminary, Washington D.C., October 1973

White Lectures, Nazarene Theological Seminary, Kansas City, Missouri, November 1973

Fiftieth Anniversary Lectures, Asbury Theological Seminary, March 1974

A Gospel for the Guiltless, Lectures, Princeton Theological Seminary, Princeton, New Jersey, July 1974

Wesley Festival, Drew University, Madison, New Jersey, October 1974

World Methodist Council Convocation on Evangelism, Jerusalem, November 1974

Fondren Lectures, Perkins School of Theology, Dallas, Texas, 1974

Heck Lectures, United Theological Seminary, Dayton, Ohio

Lectures on Theology, Kirkwood United Methodist Church, St. Louis, Missouri, January 1975

Nathaniel Taylor Lectures, Yale Divinity School, New Haven, Connecticut, February 1975

The Human Prospect and the Christian Hope, Oklahoma City University, Oklahoma, April 1975

Jones-Cadwallader Memorial Centennial Lectures, Rayne Memorial United Methodist Church, New Orleans, Louisiana, September 28, 1975

Palmer Lectures, University of Puget Sound, Tacoma, Washington, October 1975

Newnham Lectures, First United Methodist Church, Longview, Texas, November 1975

Boswell Lectures, First United Methodist Church, Dallas, Texas, 1976

The Bicentennial and the Re-Invention of America, Princeton Theological Seminary, July 1976

Gorman Lectures, University of Dallas, Dallas, Texas, September 1976

Oklahoma Ministers' Week and Bicentennial Celebration, October 1976

Wesley Institute, Evanston, Illinois, February 1977

Finch-Hunt Lectures, Memorial United Methodist Church, Western North Carolina Conference, Thomasville, North Carolina, February 1979

Heinsohn Lectures, University United Methodist Church, Austin, Texas, April 1980

Six Danforth Conferences from 1951 until 1980

Winter Lecture Series, First Presbyterian Church, Shreveport, Louisiana, January 1981

Ministers' Week, Emory University, Atlanta, Georgia, January, 1981

Fenn Lectures, Central United Methodist Church, Albuquerque, New Mexico, February 1981

Lubbock District Seminar in Continuing Education, Lubbock, Texas, March 1981

Ministers' Week, Nebraska Wesleyan, Lincoln, Nebraska, March 1981

Eighth Annual Urban Consultation Lectures, First Presbyterian Church, Dallas, Texas, April 1981

McQuaid Lectures, First United Methodist Church, Garland, Texas, May 1981

Urban Consultation, Presbyterian Church, First Presbyterian, Dallas, Texas, May 1981

Interpreting the Faith Conference, Union Theological Seminary, Richmond, Virginia, July 1981

Knowledge and Vital Piety in the Wesleyan Spirit, The Committee of 100, Emory University, Atlanta, Georgia, October 1981

Charles Lectures, Earlham College, Richmond, Indiana, November 1981

Cato Lectures, Adelaide, Australia, May 1982.

The State of the Church, University of Sydney, Sydney, Australia

Montreat Bible and Theology Conference, Montreat, North Carolina, July 1982

Asbury Summer Theological Institute, Asbury Theological Seminary, Wilmore, Kentucky, July 1982

Corpus Christi Lay Academy, Corpus Christi Cathedral, Corpus Christi, Texas, October 1982

Surtz Lectures, Loyola University of Chicago, Illinois, November 1982

Sikes-Melugin Lectures, McMurry College, Abilene, Texas, February 1983

Faculty Lectures, Texas Wesleyan College, Fort Worth, Texas, March 1983

Willson Lectures, Texas Wesleyan College, Fort Worth, Texas, March 1983

Kantonen Lectures, Trinity Lutheran Seminary, Columbus, Ohio, April 1983

Pastors' School, Macon, Georgia, June 1983

Leith Lectures, First Presbyterian Church, Auburn, Alabama, October 1983

Little Rock Trilogy, Little Rock, Arkansas, April 1984

Lectures, Cochran Chapel United Methodist Church, Dallas, Texas, October 1984

Peter Ainslie Lectures, Council on Christian Unity, Christian Church (Disciples of Christ), Indianapolis, Indiana, December 1984

Southwest Texas Conference: Seminar on Wesleyan Theology, 1984

Isthmus Lecture: "Power and Grace," Dallas, Texas, 1984

Perkins Laity Week: "Message of the Wesleys," Dallas, Texas, 1984

Boswell Lectures, First United Methodist Church, Dallas, Texas, 1984

Bicentennial Lectures, Boston University, Boston, Massachusetts, 1984

Resident's Lecture, Timberlawn Hospital, Dallas, Texas, 1984

Bicentennial Conference Sermon, Lovely Lane United Methodist Church, Baltimore, Maryland, 1984

Gilmore Lectures, First United Methodist Church, Des Moines, Iowa, 1984

Duodecim: "Towards a Post-Critical Hermeneutic," 1984

Texas Conference, United Methodist Church, Address, 1984

Central Texas Conference, United Methodist Church, 1984

Bicentennial Lecture, Trinity United Methodist Church, Beaumont, Texas, 1984

Conference on Faith and History, Southwest Baptist Theological Seminary, Fort Worth, Texas, 1984

Wesley Lectures, Wesleyan Theological Society, Emory University, Atlanta, Georgia, 1984

Staley Lectureship, Seattle-Pacific University, Seattle, Washington, 1984
University Lecture, University of Dallas, 1984
Address and panel, American Academy of Religion, Chicago, Illinois, 1984
Pacific and Southwest Conference, Rolling Hills United Methodist Church, Pasadena, California, January 1985
The Ray West Lectureship, First United Methodist Church, Corpus Christi, Texas, February 1985
Society of Wesley Studies, Randolph-Macon College, Ashland, Virginia, March 1985
Hopkins Lectures, First United Methodist Church, Denton, Texas, March 1985
Jewish-Christian Conference, Brite Divinity School, 1985
Steel-Hendrix Lecture, Hendrix College, Conway, Arkansas, October 1985
Lectures, First United Methodist Church, Houston, Texas, November 1985
Inaugural Lecture, Wofford College, Spartanburg, South Carolina, 1985
Simpson Lectures, First United Methodist Church, Wichita, Kansas, April 1986

Bibliography

1927

"A Climb in the Sunset." *The Journal*, (Wofford College) (October 1927): 13-15.

1933

"A New Deal for Presiding Elders." *Wesleyan Christian Advocate*, (23 February 1934): 6-7.

1935

Epworth Highroad, (1935).

1936

Church School Magazine, (January 1936).
"Psychotherapy in Christian Service." *Church School Magazine*, (January 1936).

1939

"Origen and the Regulae Fidei." *Church History*, Vol. 8, No. 3 (September 1939): 212-21.

1940

"The Historical Approach to Theology." *Duke School of Religion Bulletin*, Vol. 5, No. 3 (February 1940): 1-8.

"The 'Platonism' of Clement of Alexandria." *The Journal of Religion,* Vol. 20, No. 3 (July 1940): 217-40.

1942

"The Patristic Christian Ethos and Democracy." *Science, Philosophy and Religion.* Second Symposium (1942).

1943

"Comments on *The Meaning of Human Dignity From a Theological Perspective*" by Nels F. S. Ferré. *Science, Philosophy And Religion.* eds. Lyman Bryson and Louis Finkelstein. Third Symposium (1943).

"Comments on *The Unification of Specialized Knowledge in Practical Affairs*" by David E. Lilienthal. *Science, Philosophy and Religion.* eds. Lyman Bryson and Louis Frankelstein. Third Symposium (1943).

1944

The History and Mission of the Church: An Elective Unit for Young People. Nashville: Abingdon-Cokesbury (1944) (booklet).

"The Reformation and Classical Protestantism." *The Vitality of the Christian Tradition.* ed. George F. Thomas, New York: Harper (1944).

"The Problem of Religious Community in Protestantism." *The Journal of Religious Thought* 1 (Spring-Summer 1944): 117-27.

Review of *The Christian Philosophy of History,* by Shirley Jackson Case. *Church History* 13 (March 1944): 73-75.

Review of *The Doctrine of the Church in the New Testament,* by George Johnson. *Church History* 13 (March 1944): 71-73.

Review of *The Legacy of the Liberal Spirit,* by Fred G. Bratton. *Journal of Religion* 24 (April 1944): 142-43.

1945

"In the World Yet Not of the World." *Christendom* 10 (Winter 1945): 44-45.

Review of *Christianity and Classical Culture,* by Charles N. Cochrane. *Theology Today* 2 (July 1945): 265-67.

"A Christian Context for Counseling." *Counseling for Personal and Social Adjustment : Account of the Third Southern Hazen Conference, Wilson Junior College, Swannanoa, N.C., August* (Hazen Pamphlet) (1945).

1946

Review of *The Incarnation of the Word of God,* by St. Athanasius. Tr. by a Religious of CSMUS, with an introduction by C. S. Lewis. *Church History* 15 (September 1946): 237-39.

A Christian Context for Counseling, 1946.

1947

"The Church in History." *Highroad* 6 (February 1947).

Review of *The Story of Faith: A Survey of Christian History for the Undogmatic,* by William Alva Gifford. *Christendom* 12 (Winter 1947): 108-10.

Review of *The Source of Human Good,* by Henry Nelson Wieman. *Crozier Quarterly* 24 (July 1947): 248-50.

"The Unready Prophet." *Yale Divinity News* 43 (November 1947): 1-2.

1948

Review of *The Oracles of God: An Introduction to the Preaching of John Calvin,* by Parker. *Theology Today* 4 (January 1948): 575-78.

Review of *Evil and the Christian Faith,* by Nels F. S. Ferré. *Review of Religion* 12 (May 1948): 437-39.

"Teaching Christian Theology to Youth." *Workers with Youth* 1 (June 1948):2-4.

Review of *The Religion of Maturity,* by John Wick Bowman. *Christendom* 13 (Autumn 1948): 522-24.

Review of *The Protestant Era,* by Paul Tillich. *Church History* 17 (December 1948): 356-58.

Review of *Reinhold Niebuhr: Prophet from America,* by D. R. Davies. *New Haven Register* (June 1948).

1949

"Colleges, Faculties and Religion: An Appraisal of the Program of Faculty Consultation on Religion in Higher Education, 1945-48." New Haven: National Council on Religion in Higher Education, 1949. See *Educational Record* 30 (January 1949): 45-48.

Review of *The Authority of the Biblical Revelation,* by Hubert Cunliffe-Jones. *Interpretation* 3 (April 1949): 212-14.

Review of *Church, Law and Society,* by Gustaf Aulen. *Ecumenical Review* 2 (Autumn 1949): 108-10.

Review of *Christianity and Civilization. First Part: Foundations,* by Emil Brunner. *Church History* 18 (December 1949): 242-43.

1950

"The Challenge of the Church Related College." *Minutes and Addresses: National Association of Schools and Colleges of the Methodist Church, Eleventh Annual Meeting* (January 11-12, 1950): 83-94.

Review of *The History of the Primitive Church,* by Jules Lebreton. *Theology Today* 7 (April 1950): 116-18.

Review of *America's Spiritual Culture,* by Bernard Eugene Meland. *Crozier Quarterly* 27 (July 1950): 264-65.

Review of *Origen,* by Jean Danielou. *Journal of Religion* 30 (October 1950): 279-80.

Review of *Nicolas Berdyaev: Captive of Freedom,* by Matthew Spinka. *The Pastor* 14 (November 1950): 39-40.

1951

"Frontiers that Wait for Pioneers." *The Intercollegian* 68 (January 1951): 11-12.

Review of *Psychotherapy and a Christian View of Man,* by David E. Roberts. *Journal of Religion* 31 (January 1951): 74-75.

"For Us Men and Our Salvation." *Religion in Life* 20 (Spring 1951).

Review of *Early Medieval Philosophy,* by George Bosworth Burch. *Crozier Quarterly* 28 (July 1951): 281.

"The Pursuit of Happiness." *The Upper Room Pulpit* (September 1951): 3-8.

Review of *The Doctrine of the Atonement: New Perspectives in Anglican Theology,* by Leonard Hodgson. *Perkins Journal* 5 (Fall 1951): 22-25.

Review of *The Christian Sacrifice,* by Norman Pittenger. *Perkins Journal* 5 (Fall 1951): 22-25.

Review of *Systematic Theology, Vol. 1,* by Paul Tillich. *Interpretation* 5 (October 1951): 476-80.

1952

"With All We Have." *Perkins Journal* (Winter 1952): 9-13.

Review of *A History of the Cure of Souls,* by John T. McNeil. *Journal of Religion* 32 (January 1952): 66-67.

Review of *Four Philosophies, and Their Practice in Education and Religion,* by J. Donald Butler. *Theology Today* 9 (April 1952): 130-32.

"Agenda for Lund." *Ecumenical Review* 4 (April 1952).

Review of *The Church, Report of a Theological Commission on Faith and Order* by R. Newton Flew; *Ways of Worship,* by G. Van der Leeuw; and *Intercommunication, Report of a Theological Commission of Faith and Order,* by Donald Baillie.

Review of *Theology of the New Testament,* by Rudolf Bultmann. *The Pastor* 15 (May 1952): 36-37.

"The Work of the Holy Spirit." *The Christian Advocate* 127 (July 1952): 7, 27-31.

"Christian Faith and Psychotherapy." *Religion in Life* 21 (Autumn 1952): 502-12.

"A Way Forward From Lund." *Ecumenical Review* 5 (October 1952); *Perkins Journal* 6 (Winter 1953): 13-16.

1953

Review of *The Knowledge of God in Calvin's Theology,* by Edward A. Dowey. *Perkins Journal* 6 (Winter 1953): 27-28.

Review of *Christianity, Past and Present,* by Basil Willey. *Perkins Journal* 6 (Winter 1953): 28-29.

Review of *Logic For Living,* by Henry Horace Williams. *Perkins Journal* 6 (Winter 1953): 29.

1954

Psychotherapy and the Christian Message. New York: Harpers, 1954. See *Psychotherapie and Evangelieverkondiging.* 's-Gravenhage, Boekencentrum N.V., 1959.

"Psychotherapy and the Christian Message." *Pastoral Psychology* 5 (February 1954). Reprint of first chapter of the book.

"The Ecumenical Movement: Prospects of Evanston." *Perkins Journal* 7 (Spring 1954): 14-16.

"Thy Kingdom Come for This IS the Kingdom." *motive* 14 (April 1954): 2-3, 40-42.

"Theological Foundations for Christian Higher Education." *The Christian Scholar* 37 Supp. (Autumn 1954): 202-17.

Review of *Christian Hope and the Second Coming,* by Paul Minear. *The Pastor* 18 (September 1954): 39-40.

Review of *A Theology of the Living Church,* by Harold DeWolf. *Perkins Journal* 8 (Fall 1954): 33-35.

1955

Augustine: Confessions and Enchiridion. Vol. 7, The Library of Christian Classics. Philadelphia: Westminster Press, 1955.

"The Person and Work of Christ in the Thought of Saint Augustine." *A Companion to the Study of Saint Augustine,* ed. Roy W. Battenhouse, 340-70. New York: Oxford University Press, 1955.

"Some Concepts of Human Rights and Obligations in Classical Protestantism." *Natural Law and Natural Rights,* ed. Arthur L. Harding, 1-18. Dallas: Southern Methodist University Press, 1955.

Review of *The History and Character of Calvinism,* by John T. McNeil. *Perkins Journal* 8 (Winter 1955): 21-22.

"Backgrounds and Patterns in Contemporary Theology." *Perkins Journal* 8 (Spring 1955): 4-10.

"Our Faith and the Scriptures." *The Christian Advocate* 130 (16 June 1955): 11, 29-32.

Review of *Alexandrian Christianity: Selected Translations of Clement and Origen With Introduction and Notes,* by John Ernest L. Oulton and Henry Chadwick. *Church History* 24 (June 1955): 183-84.

Review of *The Self and The Dramas of History,* by Reinhold Niebuhr. *The Christian Century* 72 (June 1955): 654.

"David E. Roberts—In Memoriam." *Journal of Pastoral Care* 9 (Summer 1955): 65-67.

Review of *A Tale of Two Brothers*, by Mabel Brailsford. *Drew Gateway* 25 (Summer 1955): 246-47.

Review of *Ultimate Questions*, by Nathaniel Micklam. *Religion in Life* 24 (Autumn 1955): 629-30.

Review of *Aquinas on Nature and Grace*, ed. & tr. A. H. Fairweather. *Church History* 24 (September 1955): 280-81.

Review of *Trends and Frontiers of Religious Thought*, by Harold DeWolf. *Boston University Graduate Journal* 4 (October 1955): 24-26.

Review of *Anxiety in Christian Experience*, by Wayne E. Oates. *Pastoral Psychology* 6 (November 1955): 65.

Review of *A Commentary on the Apostles' Creed*, by Rufinus. Tr. J. N. D. Kelley. *Church History* 24 (December 1955): 372.

"The Two Halves of Freedom." *Mustang* 8 (December 1955).

1956

Review of *Martin Luther's Works, Vol. 12*, Jaroslav Pelikan. *Perkins Journal* 9 (June 1956): 29-30.

Review of *The Gift of Power*, by Lewis Joseph Sherill. *Perkins Journal* 9 (June 1956): 63-64.

"The Unity We Have." *The Christian Century* 73 (June 1956).

Review of *Conquering the Seven Deadly Sins*, by Lance Webb. *Perkins Journal* 10 (Fall 1956): 31-32.

Review of *The Grandeur and the Misery of Man*, by David E. Roberts. *Journal of Religion* 36 (October 1956): 293-94.

Review of *Philosophy of the Church Fathers, Vol. 1*, by Harry A Wolfson. *The Christian Century* 73 (October 1956).

1957

The Christian Tradition and the Unity We Seek. New York: Oxford University Press, 1957.

"Freud and the Domestication of Tragedy." *The Tragic Vision and the Christian Faith*, ed. Nathan Scott, 264-80. New York: Association Press, 1957.

Review of *The Living of These Days: An Autobiography*, by Harry Emerson Fosdick. *Pastoral Psychology* 8 (March 1957): 56-58.

"The Incipience of Faith," the Dudleian Lecture for the Academic Year 1955-56, Harvard University. Delivered at Andover Chapel, April 10, 1956. *Harvard Divinity Bulletin* 22 (April 1957): 41-60.

Comment in "Reader's Forum" on Herbert Lambert's Response to G. C. Anderson's article, "Psychiatry's Influence on Religion." *Pastoral Psychology* (April 1957).

Review of *Existentialism and Religious Belief*, by David E. Roberts. *Pastoral Psychology* 8 (April 1957): 53-54.

Review of *Dynamics of Faith,* by Paul Tillich. *Interpretation* 8 (April 1957): 473-75.

"The Challenge of Oberlin." *The New Christian Advocate* 1 (July 1957): 10-14.

"The Table of the Lord—An Ecumenical Statement." *Perkins Journal* 11 (Fall 1957): 16-20.

"Our Common History as Christians." *motive* 18 (November 1957); *Brethren Life and Thought* 3 (Spring 1958). Also in *The Nature of the Unity We Seek, Official Report of the North American Conference on Faith & Order,* September 3-10, 1957, Oberlin, Oh., ed. Paul Minear. St. Louis: Bethany Press, 1958.

Review of *Yale and the Ministry,* by Roland Bainton. *The Christian Century* 74 (November 1957).

Review of *The Religious Dimensions of Personality,* by Wayne Oates. *Pastoral Psychology* 8 (December 1957): 61-63.

1958

"The Church Unity We Have." *Christian Unity in North America; A Symposium,* ed. J. Robert Nelson, 73-80. St. Louis: Bethany Press, 1958.

Foreword to *The Crucial Task of Theology,* by Early Ashby Johnson, Richmond, Va.: John Knox Press, 1958.

"On the Methodist Standards of Doctrine." *Handbook of Selected Creeds and Confessions for Use in Seminary Studies,* 57-64. Dallas: Perkins School of Theology, Southern Methodist University, 1958. (Mimeographed).

Review of *Human Nature Under God,* by Oren Huling Baker. *Pastoral Psychology* 9 (September 1958): 58-60.

1959

"The Time Being." *Rice Institute Pamphlet* 45 (January 1959): 82-89.

"Quid Est Veritas?" *Proceedings, Council of Protestant Colleges and Universities, Kansas City, Mo., January 5-9, 1959; The Christian Century* 76 (March 1959): 258-60. See "Discursive Truth and Evangelical Truth." *Colleges and Commitments,* eds. Lloyd J. Averill and William W. Jellema, 102-6. Philadelphia: Westminster Press, 1971.

"Augustine and the Transvaluation of the Classical Tradition." *The Classical Journal* 54 (February 1959): 213-20.

1960

Ordeal of a Happy Dilettante." *The Christian Century* 77 (February 1960): 127-29. See "How My Mind Has Changed," in *How My Mind Has Changed,* ed. Harold E. Fey. Cleveland: Meridian Books, 1960, 1961, 40-54.

Love Among the Eggheads. An address to the Danforth Fellow Conference, Camp Miniwanca. Danforth Foundation (September 1960). (Pamphlet).

"What Is Evangelism?" *Church School* 13 (December 1960): 11-13.

1961

Foreword to *Protestant Patriarch: The Life of Cyril Lucaris (1572-1638), Patriarch of Constantinople,* by George A. Hadjiantoniou. Richmond, Va.: John Knox Press, 1961.

"Traditions in Transit." Chapter in *The Old and the New in the Church.* Faith and Order Commission Paper, no. 34. London: SCM Press, 1961.

"Towards a Re-appraisal of John Wesley as a Theologian," *Perkins Journal* 14 (Winter 1961): 5-14.

Review of *John Wesley's Theology Today,* by Colin W. Williams. *Perkins Journal* 14 (Winter 1961) 50-51; *Encounter* 22 (Summer 1961): 352-53.

"The Seminary for the University." Address for the Inauguration of Dean Joseph D. Quillian, Jr. *Perkins Journal* 11 (Spring 1961): 12-18.

Review of *The Social Sources of Church Unity: An Interpretation of Unitive Forces and Movements in American Protestantism,* by Robert Lee. *The Christian Advocate* 5 (2 March 1961).

"The Climate of Grace." *The Alumni Bulletin* (Bangor Theological Seminary) 3 (April 1961): 6-12.

"The Man Christ Jesus—As Divine-Human Savior." *The Christian Century* 78 (May 1961): 554-56.

"Protestant Churches Meeting the Communist Challenge." Fourth in a Series of Lectures at Highland Park Methodist Church, April 1961. Privately printed. See *Perkins Journal* 15 (Fall 1961: 33-40.

1962

"The Assemblies: A Memoir of New Delhi." *Journal of the Interseminary Movement of the Southwest* (1962): 65-70.

Review of *From Monologue to Dialogue, the Ecumenical Review,* by K. E. Skydsgaard. Vol. XIV, No. 4 (July 1962).

"The Pastoral Office." *Perkins Journal* 16 (Fall 1962): 5-7.

"The Test of Orthodoxy." *Theology Today* 19 (October 1962): 427-29.

Review of *The Rebirth of Ministry,* James D. Smart. *Union Seminary Quarterly Review* 18 (November 1962): 99-100.

1963

"Anxiety and Grace: An Augustinian Perspective." *Constructive Aspects of Anxiety,* ed. Seward Hiltner and Karl Menninger, 89-102. New York: Abingdon, 1963.

"H. Shelton Smith: An Appreciative Memoir." *A Miscellany of American Christianity: Essays in Honor of H. Shelton Smith,* ed. Stuart C. Henry, 3-21. Durham, N. C.: Duke University Press, 1963.

"Scripture, Tradition, and the Gaurdian(s) of Tradition." *Digest of the Proceedings of the Consultation on Church Union for 1962 and 1963,* Vol. 1 & 2, 83-95.

"The Shaping of the Mind of Latin Christendom." *Perkins Journal* 16 (Winter-Spring 1963): 19-22.

"Curtain Going Up?" *Mustang* 15 (March-April 1963): 19-22.

"Montreal and the Problem of Christian Tradition." *motive* 23 (April 1963): 32-34.

"Beyond Pietism: Aldersgate in Context." *motive* 23 (May 1963): 12-16.

"The 'Silent Service' Surfaces at Montreal." *The Christian Advocate* 7 (June 1963): 7-8.

"*De l'affrontement au dialogue.*" Translation of "From Disputation to Dialogue," Conference Address, Fourth World Conference on Faith and Order, World Council of Churches, Montreal, Canada, July 13, 1963. *Foi et Vie* 62 (May-August 1963). For the English text see *Ecumenical Review,* 16 (October 1963): 14-23.

"Montreal in Perspective: The Shock of Recognition," *The Christian Advocate* 8 (October 1963):10-12.

"James Allen Knight: An Appreciation." *Pastoral Psychology* 14 (December 1963): 4, 65-66.

"Knowledge and Vital Piety." A sermon preached at Highland Park Methodist Church, Dallas, March 1963. Privately printed.

Review of *Personality and the Good: Psychological and Ethical Perspectives,* by Peter A. Bertocci and Richard M. Millard. *Pastoral Psychology* 14 (November 1963): 59-61.

1964

John Wesley. A Library of Protestant Thought. New York: Oxford University Press, 1964.

"Do Methodists Have a Doctrine of the Church?" *The Doctrine of the Church,* ed. Dow Kirkpatrick, 11-28. New York: Abingdon, 1964.

"Collegiality—Key to Vatican II." *World Parish* 3 (January 1964).

"Catholics Have a Right to Dialogue." *The Christian Advocate* 8 (2 January 1964).

"What If Vatican II Succeeds?" *motive* 24 (May 1964): 6-8.

"Vatican II—An Experiment in Re-formation," *The Christian Advocate* 8 (May 1964): 7-8.

"The Sense of Tradition in the Ante-Nicene Church." *Journal of Ecumenical Studies* 1 (Fall 1964): 460-84. See *Heritage of Christian*

Thought, eds. Robert E. Cushman and Egil Grislis, 8-30. New York: Harper & Row, 1965.

"'Religious Liberty' Stand Is Called the Crucial Test of the Council." *The Oklahoma Courier,* 11 September 1964.

Review of *The Pilgrim,* by Michael Serafian. *Texas Catholic Herald,* 3 September 1964.

"Vatican II, Session iii: Early Votes Suggest Progressive Trend." *The Christian Advocate* 8 (October 1964): 23.

"What If Vatican II Succeeds: A Methodist Viewpoint." *Arena* 73 (October 1964): 6-8.

"Vatican II—Act Three: Will the Diehards Win?" *Christianity and Crisis* 24 (December 1964): 260-64.

"What Happened To Religious Liberty: A Protestant's Vatican Diary." *All-Church Press,* 31 December 1964.

Review of *Observer In Rome: "A Protestant Report on the Vatican Council,"* by Robert McAfee Brown. *The Christian Advocate* 8 (December 1964): 17.

1965

Liberta Religiosa. Roma: Fondazione S. Paolo Apostolo, 1965. (Pamphlet).

"Scripture, Tradition and Ecumenism." *Scripture and Ecumenism,* ed. Leonard J. Swidler, 9-22. Pittsburgh: Duquesne University Press, 1965.

Review of *St. Augustine of Hippo: Life and Controversies,* by Gerald Bonner. *Theology Today* 21 (January 1965): 533-35.

"Digesting Session III." Interview by Stanley Hosie. *Marist* 21 (January-February 1965).

Review of *Union et desunion des chretiens,* by J. Coppens, et al. *Journal of Ecumenical Studies* 2 (Spring 1965): 318-20.

"Vatican II—Between Acts." *Perkins Journal* 18 (Spring 1965): 318-21.

"Roman *Catholic* Not *Roman* Catholic." *U. S. Catholic* 30 (April 1965). (Excerpt from "Vatican II, Act Three"). *Christianity and Crisis* 24 (December 1964): 262.

Review of *Justification, the Doctrine of Karl Barth and a Catholic Reflection,* by Hans Kung. *The Critic* 23 (April-May 1965): 70-71.

Review of *The Church and Mankind,* by Karl Rahner and E. C. F. Schillebeeckx. Vol. 1, *Concilium. The Christian Century* 82 (May 1965).

"Doctrine of the Laity in Vatican II's Constitution on the Church." An Address to the National Council of Catholic Men, April 29, 1965. Excerpt in *Ave Maria* 101 (June 1965). See *Davenport Catholic Messenger* 24 (June 19650.

"Liberty Deferred: A Crisis at Vatican II." *Southwest Review* 50 (Summer 1965): 209-22.

"Crucial Issues in the Commission on Church Union." Digest of the address at Second Conference on Methodism in an Ecumenical Age, Lake Junaluska, N.C., July 19-23, 1965. *Central Christian Advocate* 140 (September 1965): 7-9. For a condensed, updated version, see "Fish or Cut Bait." *Together* 10 (May 1966): 13-14, and *Central Christian Advocate* 141 (1 September 1966) 7-9.

"Theodosius' Horse: Reflections on the Predicament of the Church Historian." Presidential Address, American Society of Church History, December 29, 1964. *Church History* 34 (September 1965): 251-61.

"Reformation Day Updated." *Methodist Story* 9 (September 1965): 15-16.

Review of *Unity in Freedom,* ed. Augustine Bea. *Church History* 34 (September 1965): 361-62.

"The New Ecumenical Situation: A Bibliographical Essay." *Perkins Journal* 19 (Fall-Winter 1965-66).

"'Pope Watching' Popular Indoor Sport in Rome." *The Oklahoma Courier,* 8 October 1965.

"Religious Liberty Drama Unfolds in Rome." *All-Church Press,* 8 October 1965.

"Two Rhythms Shape Council's Development." *The Oklahoma Courier,* 12 November 1965.

"Vatican II Viewpoint: Beginning of the End." *The Christian Advocate* 9 (November 1965): 23.

"Reformation Roman Style." *Our Sunday Visitor* 54 (December 1965). See "Reformation in the Roman Style." *Catholic Mind* 64 (February 1966): 15-20; "Reformatieroomse Style," *Wending* 20 (Spring 1966); *Catholic World* 204 (March 1967). Also in *American Participation in the Second Vatican Council,* ed. Vincent Arthur Yzermans, 313-18. New York: Sheed & Ward, 1967.

"A Methodist Views the Council." *Conversations in Rome: Vatican Council Observers Speaking with the Bishop of Huron.* Sponsored by the Bishop's Publication Fund. December 1965.

1966

That the World May Believe: A Study of Christian Unity. Joint Commission on Education and Cultivation, Board of Missions of the Methodist Church. New York, 1966. Excerpts in *Adult Teacher* 20 (July 1967).

Vatican II—Charter for Change. Report to Southern Methodist University and the Dallas Community, January 26, 1966. Texas Methodist Publication, 1966. (Pamphlet).

Tri-alogue on "The Death of God," by Albert C. Outler, Schubert Ogden and John Deschner. Herndon Wagers, Moderator. Ministers' Week, Southern Methodist University, February 9, 1966. Texas Methodist Publication, 1966. (Pamphlet).

"Vatican II and Protestant Theology in America Today and Tomorrow." *Vatican II: An Interfaith Appraisal,* ed. John H. Miller, 619-25. International Theological Conference, University of Notre Dame, Ind.: University of Notre Dame Press, 1966.

"A Response" (to Lumen Gentium). *The Documents of Vatican II,* eds. Walter M. Abbott and Joseph Gallagher, 102-6. Guild Press, 1966.

"Veni, Creator Spiritus—The Doctrine of the Holy Spirit," *Perkins Journal* 19 (Spring 1966): 31-40. See *New Theology,* No. 4, eds. Martin E. Marty and Dean G. Peerman, 195-209. New York: Macmillan, 1967.

"The Protestant Dilemma: A Comment on *The Christian Century*'s article on Carl Braaten's 'Rome, Reformation and Reunion.'" *Una Sancta* 23 (St. Michael and All Angels, 1966): 13-16.

"Fit for Freedom." *Emory Magazine* 42 (June-August). Reprinted in *Campus Encounter* (United Ministries in Higher Education) (Fall 1966). *Kappa Alpha Theta Magazine* 82 (Winter 1967-68).

"Called to Unity." Address to the Woman's Society of Christian Service Twenty-fifth Assembly, Portland, Ore., May 12, 1966. *Methodist Woman* 26 (July-August 1966): 28-30; *Central Christian Advocate* 141 (July 1966). *World Outlook* Old Series, 56; New Series 26 (August 1966). Excerpts in *Church School* 21 (February 1968).

"Reflections of a Council Observer." Interview by E. Gaffney. *Catholic World* 203 (September 1966).

"Vatican II—A Challenge to Protestantism." *The Critic* 25 (October-November 1966): 78-81; *Perkins Journal* 20 (Spring 1967).

Review of *Christ in Christian Tradition: From the Apostolic Age to Chalcedon,* by Aloys Grillmeier, S. J. *Theology Today* 23 (October 1966): 450-52.

Review of *Rome—Opponent or Partner?* by Rudolf J. Ehrlich. *Theological Studies* 27 (December 1966): 712-14.

"There's a Hazard in Every Advent: Pray Christmas Comes Again—To Us." *Methodist Recorder,* No. 5688 (8 December 1966).

Review of *The Second Vatican Council and the New Catholicism,* by G. C. Berkouwer. *Una Sancta* 23 (Christmas 1966): 100-102.

Methodist Observer at Vatican II. Westminster, Md.: Newman Press, 1967.

"*Die hohere Autoritat.*" *Die Autoritat der Freiheit,* ed. Johann Christoph Hampe, 51-55. Band I. Kosel-Verlag Munchen, 1967.

[Religionsfraihert als Okumenische Erfahrung in *Die Autoritat der Freiheit, III.* 231-40. Waldensian Seminary, Rome].

[Reparaturen statt Reform in *Die Autoritat, II.* 190-93. Waldensian Seminary, Rome].

"The Current Theological Scene: A View From the Beach at Ebb-Tide." Address to the World Methodist Council, August 22, 1966. *Proceedings of the Eleventh World Methodist Conference,* eds. Lee F. Tuttle and Max W. Woodward, 157-67. London: Epworth Press, 1967.

"An Uncommon Ecumenist." *One of a Kind: Essays in Tribute to Gustave Weigel,* 43-49. Wilkes-Barre, Pa.: Dimension Books, 1967.

"The Council One Year Later." *Commonweal* 85 (January 1967): 368-69.

"Unity Dialogue: How It Feels On the Inside." *National Catholic Reporter* 3 (February 1967): 6.

"The Way of the Peacemakers." *The YWC Magazine* 61 (February 1967).

"Jerusalem Institute for Ecumenical Research." *Catholic Mind* 65 (February 1967): 18-28.

"Ecumenism on the Secular Campus." *Listening* 2 (Spring 1967): 121-27.

"The Ecumenical Crisis We Face." Interview by Father John Sheerin. *Catholic World* 204 (April 1967): 20-25; *World Outlook* New Series, 27 (June 1967).

"Can We Trust Pope Paul?" *Frontier* 10 (Summer 1967): 136- 38.

"Vatican II: A Synoptic View." *London Quarterly and Holborn Review* 192 (July 1967): 188-99.

"Christian Community Begins at Home." *Methodist Story* 11 (September 1967).

"Nominal Christianity Not Enough." *The Christian* 105 (September 1967).

Review of *Vatican Politics of the Second Vatican Council 1962-65,* by George Bull. *Journal of Religion* 47 (October 1967): 357-58.

Review of *Readings in Christian Thought,* by Hugh T. Kerr. *Theology Today* 24 (October 1967): 416-18.

Review of *Challenge . . . and Response: A Protestant Perspective of the Vatican Council,* by Warren Quanbeck. *Theological Studies* 28 (December 1967): 856-58.

"Current Crisis in Belief and Identity." *Reports of the Texas Faith and Order Conference on Worship, Evangelism and Modern Man, November 3-5, 1967.*

"Worship and Christian Unity." *Music Ministry* 9 (November 1967): 3-7.

1968

Who Trusts in God: Musings on the Meaning of Providence. New
York: Oxford University Press, 1968.
"Theologische Akzente." Der Methodismus, ed. C. Ernest Sommer, 84-
102. Band 6 of Die Kirchen die Welt. Stuttgart: Evangelisches
Verlagswerk, 1968.
Foreword to *John XXIII and American Protestants,* by Eugene Carl
Bianchi. Washington: Corpus Books, 1968.
Review of *Religious Pathology and Christian Faith,* by James E. Loder.
Theology Today 24 (January 1968): 540- 42.
Review of *Moral Law in Christian Social Ethics,* by Walter Muelder.
Theology Today, Vol. 24, No. 4. (January 1968).
"Reform in the Methodist Manner." Edited text of "What Price Meth-
odist Reform?" an address to the Methodist Conference on Chris-
tian Education, Dallas, Tex., November 6-10, 1967. *The Christian
Advocate* 7 (March 1968): 7-12. See *Workers with Youth* 21 (July
1968): 14-17, 55.
"Methods and Aims in the Study of the Development of Catholic Chris-
tianity." *Anglican Theological Review* 50 (April 1968): 117-30.
"Visions and Dreams: The Unfinished Business of an Unfinished
Church." Sermon for the Uniting Conference of the United Meth-
odist Church, 23 April 1968. *Daily Christian Advocate,* 25 (April
1968). Reprinted in *Perkins Journal* 27 (Spring 1974): 36-41, and
The Wesleyan Theological Heritage, ed. Thomas C. Oden and Le-
icester R. Longden. Grand Rapids: Zondervan, 1991. Reprinted in
Albert Outler the Churchman, ed. Bob Parrott. Anderson, Ind.:
Bristol House Ltd, 1995.
"The One Man Mob." *The Log* 19 (April-May 1968).
"Falling Off the Tightrope Into the Arms of the 'Immobilisti.'" State-
ment on Pope Paul VI's Encyclical, *Humanae Vitae. National
Catholic Reporter* 4 (7 August 1968).
"Iconoclasm and the Integrity of Faith." *Theology Today* 25 (October
1968): 295-313.
Review of *Commentary on the Documents of Vatican II, Vol. 1,* ed.
Herbert Vorgrimler. *Journal of Ecumenical Studies* 5 (Fall 1968):
761-63.

1969

"Commentary on Articles 13-15 of Vatican II's Constitution on the
Church." *Vatican II's Pastoral Constitution on the Church in the
Modern World.* Holt, Rinehart and Winston, Inc., 1969.

"Methodism's Theological Heritage: A Study in Perspective." *Methodism's Destiny in the Ecumenical Age,* ed. Paul M. Minus, Jr. New York: Abingdon, 1969.

"The Mingling of Ministries." *Digest of the Proceedings of the Eighth Meeting of the Consultation on Church Union, Atlanta, Ga., March 17-20, 1969, Vol. 8,* ed. Paul A. Crow, Jr., 106-18. Princeton, N. J., 1969. See "United Methodists and COCU: The Mingling of Ministries in a United Church." *The Christian Advocate* 8 (October 1969).

"The Rule of Law and the Right of Dissent." *The Christian Uses of Conflict,* 4-5. Graded Press, Methodist Publishing House, 1969.

"Time of Danger, Time of Hope; in Quest of Community." *Our Sunday Visitor* 57 (19 January 1969).

Review of *A New Catechism: Catholic Faith for Adults. Journal of American Academy of Religion* 37 (March 1969): 100-104.

"What's Ahead for the Church?" *World Outlook* Old Series, 59; New Series, 29 (April 1969): 12-13.

Review of *Pelagius: Inquiries and Reappraisals,* by Robert F. Evans. *Commonweal* 90 (April 1969): 124.

Review of *Man's Responsibility: An Ecumenical Study,* by William Osborne. *Religion In Life* 38 (Autumn 1969): 463-64.

Review of *The End of Conventional Christianity,* by W. H. van de Pol. *Theological Studies* 30 (September 1969): 528-29.

"The Idea of Thanksgiving" and " A Summing Up Thanksgiving— Root, Flower, and Fruit." *The Spirit of. Thanksgiving;* 2,12-14 (September 1969).

Review of *After the Council; The Meaning of Vatican II for Protestantism and the Ecumenical Dialogue,* by Edmund Schlink. *Church History* 38 (December 1969): 538.

1970

"The Ordinal," *Companion to the Book of Worship,* eds. William F. Dunkle, Jr., and Joseph D. Quillian, Jr., 103-33. Commission on Worship of the United Methodist Church. New York: Abingdon, 1970.

"Crisis Coming Up." Lecture III, McFadin Lectures: COCU. *Test Case for Ecumenism in America,* Ministers' Week, Texas Christian University, February 17-19, 1970. Privately printed, 1970.

"Dedicatory Address, The Hicks Family Memorial Chapel, Pittsburgh Theological Seminary, May 11, 1970)." *Perspective* 11 (Winter 1970).

"The Crisis of Authority and the Future of the Church." *The Lamp* 68 (April 1970).

"The Jewish-Christian Dialogue: Its Ecumenical Setting." *Perkins Journal* 24 (Fall 1970): 22-29.

"The Papacy Under Fire." Review article on *Infallibility and the Evidence,* by Francis Simon and *Council Over Pope?* by Francis Oakley. *Journal of Ecumenical Studies* 7 (Fall 1970): 803-6.

"New Catholic Openness." Interview with Bob Smith. *Face To Face* 3 (October 1970): 29-32.

"Vatican II Plus Five." *The Texas Catholic* 19 (5 December 1970).

1971

Evangelism in the Wesleyan Spirit. Nashville: Tidings, 1971. Some chapters reprinted: Chapter 1–See "Wesley the Evangelist." *Together* 16 (April 1972). Chapter 2–See "On Proclaiming the Gospel." *Together* 16 (May 1972). Chapter 3–See "A Third Great Awakening?" *Together* 16 (June 1972). Chapter 4–See "A Church of Martyrs and Servants." *Together* 16 (July 1972).

"The Interpretation of the Gospels Today: Some Questions About Aims and Warrants." *Jesus and Man's Hope,* eds. Donald G. Miller and Dikran Y. Hadidian, 47-57. Pittsburgh: Pittsburgh Theological Seminary, 1971.

"A Prayer." *Bridges to the World,* ed. Harold K. Bales, 109. Nashville: Tidings, 1971.

"Does Our Abortion Stand Reflect the Church's Position?" *The Christian Advocate* 15 (September 1971): 7-8, 18.

"Pastoral Care in the Wesleyan Spirit." *Perkins Journal* 25 (Fall 1971): 4-11.

Review of *A History of the Ecumenical Movement,* by Harold E. Fey. *Catholic Historical Review* 57 (October 1971): 461-62.

1972

"How Can We Arrive at a Theological and Practical Mutual Recognition of Ministries? A Methodist Reply." *The Plurality of Ministries,* ed. Hans Kung and Walter Kasper, 83-91. Vol. 74, *Concilium.* New York: Herder and Herder, 1972.

"Introduction to the Report of the 1968-72 Theological Study Commission." *Daily Christian Advocate* (19 April 1972): 218-22. Reprinted in *Doctrine and Theology in the United Methodist Church,* ed. Thomas A. Langford, 20-25 (Nashville: Abingdon/Kingswood Books), 1991.

"Vatican II—Ten Years Later. Where is the Protestant Response?" *The Presbyterian Outlook* 154 (October 1972): 6-7.

1973

God's Providence and the World's Anguish." Chapter 1 in *The Mystery of Suffering and Death,* ed. Michael J. Taylor, 17-40. Staten Island: Alba House, 1973. (Reprinted from *Who Trusts In God: Musings on the Meaning of Providence.*)

"Revelation and Reflection: Comment in Favor of an Apophatic Theology." *Perkins Journal* 26 (Winter 1973): 14-21.

"History as Ecumenical Resource: The Protestant Discovery of 'Tradition.'" Presidential Address to the American Catholic Historical Association, December 28, 1972. *The Catholic Historical Review* 59 (April 1973): 1-15.

"The Beginnings of Personhood: 'Theological Considerations.'" *Perkins Journal* 27 (Fall 1973): 28-34.

1974

"Bio and Testimonial on Conferring Honorary Degree." *The Duke School of Religion Bulletin XXXIX,* 3 (Fall 1974): 143-44.

"An Effectual Calling." *The Duke School of Religion Bulletin,* 3 (Fall 1974): 145-52.

The New Encyclopedia Britannica, 1974. s.v. "Doctrine and Dogma."

Review of *A Religious History of the American People,* by Sidney Ahlstrom. *Perkins Journal* 27 (Spring 1974): 52-55.

"Karl Menninger and the Dimensions of Sin." *Theology Today* 31 (April 1974): 59-61.

"John Wesley as Theologian—Then and Now." *Methodist History* 12 (July 1974): 63-82.

1975

Theology in the Wesleyan Spirit. Nashville: Tidings, 1975.

"An Epochal Event Still In Search For Perspective." *The Challenge of Vatican II—Ten Years Later,* ed. Lillian R. Block, 18-19. New York: National Conference of Christian and Jews, n.d.

"Olive Branch to the Romans, 1970's Style: United Methodist Initiative, Roman Catholic Response." *Methodist History* 13 (January 1975): 52-56.

1976

"The Place of Wesley in the Christian Tradition." *The Place of Wesley in the Christian Tradition,* ed. Kenneth Rowe, 11-38. Metuchen, N. J. : The Scarecrow Press, 1976.

"The Bicentennial and The Re-Invention of America." *Perkins Journal* 30 (Fall 1976): 30-34.

1977

"'The Three Chapters': A Comment on the Survival of Antiochene Christology." *A Tribute to Arthur Voobus: Studies in Early Christian Literature and Its Environment, Primarily in the Syrian East,* ed. Robert H. Fisher, 357-64. Chicago: Lutheran School of Theology at Chicago, 1977.

"John Wesley: Folk-Theologian." *Theology Today* 34 (July 1977): 150-60.

1978

"'Gospel Studies' in Transition." *The Relationships Among the Gospels,* ed. W. O. Walker, 17-29. San Antonio: Trinity University Press, 1978.

"A Memoir and a Prospectus: The Ecumenical Movement and the Cause of Christian Unity." *Mid-Stream* 17 (January 1978): 13-23.

1979

"Facing the UMC's Accountability Crisis." *The Circuit Rider* (November-December 1979): 8-9.

Foreword to *The Apostolate of United Methodism,* by Ted Campbell. Nashville: Discipleship Resources, 1979.

1980

"The 'Logic' of Canon-making and the Tasks of Canon Criticism." *Texts and Testaments,* ed. W. March 263-76. San Antonio: Trinity University Press, 1980.

"A Fund for 'Evangelical' Scholars." *The Christian Century* (6-13 February 1980): 138-40.

"The Gospel According to Mark." *Perkins Journal* 33 (Summer 1980): 3-9.

1981

Preface to *John and Charles Wesley,* ed. with an introduction by Frank Whaling, xiii-xvii. New York: Paulist Press, 1981.

"Methodism in the World Christian Community." *Dig or Die: Papers Given at the World Methodist Historical Society Wesley Heritage Conference,* ed. James S. Udy and Eric G. Clancy, 27-36. Sydney: World Methodist Historical Society, Australasian Section, 1981.

"The Fullness of Life." *Dig or Die,* eds. James S. Udy and Eric G. Clancy, 21-26.

"The Loss of the Sacred." *Christianity Today* 25 (January 1981): 21-25.

"Response." *The Second Century* 1 (Spring 1981): 51-53.

1982

Review of *Ontology of Humor* (Philosophical Library Publishers), by Bob Parrott. "Communicators Ponder Humor." *CRS Update* (Fall 1982): 9.

"Response to 'Ecumenism in Reconstruction,' by Nikos A. Nissiotis." *Proceedings of the Fourteenth World Methodist Conference,* ed. Joe Hale, 65-66. The World Methodist Council, 1982.

1983

"Canon Criticism and the Gospel of Mark." *New Synoptic Studies,* ed. William Farmer, 233-43. Macon, Ga.: Mercer University Press, 1983.

"John Wesley's Interests in the Early Fathers of the Church." *The Bulletin* (Committee on Archives and History of The United Church of Canada in collaboration with Victoria University) 29 ([1980-82] 1983): 5-17.

"Isthmus Lectures, '82-'83: A Comment." *Perkins Journal* (Summer 1983): 1-3.

"John Wesley and Contemporary Evangelism." *Catalyst: Contemporary Evangelical Resources for United Methodist Seminarians* Vol. 10, No. 1, November 1983.

1984

The Works of John Wesley (Bicentennial Edition). Nashville: Abingdon, 1984-1987. Vols. 1-4: *Sermons I–IV.* Ed. Albert C. Outler.

"Power and Grace." *Perkins Journal* 38 (Fall 1984): 20-27.

"New Power for the Church." *Good News* (Sept.-Oct. 1984): 45-50.

"Present 'Principles' Must Not Be Abandoned." *United Methodist Reporter* (Southwest Texas ed.) 130 (November 1984): 2.

1985

Foreword to *The Early Methodist Class Meeting: Its Origins and Significance,* by David Lowes Watson. Nashville: Discipleship Resources, 1985.

"A New Future for Wesley Studies: An Agenda for 'Phase III.'" *The Future of the Methodist Theological Traditions,* ed. M. Douglas Meeks, 34-52. Abingdon: Nashville, 1985.

"After-Thoughts of a Protestant Observer of Vatican II." *The Church and Culture since Vatican II,* ed. Joseph Gremillion, 153-55. South Bend, Ind.: University of Notre Dame University Press, 1985.

"Ecumenism in a Post-Liberal Age." *Midstream* 24 (April 1985): 121-33.

"The Wesleyan Quadrilateral—in John Wesley." *Wesleyan Theological Journal* 20 (Spring 1985): 7-18.

"Toward a Post-Liberal Hermeneutics." *Theology Today* 42 (October 1985): 281-91.

Foreword to John L. Peters, *Christian Perfection in American Methodism.*
Grand Rapids, Mich.: Francis Asbury Press, Zondervan Publishing
House, 1985.

1986
"Strangers Within the Gates." *Vatican II Revisited: By Those Who Were
There,* ed. Alberic Stacpoole, 170-83. Minneapolis: Winston Press,
1986.
"Keynote Address for August 10-14 Conference of the Major Superiors
of Men." *Origins* 16 (September 1986): 253-57.

1987
"Problems of 'Selfhood' in a Christian Perspective." *The Book of the
Self: Person, Pretext, and Process,* ed. Polly Young-Eisendrath
and James A. Hall, 407-20. New York: New York University
Press, 1987.
(Untitled) *A Sense of Place: Saint John's of Collegeville,* eds. Colman
J. Barry, O.S.B. and Robert L. Spaeth (no pagination). Collegeville,
Minn.: Saint John's University Press, 1987.
Review of *Renaissance and Reformation,* by William R. Estep. *South
West Journal of Theology* 29 (Spring 1987): 44.
Review of *Jesus Through the Centuries: His Place in the History of
Culture* by Jaroslav Pelikan. *Church History* 56 (March 1987):
104-5.
"Vignettes of Church History . . . Church History by the Cube." *Mis-
sion* 20:9 (March 1987): 30-31.

1988
Albert Outler the Preacher: Sermons on Several Occasions, ed. Bob
W. Parrott. Nashville: Abingdon, 1988. Reprinted by Bristol House
Ltd., Anderson, Ind., 1995.
"The Pastor as Theologian." *The Pastor As Theologian,* ed. Earl E. Shelp
and Ronald H. Sunderland, 11-29. New York: Pilgrim Press, 1988.
"'Biblical Primitivism' in Early American Methodism." *The American
Quest for the Primitive Church,* ed. Richard T. Hughes, 131-42.
Chicago: University of Illinois Press, 1988.
"A Focus on the Holy Spirit: Spirit and Spirituality in John Wesley."
Quarterly Review 8 (Summer 1988): 3-18.

1989
"Pietism and Enlightenment: Alternatives to Tradition." *Christian Spirituality III: Post Reformation and Modern.* Vol. 18, *World Spirituality: An Encyclopedia History of the Religious Quest,* ed. Louis
Dupre and Don Saliers (in collaboration with John Meyendorf),
240-56. New York: Crossroad, 1989.

Foreword to *John Calvin's Doctrine of the Christian Life,* by John
Leith. Louisville, Ky.: Westminster/John Knox Press, 1989.
Review of *Catholicism and the Renewal of American Democracy,* by
George Weigel. *National Catholic Reporter,* (30 June 1989), 23-24.
"Pneumatology as an Ecumenical Frontier." *Ecumenical Review* 41 (July
1989): 363-74. [La pneumtologie, front de l'occumenisme in "Le
vent de l'esprit." pp. 11-28. Waldensian Seminary, Rome].

1990

"Through A Glass Darkly: Our History Speaks to Our Future." *Methodist History* 28 (January 1990): 77-91.
Review of *Christian Authority: Essays in Honor of Henry Chadwick,*
ed. G. G. Evans. *Church History* 59 (March 1990): 134-35.
"Methodists in Search of Consensus." *What Should Methodists Teach?,*
ed. M. Douglas Meeks. Nashville: Abingdon/Kingswood, 1990.

1991

John Wesley's Sermons: An Introduction. Foreword by Richard P.
Heitzenrater. Reprinted from *The Works of John Wesley,* Vol. 1:
Sermons I, 1-33. Nashville: Abingdon, 1984.
John Wesley's "Sermons": An Anthology, ed. Albert C. Outler and
Richard P. Heitzenrater. Sermon texts reprinted from *The Works of
John Wesley,* Vols. 1-4: *Sermons I-IV.* Nashville: Abingdon, 1984-
87.

1995

Reprint of *Albert Outler the Preacher. Albert Outler the Churchman*
and *Albert Outler the University Professor,* ed. Bob Parrott (Anderson, Ind.: Bristol House Ltd., 1995).

1996

Albert Outler's Christology, ed. Tom Oden (Anderson, Ind.: Bristol
House Ltd., 1996).

1997

Albert Outler's Pastoral Psychology, ed. Leroy Howe (Anderson, Ind.:
Bristol House Ltd., 1997).

1998

Albert Outler's Evangelism, ed. Billy Abraham (Anderson, Ind.: Bristol
House Ltd., 1998)

To be published are the final three volumes of *The Albert Outler
Library*: Albert Outler's edited papers on ecumenism, patristics,
and the Holy Spirit.

Endnotes

Chapter 1—Albert Finds the Church at Home

1 "Memories of Frances Isabelle Outler."
2 Related by Carla Outler to biographer.
3 Related by Albert's niece Helen Lankford to biographer.
4 Gertrude Outler, *Reminiscences Of Gertrude Outler*, 1947–48, pp. 2–4.
5 U.S. Census, Bibb County, Georgia, Enum. Dist. 16, p. 60.
6 Frances Outler, *Memories Of Frances Isabelle Outler*, p. 2.
7 *Ibid.*, p. 7.
8 Related to biographer by Helen Lankford.
9 Frances Outler, *op. cit.,* p. 9.
10 *Ibid.*, p. 7.
11 *Loc. cit.*
12 Frances Outler, *op. cit.*, pp. 8–9.
13 *Ibid.*, p. 9.
14 *Ibid.*, p. 10.
15 December 5, 1956, letter from Mrs. William Bubb to Dr. Colwell.
16 Frances Outler, *op. cit.,* p. 7.
17 *Ibid.*, p. 8.
18 H. Wayne Pipken, Interviewer, *Oral History Memoir, Baylor University Program For Oral History*, 1974, p. 2.
19 Related to biographer.
20 *Ibid.*
21 *Ibid.*
22 *Ibid.*
23 *Ibid.*
24 Pipkin, *op.cit., pp.3-4.*
25 *Ibid.*, p. 3.
26 Related by Carla Outler to biographer.
27 Gertrude Outler, *A Story of Five Acres.*

Chapter 2—Albert Becomes a Student, a Preacher, a Teacher

28 Related by Carla Outler to biographer.
29 Albert Outler, *For Goodness Sake.*
30 Pipkin, *op. cit.*, p. 5.
31 Albert Outler, *A Brief Statement Of Religious Experience and Belief.*
32 Appling County, Georgia, school records.

33 *Ibid.*
34 Albert Outler, *Kantonen Lectures*, Spring Convocation, 1983.
35 *Ibid.*
36 Albert Outler, *A Brief Statement of Religious Experience and Belief.*

Chapter 3—Albert Enters Two "Schools": Theology and Romance

37 Related to biographer by Carla Outler.
38 Quote from Carla Outler to biographer.
39 Related to biographer by Carla Outler.
40 Albert Outler, *How To Run a Conservative Revolution.*
41 Albert Outler, *A Brief Statement of Religious Experience and Belief.*
42 Pipkin, *op. cit.*, pp. 5–6.
43 Outler, *op. cit., A Brief Statement of Religious Experience and Belief.*
44 Pipkin, *op. cit.*, p. 9.
45 Albert Outler, *The Pastoral Psychology of Albert C. Outler*, edited by Leroy Howe (Anderson, Indiana: Bristol House Ltd., 1997), pp. 10–11.
46 A January 5, 1940, letter from Albert to "Jeff."
47 A March 8, 1936, letter from Albert to "Ed."
48 February 29, 1935, letter from Albert to David Stubbs.
49 February 29, 1935, letter from Albert to Bruce.
50 Pipkin, *op.cit.*, p. 12.
51 *Ibid*, p. 12.
52 *Ibid.* p. 18.
53 *Ibid.* p. 19.

Chapter 4—Albert Enters the World of Scholarship

54 *Ibid.*, p. 20.
55 *Ibid.*, p. 39.
56 *Ibid.*, p. 23.
57 Glenn Morrison, *Class Notes.*
58 Related to biographer.
59 It was much more enjoyable for Outler on Sunday, December 10, 1967, when he returned to Duke University chapel to be the preacher on a *Founders' Day Celebration* occasion. The sermon can be read in its entirety in *Albert Outler the Churchman,* second volume of *The Albert Outler Library,* Bristol Books, 1995.
60 Pipkin, *op. cit.*, p. 32.
61 *Ibid.*
62 Pipkin, *op. cit.*, p. 41.

63 *Ibid.*, p. 42.

64 *Ibid.*, pp. 41–43.

65 *Ibid.*, pp. 33–34.

66 *Ibid.*, pp. 34–35.

67 *Ibid.*, pp. 35–36.

68 Merrimon Cuninggim, *Perkins Led the Way*, pp. 9–10.

69 Faculty Minutes, September 22, 1951.

70 Attachment to Faculty Minutes, April 24, 1959.

71 Faculty Minutes, January 13, 1961.

72 Information Services Department, SMU, October 1969.

73 Senate Conference Minutes, September 27, 1969.

74 See Chapter 6, "As An Ecumenist," under "Dilettante" in Part 2 of this book.

75 Letter to "Jim."

76 Audio Tape #949J3.

77 Albert Outler, *John Wesley As Teacher.*

78 Comments given at the Thanksgiving Square celebration of *The Life and Work of Albert Outler* on October 8, 1996.

79 Audio tape #949J7, Contemporary Theology, 1970.

80 Nine books that embody Outler's advocacy of *coherent* theology as an option for our more modern *systematic* theology.

81 Audio tape #949J10.

82 Told to Outler by Bill Steele and quoted in the 1974 lecture, *Plundering the Egyptians.*

83 *Dallas Morning News,* May 30, 1974.

84 Lewis Howard Grimes, *A History of the Perkins School of Theology,* edited by Roger Loyd (Dallas: Southern Methodist University Press, 1993), p. 126.

85 Grimes, *ibid.,* p. 129.

86 The "Quillian Papers" under Outler's *Controversy File.*

87 October 8, 1997, letter from Dow Kirkpatrick to biographer.

88 *Ibid.*

89 Related to biographer by Bishop Bill Cannon.

90 From a January 6, 1998, letter to biographer.

91 *Ibid.*

92 Comments made to biographer.

93 *The Second Century — A Journal of Early Christian Studies,* Vol. 9, No. 1 (Johns Hopkins University Press, spring 1992), p. 2.

94 One of his lectures to a Church of Christ audience of students, historians, and theologians can be read in Volume 2 of *The Albert Outler Library, Albert Outler the Churchman,* pp. 94–108.

95 September 9, 1997, letter to Fred Maser.

96 Comments made to biographer.

97 The Field Bible from which John Wesley preached is passed on to each newly elected president of the Conference.

98 Audio tape # 949 B3 111-101, 111-118 W-S, 1966.

99 Speech honoring Outler at Thanksgiving Square, October 8, 1996.

100 *Ibid.*

101 *Ibid.*

102 Comments made to biographer during interview.

103 *Ibid.*

104 *Ibid.*

105 Heitzenrater's September 15, 1997, letter to biographer.

106 *Op. cit.*, Thanksgiving Square speech.

107 Robert Feaster in a telephone conversation with biographer.

Chapter 5—Albert Enters *Real* Retirement

108 October 28, 1987, letter to Dr. Richard W. Neal.

109 This was a closed chapter in his book, but not in the book of history. Read the rest of the story in Part 2, Chapter 5, "As a Methodist," in this biography.

110 "Through a Glass Darkly: *Memories, Forebodings and Faith,*" which dealt with the directions and misdirections being taken with the current Doctrinal Statement of the United Methodist Church, and may be read in its entirety in the last lecture printed in *Albert Outler the Churchman,* the second volume of *The Albert Outler Library.*

111 Outler, *The Preacher, op. cit.,* p. 36.

112 The complete text of Deschner's comments may be found in the October 1989 issue of *The Perkins Journal.*

113 *Dallas Morning News*, September 2, 1989.

114 *Ibid.*

115 *Ibid.*

116 From an editorial by Martin Marty, *The Christian Century,* Oct. 4, 1989.

Chapter 6—As a Historical Theologian (Patristics)

117 Outler, *The Hallowing of Life: Harvest Time For Secularism.*

118 Related in an interview with biographer.

119 *The Christian Century* (February 3, 1960): 127–29.

120 Audio tape # 1315/101.

121 Parker Lectures; Institute of Religion, 1987.

122 Outler, *op.cit., The Churchman,* p. 86.

123 Audio tape # 949B6 111-101, 111-118, 1966, Pt. 4C2.

Chapter 8—As a Psychotherapist

124 Albert Outler, *Psychotherapy and Christian Faith.*

125 Albert Outler, *Psychotherapy and the Christian Message* (New York: Harper and Brothers, 1954), p. 97.

126 Albert Outler, *Methodist Observer at Vatican II* (Westminster: Newman Press, 1967), pp. 80–81.

127 Albert Outler, 1987 Parker Lecture at Institute of Religion.

128 Albert Outler, *The Rise of Modern Psychotherapy and Alliances With Pastoral Care.*

129 *Ibid.,* p. 261.

130 Albert Outler, *John Wesley as Preacher.*

131 Outler, *The Preacher, op. cit.,* p. 95.

132 *Ibid.,* p. 100.

133 *Ibid.,* p. 102.

134 Outler, *Pastoral Psychology, op. cit.,* pp. 112–13.

Chapter 9—As an Arts and Sciences Person

135 Related to biographer.

136 *Ibid.*

137 Outler, *Comments on Sir John Eccles' Isthmus Institute lecture.*

138 *Ibid.*

Chapter 10—As a Methodist

139 The sermon can be read in its entirety in Volume 2 of *The Albert Outler Library, Albert Outler the Churchman,* pp. 302–12.

140 Audio tape #949 82 111-101, 111-118 W-S.

141 Audio tape #111-118 May 5, 1965 Pt. 3.

142 *The Book Of Discipline* (1984), p. 45.

143 Related to biographer.

144 Albert Outler, *Methodist Pluralism.*

145 Albert Outler, *The United Methodist Church: Our Doctrinal Heritage and Prospects; The Wesleyan Tradition.*

146 *Ibid.*

147 *The Book of Discipline,* (1988), p. 41.

148 *Ibid.,* pp. 44–45.

149 *Ibid.,* p. 47.

150 *The Book of Discipline,* (1984), pp. 72–73.

151 *Ibid.,* pp. 82–83.

152 Audio tape #949B4 111, 101, 111-118.

153 Albert Outler, *op. cit., The Churchman,* edited by Bob Parrott (Anderson, Ind.: Bristol House, 1995), pp. 456.

154 Audio tape #949 82 111-101, 111-118 W-S.

155 Outler, *op. cit.*, p. 466-67.

156 July 20, 1983, letter to Tom Thomas.

157 Outler, *Pastoral Psychology*, *op. cit.*, p. 214.

158 Outler notes.

159 Gunter, Jones, Campbell, Miles, Maddox, *Wesley and the Quadrilateral, Reviewing the Conversation* (Nashville: Abingdon Press, 1997), p. 142.

160 Related to biographer.

161 Outler notes to biographer.

162 *The Christian Century,* Feb. 6–13, 1980.

163 Statement made to Ed Robb.

164 *Op. cit., The Christian Century,* Feb. 6–13, 1980.

165 Albert Outler, *Of Human Bondage.*

166 Albert Outler, *Wilson Lectures,* 1983.

167 Teleod, *Letters*, VIII, 91.

168 Outler, *Politics and Scriptural Episkopoi*, p. 6.

169 *Loc. cit.*

170 *Ibid.*, p. 7.

171 *Ibid.*, p. 8.

172 Related to biographer.

173 Outler, *Thy Kingdom Come*, Bible and Theology Conference, Montreat, N.C.

174 Related to biographer.

175 *Ibid.*

176 *Ibid.*

177 Tom Emswiler, Jr., *Professional Personalities.*

178 Related to biographer.

179 Outler, *op. cit.*, *Politics and Scriptural Episkopoi*, p. 7.

180 Outler, *op. cit., The Churchman,* pp. 458–59.

181 January 26, 1986, letter to Bob Schuler.

182 Related to biographer.

183 January 26, 1986, letter to Bob Schuler.

184 1983 Duke Lecture.

185 Audio tape #1315/101.

186 Related to biographer.

187 Telephone interview with biographer, July 1997.

188 July 31, 1987, letter from Keith Pohl to Outler.

Chapter 11—As an Ecumenist

189 Outler, *op. cit., The Churchman,* p. 30.

190 September 16, 1997, letter to biographer.

191 Outler, *op. cit., The Christian Tradition and the Unity We Seek,* pp.70-71.

192 *Ibid.,* p. 134.

193 *Ibid.,* p. 148.

194 Related to biographer.

195 *Ibid.*

196 Grimes, *op. cit.,* p. 189.

197 Related to biographer.

198 Speech given at Thanksgiving Square in memory of Outler.

199 Albert Outler, *Methodist Observer at Vatican II* (Newman Press: 1967), p. 40.

200 *Ibid.,* p. 168.

201 Stjepan Schmidt, S.J., *Augustin Bea, the Cardinal of Unity* (Rochelle: N.Y.: New City Press, 1987), p. 783.

202 Related to biographer.

203 Related to biographer.

204 Related to biographer.

205 Pax Christi Award.

206 Albert Outler, *Confessions of an Ecumaniac,* The Kantonen Lectures, Trinity Lutheran Seminary, 1983.

207 Pipkin, *op. cit.,* p. 29.

208 Albert Outler, *The Good Shepherd — Changing Perspectives.*

209 Montreat Audio Tape: *Grace As Power.*

210 Albert Outler notes.

211 *Ibid.*

212 *Ibid.*

213 Audio tape #949J6.

214 Audio tape, Vol. 5 #10.

215 Audio tape #111-118 Feb. 24, 1965.

216 May 16, 1977, letter from Donald J. Thorman, president of the National Catholic Publishing Company.

Chapter 12—As a Community Person

217 Outler, *op.cit., The University Professor,* p. 179.

218 Outler notes.

Chapter 13—He Was Human

219 Related by Bob Schuler to biographer.

220 *Ibid.*

221 Albert Outler, *Man Alive!*

222 Related to biographer.

223 Albert Outler, *Wesley's Version of the Care of Souls.*

224 Related by Bishop Bill Cannon to biographer.

225 Heitzenrater in Thanksgiving Square speech referring to a comment made by Andy Miller.

226 Audio tape: *East and West: The Development of Byzantine.*

227 Audio tape 6B, *East and West: the Development of Byzantine.*

228 Albert Outler, *An Effectual Calling.*

229 September 9, 1977, letter to Fred Maser.

230 Albert Outler, *The University Professor*, edited by Bob Parrott (Anderson, Ind.: Bristol House, 1995), pp. 448–49.

231 Audio tape #949BI 111-101, 111-118 1966 PTI cpz.

232 *Ibid.*

233 Related to biographer.

234 Audio tape 1315/125.

235 *Ibid.*

236 Audio tape #94918.

237 Audio tape #949112.

238 Outler, *op. cit., The Preacher,* p. 57.

239 Albert Outler, *Christian Motivations in Evangelism,* p. 16.

240 Albert Outler, *Traditioning the Gospel.*

241 Albert Outler, *A Brief Statement of Religious Experience and Belief.*

242 Outler, *op. cit., Pastoral Psychology,* p. 31.

243 Albert Outler, *The Works Of John Wesley, Volume IV* (Nashville: Abingdon Press, 1987), p. 169.

244 *Dallas Morning News, Showcase, August 22, 1972.*

245 *Loc. cit.*

246 Audio tape of the reading proceedings.

247 Related to biographer by Helen Lankford, who also was a dinner guest.

248 Related to biographer by Rabbi Gerald Klein.

249 Outler notes.

250 Outler notes.

251 Audio tape 6B, *East and West; the Development of Byzantine.*

252 A transcription of tape 2, p. 34.

253 Outler, *op. cit., The Preacher,* p. 185.

254 Audio tape #1315/129.

255 Outler notes.

256 Albert Outler, *John Wesley as Teacher.*

257 Introduction to lecture: *Diagnosing the Human Flaw: Reflections on the Real Human Condition.*

258 Albert Outler, *The History and Theology of Pastoral Care.*

259 Albert Outler, *Wilson Lectures, 1983.*

260 Albert Outler, *Parker Lecture, 1987.*

261 Related to biographer in a September 22, 1997, letter from Church of Christ historian Everett Ferguson.
262 Albert Outler, "Vignettes of Church History . . . Church History by the Cube," *Mission,* 20:9 (March 1987): 30–31.
263 Albert Outler, 1987 Parker Lecture, Institute of Religion.
264 *Ibid.*
265 Albert Outler, *Ontology of Humor, Communicators Ponder Humor,* A Review, CRS *Update* (Fall 1982): 9.
266 Outler notes.
267 Related by Bishop Hunt to biographer.

Chapter 14—He Was a Bridge Builder

268 Related to biographer.
269 Albert Outler, Ecumenical Service, Shreveport, April 7, 1986.

Chapter 15—He Was a Prophet

270 Outler notes.
271 Outler, *op. cit.,* Parker Lecture.
272 Outler notes; used in various lectures as "asides."
273 Letter dated January 3, 1968.
274 Albert Outler, Kantonen Lecture, 1983.
275 Related to biographer.
276 Albert Outler, *Abortion: Dilemmas and Dimensions: Theological Considerations,* Dallas Conference on Abortion, May 15-16, 1973.
277 Amos 5:21, 24.
278 Albert Outler, *Gray Lectures,* 1983.
279 Outler, *op.cit., The Churchman,* p. 394.
280 *loc. cit.*
281 Outler notes. Used in various lectures as "asides."
282 Heitzenrater speech at Thanksgiving Square honoring Outler.

Chapter 16—He Was a Churchman

283 *The Christian Century,* February 3, 1960.

Part 4—A Retrospective

284 Related to biographer.
285 *Journal of Early Christian Studies,* The Johns Hopkins University Press, Volume 9, Number 1, p. 1.
286 Observation of the editor of the first three books of sermons in *The Albert Outler Library.*
287 Outler, *op. cit., The Preacher,* p. 238.

288 Albert Outler, *Augustine: Confessions and Enchiridion* (Philadelphia: Westminster Press, 1955), p. 16.

289 Related to biographer.

290 Albert Outler, *Repentance and Justification*, Summer Theological Institute, July 31, 1982.

291 Audio tape #6B, *East and West: The Development of Byzantine.*

292 Audio tape #260.

293 *NOTE:* A Large part of Outler's coherent theology is captured in print via his own published books and in *The Albert Outler Library,* nine books published by Bristol House Ltd.

294 Albert Outler, *op. cit., The Churchman*, p. 215.

295 Van A. Harvey, *A Handbook of Theological Terms* (New York: Macmillan Co., 1968), pp. 177–78.

296 Albert Outler, *Diagnosing the Human Flaw: Reflections on the Real Human Condition.*

297 Outler notes.

298 *Ibid.*

299 *Ibid.*

300 Albert Outler, *Why Revelation Is Not Theology in Christology.*

301 Albert Outler, *The Perennial Task of Christian Reflection in Christology.*

302 Albert Outler, *The Demand For a Non-Paradoxical Explanation— Christology.*

303 Outler, *op. cit., University Professor*, p. 110.

304 *NOTE:* A complete reading of Outler's *Christology,* the fourth volume in *The Albert Outler Library,* explains this historical process.

305 Heitzenrater, speech given at Thanksgiving Square.

306 Related to biographer.

307 Martin Luther, "A Mighty Fortress Is Our God," verse 4.

308 The sermon, "The Measure of Greatness," may be read in its entirety in *Albert Outler the Churchman,* vol. 2 of *The Albert Outler Library*, pp. 436–50.

309 Related to Biographer.

310 Audio tape #949J3.

311 Outler, *op. cit., Christology,* pp. 245–47,

312 Related to biographer.

313 *Ibid.*

314 February 10, 1984, letter to Bishop Finis Crutchfield.

315 Outler, *op. cit., The Churchman,* p. 57.

Index

A

A Foundation for Theological
Education   64, 288–290,
292–294, 328, 435, 443
A Library of Protestant Thought
149, 161–162, 195, 423, 439
John Wesley volume of   163
Abilene Christian University   382
Abingdon Press   163, 184, 188,
199, 310
Abraham, William J.   285
Academy of Senior Professionals
at Eckerd College   136
Adams, E. L.   111
Ahlstrom, Sydney   439
Ainsworth, Bishop   34, 84, 305,
361
Albert Outler Library   199, 239
Alchin, A. M., *photo of*   223
Allen, Joe   121, 143
American Academy of Arts and
Sciences   135, 261
American Catholic Historical
Association   135, 314, 343
American Society of Church
History   105, 343, 379
American Theological Society
105, 343
Anderson, Barney   143
antinomianism   282, 406
Aquinas, Thomas   146
Aristotle   148, 251
Arminian Magazine   310
Asbury, Francis   295–296
Atkins, Bishop   33
Augustine   11, 419, 427, 429
Ault, James M., *photo of*   223
Austin Presbyterian Seminary
138, 140, 172

B

Ayer, A. J.
Language, Truth, and Logic
237

Bach, Johann Sebastian   261–262
Bailey, Barry   203
Bainton, Roland   78–79, 106,
162, 237, 331, 419
Baker, Dick   96
Baker, Frank   124, 178–184, 186,
189, 358, 423–424
Outler's first encounter   163
Balas, David L.   323, 342
Barrett, Dulaney   397
Barth, Karl   71, 120, 237, 238,
308, 403, 448
Bea, Augustin   325
Beach, Robert   149
Beethoven, Ludwig van   262–263
Birmingham-Southern College 77
Blake, Bruce   216
Booth, Allan   96
Bosley, Harold   151, 401
Brahms, Johannes   263
Branscomb, Harvie   86, 89, 103,
119, 451
Bridwell Library   179, 190–191,
200, 209, 216, 257, 353,
379, 380
Broadhead, Ed   96
Brown, Kenneth   150
Brown, Robert McAfee   322
Bruebeck   262
Brunner, Emil   120
Bryan, Monk   296
Buhl, Gary W.   215
Buhman, Ronk   82
Bultmann, Rudolf   238

495